D0786635

THE CITY IN COMPARATIVE PERSPECTIVE

The City in Comparative Perspective

CROSS-NATIONAL RESEARCH AND NEW DIRECTIONS IN THEORY

edited by

JOHN WALTON

and

LOUIS H. MASOTTI

Center for Urban Affairs
Northwestern University

SAGE PUBLICATIONS

Halsted Press Division
JOHN WILEY & SONS
New York — London — Sydney — Toronto

Copyright © 1976 by Sage Publications, Inc.

Distributed by Halsted Press, a Division of
John Wiley & Sons, Inc., New York

Printed in the United States of America

Library of Congress Cataloging in Publication Data

Main entry under title:
The city in comparative perspective.
   1. Municipal research—Addresses, essays, lectures. 2. Sociology, Urban—Research—Addresses, essays, lectures. I. Walton, John, 1937-   II. Masotti, Louis H.
HT110.C5   301.36'3   76-7040
ISBN 0-470-15217-6

FIRST PRINTING

CONTENTS

PREFACE

Some of the material on the following pages first appeared as a special issue of *Urban Affairs Quarterly* ("The City in Comparative Perspective" September 1975) which I commissioned John Walton, senior editor of this volume, to assemble in my capacity as editor of the journal. It represented a major step toward the fulfillment of a commitment I made upon assuming the editorship of *Urban Affairs Quarterly:*

> In my judgment our approach to the urban condition has been too culture-bound; we have restricted ourselves unnecessarily to American (and the United States at that) versions of the urban world. I am, therefore, actively soliciting manuscripts which explore urban phenomena cross-culturally in order to provide a broader urban perspective.

Because of space limitations in *Urban Affairs Quarterly*, we were able to include only a few of the many excellent papers submitted for the colloquium. After publication of the special issue and its very favorable reception by comparative urban scholars, we approached Sage Publications and Halsted Press with a proposal to publish an expanded version of the journal as a full-length book. We argued that despite the recent publication of some very fine comparative books (including Sage-Halsted's own *Comparative Community Politics*, T. N. Clark, ed.), the volume we proposed broke significant new ground in the growing debate over theory and method in comparative urban research.

We are obviously pleased that Sage and Halsted accepted our judgment and agreed to publish what we like to think is an important collection of interdisciplinary perspectives on comparative urbanization. We are also exceptionally fortunate to be able to include the most recent work of such a perceptive and insightful group of international urban scholars. Except for essays which first appeared in *Urban Affairs Quarterly* (by Abu-Lughod, Jacob, Aiken, and Evers) and the paper by Castells, which is a revised and expanded version of a manuscript first published in *Comparative Urban Research* (and reprinted here with the gracious permission of the Editor, William John Hanna), the papers which follow were especially prepared for this volume.

We are grateful to the staff, and in particular to Deborah Ellis Dennis, of the Center for Urban Affairs, Northwestern University, for assistance in the preparation of the manuscripts for publication. Special appreciation must go to Rhoda Blecker of Sage Publications for her extraordinary patience in the face of my ordinary procrastination.

LHM

Evanston, Illinois
January 6, 1976

COMPARATIVE URBAN RESEARCH
The Logic of Comparisons and the Nature of Urbanism

LOUIS H. MASOTTI
JOHN WALTON

In the prefatory remarks to collections of this sort it is usually noted that the topic of concern is enjoying a new and unprecedented amount of scholarly attention. One must always be skeptical about such projections; often they tell us more about the agenda of the editors than about trends in research. Moreover, social science is fickle and the emergent concerns of one year frequently devolve to the backwash issues of the next. Recognizing the pitfalls of such prognoses, it would still appear safe to argue that the field of comparative urban analysis is growing rapidly. If one had attempted to teach a comparative urban course in the early 1960s, the available materials would have been limited, scattered and in many cases fugitive. Since then there is considerable impressionistic evidence that the field is developing on a variety of fronts; witness the publication of books such as *The Human Consequences of Urbanization* (Berry, 1973); *Modernization, Urbanization and the Urban Crisis* (Germani, 1973); *Urbanism, Urbanization and Change: Comparative Perspectives* (Meadows and Mizruchi, 1969); *Urbanism in World Perspective* (Fava, 1968); *The City in Newly Developing Countries* (Breese, 1969); *Comparative Community Politics* (Clark, 1974), *An Urban World* (Tilly, 1974); and *Comparative*

Urban Structure (Schwirian, 1974), the appearance of journal issues devoted to comparative urban research, e.g. *The New Atlantis* (Winter 1970), *Urban Affairs Quarterly* (September 1975), and the *Journal of Comparative Administration* (November 1972 and February 1973), and an increasing number of articles in both the disciplinary journals and the special focus journals (e.g. *Comparative Political Studies, Studies in Comparative International Development*). Similarly, the appearance of a new journal— *Comparative Urban Research*—seems to have struck a responsive chord among comparative scholars, and provides a lively forum for their activities, projects, and research.

If, indeed, there is a trend toward understanding urban phenomena in comparative perspective it is long overdue. The great majority of urban research has been incredibly parochial and this seems to apply as much to the work of U.S. scholars as to other national traditions. If urban research in the United States is more commonly charged with ethnocentrism, the explanation may be simply more support there for more people to pursue parochial concerns.

The parochialism of urban research is reflected in two distinctive forms. First, and most obvious, it appears in work that has been confined to a single, "native" national setting and which pursues explanations for arrangements or events that are likely quite unique given the fact that fundamental socio-cultural influences on urban forms are not allowed to vary. Illustratively, a great deal of research has been done in the United States on the performance of urban governments in the provision of public services. But even comparative studies *within* this society deal with an extremely limited range of public responsibility for urban services by contrast to European cities and therefore cannot address general societal explanations of the sources of variation.

Second, and perhaps more serious, parochialism appears when researchers venture into "foreign" settings with a prefabricated set of theoretical and methodological tools which presuppose the order and meaning of events. For example, another venerable tradition in U.S. urban studies is social area analysis or urban ecology. Theoretically, this approach is heavily influenced by uniquely North American views on dominance and competition. Patterns of land use and urban social structures are viewed as outcomes of competitive forces in the market place. The distribution of groups and classes in urban space is a function of their unequal resources and value choices. While there would appear good reason to question these assumptions even in the U.S. case, they become much less credible when applied to Third World cities whose social ecology is more typically the consequence of colonial dominance and the power of internal, dependent elites.

Clearly the solution to both of these problems lies in more extensive comparative work premised on a broader range of theoretical viewpoints. The myopia of parochialism will be overcome to the extent that critical comparative work can demonstrate that our present knowledge is inadequate to explain urban forms and processes because it has either precluded examination of fundamental causal forces by focusing on special cases, or because it has misinterpreted those causal forces. As we shall suggest below, the first of these alternatives is now being actively explored and the second is emergent.

If the impression has been conveyed thus far that the proliferation of comparative urban research is an unmixed blessing, this should be promptly qualified. One obvious and discouraging consequence of this activity has been the extreme fragmentation of comparative work. Researchers with separate interests and little mutual awareness have variously construed comparative urbanism as the study of migration and migrant adaptation, social ecology, land use and planning, location theory, economic function, politics and participation, life styles and modernization, and the like. In short, there is no "field" of comparative urban analysis as distinct from a disparate ensemble of disciplines, substantive concerns, methods, and theories that are unreliably classified under the reified category.

Of course, many would argue that this is unavoidable, necessary, or even desirable; we need an urban anthropology to study migration and settlement patterns, an urban geography to study location, an urban political science to study government and participation, an urban sociology, an urban economics, an urban psychology, and so on. But what this disciplinary balkanization implies is that there is nothing *distinctively urban* to be understood or explained; rather the urban *milieu* is merely a setting for the study of a variety of processes defined by other criteria. The city per se as an historical, social form is less the object of interest than a variety of activities that happen to go on there with greater regularity or in more intensified ways than elsewhere. Consequently "urban" this or that is a convenient yet specious label for the "real" this or that. It appears that the latter view predominates in comparative urban research, which may be at the root of much of our theoretical confusion. Assuming that some principled bases could be established for urban phenomena qua urban phenomena, it should then be possible to advance the field significantly by integrating various approaches within a common framework or a limited set of competing frameworks.

THE SUBSTANCE OF URBAN RESEARCH: FOCUS AND LOCUS

The essays which follow were selected for inclusion in this volume based on their individual quality and their collective expression of contrasting viewpoints. They also represent, appropriately enough in a book on comparative perspectives, a wide range of substantive urban phenomena in a variety of locations around the world. The collection is in fact organized around four substantive themes—"Theory and Method in Comparative Urban Ecology"; "The City in Developed Societies: Comparative Politics"; "The City in Developing Societies: Systemic Approaches"; and "New Direction in Theory." However, as we shall attempt to show in the following section, the essays can also be profitably arranged in terms of significant analytic and methodological categories.

The research foci represented in the following chapters range from the individual as unit of analysis through urban groups, cities, and nation-city interactive systems to global political economies. Substantively, the studies reported here deal with such disparate urban activities, groups, and processes as political orientations, transformations, participation, and parties (Aiken, Jacob, and Koehn); housing, landownership, and squatter settlements (Bryant and White, Leeds and Leeds, Evers, Pickvance, and Cornelius); social ecology and social change (Abu-Lughod, London and Flanagan, Edari); and economic foundations of urbanism (Castells, Walton, Pickvance).

All but two of the papers (Castells, Walton) report on specific urban systems and collectively they range around the world, including large segments of both the developed world (United States, Great Britain, France, Italy, Yugoslavia, Poland, the Netherlands, and Belgium) and the Third World (Ethiopia, Kenya, and North Africa; Mexico, Chile, Peru, and Brazil; India, Indonesia, and Singapore).

Because many of the papers cut across several of the themes we are attempting to deal with, we have had to make some difficult choices in ordering the papers. Although it may not appear so upon first glance at the table of contents (e.g., there are essays on housing in each of the last three sections), there is a logic to our topical organization. All three papers in Section I are clearly focused on urban ecology and "hang together" as a group. Section II is made up of four papers which share at least two characteristics—a focus on comparative urban political activities and a locus in the developed world. The essays in the section on "The City in Developing Societies: Systemic Approaches" have in common, in addition to the fact that they are Third World oriented, a concern with the dynamic interaction of elements *within* the urban system (e.g., in Cornelius, urban land and housing markets, government interventions and the housing options of the urban poor in Mexico City), or *between* the urban and national systems (e.g., Koehn's focus on the interaction of urban elites and national policy in Ethiopia).

The last section of the book groups three essays on an emergent theoretical approach to urban analysis. The emphasis here is on neo-Marxist, structuralist or political economy perspectives which attempt to explain the broader societal origins of contemporary patterns of urbanism and urbanization particularly in advanced capitalist countries. Although each of these attempts to develop some new theoretical ideas, they also point to some of the unique methodological implications of their views.

THE LOGIC OF COMPARISONS

In our judgment it made good sense to order the thirteen chapters in this collection as found in the table of contents for the reasons stated above. Without seeming to contradict our own rationale for presentation of the book's essays, we would like to suggest two alternative ways—one methodological and the other theoretical—in which the papers in this volume and comparative urban research in general can be approached.

The methodological alternative argues for an evaluation of the papers using as a criterion the "logic of comparison" employed by the author. Theoretically, the essays might appropriately be analyzed and compared in terms of their fundamental conception of "urbanism"—i.e., an assessment of the most significant causal influences affecting the urban phenomena in question.

Given the nascent stage in which we find comparative urban analysis, it seems most appropriate to address the logic of comparisons question head-on. The logic of comparisons refers to the rationale employed to support the claim that x and y have sufficient properties in common and/or properties that differ along specified dimensions to allow meaningful, convergent comparisons. Conventionally, the former is referred to as "conceptual equivalence" (Sears, 1961) and is considered a matter of inference, not of direct observations (Przeworski and Teune, 1970: 118). Given cross-cultural variability in social reality, the problem for the social scientist is to design research or arrange existing data in such a way as to yield the most meaningful generalizations. In the present context, this means comparative analysis and that in turn implies informed selection of appropriate units and levels of analysis as well as the establishment of appropriate measures of conceptual and measurement equivalence across the entities being compared.

Most comparative studies begin with known differences among social systems and evaluate the effect of these differences on some other social phenomena which occur within these systems. Przeworski and Teune (1970) have elaborated an alternative strategy for comparativists: taking system differences into account as they are encountered in the process of explaining observed social phenomena in the systems. They offer two research design strategies: "most similar systems" and "most different systems." In the former, which Naroll (1968) has called "concomitant variation," systems as similar as possible with respect to as many characteristics as possible are the optimal samples for comparison. Common systemic characteristics are considered "controlled for" and intersystemic differences become explanatory variables. In "most different systems" designs those factors differentiating social systems are eliminated by formulating statements that are true regardless of the system within which observations are made:

> As long as these statements continue to be true in all systems, no reference to systemic characteristics is made. As soon as additional statements cannot be validly formulated across systems, however, the hypothesis concerning no difference among systems has to be rejected and the level of analysis is shifted to systemic factors [Przeworski and Teune, 1970: 39].

Among the papers in this volume, the "most similar systems" approach, or some varient of it, is employed by Abu-Lughod, Leeds and Leeds, Aiken, and Bryant and White. Jacob (because of his focus on the individual as unit of analysis) Evers, and London and Flanagan (seeking "cross-cultural universals"), appear to utilize a "most different systems" approach to comparative analysis.

Abu-Lughod argues for "legitimate comparisons"—i.e. comparative research on cities carefully selected on the basis of identifiable similarities (such as North African location and common historical or cultural features) as well as specified differences.

> I would therefore like to argue strongly for a strategy which moves in disciplined fashion from the very specific to the somewhat more general to the even more general via the semi-controlled "experiment" and which attempts to illuminate the similarities and differences uncovered by this research strategy by means of common mechanisms of process.

The three North African capital cities in which she did her research (Cairo, Tunis, and Rabat-Salé) allow for such controlled comparisons.

Aiken analyzes class politics in a large number of European cities within four countries and "stratified" or controlled on the key dimension of multiparty electoral systems. Moreover, where cross-national differences emerge, he provides explanations based upon unique and contrasting features of the societies.

In their study of squatter settlements in three Latin American countries (Brazil, Chile and Peru) the Leeds' argue for a "comparison of cases."

> These cases are choosen not merely because of some accident of having two or three units of study with which we happen to become familiar, but on the bases of some attempt to use criteria of comparability to select them. Although the selection procedure is admittedly still crude, it is far from merely *ad hoc* and represents a step in the direction of a proper comparative method whether for political, social, or other analyses.

For the Leeds', the key independent variable distinguishing the three political systems is the extent to which there is a mass base for political parties.

The approach taken by Bryant and White in their comparative study of housing policies and politics in two somewhat similar systems—Great Britain and the United States—is to compare group *response* to similar policy stimuli. In their effort to explain differences in housing policies across the two societies, they reject policy output (system resource allocation) analysis and political culture. Instead, they argue that at least in the case of housing in Great Britain and the United States the most productive approach is to examine the options or strategies available to relevant groups.

> The assumption is that [groups] behave rationally in response to perceived trade-offs between costs and benefits. It is this explanation that appears most useful in understanding the different degrees of popular concern and activity over the housing issue. Approached in this way the resources of the system and the culture become two of a variety of factors which enter into a group's calculus as to which issues to pursue, and by what method.

In their analysis, they identify three political factors which constitute the "strategic situation" for housing: the extent of the constituency, whether or not the issue is a partisan one, and the impact of the policy.

The chapters by London and Flanagan and Jacob do not fit the "most similar system" design category. The former, by implication, and the latter, by design, are "most different systems" approaches to comparative analysis. London and Flanagan, in their survey of the literature on urban ecological structure in Latin America, Southeast Asia, and tropical Africa conclude, not unexpectedly, that there seem to be no universal patterns. They quickly add that such a conclusion, reached as a result of a static, cross-sectional description of ecological structures, misses a very basic point—i.e., that cities are dynamic, constantly growing and changing. They argue for a "dynamic approach" and an historical perspective which together might prove fruitful in the search for cross-cultural generalizations: "The fact that an evolutionary sequence or convergence hypothesis is not easy to 'prove' should not block our efforts in this direction."

London and Flanagan had set out to seek "cross-cultural universals" in the relationship among those forces and factors in society which influence the ecological structure of cities, their dependent variable. Having discovered that no universal pattern exists, they realistically readjusted their thinking to a more discriminate typology of city forms on the one hand and a recognition on the other of the influence of historical-dynamic processes on spatial ecology.

In the Jacob paper we find a fundamental qualitative shift in comparative logic. Here the research design boldly attempts to compare (like Aiken) a large number of communities stratified by size and economic level in four nations, but nations vastly different in contextual properties (i.e., India, Poland, Yugoslavia, and the United States). Across thirty communities in each of the four nations Jacob's units of analysis are local political leaders ($N = 3,930$) and it is at the level of these individuals, their attitudes and values, that he finds the justification for this ambitious comparison, i.e., factor analytic studies indicate a common dimension of political orientations which is termed "activeness." As a result, Jacob's analysis of the "anomaly" of individual autonomy and collective responsibility lays more emphasis on generalizations common to these societies rather than on differences among them. This, obviously, is a bold and instructive effort. It is important to note, however, that the author himself points out some of the hazards of this strategy in the following words:

> The case is not altogether convincing that activeness as measured in one country was indeed comparable to what was measured in another (the combinations of indicators were actually so diverse across countries as to throw doubt on the intriguing theoretical argument for comparability.

Unlike other ambitious students of cross-national political attitudes (e.g., Almond and Verba, 1963), Jacob is candid enough to call attention to the problem of conceptual equivalence which plagues all comparative analysis to a greater or lesser degree.

It will be noted that this discussion of comparative method has not dwelled on particular research techniques or methodologies. This omission was intentional, since we believe that the real methodological issues have less to do with whether surveys are taken, participant observation strategies are employed or historical insight is creatively used; rather the issue centers on the costs and benefits of the comparative logic employed. In fact, the papers to be found in this collection reflect a variety of methodological techniques. Aiken employs public data sources on voting behavior and correlates, and wisely uses longitudinal designs; Jacob bases his analysis on an exceptionally large cross-sectional survey while Edari uses a small stratified sample; Bryant and White, Cornelius, and Koehn base their respective analyses on a well executed combination of fieldwork and elite interviews; Leeds and Leeds employ extensive fieldwork and considerable insight in three countries; London and Flanagan report on an extensive literature review; Evers marshals his own and other research evidence on land use, value and landownership; Abu-Lughod's approach is largely historical employing many fugitive materials, though clearly her paper is informed by her work in social ecology. In addition to Abu-Lughod, at least four other contributors to this volume make a strong argument for an historical perspective—London and Flanagan, Edari, Castells and Pickvance.

While not exhaustive, this is an instructive spectrum of techniques, methodologies and approaches that have been, and continue to be, put to good use in comparative urban research. Given the high cost of doing elaborate cross-cultural urban research (it is reliably estimated that the Jacob Community Values project cost upwards of two million dollars), efficient methodologies which produce reliable and valid data should be a major concern as the field of comparative urban research develops.

THEORETICAL DIMENSIONS OF URBANISM

Although only the three chapters in Section IV specifically address themselves to the fundamental question of the nature of urbanism, each of the papers at least implies a theoretical position with respect to the major causal forces at work on the phenomena they seek to explain in a deliberately chosen urban setting; therefore, each implies a position on the part of the author as to what he or she considers distinctively urban. For the sake of contrast and recognizing that the authors do not always identify themselves with these positions, we suggest that three general theoretical approaches characterize the material. Moreover, each of these embodies a distinctive conception of what is "urban", what makes the city the appropriate locus or focus of investigation. The three categories we shall employ are *Contemporary Approaches to Participation and Resource Competition, Historical-Systemic Approaches to Urban Process,* and *Structuralist Approaches to the Production of Urban Forms.*

CONTEMPORARY APPROACHES TO PARTICIPATION AND RESOURCE COMPETITION

This is the least explicit of our approaches since it includes most of the analyses which simply assume rather than develop a theoretical stance. Nevertheless, within limits it can be shown that certain assumptions and procedures characterize the approach. They tend to focus on contemporary events rather than historical process and, in a positivistic vein, to employ a set of independent variables to account for some consequent dependent variable. Urban settings are selected for this research since the dependent variable of concern, while not necessarily unique to the city, is magnified and made more salient there. Particularly, a variety of interests are compressed in close proximity leading to a keener competition for available resources. Key issues become how these interests are mobilized to participate and what factors shape their inter-competition and its outcome.

Illustratively, London and Flanagan engage in a review of the literature on urban ecology most of which is based on classical ideas of dominance and competition. The key resource here is urban land as well as the amenities attached to various locations; the problem is to account for land use and, therefore, spatial arrangements as a consequence of the competitive advantage of various interests. Aiken employs a similar resource competition model, although here the prizes to be won are not only the use of space but the broader set of resources allocated by the political system and its partisan elected officials. Political parties, socioeconomic interests, and, in Aiken's case, class and religious groups characterize the urban environment through their competition for public policy advantages. In a related fashion Jacob studies public officials and the factors that influence their initiative or responsibility in policy making.

In general, this approach, which has been most prevalent in North American social science, is not specifically "urban." Social ecology, political participation, electoral and party competition, etc., are general societal processes and their examination in the urban locus is somewhat a choice of convenience. Consequently, this approach has the least developed concept of urbanism apart from certain general notions of greater interdependence and need for regulatory policy.

HISTORICAL-SYSTEMIC APPROACHES TO URBAN PROCESS

A second and more distinctive approach lays great stress on the city as a complex interactive system which cannot be understood with static or positivistic models.

In essence, the systemic approach to urban processes argues for an analysis of urban phenomena which takes into account its context. Phenomena and context are dynamically inter-related in an ongoing way which normally involves mutual causation. An exceptionally cogent and convincing argument on behalf of systems analysis or what they call "holism" is offered by Anthony and Elizabeth Leeds in their stimulating contribution to this volume. The specific purpose of their paper is to account for the variation in forms of behavior of residents of squatter settlements and related types of urban occupation when confronting the political systems of their respective countries (Brazil, Peru, and Chile) given the fact that the squatters are interested in extracting goods and services from the policy. The Leeds' argue that previous explanations have almost always been in terms of the *immanent* characteristics of the population themselves rather than being accounted for in terms of the variation in the forms of political systems with which they deal. In general the Leeds' argue that the political action of any actor is "conditioned, constrained, and even perhaps, determined" by a wide range of external variables of the "inclusive polity." This influence or mutual causation works in both directions, since one actor's context is most likely another actor who in turn is within the contextual vortex.

While the Leeds' applied the systemic approach to squatter settlements in their contest for goods and services vis-a-vis the political systems of Latin America, Koehn applied a similar kind of analysis to the dynamic interaction of urban elite and national policy making. While urban elites clearly have significant influence by taking national political roles, he argues convincingly that changes in national policy had a transformation effect on urban politics and particularly on the quality of life in those communities.

The chapter by Bryant and White argues for an analysis of housing policy and politics in terms of "strategic situations" with which housing groups must cope. They discussed three specific political factors which influenced this strategic situation. The extent to which a housing constituency exists or needs to be mobilized, the existence of differences among the policy makers which provide more or less access for interest groups, and the impact of housing policy in terms of the degree and concentration of benefits. In other words, Bryant and White seem to be arguing in a fashion similar to the Leeds' that housing interest groups are more or less predictable depending on the degree to which their adversaries are predictable. Put in still other terms, it is being argued that the differentiated forms of behavior can be accounted for effectively in terms of the variation in the forms of the political systems which are confronted. The Leeds' would argue, and Bryant and White would no doubt agree, that it is quite unnecessary to look to the immanent characteristics of the groups or their members in order to explain the variations in behavior.

Cornelius also employs a systemic approach to the processes involved in Mexico City housing markets and land speculation. The combined effects of governmental land use and housing policy (e.g., "urban renewal"), financial institutions which control credit, private real estate interests, and the construction industry has been to create an acute shortage of low-cost housing opportunities for the urban poor just as it has fueled land speculation. In reaction the homeless have illegally occupied and settled properties where they feel the government will not evict them. But, ironically, even these squatter settlements are sometimes encouraged by land speculators when they make possible the acquisition of surrounding properties debased in value.

Finally, the papers by Abu-Lughod and Edari are the most explicit with respect to the historical dimensions of systems analysis. While the Leeds' trace the recent history of political parties in their three Latin American countries, these two papers insist that contemporary African cities have thousand-year histories including such fundamental watersheds as European colonialism. Abu-Lughod indicates that the evaluation of "modern urbanism" must contend with patterns of social and spatial differentiation created under colonialism and perpetuated by internal elites. Edari argues that migration, socio-economic differentiation, and ethnic contact assume different forms under different historical influences. Urban migration, for example, is changing from the stream of unskilled, temporary sojourners of the Colonial Era to a more selective attraction of young and better educated males seeking skilled and industrial employment. Any cross-sectional correlation of socio-economic status and length of urban residence would conceal this trend by "averaging out" early and later patterns.

Summarizing, the systemic approach treats urbanism as the outcome of a variety of historical forces whose consequences have been to differentiate urban society into a complex melange of groups separated by space, ethnicity, social class, and power. The present circumstances and future prospects of any one group must be understood in the context of its relationship to a variety of others and, therefore, the conception of urbanism provided is one of a highly interdependent population engaged in strategic moves and calculations. Unlike the previous approach, urban social organization is not to be viewed as the form in which competing interests resolve themselves since the systemic approach would regard competition itself (including its absence or delimitation) as proscribed and conditioned within limits set by historical possibility and the societal distribution of power. Urbanism is understood as the adaptation of a diversified population to these influences; as a "way of life" based on kinship, ethnicity, and class; as a political culture based on the realities of power; and, at the structural level, as a pattern of geographic and occupational differentiation based on the political economy.

STRUCTURALIST APPROACHES TO THE PRODUCTION OF URBAN FORMS

A third set of papers in this volume represent new "structural" or political economy theories concerned with explaining urbanization and the various sociospatial forms that cities assume. This approach has much in common with the systemic, particularly its stress on holistic analysis, but it also differs in several ways. It recognizes mutual causation but choses to begin with the economic foundations and functions of urbanism tracing their implications through the political system to the manner in which social classes are distributed in space. It is intimately concerned with urban processes such as political struggles and social movements, but attempts to locate these in the contradictions of the larger political economy. It is historical but, in addition to focusing on the histories of particular cities, it attempts to explain the origins of urbanization and, particularly, the origins of the contemporary capitalist city.

The paper by Pickvance provides a brief sketch of the theory and then goes on to review some recent French work in the area of housing as illustrative of the type of research that stems from the approach. Pickvance feels that this is a promising avenue for future research and one that can be pursued by Marxists and non-Marxists alike. Evers' paper earlier in the volume is an excellent example of the kind of research that would stem from this framework. Castells' short paper is a condensed version of some of his ideas on the theoretical bankruptcy of urban sociology and politics. While this work has enjoyed wide exposure in Europe, it is just beginning to appear in the United States and English language media. Castells argues that urban research has lacked a valid "scientific" and "real" object; that it has spuriously regarded certain phenomena as "urban" when in fact they are societal and that it has failed to develop nontautological explanations for those phenomena that may be uniquely urban. He goes on to suggest some theoretical alternatives. Walton's concluding paper attempts to synthesize a variety of contributions to the new political economy approach and move on to suggest how it might be applied to comparative work.

The structuralist approach regards the city as a particular social formation conditioned by the economy. In particular, under advanced capitalism urbanization increases markedly as a mechanism for concentrating the labor force and the means of production so as to reduce the time and costs of the circulation of capital; it is a social form for enhancing capital accumulation. The capitalist city at once concentrates and segregates the urban population in ways that enhance profit but also lead to conflicts and the need for state intervention; e.g., to provide housing or other necessities for the reproduction of the labor force. Yet cities are not unique to capitalism nor are all capitalist cities alike in urban structure. As Walton's conclusion suggests, more elaborate conceptualization of urban forms and economic-system "mixes" is necessary before the theory's explanatory power can be demonstrated, and this suggests a number of important research topics. Similarly, more attention must be given the interplay between economy and polity; the extent to which the State merely reflects the demands of accumulation, or mediates between these and the interests of the larger population, or acts in some relatively autonomous fashion.

This approach has the advantage of developing an explicit explanation of urbanism and of integrating other systemic approaches to more discrete topics. In that sense it has theoretical promise; it may open up some avenues of interpretation that are badly needed in a field whose empirical thrust has far outrun its theoretical capacity for organization and explanation.

CONCLUSION

In what has just been said our intention is not to advance some new orthodoxy. Quite the reverse. Among the comparative strategies and theoretical approaches spanned by the articles in this volume, all have merit depending upon the constraints of the research situation and the type of questions posed. We hope that these remarks will contribute to critical thinking about method and theory. This introduction intends to provide one set of coordinates that might be useful in contrasting alternative methods and theories in comparative urban research. Doubtless readers will generate their own schemes for contrasting these materials. Our own belief is that the originality and quality of the contributions provide an excellent opportunity to think further the issues in comparative urban work and for this we are grateful to the authors.

REFERENCES

ALMOND, G. A. and S. VERBA (1963) The Civic Culture: Political Attitudes and Democracy in Five Nations. Princeton: Princeton University Press.

BERRY, B. J. L. (1973) The Human Consequences of Urbanization. New York: St. Martin's Press.

BREESE, G. [ed.] (1969) The City in Newly Developing Countries. Englewood Cliffs, N.J.: Prentice-Hall.

CLARK, T. N. [ed.] (1974) Comparative Community Politics. New York: Halsted Press (a Sage Publications book).

FAVA, S. F. [ed.] (1968) Urbanism in World Perspective: A Reader. New York: Thomas Y. Crowell.

GERMANI, G. [ed.] (1973) Modernization, Urbanization and the Urban Crisis. Boston: Little, Brown.

Journal of Comparative Administration (1972) "Comparative Urban Politics," Part I. (November).

––– (1973) "Comparative Urban Politics," Part II. (February).

MEADOWS, P. and E. H. MIZRUCHI [eds.] (1969) Urbanism, Urbanization and Change: Comparative Perspectives. Reading, Mass.: Addison-Wesley.

NAROLL, R. (1968) "Some thoughts on comparative method in cultural anthropology," in H. M. Blalock and A. Blalock (eds.) Methodology in Social Research. New York: McGraw-Hill.

New Atlantis (1970) "Comparative Research on Community Decision-making." (Special issue, Winter).

PRZEWORSKI, A. and H. TEUNE (1970) The Logic of Comparative Social Inquiry. New York: John Wiley.

SCHWIRIAN, K. P. [ed.] (1974) Comparative Urban Structure: Studies in the Ecology of Cities. Lexington, Mass.: D. C. Heath.

SEARS, R. (1961) "Transcultural variables and conceptual equivalence," in B. Kaplan (ed.) Studying Personality Cross-Culturally. Evanston, Ill.: Row, Peterson.

TILLY, C. [ed] (1974) An Urban World. Boston: Little Brown

Urban Affairs Quarterly (1975) "The City in Comparative Perspective." (September).

Chapter 2

THE LEGITIMACY OF COMPARISONS IN COMPARATIVE URBAN STUDIES
A Theoretical Position and an Application to North African Cities

JANET ABU-LUGHOD

An old controversy, never resolved, lies at the root of present difficulties in the burgeoning field of comparative urban studies—a field marked by a great deal of motion but not too much progress, if by the latter term we mean coherent and systematic movement toward an agreed-upon goal. The controversy goes back at least to the nineteenth century and was generated by the tendency of early anthropologists to make elaborate files of "interesting" culture traits (gathered from as many points on the globe as explorers had written home about), and then to construct simplified theories concerning the evolution of given institutions over time by assiduously inserting selected bits of cultural evidence into the strata of their (assumed) evolution. Needless to say, evolutionary progress always conveniently culminated in the form that happened to be prevalent in Western Europe at this time (Nisbet, 1970).

In statistics, this is known as converting cross-sectional data into a theoretical model of change, a perfectly legitimate operation so long as several rather critical caveats are strictly respected. First, the theoretical model of change must not then be treated as if it had been empirically derived over time. Second, the dating sequence must be established rather

AUTHOR'S NOTE: *The research on North African cities has been partially supported by funds from the Center for Studies of Metropolitan Problems, National Institute of Mental Health, Grant 1-RO1-MH21511. An earlier version of this paper was presented to the Comparative Urban Studies and Planning Program, School of Architecture and Urban Planning, University of California (Los Angeles) in February 1974.*

unambiguously and, preferably, independently (i.e., in demographic cohort analysis, sequence is given, since old age always follows childhood; in archaeology, the strata are dated wherever possible by supplementary measures such as Carbon 14 or numismatics rather than simply judgmentally ordered). And, finally, there must be good and substantial reason to believe that the items being arranged on a continuum are all members of the same universe or "set." It was, indeed, the cavalier violation of these caveats which led to the low esteem into which such anthropology pioneers as Spencer, Morgan, Tylor, and Frazer have fallen.

Anthropologists eventually reacted violently against this older method which systematically assigned randomly selected culture traits to "prove" cultural evolution. They began to insist on the integrity of the case study and upon the indivisibility of "the system," an insistence which led straight into functionalism as a theory and to the frenzied search for isolated communities where ethnographers could probe the depths of integrated systems before they were contaminated by impingements and "distortions." In this overcompensatory swing, they left themselves open to three accusations. First, the power of their method for comparative purposes was almost totally eroded, for on what grounds does one compare unique total systems? Second, the emphasis on cultural integration led many scholars to neglect or minimize the issue of change. And third, since most societies existed in nonisolated conditions and, indeed, pristine communities were becoming increasingly difficult to find, anthropologists were in danger, at best, of producing irrelevant findings, and, at worst, of putting themselves out of business.

The field of comparative urban studies has been haunted by the same set of unpalatable alternatives, although they have nowhere been stated as explicitly as in anthropology. However, if a theory of urban change and process is to be developed to guide comparative urban studies, that theory will have to steer a more careful course between the Scylla of grand theory and the Charybdis of the pristine case study. Let us try to apply these remarks more specifically.

One of the primary characteristics of evolutionary theory was that it sought a common origin for a given cultural institution. Has this been the usual approach in the study of urbanism? I think so. Whether the answer has been sought in geomorphology—i.e., river transport or basin irrigation systems (Adams, 1965; Wittfogel, 1957); in geopolitics—i.e., symbiosis between mountain predators and plains cultivators (Mumford, 1961) or even new methods of control to extract surplus (Adams, 1966); in religious shrines and sanctuaries (Fustel de Coulanges, 1955; Wheatley, 1971); in economic exchange—i.e., the city as exchange point for surplus nuts and berries (Jacobs, 1969; Pirenne, 1925); or in technology, chiefly inventions that create surpluses (Childe, 1950, 1951), the search has been for a "common ancestor" of urbanism. Rather than search for a single progenitor, I suggest we get on with the real business at hand—namely, to investigate the conditions under which cities in various types of terrain and under differing systems of social organization and at differing levels of technological competence depended in varying degrees upon each of these impetuses for their origin and early development. The emphasis would be on common process, rather than on evolutionary line or simplified congruence.

A second characteristic of early evolutionary thought was to assume that a single prime mover was operative and therefore to classify culture traits along a continuum related to that prime mover, and, further, to assume that the existence of these traits implied a whole set of other characteristics in common—i.e., to use the continuum as a basis for a taxonomy. In urban studies, it is significant that perhaps the most influential book to have come out in comparative urbanism during the present generation has been Gideon Sjoberg's *The Preindustrial City* (1960). What Sjoberg's brilliant book did was to take technology (and more specifically, energy source) as the prime mover and basis for constructing a hierarchical taxonomy of urban types, and then to concentrate on the preindustrial city as occupying a position in that hierarchy. He explored the cultural and social as well as the morphological similarities of cities categorized together on the basis of technological level. In the process, significant differences were glossed over, and both the critical antecedent and coexisting variables received little attention.

A third characteristic of evolutionary thought is its much-maligned tendency to draw culture traits at random and to "collapse" whole societies or parts of societies into the same category (and presumed same causation) on the basis of similarities in appearance and labels. Some of our work in comparative urbanism has been guilty of just this inadmissible approach. Let me give one example.

Throughout much of the developing world, researchers have been identifying types of housing developments which, while variously named, are classified as squatter settlements. With perhaps too much ease, these developments, having roughly the same morphology and dubious legal status, are assumed to have arisen from similar causes, to serve similar sociological functions, to have similar social organization, and, finally, to produce similar consequences. I am not certain that some of the generalizations we have been making in this area of comparative urban studies are at all justified. There seem to be critical differences in traditions of land ownership and therefore the legal status of squatting, in patterns of political power and therefore the relationship of squatters to the state, in the sources, motivations and circumstances of migration and therefore selectivity and characteristics of squatter populations, which ought to yield place-specific variations. Differential government policies are a final source of variation. Nevertheless, we keep attempting to generalize about what does or does not go on in urban subareas so ostensibly similar in type. I suggest we worry more about accounting for the differences.

A final characteristic of evolutionary thought was that it assumed that the institutional form found in the culture of the theorist represented the ultimate point toward which institutions elsewhere were moving and that, therefore, examples could be arranged along a continuum on the basis of how "close" or how "far" they were from the point toward which they were inevitably headed. Much of what goes on under the rubric of "modernization," whether related to economic development or comparative urban studies, takes this assumption of convergence as its hidden premise. (I am not denying that certain types of convergence may in fact exist; I am only insisting that this should be a subject for empirical investigation rather than an a priori assumption, as it often is.) Thus, we have in comparative urban studies an assumed continuum stretching from the "primitive city" of Timbuctu to the post-modern "city without a center" of Los Angeles. This continuum is no more useful than the other old continuum we tried but failed so miserably to apply with profit to cross-cultural studies—namely, the rural-urban continuum. What is "modern" in the sense of being most *recent* within a given city is quite different from what is "modern" in the sense of being most similar morphologically to the patterns found in industrial and postindustrial cities in the West. The two are not coterminous, and to act as if they were is to stack the deck against ever being able to identify the new forms of urbanism emerging in places outside Europe and the United States.

If to some extent comparative urban studies have erred in the direction of the nineteenth-century social Darwinists, to some extent they have also erred in the opposite direction. Parallel to the anthropologists who fought for the recognition of the integrity of holistic cultural systems have been the historians of specialized culture areas and of particular cities within them. But even these have erred in two opposite directions: first, they have tended to focus on biographical descriptions of individual cities and to emphasize their incomparable qualities; but then they have also fallen into the easy trap of describing an ideal generic type which often turns out to have been abstracted chiefly from their one case. This has certainly been the tendency in the area of urban research nearest to my heart—the so-called "Islamic city." Ideal-type descriptions abound (Berque, 1958; von Grunebaum, 1955; G. Marçais, 1940, 1945; W. Marçais, 1928; de Planhol, 1959), each distorted by the loose tendency to specialize on one city, the cities of a given subregion, or cities at a given point in Islamic history, to generalize findings to a mythological beast called "the Islamic city." And, as happened to the anthropologists who took as sacrosanct the isolated case study, there was a natural tendency to focus more on the persistence of forms than upon the changes. Hence, the literature abounds with discussions of the Islamic city not only generalized to large geographic regions (as if important influences were not at work differentially over the wide expanse of Islam) but also generalized over time (as if somehow change and development were urban phenomena whose appearance on the scene coincided with the advent of Western urban forms). The Islamic city thus became the "traditional city" and was assumed to have had only minimal development over time.

All this brings me to the theoretical position I wish to take and to my recommendation that comparative urban studies backs up a bit from the too ambitious task it has taken upon itself and sets more precise limits to its activities—limits which will distinguish legitimate comparisons from illegitimate comparisons, given the present state of the art. I would therefore like to argue strongly for a strategy which moves in disciplined fashion from the very specific to the somewhat more general to the even more general via the semi-controlled "experiment," and which attempts to illuminate the similarities and differences uncovered by this research strategy by means of common mechanisms of process. I shall first try to explain a little better what I mean by this somewhat dense sentence, and then attempt a demonstration analysis, utilizing the material I have been working on for the past several years (nowhere near completed): a comparative analysis of three North African capital cities—Cairo, Tunis, and Rabat-Salé.

First, what is meant by a semi-controlled experiment? What is being proposed is a procedure for tracing the operation of common variables *within* specific parameters set by a culture area and a level of technological competence *before* jumping ahead to taxonomies and theories of comparative urbanism which "throw into the hopper" all cities at all times from all over to see which traits and isolated characteristics appear congruent or divergent. In any semi-controlled experiment, the parameters are those variables which are taken to be roughly constant, so that the operation of other variables can be examined in more disciplined fashion. In the present comparisons, climatic zone, political role, and the cultural-legal normative system are treated as common parameters, enabling us to test the operation of such variables as situs, trade patterns, centrality-peripherality vis-à-vis the wider Islamic world, differential linkage to pre-Islamic and non-Islamic systems, and imposed or diffused impingements from Europe. These changes can then be analyzed over time with specific attention to increased technological sophistication.

What do I mean by attention to common mechanisms of process? I mean that if we are to develop real generalizations and theories in the field of comparative urbanism, these should be sought on the level of "becoming" rather than on the level of "being," to borrow a distinction from the ancient Greeks. The empirical generalization that upper-income districts are found near water (or on hilltops, or whatever) is *not* a process statement. A process generalization would state the conditions under which the presence of a body of water leads to certain types of land-use developments and the reasons why specific hypothesized differences in outcomes should be expected under specified climatic, normative, and economic variations. The empirical generalization that central business districts contain the highest (or the lowest) densities has nothing to do with process. A process generalization would discuss the relationship between processes of concentration and dispersion and the mechanisms whereby differential valuations and mini-max decisions are cumulatively translated into centripetal or centrifugal movements. An empirical generalization that subgroups within cities are segregated according to familism, ethnicity, and/or class in a specific way is *not* a process statement. A process generalization would involve explaining the conditions under which and the processes whereby given social structures are translated into given spatial patterns. The empirical generalization that urban primacy (so-called "overurbanization," a clearly value-added gratuity) is found chiefly in small developing countries is *not* what is meant by process. A process generalization is one which would trace shifts in the pattern of core-periphery balance over time under conditions of changing patterns of transportation, communication, and the distribution mechanisms for money and power.

With all of this in mind, let us turn to the case of North African urbanism, and more specifically to a comparison of the cities of Cairo, Tunis, and Rabat-Salé, looking first at what they have in common, then at the major differences among them, and, finally, at the common processes (applied in variable degrees) which have led to the wide and very real differences we now find. The analysis will be highly tentative, for much work remains to be done. It will be highly general, since space does not permit a fuller explication (see Abu-Lughod, 1975b for illustrations).

I

THE PARAMETERS

The three cities under study are located in North Africa, which has a roughly common semi-tropical climate, coolest for Rabat-Salé and warmest for Cairo, wettest for Rabat-Salé and dryest for Cairo. The countries in which the cities are located are each characterized by a sharp demarcation between the "desert" and the "sown," although the line between the two has shifted significantly over time due to the alternating processes of dessication and irrigation, and mountains intervene between the two in Morocco. This demarcation is translated into socioeconomic and ethnic cleavages within the national populations, of greatest significance in Morocco, of least (current) significance in Egypt. The three cities are each located next to significant bodies of water (Cairo on the Nile, Tunis on a saline lake extension of the Mediterranean, Rabat-Salé at the Atlantic coast on either side of a river estuary) and have served, albeit not continuously, as port entrepôts, although the port function remains significant today only for Tunis.

The three cities occupy sites which were historically receptive to urban developments long before Islamic times. Cairo is relatively close to Pharaonic Memphis, Tunis is near Phoenician-founded Carthage, and Rabat-Salé occupies a district containing the ruins of the Roman (and possibly Phoenician before that) outpost of Sala. Nevertheless, each of the three cities demonstrates an historic discontinuity between the pre-Islamic settlement which had virtually disappeared and the Islamic settlement which, for all intents and purposes, can be considered to be a newly founded city. All, in addition, were founded or refounded by Muslim military governors imbued with religious fervor and dreams of glory. Thus, each combined in its earliest symbolic character both God and the sword; considerations of economic base came later.

All three cities, having been reconstituted during the first few centuries of Islam, were fundamentally shaped by a common legal system. And, to my mind, this common legal system is the only legitimate basis for the real, rather than merely nominal, classification called the "Islamic city." The cities grew and developed under a normative system which defined forms of ownership and rights of development, which dictated similar distinctions between private and public space and established common rules of deportment in each, and which allocated in similar fashion the rights and responsibilities for urban affairs among occupants, private proprietors, and the quasi-religious state. Since this legal system was substantially different from the system of Roman Law from which most medieval European cities derived their patterns of organization and development, there is good reason to examine the three cases together and to distinguish them from European models.

And, finally, each of the cities now serves as the political capital of the country in which it is located and is therefore the seat of political rule, the home of most government employees (and the public employment sector in each country is formidably large), and the display arena most sensitively projective of a national image to the rest of the world.

The similarities noted above have yielded certain common problems and mechanisms for solutions which suggest that the cities constitute a theoretically defensible "set" within which it would be legitimate to make comparisons. Furthermore, the three cities differ substantially enough from one another on other equally important variables so as to make the comparative analysis of their contemporary state and emerging problems fruitful. While some of these differences may be incomparable, others allow us to array the three cities on several continua and to trace their emergent differentiation. Our task will be to demonstrate how these divergent patterns came about and to examine the historical and other influences which account for the differences.

THE VARIATIONS

With respect to size, Cairo, with close to 7 million inhabitants, is by far the largest and most important city, not only within its nation-state of almost 40 million people but indeed in all of Africa and the Middle East. It obviously serves regional functions that extend far beyond the national frontiers of Egypt. Needless to say, it is several times more populous than Alexandria, the Egyptian city of second rank.

Tunis occupies a similar primate position within Tunisia, although because of the smaller size of the national system (the population of Tunisia is only about 5 million) and the city's much more limited role with respect to a hinterland beyond national frontiers, its population—even within the generously bounded district of Greater Tunis, including extensive suburbs and satellites—still falls slightly below 1 million. The Tunisian city of second rank, Sfax, is by contrast a mere dwarf, and core-periphery relations are marked by the tremendous concentration of goods and services in Tunis. All transportation and communication lines in the country focus squarely on Tunis.

Morocco, while considerably larger and more populous than Tunisia, has remained far more decentralized, for compelling geographic and political reasons. Several good-sized cities are scattered throughout this country of 15 million persons, and each, at one time or another, has served as the region's most important urban center. Currently, the largest city in Morocco and its undisputed economic giant is *not* Rabat-Salé but rather the twentieth-century and largely European-founded metropolis of Casablanca with over 1.5 million inhabitants. Cities in the second-tier rank include Fez, Marrakech, Meknes, and Rabat-Salé, all of which contain several hundred thousand inhabitants apiece. Interestingly enough, during the nineteenth century these four cities constituted simultaneously the capital cities of Morocco, under a unique system of court rotation. It was not until its twentieth-century designation as the *only* capital city that Rabat-Salé's population gradually inched ahead of the others. Its metropolitan area, which includes not only the twin cities but surrounding suburbs and farmland, now contains well over a half-million inhabitants and is growing quite rapidly.

With respect to internal arrangement, we find that all three cities are characterized by ecological discontinuities and the juxtaposition within them of three fairly distinct models of city-building and urban life (Abu-Lughod, 1971b). However, the degree to which the historical nucleus (the medieval Islamic city), the nineteenth- and twentieth-century "Western-style" extensions of that core, and the peripheral "squatter" or semi-rural quarters are ecologically disjunctive varies significantly from one city to the other.

Cairo shows the greatest degree of integration among the quarters, the fewest sharp boundaries between adjacent types of quarters, and the smallest range of variance between zones of highest and lowest status as measured by quality of housing and characteristics of residents. As has been demonstrated in our earlier sequential analysis of the evolving ecological structure of Cairo (Abu-Lughod, 1971a), considerable blending and equalization occurred between 1947 and 1960, a process which has apparently continued at an even faster pace during the subsequent period.

Tunis is still substantially more segregated than Cairo, although less so than Rabat-Salé. The historic nucleus is ecologically distinct, even though the wall which formerly marked its boundary was removed before the end of the nineteenth century and a transportation system along its course has provided peripheral access to the old city throughout the twentieth. Transitional zones have grown up between the most Westernized quarters and the medieval core; indeed, the "historic" city has made substantial inroads into the colonial quarters which Italian and French settlers constructed on the muddy flats between the former "port gate" and the lake. On the other hand, whereas earlier cultural and ethnic cleavages have blurred, the ecological lines drawn along economic cleavages have strengthened. Much of the older city is being "proletarianized," as migrants from the rural zones of Tunisia take the place of the Tunisian Muslim bourgeoisie, almost all of whom have left the medina for homes either in the colonial-founded city or in the now-burgeoning suburban zones to the west and northeast. (It is interesting to note that this process occurred in Cairo almost fifty years earlier.) Peripheral proletarian zones, both squatter-type and government-constructed, are heavily concentrated near sites of heavy industry or on environmentally unattractive sites along the odiferous saline lakes. These remain ecologically segregated and indeed may be becoming even more sharply cut off from areas of high- and middle-income residence by the "judicious" creation of barriers, such as walls, superhighways, and the like. The range between quarters is significantly great on most social indicators, although nowhere as obvious and marked as in Rabat-Salé.

Rabat-Salé, by virtually every criteria available, is characterized by the most extreme and marked discontinuities. Its ecological pattern sensitively reflects social cleavages which have barely begun to be integrated in a society where the range of class differences, ways of life, and, indeed, separate economies remains almost as extreme as it had been during the decades of colonial rule. Segregation is along both economic-class and "style-of-life-ethnic-linguistic" group lines, and the three types of city form—the historic core city, the Western-styled colonial city, and the bidonville or peripheral squatter settlement—coexist with a remarkably small degree of interpenetration and transactional frequency (Abu-Lughod, 1974).

Both man-made and topographic barriers reinforce this trifurcation of specialized and nonintersecting life styles. First, the river estuary itself has served historically as the most important boundary. On one side was the rectangularly-walled town of Salé, already quite prominent by the eleventh century as a center of religion, production, and trade. Across the river, on the site of an older Islamic monastery *(ribat)*, the Almohads constructed during the second half of the twelfth century a staging port for their invasion of Spain, which was expanded to form the princely city of Ribat al-Fath. The settlement was abandoned soon afterward, not to be revived until the beginning of the seventeenth century, when the last remaining Muslims were expelled from Spain. Some of these Andalusians went to Tunis, where they infused the medina with new traits; others went to Salé but were quickly exiled to the other bank of the river where they first rebuilt the walled ribat (the so-called Qasba of the Oudaia), and then the city core just below the Qasba (Caillé, 1949: vol. I). Ignored by the French occupiers in favor of Rabat, the town of Salé remained even more isolated from its neighbor than ever before (Naçiri, 1963; Brown, 1969). Today it is an almost exclusively lower- to middle-class zone, despite attempts to build suburban villa quarters on the highlands beyond the city walls. Rural migrants have crowded into its walled quarter, and bidonvilles and *trames sanitaires* (low-cost public housing) proliferate on its agricultural periphery. Quarrying, pottery-making and brick works constitute the heavy polluting industries which supplement the handicraft production of its declining economic base.

City walls are the second barriers delimiting ecological zones. Within the city of Rabat, the extreme northern corner constitutes the medina proper, still fully walled (flanked on two sides by water, on a third by the twelfth-century wall of Ribat al-Fath, on the fourth by the seventeenth-century wall built by the Spanish emigrants). These walls were left intact and indeed strengthened by the French, who considered them both a legal and a symbolic barrier between "the natives" and themselves (for details, see Abu-Lughod, 1975a). Interestingly enough, while some earlier walls (such as the extention of the twelfth-century wall which intersects but does not divide two European-style quarters) now serve only decorative functions, new walls (such as those which shield from view a number of the peripheral bidonvilles adjacent to the highways that lead to Casablanca) have actually been constructed in the present century to isolate incompatible ecological conclaves. Thus, the wall is clearly not a "natural" barrier so much as it is a device to maintain segregation when it is considered useful.

Topography has also served this function. While Rabat is certainly not hilly, it is on undulating terrain, considerably higher than either the riverbed or the sandflats on which Salé is built. Sharply pitched slopes descend precipitously to the saline shores. And it is on these slopes, largely hidden from view by topographic features, that one finds a series of bidonvilles sharply differentiated from adjacent quarters.

Recently there have been the first signs of mending in the tattered social fabric of Rabat-Salé. The river, formerly a barrier of the first order, is now traversed by several bridges whose congestion at rush hours indicates the increased economic and labor linkages between the two cities. The walls surrounding the medina of Rabat, while still standing, are becoming less functional as a dividing line between the Islamic core and the Western-style city and more functional as a decorative element. Suq-retailing practices have spilled over from the old city to the first few blocks of the new city beyond the Andalusian walls, and life in Océan, a modest quarter just beyond the Almohad walls that had originally been the home of European skilled workers has become less and less differentiated from the type of life found in the medina. Thus, a process which is very far advanced in Cairo and which is a few decades old in Tunis appears to be beginning now in Rabat.

A third continuum along which the three cities may profitably be arranged is in terms of their economic bases, with Tunis having the firmest multibased economic centrality, Cairo sharing her functions with the rival magnet of Alexandria, and Rabat virtually overshadowed by and dependent upon the "real" economic capital of Casablanca, less than 100 kilometers away. To some extent, the relationship of each city with its waterway and with external trade constitutes the underlying variable.

Tunis began in the Islamic era as a crucial port and ship-building arsenal. Furthermore, the city's location, at the crossroads of a fertile coastal strip which rounded the bend at Bizerte, meant that even before Islam it functioned economically as a logical stopping place for traders as well as a point of economic exchange. In Berber, Tunis meant "the place where one spends the night" (Pellegrin, 1955: 4). By the twelfth century, long after being well-established as both a port for water traffic and an exchange center for land trade, Tunis added the political function. It was proclaimed capital of Ifriqiya, a role which it has retained to the present. The port continued to be central to its existence and strongly stimulated the development of industry and commerce in the city.

Both Cairo and Rabat, on the other hand, experienced radical reversals in their status as centers of water-borne trade, Cairo somewhat earlier than Rabat and with less drastic consequences for its economic base. Like Tunis, both cities had been ship-building arsenals from the beginning, but unlike Tunis, both were equipped to handle ships of shallow draft only. Once the technological shift to steam and heavier-draft ships occurred, their respective ports ceased to be important.

By the sixteenth century, Cairo's port functions had already become relatively insignificant. Though it had been the major break-in-bulk trans-shipping point for the rich spice trade of the orient before the African Cape was rounded in 1498, it was reduced to a minor connecting stage between points on the Mediterranean and those on the Upper Nile. Later, in the eighteenth and even more in the nineteenth centuries, when direct trade with Europe became more important and when shipping converted to steam, the last vestiges of its significance as a port were transferred to Alexandria. The construction of the Suez Canal, which bypassed the trans-shipping point at Cairo, simply completed the gradual process of erosion that had long been under way.

Rabat's port functions were always more central to its existence and were lost more precipitously. The city originated in the twelfth century as a staging point for the Almohad campaigns in Spain, and its seventeenth-century revival, similarly, was linked to the expulsion of the Hornacheros and other Muslims from that country. These refugees went into an industry that was definitely water-linked—namely, piracy. The so-called Sallee Rovers of English sea chanty fame were, indeed, the corsairs of Salé (Caillé, 1949: vol. I). But it is important to note that the ships which darted out of the BouRegreg harbor to harass European vessels were manned not by the stolid urbanites of traditional Salé but by the Spanish-descended adventurers of Rabat. Piracy out of this port on the western coast of Africa became important at just about the time that Cairo's port functions dried up. The cause of both events was the same—the basic shift in world trade routes.

During the seventeenth century, then, Rabat gained considerable importance, but its revival was short-lived. The hazardous sandbar in the harbor and the turbulence of the sea—factors which had indeed protected raiding ships from retaliation—were both intensified by an earthquake in 1755 which virtually ruined the harbor. In addition, the insurrectionist independence of the Rabatis stimulated the Sultan of Morocco to later establish at the new coastal town of Mogador a more southerly port which could be more directly under his control. Even later in the nineteenth century, Europeans, who were by then establishing firm trade footholds in Morocco, began to conduct more of their business through Casablanca (hitherto the unimportant town of Anfa), and once the Protectorate was established, huge sums were invested in deepening that harbor to eliminate the inconvenience of lighterage (Adam, 1968).

In the case of Cairo, removal of the port function did not leave the city without an alternative economic base, even though it did result in a tremendous expansion of Alexandria's role in the national economy. Rather, both Cairo and Alexandria received economic infusions from the development of the international cotton trade and from the food- and fiber-processing industries which were generated during the late nineteenth and early twentieth centuries. Furthermore, Cairo remained the capital of Egypt and, as the state strengthened and eventually gained independence from British colonial rule, her governmental functions were significantly increased. Thus, the port was only one among many reasons for her economic viability, and the city eventually survived the decline initiated by its disappearance.

Not so with Rabat. The volatile fluctuations in its history had always been linked to the port, and when this function was undercut, stagnation was inevitable. But Rabat's decline to modest status was dramatically reversed by an "act" which suddenly replaced its port function by an administrative one. In 1912, following a number of outrageous gunboat-diplomacy incidents, France succeeded in establishing a Protectorate over most of Morocco. The original intention of Maréchal Lyautey, the newly appointed French Résident Général, was to establish his capital at Fez, certainly the country's most important city. But the strength of nationalist resistance there and Fez's clearly indefensible location in the interior quickly forced him to retreat to Rabat, where he set up his official headquarters. It was then an almost exogenous factor, and one linked more to political and military expediency than to an economically rational choice, that finally transfused Rabat with the economic base that has continued to sustain it. Ever since, Rabat's situation has been essentially akin to that of Washington, D.C., which, like Rabat, would experience virtual economic collapse if the seat of government were suddenly to be removed.

This has created for Rabat in the contemporary period types of problems which it does not share with either Tunis or Cairo, capitals whose present status was neither so capriciously established nor so fragily sustained. Whereas all three capitals have attracted disproportionate numbers of rural migrants, drawn to the seat of power in the hope that their needs will be more visible and therefore preferentially met, only Rabat has been yet unable to absorb most of these newcomers into the modern industrial sector associated with economic development. That development continues overwhelmingly to be drawn to Casablanca, with its already well-endowed infrastructure and now increasingly to more decentralized, resource-rich centers in the interior.

In the preceding sections, we have alluded repeatedly to the obvious fact that cities and the countries of which they are a part are scarcely "closed systems." Therefore, to comprehend the factors which underlie individual urban changes requires careful attention to the contexts within which such changes are generated. Let us take for example one aspect of the geographic context. It is significant to note that the pre-Islamic linkage of each of the capitals was not latitudinally with one another but rather with quite different and longitudinally ordered subregions of the Mediterranean and Africa.

Morocco's significant neighbors were to the south (the trans-Saharan routes to Timbuctu, the early significance of Sijilmasa, the nomadic waves across the Sudanic belt) and only secondarily to the north (the Roman Empire and later Spain and France). Only occasionally was the city drawn organically into the "natural" sphere of the wider Maghrib—i.e., Algeria,

Tunisia, and sometimes western Libya—and then largely through the overland Taza corridor which constituted a gaping hole in the otherwise fortress-like mountain defenses.

Tunisia, lacking natural defenses and limits, was always more a crossroad than an autonomous entity, and this fact is reflected in the fluid state of its relations first with one and then another part of the Mediterranean. In general, he who controlled the "middle sea" controlled Tunisia. In addition, it was through Tunisia that the Mediterranean world occasionally linked up with the African interior via several critical caravan routes that went directly through the country. During the Islamic period, Tunisia proved an equally important crossroads for lateral traffic across North Africa. It constituted the first consolidation point beyond Egypt of the Arab advance during the first centuries after Muhammad; it was the source out of which the Fatimids moved eastward to establish their dynasty at Cairo; and it was Tunisia which absorbed the main brunt of the devastating incursions by the Beni-Hilal. At times the country was master of parts of Algeria, at times subject to either Algerian or more often Moroccan hegemony. Only at rare moments was it able to take advantage of fragmenting empires to become a fairly autonomous province within a larger but only nominal system.

Egypt, like Morocco, always constituted a more natural region sufficient unto itself, one which followed strictly the north-south axis established by the Nile. Whenever it was strong it expanded its control both southward into the Sudan and northeastward into the fertile crescent and beyond. When it was weak, it retracted to its boundaries and became superficially (and unreliably) a subject state of whoever controlled the eastern Mediterranean. On the other hand, when the Islamic Empire reached its periodic heights, Cairo served as so vital a magnet for scholars, religious thinkers, and politically ambitious rulers that it cross-fertilized within its gates the economic, cultural, and aesthetic creations generated in territories over which it exercised little if any political control.

These geographic facts created quite distinct consequences for the three cities. Architecturally, each of the older cities is a unique amalgam of differential inspirations. Rabat-Salé on the surface would appear least cross-pollinated by virtue of its almost exclusive Andalusian base, but even here it would be a false simplification to forget that the ninth-century Omayyad dynasty of Spain came directly from Damascus and that, consequently, Syrian styles infused not only the cities founded by the Caliphate of Cordoba but the Moroccan cities that developed over the centuries during which Morrocco and southern Spain constituted a unified cultural-geographical region.

Tunis absorbed architectural and social patterns from the most diverse sources, as one might expect from its geographical position at the crossroads. Indigenous, Arab, Andalusian, and even Roman and later Italian forms amalgamated to form the basic pattern of Tunis, over which the Ottomans laid their superficial stamp by building palaces and government structures. All of these influences, however, were as much modified by local esthetics as Tunis was transformed by them. The Tunisian instinct for delicacy and good taste simplified the florid excesses of Alhambra and lightened the heavy solidity of the Ottoman style to yield a distinctively Tunisian architectural genre.

In Cairo, the medieval heritage was of an entirely different order. No trace of al-Andalus is to be found and only a few signs of early Arab or Fatimid influence remain. The dominant Islamic tradition came from the vicinity of Anatolia, and the remaining architectural monuments are chiefly those left by Saladin, the Mamluks, and later the Ottomans. However, their straighter lines and the often starkly simplified use of mass make them reminiscent more of pharaonic monuments than of either the lacy Syrian-Andalusian arched extravaganzas or of the heavy earth-hugging Ottoman domes.

Architecture is only one of the more visible areas through which one may observe the results of diffusion via geography. Similar analyses can be made of the diffusion of social and cultural patterns, although these are perhaps somewhat more subtle and harder to establish. One might, for example, compare municipal institutions and urban officers to show in what ways the prior Byzantine patterns influenced eastern Islam but failed to modify the Maghrib.

Geographic factors, as we have thus seen, greatly affected the type of urban development each of the cities experienced during the long centuries of its existence. In more recent times, political factors seem to have played an even more decisive role, beginning perhaps with the Ottomans of the sixteenth century, who succeeded in drawing into their orbit both Egypt and Tunisia (as well as Libya and Algeria) while being incapable of extending any dominion over Morocco. The unity of the Islamic world and of the Maghrib was thereby forfeited.

From the sixteenth century onward, Cairo and Tunis shared a common linkage with Istanbul. Despite the resurgence of local aristocracies in both Cairo and Tunis, and despite much de facto political autonomy, both cities shared a set of similar institutional reforms and were exposed to a similar set of modernizing influences linked to their participation in the Ottoman Empire. Both benefited from the reintroduction of wheeled vehicles, a method of transport which had virtually disappeared from the Fertile

Crescent and North Africa due to the introduction of the camel (Bulliet, 1973). The absence of the wheel had marked effects on the evolving street system in early Islamic cities, and its reintroduction was similarly influential in generating a demand for wider and straighter streets. More important, Cairo and Tunis were both affected by the Turkish Tanzimat reforms of 1858 which strengthened private ownership of land, modified the system of taxation, and provided new models for municipal administration.

And perhaps of greatest significance, Tunisia and Egypt paid the price for the decline in Ottoman power, a decline which left their provinces open and defenseless in the face of European colonial adventures during the nineteenth century. Algeria, the farthest province, was of course the first to fall (in 1830). Half a century later, both Egypt and Tunisia lost their independence, the former to Great Britain, the latter to France.

The deviant status of Morocco during these centuries was increasingly confirmed and intensified. It was virtually isolated. One indication of its isolation is that the wheel remained unused in Morocco until the opening years of the twentieth century—that is, more than a century after its reintroduction into Egypt. It would be a mistake, however, to overemphasize the isolation. The European powers were locked in bitter competition over Morocco, and it is perhaps more to the standoff they achieved than to its own not insignificant capacity to resist conquest that its delayed colonization must be attributed. Economic colonialism, in the form of unprotected markets and extraterritorial consular rights (similar to those which Europeans enjoyed in Tunisia and Egypt by virtue of the Capitulations signed with the Ottoman Porte), certainly existed in Morocco during the nineteenth century, and already by then native industries were declining under the impact of cheaper, foreign-manufactured goods. But the 1880 Treaty of Madrid and the later Act of Algesiras (1906) had established an elaborate system whereby colonial powers shared in exploiting the country. It was not until 1912 that France established monopoly rights through its Protectorate over the largest portion of Morocco. It yielded the northern corner to Spain, and thus until the 1950s the natural region of Morocco was artificially subdivided into two political zones—a fact which perhaps strengthened the country's already strong tendencies toward decentralization and which led to the elaboration of two types of European-styled cities within its boundaries: those such as Tangiers, Tetuan, etc., on the Spanish model; and the remainder, including Marrakech, Fez, Rabat, etc., on the French model.

Given the political factor of colonialism, one would expect that Egypt, because it was under British rule, would have followed a quite different path from either Tunisia or Morocco, both of which were under French rule. Upon closer examination, however, this political variable turns out to be, if not spurious, at least of surprisingly minor significance. To some extent, the explanation is to be found in the legal codes used by the colonizing powers. The laws of local government, administration, and town planning which were introduced in 1883 by the British in Egypt (the so-called Organic Laws) were virtually identical to the laws imposed by the French in Tunisia in the same year. Indeed, the very same legislation appears in 1883 in British-administered India. It is possible to translate from French to English or vice versa with little difficulty, and it appears that the English administration simply adopted the French legislation. Morocco, in addition, was not particularly deviant in this instance. For example, the first local government and planning laws introduced into that country in 1914 were acknowledged to have been based on the Egyptian model (Sablayrolles, 1925: 39, 58). And the laws which governed land registration under French-administered Morocco were copied from the Torrens Act, which had been developed in Australia.

In short, the facts that Britain was the colonial power in Egypt and that France occupied the counterpart position in Tunisia and later in Morocco did not in themselves result in particularly distinctive patterns of control over "the natives" nor necessarily in different patterns of urban development. Several other factors were of much greater significance. The first of these was the time period during which the first "Western-style" additions were made to the cities. The second was the proportion of the urban population who were foreigners and who therefore sought to be accommodated in the new additions. The third factor was the ideological position of the colonists which defined the degree to which local elites were allowed to adopt European styles of life and to assimilate to the foreigners during the colonial period.

Because Tunisia and Egypt were integrally linked with the Ottoman Empire, they experienced both the indigenous impulses toward modernization endemic in that empire during the latter half of the nineteenth century and the direct contacts with Europe which were becoming increasingly frequent and, indeed, unavoidable. The Khedive of Egypt, Isma'il, began in the 1860s to expand the city of Cairo onto relatively open land between the western limit of the medieval city and the Nile which, as it receded, had left high and dry land in its wake. French city planners worked with Egyptian engineers to design this new addition, the major lines of which were already laid out long before the British established their rule. This accounts for the fact that the first (and indeed later as well) additions to Cairo in the modern era followed the French mode of city planning (Abu-Lughod, 1971a).

A similar although less extensive effort was made in Tunis, prior to the institution of French colonial rule, to develop a Western-style city expansion on the muddy flats which, through landfill, were being recovered from the elongated edge of the Lac du Tunis. However, since most of the foreign population in the city was *not* French, but rather Italian, the earliest plans were on the grand Roman pattern. It was not until later that the full lines of this urban expansion were laid out, and even then the French colonial administration employed some Italian planners to help them in their designs.

In contrast, before the establishment of direct French rule in 1912, none of the cities of Morocco (with the exception of Casablanca whose deviant status has been described) contained any quarters designed along European lines. After Lyautey was appointed Résident Général of Morocco, he recruited French city planners and delegated to them the responsibility for drawing up master plans for several new towns to be built entirely on the French model and for urban extensions to practically every indigenous Moroccan city. His policy was explicit. These new extensions were to be clearly separated from the existing "native" cities which were to be touched as little as possible, and were to be planned to maximize modernity and efficiency, although architectural controls were imposed to require that façades in the newer quarters blent esthetically with the Moroccan architecture he so admired.

Once built, the new European-style communities met a different fate in each of the cities, largely dependent upon whether the foreign community was large enough to sustain a fully self-contained urban system or was so small that such a system could be maintained only by allowing (or encouraging) natives to help support it. In Cairo, the number of foreign residents remained quite small, and despite their virtually complete segregation in the "colonial" city they constituted at their peak only about half the residents of the new quarters. Furthermore, their number peaked in the early decades of the twentieth century and declined drastically after the first World War. From the beginning, then, Egyptians lived in the European-style quarters, a fact reflecting the degree to which British rule was based upon its alliance with not only the monarchy but with a large upwardly mobile class of local persons. Egyptianization of the colonial city, then, took place from the very beginning and extended over a fairly long period of time. The final phase of Egyptianization, and a relatively minor one in terms of overall urban development, occurred in 1956 when many foreign nationals had their properties nationalized in retaliation for the British-French-Israeli invasion of Suez and left the country.

In Tunis, foreigners constituted a much larger proportion of the total population and their numbers, supplemented by the aristocratic Jews of Italian origin who deserted the medina quite early to live in the European quarters, were sufficient to maintain an almost self-contained and self-sufficient city outside the original town. Foreign nationals, furthermore, were not all members of the elite. A fairly sizable number of them were Maltese and Sicilian workers who had settled chiefly in the interstitial zone between the predominately Muslim medina and the more French Christian upper-class zone that advanced westward on the former site of the receding lake. The European-style city thus was subdivided ecologically into numerous zones along ethnic and class lines. This meant that it was never as completely dependent upon the old city for its services and menial workers as was true in Cairo where the Western-style city was the almost exclusive preserve of the elite. When the foreign community of Tunis was decimated at the time of independence in the 1950s, some lower- and middle-class foreigners remained behind, and many areas containing varied levels of housing quality and cost were made available to Tunisians wishing to relocate outside the medina.

Rabat-Salé experienced an entirely different set of conditions with respect to the European-style city which the French had built for their own use and which the Moroccans inherited when many Frenchmen left the country after independence was gained. From the very beginning, it was assumed that the new cities would be for the exclusive use of the French colonists—for in Morocco as in Algeria, France intended to colonize, not merely to rule. At first, indeed, a concerted effort was made to prevent any mixing of the native and colonial populations. Foreigners were enjoined from residing in the medinas, and natives were actively discouraged from entertaining any pretensions regarding residence in the new quarters which were being so generously funded through confiscation of their lands (Abu-Lughod, 1975a).

The avowed policy of apartheid was never realized, but not for lack of administrative efforts. First, just as there existed groups in Egypt and Tunis which fell somewhere between the foreign elite and the "natives," so in Morocco a marginal group, consisting of the so-called "protégés" (Bowie, 1970), created the first anomaly in the dichotomous classification;

many of them settled in the newer quarters. In addition, wealthier Jews who were subject to cooptation by the Protectorate also took the opportunity to leave the ghettoes to which they had been confined at the beginning of the nineteenth century. The flood-gates to the newer quarters were forced open, however, by the fact that a massive migration of Moroccans to the cities had begun, the cities had in fact made no provision for them at all. Into many quarters, sometimes belatedly planned but often left to the expediential device of squatting, came large numbers of workers drawn to the factories and other jobs opening up in construction and service. Once the medinas became saturated with their numbers, some of the residents of the older quarters joined newly arrived migrants in the patches of the new city which became exclusively Muslim quarters. Most often, these patches were to be found some distance from the old medinas; they had leapfrogged over the elegant European city to the outskirts.

Nevertheless, the number of foreigners was always adequate to permit the European-style city to develop a relatively self-contained life, albeit one which had increasingly to be lived out in the wedges between the growing Moroccan quarters. When independence was declared in 1956, these European-dominated zones began to empty out, and Moroccans inherited the urban plant which their exploitation had helped to subsidize into existence. Transformation of these zones is going on quite rapidly now, and the Moroccan elite is beginning to move to areas of "second settlement," beyond the European-style colonial city to the suburban outskirts of Souissi, and even beyond the university where, indeed, today's master planners of Rabat envisage a new city center and planned community to be built on hitherto vacant land.

It is easy to note parallels here, for the open land has the same reddish hue as Hamra, that modern Arab subsection of Beirut which Palestinian emigrees boomed into existence overnight in the 1950s (see Khalaf and Kongstad, 1974), and the plans are as ambitious as those which Cairo executed first in Heliopolis and then in the newer Nasr City adjacent to it. It reminds one of the suburban development around the Belvedere quarter of Tunis. In short, despite all the heavy past and the arcane histories of these cities, the communities which are evolving from them in the modern age have unique qualities which have more in common with one another and with other cities in the Arab world than they have with New York or Los Angeles.

II

The material in the preceding section can be expanded almost infinitely, but it has not been my intention to give anything more than a very preliminary analysis of some of the items which have taken on importance to me as I continue my study of the cities of Cairo, Tunis, and Rabat-Salé and attempt to describe their patterns and seek causal explanations for their different routes to modern urbanism. By now I have probably not only annoyed specialists on these cities with too many as yet unsupported and possibly erroneous generalizations, but also bored comparative urbanists who now know more about these three cities than they ever cared to.

I shall not apologize, for this was my intent. Too often the urban biographer fears generalization, for some of the details of historical growth, wrested with such great pain from fragmentary historical evidence and often found only in sources in "difficult" languages, must by definition be lost when the canvas is expanded to comparison. And too often, unfortunately, the specialist in comparative studies prefers to treat cities as if they were, if not acts of God, at least natural phenomena which follow natural laws and can therefore be analyzed without reference to their heavily encrusted, man-made histories.

My intention, then, was to demonstrate that comparative urban studies, even within the more limited agenda and goals set in the first part of this paper, is a complicated task, requiring knowledge of many more disciplines and facts than specialists are usually trained to handle. To my knowledge, we have thus far failed to train persons in this type of research and analysis. I hope I have not discouraged too much by my remarks those readers who hope to advance the infant field of comparative urban studies. An enormous amount of work remains to be done, but the contribution of such work to a deeper understanding of urban process cannot be overestimated.

REFERENCES

ABU-LUGHOD, J. (1975a) "Moroccan cities: apartheid and the serendipity of conservation," in I. Abu-Lughod (ed.) African Themes. Northwestern University Program of African Studies, Evanston.
——— (1975b) untitled article forthcoming in Ekistics.

——— (1974) "Factorial ecology as a technique for comparative analysis: Rabat-Salé, Morocco, an example of a post-colonial caste system." Northwestern University Comparative Urban Studies Program, Evanston. (mimeo)

——— (1971a) Cairo: 1001 Years of the City Victorious. Princeton: Princeton Univ. Press.

——— (1971b) "North African cities blend the past to face the future." Africa Report 16 (June): 12-15.

ADAM, A. (1968) Casablanca: Essai sur la transformation de la société marocaine au contact de l'occident. Paris: Centre de récherche scientifique. 2 vols.

ADAMS, R. M. (1966) The Evolution of Urban Society, Chicago: Aldine.

——— (1965) Land Behind Baghdad. Chicago: Univ. of Chicago Press.

BERQUE, J. (1958) "Médinas, villeneuves et bidonvilles." Les Cahiers du Tunisie (Nos. 21-22): 5-42.

BOWIE, L. (1970) "The impact of the protégé system in Morocco, 1880-1912." Ohio University Center for International Studies, Athens. (mimeo)

BROWN, K. (1969) "The social history of a Moroccan town: Salé, 1830-1930." Ph.D. dissertation. University of California (Los Angeles).

BULLIET, R. (1973) "Why they lost the wheel." Aramco World Magazine (May/June): 22-25.

CAILLE, J. (1949) La ville de Rabat jusqu'au protectorat Français: histoire et archéologie. Paris: Vanoest. 3 vols.

CHILDE, V. G. (1951) Man Makes Himself. New York: NAL.

——— (1950) "The urban revolution." Town Planning Rev. 21 (April): 3-17.

FUSTEL DE COULANGES, N. (1955) The Ancient City. Garden City, N.Y.: Doubleday Anchor.

VON GRUNEBAUM, G. (1955) "Islam: essays in the nature and growth of a cultural tradition." American Anthropological Association Memoir 81.

JACOBS, J. (1969) The Economy of Cities. New York: Random House.

KHALAF, S. and P. KONGSTAD (1974) Hamra of Beirut: A Case of Rapid Urbanization. The Hague: Mouton.

MARCAIS, G. (1945) "La conception des villes dans l'Islam." Revue d'Alger 2.

——— (1940) "L'urbanisme musulmane." 5º Congrès de la Féderation des sociétés savantes de l'Afrique du nord. Algiers.

MARCAIS, W. (1928) "L'Islamisme et la vie urbaine." L'Académie des inscriptions et belles-lettres: Comptes Rendu (Jan-Fev).

MUMFORD, L. (1961) The City in History. New York: Harcourt, Brace & World.

NACIRI, M. (1963) "Salé: étude de géographie urbaine." Revue de géographie du Maroc Nos. 3-4: 13-82.

NISBET, R. (1970) Social Change and History. London: Oxford Univ. Press.

PELLEGRIN, A. (1955) Histoire illustrée de la ville de Tunis et de sa banlieue. Tunis: Saliba Editions.

PIRENNE, H. (1925) Medieval Cities. Garden City, N.Y.: Doubleday Anchor.

DE PLANHOL, X. (1959) The World of Islam. Ithaca: Cornell Univ. Press.

SABLAYROLLES, L. (1925) L'Urbanisme au Maroc: les moyens d'action-les resultats. Albi: Imprimerie Cooperative du Sud-Ouest.

SJOBERG, G. (1960) The Preindustrial City. New York: Free Press.

WHEATLEY, P. (1971) The Pivot of the Four Quarters. Chicago: Aldine.

WITTFOGEL, K. (1957) Oriental Despotism. New Haven: Yale Univ. Press.

Chapter 3

COMPARATIVE URBAN ECOLOGY
A Summary of the Field

BRUCE LONDON
WILLIAM G. FLANAGAN

Since World War II, a considerable literature has emerged on the spatial ecology of cities in countries other than the United States. The bulk of this writing in comparative urban ecology has been concerned with cities in developing, rather than developed, countries. Moreover, this body of literature tends to revolve around or focus upon several recurring themes and issues. Perhaps the main impetus to the emergence of a comparative urban ecology was the now well-recognized ethnocentrism of much of what has been called "the classical school" of human ecology. Viewed in the aggregate, the comparative literature constitutes a critique of aspects of Burgess' concentric zone hypothesis (Burgess, 1925).

Burgess was attempting to answer the question of whether or not cities, despite obvious variations, have an underlying "ideal typical" form by which they may be described. With his series of five concentrically arrayed zones, he implied a direct relationship between socioeconomic status and distance from the city center. Although Burgess' description of the residential distribution of social classes is only one aspect of his model, it is the one most frequently treated in the comparative literature. Therefore, we will focus our attention on this gradient hypothesis.

Empirical studies of both American and foreign cities have demonstrated that the Burgess construct was both time-bound and culture-specific, and, perhaps, limited more specifically to the description of only a certain selection of North American cities at a particular point in their developmental histories. Thus, Burgess' theoretical construct does not have the degree of universal applicability which urban sociologists of an earlier day (and perhaps Burgess himself) attributed to it (Dotson and Dotson, 1957: 1-5).

The search for ideal types or cross-cultural universals, like many such theoretical endeavors, ultimately reduces to a question in the realm of the sociology of knowledge—is cross-cultural generalization possible? Or, are all such attempts at generalization subject to the pitfalls of historicism or cultural relativism? Criticisms of Burgess' attempt to form an inclusive generalization have thus evolved into a debate over the relative import of unique cultural variables (indigenous to a given society) on the spatial structure of a given city in that society. For analytical purposes, we can distinguish two divergent schools of thought. On the one hand, researchers such as Dotson and Dotson (1954, 1956, 1957), and Caplow (1949, 1952)—generally writing prior to 1960—emphasize the empirical refutation of Burgess' hypothesis in cities in developing countries, and cite certain culturally "unique" variables such as land-use planning and value orientations as the ecologically relevant forces which determine either a nonzonal or an inversion of the zonal pattern posited by Burgess. On the other hand, researchers such as Schnore (1965, 1972), and Hawley (1971)—writing more recently—recognize the import of the culturally unique, but emphasize the need to search for more inclusive generalizations in spite of the difficulties inherent in such an endeavor.[1] While these authors tend to view the Burgess construct as a heuristic device of limited empirical validity in itself, they also see it as an example of the type of generalization to be most profitably sought after.

The tension between "the unique" and "the general" creates a potentially profitable dialectic for sociology. Rather than attempting to reconcile the rather sterile polemic which continues between advocates of these two views, our perspective entails an acknowledgement of the significance of both emphases, and an effort to explore the possibility of formulating qualified generalizations.

THE BURGESS AND SJOBERG IDEAL TYPES:
A THEORETICAL FRAMEWORK

Given this debate as the initial impetus to comparative ecological studies, certain other analytical divisions may be discerned in the literature. There are two general and distinct areas of urban ecological concern. Some studies focus on city-hinterland relationships (Keyfitz, 1961, 1965), while others are concerned mainly with the internal spatial structure or distribution of demographic and ecological factors within a city. Since we are exploring the applicability of the Burgess hypothesis, our emphasis will, of course, be on the latter. This subarea can be further broken down itself in terms of criteria for the analysis of the distribution of particular land uses. Some studies, using type of residence as an indicator of socioeconomic status, plot the distribution of social classes throughout a city (Dotson and Dotson, 1954, 1956, 1957). Others distinguish between the locus of residence and that of industry (Gist, 1957, 1968); symbolic or religious land use and commercial land use (Firey, 1947); or among various ethnic groups, age groups, sex ratios, and other demographic and ecological variables (Redick, 1964). Finally, the most recent additions to the literature are studies which exploit the increasing ability to apply aggregate statistical techniques to the analysis of census data in order to identify the key organizational and spatial dimensions of the internal structure of cities.[2]

It would be desirable to incorporate elements of all these factors in any attempt at a comprehensive description of the ecological structure of a given city. It is necessary here, however, to create a more narrow focus. We have chosen the general criterion of the residential centralization, decentralization, and segregation of homogeneous status groups for this purpose.

It would be advantageous to have an ideal type with which to contrast the Burgess construct. As a quasi-theoretical framework, we would then have two distinct ideal types, each standing at opposite ends of a hypothetical continuum. Empirical cases would be assumed to fall somewhere between the extremes.

Sjoberg (1960) has provided just such a device in his description of the spatial ecology of the preindustrial city. Typically, this city was walled, with its central area containing the prominent governmental and religious structures and the main marketplace. The city also tended to be sectioned off along ethnic and occupational lines (with the two often coinciding). However, of central concern here, there was an indirect relationship between power and wealth, and distance from the center of the city—exactly the reverse of the socioeconomic status gradient posited by Burgess.

Approaching cross-cultural generalization within a historical perspective, the empirical question becomes not one of determining whether Burgess or Sjoberg is "right" or "wrong." Rather, it becomes a matter of determining just where on our continuum a particular city (in a particular society at a particular time) lies. In effect, we are attempting to reconcile the two opposing types within a single framework. Two such attempts are particularly noteworthy: Schnore's evolutionary sequence hypothesis (1972: 17-21), and Hawley's multilinear convergence hypothesis (1971: ch. 13).

After reviewing the literature on Latin American cities and noting that their spatial structures conform to neither Burgess' nor Sjoberg's types, Schnore (1972: 21) advances the possibility that these two types "are special cases more adequately subsumed under a more general theory of residential land uses in urban areas." More specifically, he feels that it may be possible to demonstrate that, starting with a pattern similar to that of the preindustrial city, the residential structure of the city evolves in a predictable direction (toward the structure posited by Burgess) as city and nation experience the process of development.

In a similar but more explanatory vein, Hawley (1971: 294, italics added) advances his multilinear convergence hypothesis.

> The case for the convergence hypothesis lies in the implications of the growth and ramifications of regional interdependencies. It assumes that increasing participation by initially differentiated societies in a common technology, common markets, and a common universe of discourse exerts a powerful generalizing and standardizing influence. Social units that engage frequently and regularly in mutual exchanges tend to acquire *counterpart functions and matching structures*, for to do otherwise impedes communications, raises the cost of exchanges, and preserves inequality of opportunity. This is not to say . . . that the convergence hypothesis implies that there is a "stable destination." It proposes rather that different lines of development will become increasingly similar as they become less separate.

Hawley notes that there is one serious difficulty involved in attempting to gather evidence in support of such an hypothesis: "In few if any places in the non-Western world has urbanization advanced to the same stage as that attained in the West. Hence, actual convergences cannot be conclusively demonstrated" (1971: 295). On the other hand, an examination of a wide variety of studies describing residential distributions in particular cases of cities exemplifying various stages in the developmental process might accomplish what individual cross-sectional or descriptive case studies could not.

The strategy employed in this paper, therefore, has been to review the literature in order to see if certain evolutionary processes are evident in the spatial structure of cities in developing countries.[3] Do cities, early in their histories, display a spatial structure similar to Sjoberg's preindustrial city type in which centralization of upper-class residence, and a corresponding decentralization of lower-class residence, is the general rule? Do these same cities, later in their histories, display a spatial structure similar to Burgess' concentric zone type in which centralization of the lower classes, and decentralization of the upper classes, is the rule? Of course, we would expect any empirical case to be somewhat of a combination or mixing of elements of both types.

Therefore, if any initial support for an evolutionary sequence hypothesis is to be gleaned from the literature, we must observe the changes that particular cities undergo over time in order to discover if, or to what extent, the assumption of elements of the Burgess pattern has taken place. If the cities examined were initially preindustrial in form (at least in terms of the status gradient which is our central focus), then we can proceed to support or refute the evolutionary sequence hypothesis to the extent that the following two corollaries are accepted or rejected.

C1: As cities in developing countries become more and more "modernized," a certain amount of decentralization of the upper classes becomes theoretically possible (due minimally to advances in transportation technology). This may be seen empirically in the emergence of relatively homogeneous middle- and upper-class enclaves ("suburbs") on the periphery of such cities.

C2: As cities in developing countries become more and more "modernized," a certain amount of centralization of the lower classes becomes theoretically possible as members of the upper classes evacuate locations in the central areas of cities. This may be seen empirically in the appearance of relatively homogeneous lower class residential enclaves ("slums") near the center of such cities.[4]

What evidence, then, does the literature on the spatial structure of cities in developing countries present on these migratory processes of expansion, invasion, succession, and segregation?

LATIN AMERICA

Even those Latin American studies which—by contrasting Anglo and Latin "cultures"—emphasize the importance of culturally unique factors in determining a city's internal spatial structure, provide "evidence" which supports an evolutionary sequence or convergence hypothesis when interpreted in light of our two corollaries. After reviewing the literature on the spatial structure of Latin American cities,[5] Schnore (1965: 358) noted that in *all* the studies reviewed the traditional or colonial pattern (characterized by a "preindustrial" status gradient) was "reported to be in one or another stage of breakdown," with an apparent tendency to shift in the direction of the North American pattern.

This observation was reported as early as 1934 in Hansen's (1934) study of Merida. Hansen felt that the traditional relationship between status and residential location with reference to the center was reversing over time largely because of population growth and concomitant organizational change. Caplow (1949: 132)—after reviewing much the same literature as Schnore—augments Hansen's initial insight by pointing out that, after arranging all the Middle American cities upon which some ecological data are available in order of size, "it is at once apparent that the larger the community the further it has departed from the traditional colonial pattern."

This is not to imply that Caplow is optimistic about the possibility of cross-cultural generalization. He feels that the reverse gradient persists in Guatemala City despite rapid growth (1949: 123); and that the syndrome of changes in land use common to the North American "crescive city" does not exist in Guatemala City (1949: 127), largely because of a tradition of land-use planning and an elite value system which leads them to "cling to central location." Nevertheless, Caplow cannot avoid pointing out that there are distinct indications that the North American pattern may develop in the future for there is already some displacement of upper classes from their traditional central location (1949: 125).

Not unlike Caplow, the Dotsons (1956, 1957) attribute causal primacy to culturally unique variables in determining the spatial structure of Mexican cities. They, too, however, cannot avoid citing descriptive evidence which, in light of our two corollaries, lends support to an evolutionary sequence hypothesis. They cite the importance of the upper-class view that the urban life is "the good life," claiming that such a value system is one key to the persistence of a reverse gradient. In a similar vein, Johnson (1967: 186) says that

> an awareness of local circumstances is always important for an understanding of the urban geography of a particular area. Differing societies make varying assessments of what constitutes an amenity, different technologies produce distinctive patterns of accessibility, and different assumptions about the nature of land ownership cause variations in the operation of the urban market. As a result the detailed structure of a typical city may well vary from culture to culture, and the factors which explain its form may also differ in emphasis.

As the Dotsons emphasize, "No theory of the nature of cities which neglects this cultural factor . . . can hope to be successful" (1957: 18).

However, an awareness of this should not preclude attempts at generalization, and the Dotsons themselves provide evidence. They point out how the elite urbanite is often "forced" from his traditional location by the expansion of the central business district. There comes a point at which culturally defined ideals are no longer able to withstand the economic pressures of growth. Again in agreement with Caplow, the Dotsons recognize "a correlation between the degree of deviation from the colonial pattern and the size and rate of growth of the city" (1954: 367). In smaller cities such as Piebla, we do not find some of the "new ecological tendencies." Guadalajara, however, has a mixed pattern in which most of the housing near the center is middle- or upper-class; and the periphery is the locus of the poorest housing; *but* the very best housing is partly located on the edge or outskirts of the city. Finally, Mexico City displays the most marked shift toward the North American pattern, including much new middle-income housing on the fringes; suburbs for the wealthy ten miles from the central business district (Hayner, 1968: 166); and, most significantly, a considerable deterioration of parts of the central business district which is very reminiscent of Burgess' zone of transition.

Rather than interpret this in terms of convergence with the North American pattern, the Dotsons view it in terms of the emergence of "an essentially new ecological form." As indicated earlier, there simply is no way to conclusively demonstrate ultimate convergence (until such time—if that time ever comes—as it actually happens). Nonetheless, this new ecological form may just as easily be interpreted as a shift *toward* the North American pattern, especially in light of the fact that this form, although new to Mexico, is probably very similar (in terms of its mixed residential distribution) to American industrial cities of the nineteenth or early twentieth centuries. Indeed, recent studies by Schwirian and Rico-Velasco (1971) and Schwirian and Smith (1974) of the three largest cities in Puerto Rico make just this point by linking the centralization patterns of a city's status groups to, first, a society's position in the economic development process, and second, a city's position in that society's urban hierarchy. Just as Caplow and the Dotsons found larger communities departing further and further from the Sjoberg pattern, the Puerto Rican studies reveal that "Mayaguez . . . the smallest of Puerto Rico's metropolitan centers . . . shows an ecological pattern characteristic of the traditional city"; while the somewhat larger city of "Ponce is in the midst of a spatial shift in population distribution" such that "the traditional spatial pattern is disrupted while the more modern has yet to emerge"; but that "the ecological patterning of San Juan—the primate city—is very similar to that of cities in highly developed societies" (Schwirian and Rico-Velasco, 1971: 334). Indeed, "in San Juan the most centralized groups are generally those of lowest status" (Schwirian and Smith, 1974: 420).

Amato's (1969a, 1969b, 1970) studies of the South American cities of Bogota, Quito, Lima, and Santiago generally reinforce the emerging image of a clear shift away from traditional elite centralization toward a rather mixed pattern marked by the persistence of some elite centralization and low-status decentralization, a frequently sectoral decentralization of elite groups to environmentally desirable locations, and a delayed but increasing centralization of low-status groups.

SOUTH AND SOUTHEAST ASIA

A considerable body of literature has emerged on the morphology of South and Southeast Asian cities. Generally, an emphasis on culturally and situationally unique factors, tempered by descriptions of that mixed residential land use which may herald convergence, is as common to the Asian literature as to the Latin American.

Berry and Spodek (1971) present an excellent description of traditional Indian residence patterns. The physical structures of both the ancient town and contemporary villages correspond with the Sjoberg type, as "favored" castes reside near either the spatial or symbolic center, while those considered "outsiders" are located on the fringe. In contrast, the ecology of many large Indian cities has been described by Brush (1962) as a "dual structure." Implied here is the sharp contrast between the patterning of the indigenous areas of these cities, and that of the areas "grafted on" to these by the British. In the old, indigenous cities the residential areas of the high castes were centralized, while those of the laboring castes and outcastes were located on the outskirts (Brush, 1962: 60). The British military and railway towns (which often were located adjacent to extant indigenous towns), however, were usually preplanned in a grid pattern with a rigid hierarchy of status in which the highest ranks resided furthest from the center of town (Brush, 1962: 63). Despite this juxtaposition of indigenous and alien forms, such cities function as units, and, in this sense, the city as a whole is moving toward the Western pattern. As in Latin America, however, not all contemporary Indian cities evidence an evolution toward the Western pattern. Prior to 1960, Bangalore, for example, had a fairly uniform centralization of upper classes and decentralization of lower classes (Gist, 1957: 361). Howrah, too, has had little residential decentralization of higher castes despite modern development of road transport (Berry and Rees, 1969: 445).

However, even though most observers generalize that the *dominant* spatial pattern is one of high-status neighborhoods in central areas and low-status neighborhoods at the periphery, for cities such as Calcutta (Berry and Rees, 1969; Berry and Spodek, 1971), Bombay (Mehta, 1968; Berry and Spodek, 1971), Poona (Mehta, 1968; Berry and Spodek, 1971), and Madras, Kanpur, and Ahmedabad (Berry and Spodek, 1971), these same studies *describe* an increasingly mixed pattern. Some limited decentralization of higher-status groups has been documented for Poona (Mehta, 1968: 404, 407; Berry and Spodek, 1971: 365), Madras (Berry and Spodek, 1971: 354, 358), Ahmedabad and Kanpur (Berry and Spodek, 1971: 359), and Bombay (Berry and Spodek, 1971: 361).

On the other hand, some centralization of lower-status residence has occurred in Calcutta (Ghosh, 1950: 257) and Poona (Mehta, 1968: 404 Berry and Spodek, 1971: 367). In general, the Sjoberg or preindustrial gradient applies to Indian cities because of factors such as low growth rates, the general poverty of in-migrants, the minimal deterioration of central neighborhoods, and the tendency for industry to locate on the periphery. However, deviations from this pattern are increasingly common as Indian cities are evolving away from the traditional spatial pattern with the emergence of new elements.

In his description of the ecological structure of Rangoon, Burma, Redick (1964) makes the point—supported by McGee's (1967: 107-108) study of Southeast Asian cities—that some of Rangoon's better residential areas have come to be located beyond the city's central core, although most of the housing in these peripheral areas is lower status. Redick emphasizes that the outlying areas have a higher rate of growth than the central areas. This is not due to the "depopulation" of a central core as in the Western city, but rather to a complete saturation of the center which forces the growing urban population to expand outward. The result is a very mixed residential status pattern on the periphery as upper-status groups escape central congestion, while rural in-migrants settle in peripheral squatter areas which are often adjacent to elite "suburbs." In this light, it is apparent that elements of the so-called Western pattern are evolving (elite decentralization) but for very different reasons from those behind their initial emergence in the West, and with a less homogeneous "suburb" as the result.[6]

The literature on Indonesian cities (Keyfitz, 1961: 349-350; McGee, 1967: 71, 146; Sendut, 1969: 468-470) indicates that early in their histories they were typically marked by the centrality of noble and upper-class residence. This characteristic apparently persisted until the decade following World W ar II when rapid growth led to the emergence of the new ecological residential elements of suburbs and squatter settlements in cities such as Kuala Lampur and Singapore.

Bangkok, Thailand, has also undergone an apparent shift away from a preindustrial and toward a more industrial type pattern (London, 1973). Since its emergence as the prototypical walled palace city surrounded by the market gardens and rice fields of the peasantry, Bangkok has experienced considerable crescive growth. At present, relatively homogeneous peripheral residential areas exist for Thai elites, the Western commercial-military elite, and lower-status, marginally occupied urban workers and squatters; while relatively homogeneous central residential areas as well exist for both traditional elites and entering poor. Thus, Bangkok, too, has that mixed distribution of "the poorest and the wealthiest elements of the city in both the core and outer areas" which seems to indicate that the city is in some stage of transition between our two ideal types—the historic centralization of elites and decentralization of the poor is no longer the norm.

TROPICAL AFRICA

As well as sharing the many variable influences on residential patterns with the other world regions we have discussed, additional considerations seem to be in order for Tropical Africa.[7] Any general tendency for status centralization or decentralization is obscured by such factors as colonial policies of racial segregation, ethnic residential clustering across economic category, religious clustering around centers of worship, pronounced effects of topography, the extent of indigenous precolonial urban development, the extent and intent of the colonial or independent governments' urban design or planning schemes (a command interference with market mechanism), the provision of government and private business-sponsored housing for employees near place of work, and central concentration and peripheral scarcity of services. Not surprisingly, little can be said about the ecology of the African city that escapes exception.

The city of Kampala in Uganda shows the effect of many of these variables. The topography of the region consisted of a number of adjacent hills separated by malarial swamps. The grant by the ruler of Kampala hill to the British for the building of a fort led to the familiar "grafted-on,"

dual center pattern of development, but without immediate dominance of
the royal capital (Mengo) by the British settlement which remained "an
insignificant adjunct of the Ganda capital" for fifteen years. "But, after
that, Mengo became increasingly overshadowed by the cuckoo in the nest"
(Southall, 1967: 301).

Kampala developed, by Southall's account, from hill to hill, by cells,
with each *mutala* (hill) developing a dominant institutional theme. These
developed almost as subcommunities with employment, residents, and
markets clustering around the university, hospital, or the various religious
institutions (Southall, 1967: 306 ff.). The result was the emergence of a
cellular "micro" residential ecology. "The residential hills in particular, are
divided into concentric zones where the housing is graded from the most
luxurious at the top, to low standard housing on the lowest slopes that
were marshy until recently" (Gugler, 1972: 18).[8]

An overall residential ecology begins to appear in the 1950s as the CBD
(moved from Kampala to the larger Nakasero hill) came to provide an
urban focus. Europeans and Asians invaded nearby high ground formerly
occupied by Sudanese and developed a residential pattern whereby the
best homes were constructed further from the new center (Southall, 1967:
306). In the overall view of Kampala, the lowland/low-grade housing can
be seen occurring according to a general, familiar pattern. Wandegeya
emerged adjacent to major areas of employment (Southall, 1967: 312), as
did Kisenye. This latter development grew just outside Kampala's irregular
municipal boundary under the less effective restrictions of the old and
separate town of Mengo (Gugler, 1972: 22-23). Gugler (1972: 7) makes
the critical observation that poor Africans are driven to the periphery of
the city by the unrealistic building standards that regulate habitation
within the municipal boundaries.

Other East African capitals are sited on less dramatic terrain and
present a simpler residential ecology, although the effect of central-
peripheral versus topgraphic factors is no clearer.

The high ground in Nairobi lies to the east of the city center. This
became the European area. The African and Asian population, as a result
of segregationist colonial policy, clustered on alternate sides of the industrial and commercial areas, thus creating three distinct social Nairobis
(Tiwari, 1972: 43).

Based on the single indicator of population density alone, and to the
extent this is an accurate indicator of economic status, there is an overall
gradient correlating lower density and distance from the center which
holds over the period 1963 to 1969, though the gradient is less radical by

the later date. For the European population, however, the gradient becomes more radical through the sixties.[9] The Asian population shows little variation over time. But for Africans the gradient has reversed itself between 1963 and 1969, and now the density of this population *increases* with distance from city center. Tiwari (1972: 44) attributes this development to more intense use of existing dwellings (i.e., more occupants per room) throughout the African-predominated areas, plus the erection of poor shelters for rent, added to by the growth of the large squatter development in the Mathare valley. "Suburbanization" holds quite different ecological implications for the formerly exclusively European Upper Nairobi expanding to the west, and the growing numbers of African poor aggregating on the edge of accessibility to the city.

Dar es Salaam is described by de Blij (1963: 20) as having formally had a somewhat concentric residential structure along the lines of the preindustrial or colonial model. High-, middle-, and low-quality residence, with the usual (for East Africa) racial correlate (European, Asian, African) worked back from the most salubrious point by the sea. Suburbanization did not follow the concentric pattern, but destroyed it, as the high-quality residences grew northward, along the shore and contiguously with older high-quality residence. Middle- and poor-quality residences have developed westward away from the sea in a mixed segment occupying lower, marshy ground. To the south, the last wedge of land is occupied by transport and industrial areas (de Blij, 1963: 29-32).

The city of Khartoum on the Nile reiterates the import of physical features, high ground, and waterfront, in evolving residential ecologies in the tropics.[10] Hamdan (1960: 24) identifies the "three Khartoums" located on the confluence of the White and Blue Niles.

It is the case, for each town, that the nucleus of urbanization was along the waterfront and grew annularly and concentrically away from it (Hamdan, 1960: 25). The result, says Hamdan (1960: 27), is fundamentally similar to the Burgess model, more pronounced in the more mature structure of Khartoum than the other towns, except the Niles have replaced Chicago's Lake Michigan in enforcing semi-circular rather than circular patterns (Hamdan, 1960: 30). The residential gradient (for each town) proceeds not so much from the core as it varies directly with distance from the river. And, in our terms, it is *not* the Burgess pattern that it follows, but the preindustrial one.

The best residences were built close to the river (where access was not blocked by administrative buildings) and ran back along a ridge on the east when riverside development was blocked by the substantial British army barracks and airport in this direction. Class II residences reach back from the central core administrative/commercial area to the railroad loop and beyond, along and adjacent to the best residences on the east. The downward gradation continues away from the river to the south, through "Khartoum III" and the New Deims-a grid of "substandard" mud brick shelters housing Khartoum's poor. Beyond these and along the municipal boundaries were the shanties of the Fellata village, the worst of all living areas (Hamdan, 1960: 38).

When the possibilities on the eastern side of the city were exhausted, a new site for better residences was not developed to the south beyond the ring of poverty, but the new site followed the Nile west. "Suburbanization" hardly describes the then newly developed area which begins only a half mile from where the core ends. The relatively well-to-do chose to face the threat of periodic inundation with uneconomical land reclamation rather than move from the city "center" and the waterfront (Hamdan, 1960: 38-39).

In West Africa, a long tradition of urban living predated European conquest and colonization. The meeting of these distinctive urban traditions generally meant the eventual relegation of the indigenous portion to secondary importance. Actually, the amount of influence of expatriate activity on the indigenous town design and land-use pattern varied a great deal by individual case.

For instance, when Miner visited Timbuctoo in 1940, after it had suffered a long period of economic decline and decades of French rule, he found what may be recognized from his description as a typical preindustrial pattern. The best mud brick residences were located near the center, grading out through an intermediary area of less well kept buildings to the straw huts of the periphery (Miner, 1965: 45-46). The French grafted on their dwellings and other buildings to the south (Miner, 1965: 39), with apparently little influence on the preindustrial gradient pattern. This situation can be compared to that of Maradi (Niger) where, under the command of French authorities (and the protest of inhabitants) the city was moved to a higher site and laid out in a nineteenth century geometrical French town plan (Thom, 1972).

An almost equally devastating intervention occurred with the European invasion (ecological) of the Yoruba fishing and trading town at Lagos.[11]

Mabogunje (1968: 274) describes Lagos, in its early post-European-contact development, as approaching the twin-center model of side by side indigenous and European development. The African sector was substantial enough in the colonial era that a policy of racial separation meant that the better European residential area developed in a ring, more or less, around and separated from the Nigerians (Sada, 1972: 12). The explosive growth of Lagos after 1951 engulfed and disrupted this simple pattern, as it did many formerly outlying areas.

As a result, the low-grade housing that shelters the poor was found both in the central city, where descendants of the original grantees were ever more crowded due to growth in numbers, and on the periphery (Sada, 1972: 23), beyond the city boundary and authority. Of the twelve high-grade housing estates, only three were peripheral. Middle-grade locations showed little general patterning.[12]

The relatively more recent supply of access and services to the suburbs, and the relatively more recent growth of high-grade residences there may be predictive of a future trend. But we can expect the number of poor, with no other choice, to grow on the periphery as long as Lagos remains such an attractive target for migrants. The likely nucleation of various groups around sectors of Lagos' remarkable ribbon development promises to maintain the complex residential pattern of the city.

Another Yoruba development, Ibadan, presented a much larger and less passive obstacle to the development of a "Western" urban pattern. The growth of the new portion of the city has, typically, taken place on the edge of the old walled town. In fact, when Splansky (1966) applied the Burgess model to the city of Ibadan, he focused on the new, tacked-on portion—a perspective which led him to view the old section as not so much a part of the city as it was synonomous, in effect, to Lake Michigan in the original case. That is, he saw in the new city not circles, but the crescents of inner core, zone of transition, with a merged third band of better and poorer residences.

When Mabogunje wrote of the same city in 1962, he took the center of the old city as the "core" of the new and old agglomeration. In the middle of the nineteenth century, this core, surrounded by an inner wall, was observed to be not so fine an area as those suburbs, more spaciously laid out with gardens and fruit trees, that lay between the inner and outer wall (Mabogunje, 1962: 66). These suburbs and additional areas within the outer wall, came to be built up and congested, and "suburbanization" of better residences continued out to and beyond the wall over time. The new Gbagi business district grew adjacent on the western side, providing an eccentric economic focus with regard to the old town.

The result is that Ibadan has developed two city centers that function "almost despite each other" (Mabogunje, 1967: 44), and for which, Mabogunje argues, the Burgess model is neither wholly irrelevant nor adequate, since what is required is a scheme capable of dealing with the twin-centered Nigerian towns where extensive endogenous development had taken place (1968: 179, 205).[13] Mabogunje's generalizations regarding residential distribution for Ibadan indicate, in their superficial aspect, a certain conformity with the Burgess model.

The more central portions of the old city, described by Mabogunje as a physical, although not a sociological, slum (i.e., the most substandard and decaying buildings and the most well-integrated community) provides a ready-made capsule of poor labor adjacent to the new center (although the large population of the old town is, of course, economically heterogeneous). Beyond, both inside and outside the wall, are the low- to medium-quality residential districts (Mabogunje, 1968: 225). Yet there is the suggestion that this describes either an immature gradient on the model posited for developed countries, or an altogether unique development because the gradient described by Mabogunje did not proceed from the new CBD—indeed, the new CBD was engulfed by it. The gradient proceeds instead from the core of the old, preindustrial, walled Yoruba city of Ibadan.

The city of Ibadan, as do the other cases profiled here, underscores the necessity for understanding present patterns as the current embodiment of historical processes. General ecological principles of centralization and decentralization operate, but face additional factors of resistance in tropical Africa. These may require more qualification in this region than elsewhere with regard to general ecological principles, not the abandonment of these principles.

LEVEL OF DEVELOPMENT AND SPATIAL STRUCTURE: THE "FIRST AND SECOND WORLDS" IN CROSS-HISTORICAL PERSPECTIVE

We would suggest that the patterns of residence in the cities studied— patterns which, at least to some growing extent, "include a mixture of the poorest and the wealthiest elements of the city in both the core and outer areas—represent some stage of transition between our two ideal types. An underlying assumption of this argument would imply in very general terms a correlation between some "level of *national* development" (on our preindustrial/industrial continuum) and urban spatial structure. Thus, to round out our arguments, we must be able to demonstrate that, at earlier points in their developmental histories, cities in the now-developed nations were structured like cities in the now-developing countries. In effect, this amounts to an attempt to "control" for "level of national development."

Indeed, there is a fair amount of literature on early American cities to support this assumption. North American cities of the past, developing prior to the "transportation revolution," had their middle- and upper-class residences much closer to the center. Actually, the city itself was so necessarily compact—"everyone" had to walk to work—that all classes lived close to its geographical center. Differentiation was more by "neighborhood" than by distance from the center. Apparently, there was little choice involved on anyone's part, except perhaps those wealthy enough to maintain both town and country residences. It is in this context that we see Burgess describing the present zone of transition as once containing the homes of the "best families" (1925: 50-51). Similarly, Hoyt (1933, 1939), Warner (1962), and Heberle and Bertrand (1948) describe Chicago, Boston, and cities in the South as having the homes of the socially prominent *originally* just outside the central business district, but increasingly on the periphery as time, improved transportation technology, congestion at the center, and the financial means to actualize a "rural ideal" (Warner, 1962: 5) permitted.[14] Indeed, Haggerty (1971) points out that even those newer U.S. cities which have an inverse status gradient are likely to conform to the Burgess pattern over time. To this extent, cities in the United States were once much like cities in the now-developing countries.

A consideration of the literature on European cities, however, casts some doubts on the potential conclusion that "a general theory of residential land uses in urban areas," emphasizing that the residential structure of the city evolves in a predictable direction, may be forthcoming. European cities are much older than American cities. Built on a long-established preindustrial base, they have an ecological foundation which in many cases resists change in the direction of the United States industrial city's pattern (Thomlinson, 1969: 169).

Those European cities such as Oxford (Collison and Mogey, 1959), Rome (McElrath, 1962), Prague (Moscheles, 1937), and, in general, French cities (Caplow, 1952) and cities of the Alfold (Beynon, 1961b), which had not undergone particularly rapid growth, retained a preindustrial gradient. However, even those large cities which are growing rapidly and which thus might be expected to conform to the American pattern because of a need to "create" locations for the expanding middle class and for industry— cities such as London, Paris, Vienna, Stockholm (Hauser, 1968), and Budapest (Beynon, 1961a)—exhibit a tendency for the middle and upper classes to remain centralized as industry locates on the periphery near the working-class areas.

This stands in sharp contrast to the American response to industrialization. Hauser (1968) feels that this is because the American city did not build to as great an extent on a truly preindustrial base.[11] Also, the less restricted operation of market forces in the United States contrasts with the European emphasis on government urban planning.[16]

One might conclude that there is no uniform pattern to be observed everywhere, and, as far as it goes, this would be correct. This point of view would logically posit the need for the creation of a typology of city forms in order to help understand why certain cities have certain residential land-use patterns. Among the many forces and factors which seem to "determine" the ecological structure of a city are growth *on* an industrial versus preindustrial base (i.e., this "determines" whether industry will locate centrally or peripherally); colonialism versus independence (i.e., this "determines" the appearance of a "grafted-on" or "dual" structure); and level of economic and technological development at the time of growth. Using just these criteria, the following are some "types" of cities which would currently be expected to exhibit differing ecological structures:

(a) preindustrial cities influenced by colonialism (Mexico, India, Africa);
(b) preindustrial cities uninfluenced by colonialism, having indigenous invention of industrial technology (Europe);
(c) preindustrial cities uninfluenced by colonialism, *not* having indigenous invention of industrial technology (Bangkok);
(d) cities reflecting the "pure" impact of industrial technology (United States).[17]

The choice of forces and factors, and the ultimate listing of city types, is an arbitrary matter. The key point here is that any such exercise (although of some conceptual utility) results in a purely static, cross-sectional description of ecological structures. Thus, simply to conclude that there is no uniformly observable pattern misses a very basic point. "It is important not to confuse a specific pattern of spatial distribution with the general principles of . . . ecology" (Theodorson, 1961: 330). Ecological principles must reflect the fact that structure arises out of *process*. The city is a dynamic emergent, growing and changing. This processual nature has meant that the spatial relationships among groups within the city are constantly in flux. Any static, cross-sectional description of what is the most recently valid pattern of residential land use will soon be outmoded. Indeed:

> Large American cities are beginning to show what may be a modification of
> the typical ecological pattern of the past . . . rejuvenation and reorganization
> of the central areas . . . gradual movement of industrial plants to outlying areas
> and the large-scale construction of low cost housing, which attract lower-
> income groups to the suburbs [Theodorson, 1961: 330].

Probably as a result of this dynamic reversal, recent studies of the
ecology of North American cities—studies combining the techniques of
classic spatial ecology and factorial ecology (Schwirian, 1974: 9)—are
finding that, although some ecological factors are distributed by distance
gradient from the center, social status appears to be distributed *sectorally*
(Anderson and Egeland, 1961; Schwirian and Matre, 1974). This sectoral
distribution *still* reveals a differentiation into homogeneous class residential areas. That the spatial distribution of these areas is less susceptible to
description in terms of distance gradients is a function of the increasingly
mixed pattern found in North American cities. On the one hand, just as
cities in the Third World are moving away from the Sjoberg pattern, on the
other hand, cities in North America are transcending the Burgess pattern.
Even though both are evolving under the impetus of different causes, each
is incorporating what were *once* solely elem ents of the other's ideal status
gradient pattern, and are thus becoming structurally more and more
similar. Thus, the hypothesis that some sort of overall convergence toward
similarity is taking place, or that the residential structure of the city is
evolving in a predictable direction, should be neither constrained by the
reification of a given "ideal type," nor precluded by the fact that there is
now no uniform pattern observable everywhere.

The dynamic approach and the historical perspective have the potential
to merge in the search for cross-cultural generalizations. The fact that an
evolutionary sequence or convergence hypothesis is not easy to "prove"
should not block our efforts in this direction. In fact, much of the
evidence gleaned from the literature presents these hypotheses as promising organizing conceptualizations for research.

DISCUSSION

Throughout our review, the ecological structure of cities has been
viewed as a dependent variable. The main thrust of the research has been
to discover those forces and factors which contribute to both cross-
cultural similarities and differences in that structure. In this regard, it may
be accurate to point out—as an initial observation—that the accumulated

evidence indicates that economic and technological factors are the dependent variables which tend to produce ecological similarities; while culturally unique factors are the independent variables which tend to foster ecological differences. Sjoberg (1965: 250), for example, emphasizes that convergence theorists focus on similarities because they stress technological factors; while his "antagonists," the cultural relativists, focus on differences because they stress "cultural values as an independent variable."

Such an "explanation" is perhaps descriptively accurate, and hence, intuitively appealing. However, it does not cut to the core of the matter. It is not a causal explanation. To come closer to a true explanation of this convergence phenomenon, we must reduce the situation under examination to its lowest common denominators, to its "elements." It is at this point that we return to the statement made earlier about the analytical separation of "social" and "cultural" phenomena (see note 1), for these are the elements upon which our attempt at explanation will ultimately be built.

For analytical purposes, we should distinguish between the social and cultural components of social phenomena. Culture refers to shared behavior, but behavior can in turn be reduced analytically to ideas. Thus, in terms of content, culture becomes a mental component (shared mentality) since, analytically, the lowest common denominator of all material as well as nonmaterial culture is symbolic forms. Thus, those *normative* ideas which prescribe the ideal patterns for social relationships are *cultural* phenomena. The social component, on the other hand, is the active, concrete, experiental process of interaction between people. As distinguished from our cultural component, this is a decidedly nonnormative element. In certain new or unstructured situations, interacting individuals and groups each brings its own distinctive normative or cultural contents to the arena of interaction. In many such cases, individuals or groups with no previous contact with each other have developed no shared ideas to guide their interactions (this is especially true of interacting cultures). Contact is in this sense nonnormative. Thus, norms may define the ideal patterns for most social relationships, but what actually happens when real people and groups interact is often very different from that ideal.

The crux of our present problem is that an analytical separation of economic and technological variables from cultural variables creates a false dichotomy. Although one aspect of economics may well be contact or interaction of a nonnormative sort (a strictly social component), a more fundamental aspect is decidedly normative (hence, subsumed under our cultural component)—e.g., the *norms* governing property and market relationships and so on. Technology (as a complex of cultural traits), too, can be subsumed under the heading of our cultural component as all material and nonmaterial technology can be reduced to *ideas*. A given economic system and technological capability are nothing more nor less than parts of the content of a given culture. In this light, to state that economic and technological variables produce spatial convergence, or that cultural variables retard such convergence, is a somewhat misdirected argument precisely because economic norms and technological ideas are as much cultural variables as are those *attitudes* and *values* which specify a "rural ideal" or "pro-urbanism." In other words, such an argument fails to go beyond the influence of strictly cultural variables in determining spatial structure.

To complete our picture, we must show the contribution of some strictly social component to the morphological changes we have been observing. This component is not that difficult to isolate. It is analytically extant in the form of contact between or among cultures. All cultures are products of unique historical pasts. At the moment any two cultures come in contact, each possesses a historically evolved cultural content—not only value systems, but economic and technological systems as well. In contact, two cultures tend to face each other as conflicting or competing interest groups. In most cases, one will emerge as dominant, the other as subordinate, depending largely upon the "superiority" of one cultural content (its material, and especially technological, capabilities)[18] over the other. Once this point has been reached, a process of diffusion and acculturation begins, and, even though both cultures are likely to change, it is the subordinate which assumes or incorporates (when possible) those elements which enabled the dominant culture to achieve its ascendant position in the first place. Empirically, these borrowed elements are usually of an economic or technological nature (for example, a particular mode of production, and the means of production which go along with it). Armed with these new means, the subordinate will change, and change under these circumstances will necessarily appear to be making the subordinate ever more similar to the dominant. However, a proper evolutionary or dialectic perspective recognizes that, through contact, a synthesis emerges which neither wholly reflects nor wholly obliterates the forms of either extant alternative. Thus, both similarities and differences persist as social *and* cultural components interact.

Perhaps the following quote from Hawley (1971: 311 ff.) will bring this rather abstract discussion back to a more empirical level, indicating its relevance to the topic of the convergence hypothesis:

The regions and nations of the world are being absorbed into an expanding world ecumene. As one society after another has yielded to the superior economic and political power of an industrialized market economy, it has been thrust along a path toward a drastic internal reorganization. For it could not remain in its traditional pattern and at the same time participate in a highly rationalized network of interregional relationships. Participation in the world economy has demanded of every society the adoption of a new technological regime, a reorientation to resources, a fundamental reconstitution and realignment of social units, and a broad-scale redistribution of its population. Urbanization is a more or less localized manifestation of this region-wide or multi-regional transformation. . . . Although urbanization begins in very different cultural contexts, in each instance the trend soon begins to reproduce phases and patterns that have occurred in other times and places. The convergence tendency penetrates surface features, such as spatial arrangements—though even those are not as arbitrary as an uncritical view might lead one to suspect.

NOTES

1. We suggest that the proponents of the former point of view are products of the prevailing ideas of the first three or four decades of twentieth-century sociology—especially the rather uncritical application of the anthropological conception of culture to all social, behavioral, and symbolic phenomena. This might explain their reluctance to search for the inclusive generalization, and their emphasis on the extreme variability of cultures. The proponents of the latter point of view are similarly products of their era, for, in recent decades, sociologists have begun to differentiate between "social" and "cultural" phenomena, and this division of labor has served to kindle an awareness of both the possibility of and the need for more inclusive cross-cultural generalizations. This general trend toward the tempering of historical specificity with historical generalization may also be seen as a dialectic characteristic of the history and evolution of all social thought. The thesis of extreme relativism has been challenged by the antithesis of the possibility of generalization, and the emerging synthesis is exemplified by the "evolutionary sequence" and "convergence" approaches of Schnore (1965, 1972) and Hawley (1971).

2. Schwirian (1974: 3-32) provides an excellent overview of these trends in the ecological literature, especially his discussion of the recent syntheses of social area analysis and factorial ecology.

3. Note that this does not preclude an analysis of U.S. cities early in their histories.

4. Note the implication in both corollaries that new groups are coming to occupy locations which either were previously unoccupied or were occupied by groups having very different SES characteristics.

5. Including Hansen (1934); Hayner (1944: 1945); Leonard (1948); Hawthorn and Hawthorn (1948); Caplow (1949); and Dotson and Dotson (1954), most of which displays a "cultural emphasis."

6. Interestingly, the recent demise of suburban homogeneity in the United States occurred in just the reverse order, with the decentralization of working-class groups to an already upper-class location. At any rate, despite the differences in the temporal ordering of status group decentralization in the two situations, the peripheries of both U.S. cities and larger cities in the Third World are assuming a very mixed pattern.

7. There is some literature on the ecological structure of African cities outside tropical Africa (Abu-Lughod, 1969; Latif, 1974a 1974b; Kuper et al., 1958). For reasons of homogeneity and brevity, we will not deal with this literature here. In general, however, these studies do describe the aforementioned mixing of the poorest and the wealthiest groups in both the city's core and periphery.

8. The construction of higher- and lower-status government housing estates in the eastern suburbs carries out this pattern of hilltop ecology in the adjacent Nakawa (lower) and Naguru (upper) estates (Southall, 1967: 317): "At Nakawa the bed spaces intended for single migrant laborers are at the bottom of the slope and the inhabitants differentiate the status of Upper and Lower Nakawa. In Naguru also, the newer, larger and more prestigeful homes are fairly consistently on the upper slopes. There is some overlap in socio-economic status between the two estates and certain ethnic or occupational characteristics tend to partly override status gradients, but in general there is a rise from Lower to Upper Nakawa and on through Lower to Upper Naguru."

9. Suburbanization continued through the sixties as the flatter lands beyond the best Upper Nairobi highland developed. The pattern was linear, moving beyond European rather than encircling Asian and African pre-dominated lands (Halliman and Morgan, 1967: 106).

10. For a similar discussion of environmental quality as an ecological variable outside tropical Africa, see Amato (1969b).

11. Sada (1972: 3) contends that "New African urban centers are unique in their internal spatial attributes and require different theoretical models for their study and planning," and identifies a number of problems for applying the models of Western experience to cities like Lagos. The command power of government in the purchase of urban land for planning purposes, and old grants that were made long ago to inhabitants on the basis of their occupation of that land, affect the possibility of generalization about land use based on the assumption of freely operating market mechanisms (Sada, 1972: 7-8). Conveniently located accommodations provided by employers, the effect of common family holdings on geographic mobility within the city, the comfort of family, village, or ethnic neighborhood surroundings, and the insecurity of suburban locations (with their *higher* crime rates) and lack of amenities and services all play a role in determining the residential ecology of Lagos.

12. Taking population density as one index of residential gradient, Sada observes no steady decline with distance from the center. Density goes down, then rises, at the city boundary, then drops again. The correlation between distance from the center and land rent is .0049 distance/land value, and .064 distance/house rent (Sada, 1972: 23). The "flatness" of these indicators is likely due in great part to the large numbers of migrant poor on the edge of town.

13. The twin towns of the central African copperbelt, which have been excluded from this discussion for reasons of space, require a similar conceptual scheme.

14. For extended references to the literature on the ecological structures of American cities, see Abbott (1974) and Schwirian (1974).

15. Interestingly, industry tends to locate on the peripheries of large, *old* Third World cities, just as in Europe (Mehta, 1968; Berry and Rees, 1969; Berry and Spodek, 1971). This would seem to be a function of rapid growth on a preindustrial base.

16. In this regard, a recent study of the ecological structure of Moscow in 1897 is of interest (Abbott, 1974). The urban structure of Moscow clearly resembled the Sjoberg pattern, but "may have been in the process of changing towards a modern structure." We are only able to speculate as to the nature of contemporary status gradients in cities in self-described classless nations.

17. This listing, of course, does not represent all possible permutations and combinations of the three variables chosen. However, the "typology" is meant to be more suggestive than inclusive.

18. As used here, "superiority" connotes nothing more nor less than the fact that steamships, cannons, and guns have with some regularity overpowered canoes, spears, and slingshots.

REFERENCES

ABBOT, W. F. (1974) "Moscow in 1897 as a pre-industrial city: a test of the inverse Burgess zonal hypothesis." Amer. Soc. Rev. 39 (August): 542-550.

ABU-LUGHOD, J. L. (1969) "Testing the theory of social area analysis: the ecology of Cairo, Egypt." Amer. Soc. Rev. 34 (April): 198-211.

AMATO, P. W. (1969a) "Population densities, land values and socioeconomic class in Bogota, Columbia." Land Economics 40 (February): 66-73.

——— (1969b) "Environmental quality and locational behavior in a Latin American city." Urban Affairs Q. 5 (September): 83-101.

——— (1970) "A comparison: population densities, land values and socioeconomic class in four Latin American cities." Land Economics 41 (November): 447-455.

ANDERSON, T. R. and J. A. EGELAND (1961) "Spatial aspects of social area analysis." Amer. Soc. Rev. 26 (June): 392-399.

BERRY, B.J.L. and P. H. REES (1969) "The factorial ecology of Calcutta." Amer. J. of Sociology 74 (March): 445-491.

BERRY, B.J.L. and H. SPODEK (1971) "Comparative ecologies of large Indian cities." Econ. Geography 47 (Supplement, June): 266-385.

BEYNON, E. D. (1961a) "Budapest: an ecological study," pp. 357-370 in G. A. Theodorson (ed.) Studies in Human Ecology. Evanston, Ill.: Row, Peterson.

——— (1961b) "The morphology of the cities of the Alfold," pp. 355-356 in G. A. Theodorson (ed.) Studies in Human Ecology. Evanston, Ill.: Row, Peterson.

BRUSH, J. E. (1962) "The morphology of Indian cities," pp. 57-70 in R. Turner (ed.) India's Urban Future. Berkeley: Univ. of California Press.

BURGESS, E. W. (1925) "The growth of the city: an introduction to a research project," pp. 47-62 in R. E. Park (ed.) The City. Chicago: Univ. of Chicago Press.

CAPLOW, T. (1949) "The social ecology of Guatemala City." Social Forces 28 (December): 113-133.

——— (1952) "Urban structure in France." Amer. Soc. Rev. 17 (October): 544-550.

COLLISON, C. and J. MOGEY (1959) "Residence and social class in Oxford." Amer. J. of Sociology 64 (May): 599-605.

DE BLIJ, H. J. (1963) A Study in Urban Geography: Dar es Salaam. Evanston, Ill.: Northwestern Univ. Press.

DOTSON, F. and L. O. DOTSON (1954) "Ecological trends in the city of Guadalajara, Mexico." Social Forces 32 (May): 367-374.

——— (1956) "Urban centralization and decentralization in Mexico." Rural Sociology 21 (March): 41-49.

——— (1957) "The ecological structure of Mexican cities." Revista Mexicana de Sociologia 19.

FIREY, W. (1947) Land Use in Central Boston. Cambridge: Harvard Univ. Press.

GHOSH, S. (1950) "The urban pattern of Calcutta." Econ. Geography 16 (January): 257.

GIST, N. P. (1957) "The ecological structure of an Asian city: an East-West comparison." Social Forces 35 (May): 356-365.

——— (1968) "The ecology of Bangalore, India: an East-West comparison," pp. 177-188 in S. F. Fava (ed.) Urbanism in World Perspective: A Reader. New York: Thomas Y. Crowell.

GUGLER, J. (1972) "Urbanization in East Africa," pp. 1-26 in J. Hutton (ed.) The Urban Challenge in East Africa. Nairobi: East African Publishing House.

HAGGERTY, L. J. (1971) "Another look at the Burgess hypothesis: time as an important variable." Amer. J. of Sociology 76 (May): 1084-1093.

HALLIMAN, D. M. and W.T.W. MORGAN (1967) "The city of Nairobi," pp. 98-120 in W.T.W. Morgan (ed.) Nairobi City and Region. London: Oxford Univ. Press.

HAMDAN, G. (1960) "The growth and functional structure of Khartoum." Geographical Rev. 50 (January): 21-40.

HANSEN, A. T. (1934) "The ecology of a Latin American city," pp. 124-142 in E. B. Reuter (ed.) Race and Culture Contacts. New York: McGraw-Hill.

HAUSER, F. L. (1968) "Ecological patterns of European cities," pp. 193-216 in S. F. Fava (ed.) Urbanism in World Perspective: A Reader. New York: Thomas Y. Crowell.

HAWLEY, A. H. (1971) Urban Society: An Ecological Approach. New York: Ronald Press.

HAWTHORN, H. B. and A. E. HAWTHORN (1948) "The shape of a city: some observations on Sucre, Bolivia." Sociology and Social Research 33 (November/December): 87-91.

HAYNER, N. S. (1944) "Oaxaca: city of old Mexico." Sociology and Social Research 29 (November/December): 87-95.

——— (1945) "Mexico City, its growth and configuration." Amer. J. of Sociology 50 (January): 295-304.

——— (1968) "Mexico City: its growth and configuration, 1345-1960," pp. 166-177 in S. F. Fava (ed.) Urbanism in World Perspective; A Reader. New York: Thomas Y. Crowell.

HEBERLE, R. and A. BERTRAND (1948) "Social consequences of the industrialization of Southern cities." Social Forces 20 (October): 29-37.

HOYT, H. (1933) One Hundred Years of Land Values in Chicago. Chicago: Univ. of Chicago Press.

——— (1939) The Structure and Growth of Residential Neighborhoods in American Cities. Washington: Federal Housing Administration.

JOHNSON, J. H. (1967) Urban Geography. Oxford: Pergamon.

KEYFITZ, N. (1961) "The ecology of Indonesian cities." Amer. J. of Sociology 66 (January): 348-354.

——— (1965) "Political-economic aspects of urbanization in South and Southeast Asia," pp. 265-309 in P. M. Hauser and L. F. Schnore (eds.) The Study of Urbanization. New York: John Wiley.

KUPER, L., H. WATTA, and R. DAVIES (1958) Durban: A Study in Racial Ecology. London: Jonathan Cape.

LATIF, A. H. (1974a) "Factor structure and change analysis of Alexandria, Egypt, 1947 and 1960," pp. 338-349 in K. P. Schwirian (ed.) Comparative Urban Structure: Studies in the Ecology of Cities. Lexington: D. C. Heath.

——— (1974b) "Residential segregation and location of status and religious groups in Alexandria, Egypt," pp. 423-432 in K. P. Schwirian (ed.) Comparative Urban Structure: Studies in the Ecology of Cities. Lexington: D. C. Heath.

LEONARD, O. E. (1948) "La Paz, Bolivia: its population and growth." Amer. Soc. Rev. 13 (August): 448-454.

LONDON, B. (1973) "The residential ecology of Bangkok, Thailand." Research report, Department of Sociology, University of Connecticut, Storr. (unpublished)

MABOGUNJE, A. L. (1962) "The growth of residential districts in Ibadan." Geographical Rev. 52 (January): 56-77.

——— (1967) "The morphology of Ibadan," pp. 27-56 in P. C. Lloyd et al. (eds.) The City of Ibadan. London: Cambridge Univ. Press.

——— (1968) Urbanization in Nigeria. London: Univ. of London Press.

McELRATH, D. C. (1962) "The social areas of Rome: a comparative analysis." Amer. Soc. Rev. 27 (June): 376-391.

McGEE, T. G. (1967) The Southeast Asian City. New York: Praeger.

MEHTA, S. K. (1968) "Patterns of residence in Poona (India) by income, education, and occupation (1937-65)." Amer. J. of Sociology 73 (January): 496-508.

MINER, H. (1965) The Primitive City of Timbuctoo. Garden City, N.Y.: Doubleday. (First published in 1953.)

MOSCHELES, J. (1937) "The demographic, social, and economic regions of greater Prague: a contribution to urban geography." Geographical Rev. 27 (July): 414-429.

REDICK, R. W. (1964) "A demographic and ecological study of Rangoon, Burma," pp. 31-41 in E. W. Burgess and D. J. Bogue (eds.) Contributions to Urban Sociology. Chicago: Univ. of Chicago Press.

SADA, P. O. (1972) "Residential land use in Lagos: the relevance of traditional models." African Urban Notes 7 (Winter): 3-25.

SCHNORE, L. F. (1965) "On the spatial structure of cities in the two Americas," pp. 347-398 in P. M. Hauser and L. F. Schnore (eds.) The Study of Urbanization. New York: John Wiley.

——— (1972) Class and Race in Cities and Suburbs. Chicago: Markham.

SCHWIRIAN, K. P. (1974) Comparative Urban Structure: Studies in the Ecology of Cities. Lexington: D. C. Heath.

––– and M. MATRE (1974) "The ecological structure of Canadian cities," pp. 309-323 in K. P. Schwirian (ed.) Comparative Urban Structure: Studies in the Ecology of Cities. Lexington: D. C. Heath.

SCHWIRIAN, K. P. and J. L. RICO-VELASCO (1971) "The residential distribution of status groups in Puerto Rico's metropolitan areas." Demography 8 (February): 81-90.

SCHWIRIAN, K. P. and R. K. SMITH (1974) "Primacy, modernization, and urban structure: the ecology of Puerto Rican cities," pp. 324-338 in K. P. Schwirian (ed.) Comparative Urban Structure: Studies in the Ecology of Cities. Lexington: D. C. Heath.

SENDUT, H. (1969) "The structure of Kuala Lampur, Malaysia's capital city," pp. 461-473 in G. Breese (ed.) The City in Newly Developing Countries. Englewood Cliffs, N.J.: Prentice-Hall.

SJOBERG, G. (1960) The Preindustrial City: Past and Present. New York: Free Press.

––– (1965) "Cities in developing and industrial societies: a cross-cultural analysis," pp. 213-263 in P. M. Hauser and L. F. Schnore (eds.) The Study of Urbanization. New York: John Wiley.

SOUTHALL, A. W. (1967) "Kampala-Mengo," pp. 297-332 in H. Miner (ed.) The City in Modern Africa. New York: Praeger.

SPLANSKY, J. (1966) "The concentric zone theory of city structure as applied to an African city: Ibadan, Nigeria." Assn. of Pacific Geographers 28 (Yearbook): 135-146.

THEODORSON, G. A. (1961) Studies in Human Ecology. Evanston, Ill.: Row, Peterson.

THOM, D. J. (1972) "The morphology of Maradi, Niger." African Urban Notes 7 (Winter): 26-35.

THOMLINSON, R. (1969) Urban Structure. New York: Random House.

TIWARI, R. C. (1972) "Some aspects of the social geography of Nairobi, Kenya." African Urban Notes 7 (Winter): 36-61.

WARNER, S. B., Jr. (1962) Streetcar Suburbs: The Process of Growth in Boston, 1870-1900. Cambridge: Harvard Univ. Press.

Chapter 4

URBAN EXPANSION AND LANDOWNERSHIP IN UNDERDEVELOPED SOCIETIES

HANS-DIETER EVERS

URBAN LANDOWNERSHIP, A NEGLECTED ASPECT IN THE STUDY OF URBANIZATION

There has certainly been no lack of studies on urbanization and urban life after the turn of the century. Many aspects have been discussed, and considerable progress has been made in understanding the process of urbanization and the change of urban social structure over time. One aspect has, however, been curiously neglected—namely, urban landownership. This is even more surprising as there is an abundance of studies on *rural* land tenure. Neither classic sociological studies like Max Weber's "The City" nor the far-reaching ecological studies of the Chicago School in the 1920s and 1930s have placed any great emphasis on the ownership and transmission of land in urban areas. Whereas the questions of how urban land is used, who occupies it, and what price it fetches on the urban land market have been discussed in great detail, the question of who owns the land has hardly ever been touched upon since an early interest in the late nineteenth century (Marx, 1955; Liebknecht, 1876; Weber, 1904) had quickly lapsed.

Modern studies of the Shevky-Bell-type social area analysis have introduced many variables and factor-analyzed them. But neither the

AUTHOR'S NOTE: *This paper was prepared while I was Visiting Professorial Fellow at the Centre for Policy Research, Universiti Sains Malaysia, Penang. I should like to thank K. J. Ratnam, Kamal Salih, Goh Ban Lee, Ed Bruner, and Erik Cohen for comments on various drafts of this paper.*

earlier studies of Shevky and Bell nor recent more advanced studies like Berry and Spodek's (1971) factoral ecology of large Indian cities has introduced landownership as one of their main variables. A brief survey of summary works and readers on urbanization and urban society in Africa, Asia, and Latin America show that patterns of landownership and related problems of concentration of ownership and its dispersion are hardly mentioned.

General works surveying a field of urbanization in newly developing countries like Breese (1969) or McGee (1967) neglect the problem of landownership altogether. This neglect is difficult to explain. There is certainly no lack of political or social problems connected with urban landownership. To mention just a few: Urban unrest is often based on landlord-tenant conflicts; urban planning is frequently obstructed by powerful landowners; there is frequently rampant corruption in relation to urban land questions and urban planning (Janssen and Ratz, 1973); there is increasing land speculation and, resulting from all these problems a growing discussion on the need to nationalize city land in Europe and the United States (Hofstee, 1972; Barras et al., 1973).

But even in socialist countries where radical land reform programs have been instituted, a change of urban landownership appears to be difficult. Thus, even in the People's Republic of China, urban land had not, by the middle of 1966, been nationalized, and many landlords still drew rent from their property, although at controlled rates (Wheelwright and McFarlane, 1970: 104). Without bemoaning the lack of attention to problems of urban landownership any further, I shall try to survey the field and present some preliminary ideas on urbanization and urban landownership based on the few available studies.[1]

URBAN EXPANSION AND LAND
FRAGMENTATION (SUBDIVISION)

Urban ecologists have found it useful to distinguish between two major aspects of the urbanization process—"expansion" and "aggregation" (Quinn, 1971). The first refers primarily to the spatial growth of the urban complex and the latter to the increasing population concentration in urban areas. In this paper, I shall devote my attention to the first aspect of spatial urban growth, or "expansion" only.

A few studies address themselves to the question of what happens to the ownership of urban land when urban expansion takes place. All these studies conclude that urban expansion is accompanied by land subdivision and fragmentation of landownership. McTaggart (1966) provides us with a detailed study of the development of landownership of Noumea, the capital of French Caledonia, covering the period from 1880 to 1960. He concludes that "as a rule, in the conversion of land from rural to urban there is fragmentation of ownership" and "once achieved, patterns of land fragmentation in urban areas are remarkably persistent" (1966: 189). In this process, the percentage of large-scale landowners in Noumea has declined and that of small-scale owners has increased (1966: 191). Several earlier studies on urbanization in the United States show that this process of subdivision in the suburban areas produces a concentration of owner occupancy on the city fringe, whereas the city core has higher tenancy rates (Quinn, 1971: 468).

Wolfe's study (1967) of a Seattle, Washington, suburban area also shows this process of subdivision but adds some further refinements. As the city moves out into the suburbs, subdivision of large estates takes place at first. But then a short period of reassembly occurs when urban developers buy up land for housing estates. "Consequently a myriad of small ownerships now exists even though a 'momentary' reassembly did occur," concludes Wolfe (1967: 280).

A somewhat similar pattern emerges from our study of Upper Orchard Road, Singapore, an area which developed recently into a subsidiary town center (Lim, 1972). In the wake of urban expansion, subdivision took place. Eventually big developers bought up land and assembled lots for large-scale commercial enterprises and hotels.

The Upper Orchard Road study covers only a minute section of the city of Singapore. The results of the study do, however, help to explain the land fragmentation profiles of another study area, a small town on the east coast of West Malaysia. Land fragmentation is highest in the city center and in several fast-developing suburban areas. Subdivision is less in the area surrounding the center. This area is partly used for government offices, schools, graveyards, and hotels and partly as a village-type residential quarter (Kampong). This process of leaving areas of almost rural land use and landownership patterns within the urban area has been described as "leap-frog development," as urban growth "jumps" across these areas and leaves them at least temporarily intact.

It can also be learned from these studies that subdivision usually precedes urban development, though on some occasions the expected urban development might not take place at once as the studies by Parson (1972) on Northern California, and by Fellmann (1957) show.

A concentration on the process of subdivision of land and fragmentation of landownership seems to be somewhat limited in scope. A host of more important problems can be posed. If urban expansion and subdivision occur, what impact has the existing land tenure system of the surrounding rural areas on the emerging patterns of urban landownership? It surely makes a difference whether urban expansion takes place in an already highly fragmented and densely populated rural area or into almost open space as in the Middle West of the United States during the past century. Does subdivision of land into smaller plots really mean a deconcentration of landownership, as suggested by McTaggart (1966)? As land values rise, the ownership of a fairly small plot of land can be far more significant than owning a large tract of low-value property. Who are the owners of land before and after urbanization, or, more generally, what is the link between urban social structure and changing patterns of landownership?

I shall try to go into some of these questions as far as data are available.

URBAN EXPANSION AND
LAND SPECULATION

Differences in the urbanization process between developed and underdeveloped countries have frequently been pointed out. In order to stress these differences, the somewhat unfortunate terms "pseudo-urbanization" (McGee, 1967: 17) or "over-urbanization" (Sovani, 1969) have been used. Those terms refer to the fact that, in many underdeveloped areas, urbanization takes place without industrialization and exceeds the rate that might normally be warranted by the internal economic and social structure of the respective countries. The social and economic structure of Third World cities tends to be determined by the preponderance of government administration and by the commercial links with the world-capitalist system. Relations with the peasant sector of the hinterland are very often primarily extractive or exploitative. Cities attract resources from rural areas in the form of migrants or deliveries of victuals. Very little returns to rural areas in form of private investment or government subsidies. Quite often, cities tend to be inhabited by foreign or local ethnic minorities, adding a further dimension to urban-rural differences (Kimani, 1972).

All this has serious consequences for urban landownership patterns. The local urban bourgeoisie that profits from commercial transactions with the world-capitalist system finds it difficult to invest profits from commerce and corruption as there are few industrial enterprises in the country itself and open investments abroad are normally restricted by currency regulations and tax considerations. There is also inflation, a lack of expertise and a general mental block to seek investment in industrial enterprises or in areas far away from the city of origin. The result is conspicuous consumption, the use of land as a status symbol, and investment in property. The pressure on urban land is thus increased not only by the growing urban population but also through the lack of alternative investment opportunities. Land prices spiral, and Third World cities are hit by waves of land speculation as soon as some economic development takes place. This is pointed out in a United Nations report as follows: "Speculation in land in the very largest Asian metropolitan centers has indeed risen to such an extent that urban land prices are higher in the developing countries in Asia than even in the most developed countries" (United Nations, 1968: 52).

In the wake of increasing speculation, land transactions tend to become largely "institutional," that is between speculators, rather than "terminal," that is between the speculator and ultimate resident. This became apparent in our study of Georgetown, Penang, Malaysia, an area that was hit by a wave of land speculation in the early 1970s (Goh, 1975). Detailed data on this process are also provided by Sargent (1972) on Buenos Aires. The institutionalization of land speculation reduced the ability of poor migrants to buy land for residential purposes in the rural-urban fringe as these areas tended to become the object of land speculation rather than urban expansion and urban development. This led among other things to an overcrowding of the city center and the formation of working-class slums (Sargent, 1972: 368). Another outcome of land speculation and increase in land prices may be an extension of squatter areas (that is, a breakdown of the norms of landownership) and "leap-frog" development.

This process, however, does not stop at the lower classes, but eventually reaches the middle class. Singapore provides a good example. Despite largely foreign-induced industrialization, land speculation became rampant at the end of the 1960s and beginning of 1970s. According to a report in a Singapore trade journal in 1969/70, "Middle income earners woke up with a jolt to find that they had been priced out of the housing market" (Singapore Trade and Industry, 1973: 21), whereas advertisements lure millionaires to upper-class areas with a promise to "pamper them with a palatial home priced at $1 Million and over" (1973: 11). Prospective homeowners are thus reduced to tenants or seek investment in land elsewhere. As a consequence, small-scale investors join large speculators to increase the pressure on prospective urban land, and speculation is directed to new areas. Though exact data are difficult to obtain at present, there are nevertheless indications that *waves* of speculation extend from major urban centers to secondary towns and rural areas, sometimes even transcending national boundaries. Preliminary data from the study of Georgetown, Penang, substantiate this argument.

URBAN EXPANSION AND RURAL
LAND TENURE

Though absentee landlordism is, of course, a long-established feature of most predominantly agrarian societies, chances are that more and more land in the immediate vicinity of large towns is going to be owned by an urban elite, as soon as economic development takes place. In Southeast Asia, both Burma and South Vietnam provide us with early examples of a growing loss of land to absentee landlords. In colonial Burma, large tracts of farm land had been acquired by Chettiars living in Rangoon and early Burmese nationalism focused very much on this issue of land tenure (Mahajani, 1960: 68). In South Vietnam, an estimated 70% of all farmers owned no land any more in the 1950s. A study of a fairly representative village some thirty miles from Saigon showed more than one-third of all rice land was owned by only one absentee landlord (Hendry, 1964: 34). Some paddy land was also held by nonresident teachers or minor government officials as a "supplemental source of income" (Hendry, 1964: 38). The impact of land speculation by an urban-based elite on the rural areas surrounding the cities can also be demonstrated by more recent examples taken from Thailand and Indonesia.

When the then Thai Prime Minister, Field Marshal Sarit, died in December 1958, it was disclosed that he and his wives owned vast tracts of land especially along highways leading out of Bangkok, the Thai capital. But other members of the Thai urban elite had also bought up land, particularly along the roads and canals leading out of Bangkok. The result has been increasing landlessness and a growing rural proletariate in the vicinity of Bangkok. This is substantiated by reports from F.A.O., U.N.D.P., and the Bangkok Bank, which state that "tenancy in the central plain is spreading largely because of land speculation (generally by urban residents) and mortgage foreclosures" (U.S. Department of Agriculture 1972: 18).

An earlier report of the Thai Ministry of National Development (1964) states that in the central plain area surrounding Bangkok 19% of the paddy farmers owning no land at all had sold their land only recently. In the early 1960s, when the data were collected, about one-third of all peasants were already landless. This figure is much higher than the national average. Problems of land tenure were not acute in Thailand until recently, and tenancy and absentee ownership were not widespread, except perhaps here and there in the Northeast (Luther, 1970) and in the Bangkok area. Nationwide, nearly 82% of the Thai farmers owned all or part of the land they cultivated (U.S. Department of Agriculture 1972: 17). This demonstrates very clearly that absentee landlordism is here primarily an *urban*-induced phenomenon. A discussion of rural land tenure without taking urbanization and urban social structure into consideration would thus be misleading.

For Java, Indonesia, exact information is even more difficult to obtain. Data from an agricultural survey and the 1971 census at least give some rough indication. As Table 1 shows, the higher the urban population in a province, the higher the percentage of land under rent or sharecropping. This gives at least some indication that urbanization and the growth of urban elites may result in an increase in absentee landlordism or landlessness.[2]

It is also an open secret that land speculation is rampant in Jakarta and its vicinity. It appears that higher civil servants and military officers are now engaged in buying up agricultural land in villages. This is aided by the 1960 Land Reform Laws that state that only members of the Armed Forces and government officials are allowed to own land outside the district of their residence. Also here absentee landlordism appears to be on the increase as a result of urban development and the growing relative affluence of an urban upper class (Evers, 1973). There are also several cases where urban residents tried to regain control of their former rural

TABLE 1

	% Urban pop.	% Land (paddy, etc.) rented or sharecropping	Average size of owner-cult. plot in ha
W. Java & Jakarta	28	17	0.5
Jogjakarta	16	14	0.5
E. Java	15	12	0.7
C. Java	11	13	0.6

landholdings, which had been confiscated under the 1960 land reform laws prior to the coup of 1965.

We may thus tentatively conclude that the specific type of "development" taking place in the urban centers of Third World countries leads to increased land speculation, the enrichment of a land-owning urban elite, increased absentee landownership in rural areas surrounding the city and thus a growing social and economic dependence of rural areas on the dominant city. Urban expansion thus reaches much further than the immediate suburban fringe, where subdivision and urban development might take place, as discussed earlier.

URBAN EXPANSION AND CHANGING CONCEPTS OF LANDOWNERSHIP

In the process of land speculation, a landed urban elite attempts to reach out into the rural urban fringe and beyond. But there is not only an increase in absentee landownership and a growing control of the city over the countryside, but also a cultural change in legal norms governing landownership. The process of urban expansion and the physical extension of built-up areas has so far been analyzed in terms of an increasing subdivision of land on the rural urban fringe and the spatial extension of the power of a land-owning urban elite. We now have to add the third aspect of urban "cultural expansion." The diffusion of urban cultural patterns into the countryside can take many forms. In the context of this paper, we shall refer only to norms of ownership as an important aspect of this cultural pattern.

The concept of "ownership" of land as incorporated in most legal codes today is of relatively recent origin. During the European Middle Ages and still in many parts of Asia and Africa today, land is held for use rather than "owned" (Vance, 1971: 107). Rights to the use of land were either an integral part of citizenship or of membership in a kinship group. It was only with the development of mercantilism and capitalism that pieces of territory came to be viewed as commodities capable of being bought, sold, or exchanged at the marketplace (Soja, 1971: 9). Ownership of land, in fact, was the basis out of which the dominant position of private property in modern capitalism developed (Marx, 1955: 91). The city, however, was the center of this development (Weber, 1958: 97). Urbanization and the development of the concept of private property are thus intrinsically linked.

Wherever colonial cities were founded, this European concept of private property was implanted and expanded with urbanization. One of the first tasks a colonial government tended to undertake was the measurement and registration of urban land. The outcome of the introduction of a Western concept of property was usually a dual system of land rights differentiating between Western individual property rights in the city and "native land rights" in the rural areas.[3]

Conflict between the two systems was and is frequent and becomes particularly pressing in the rural urban fringe where land developers and land speculators expand the capitalist concept of individual property rights against a peasantry that still maintains a socially bounded concept of customary land rights. The outcome of this struggle depends very much on the political situation, but frequently the urban speculators, aided by professional lawyers, courts, and police, remain victorious. Gananath Obeyesekere (1967), e.g., describes how lawyers use Roman Dutch law to overrule intestate succession to land according to Kandyan customary law. In this way, they manage to reap monetary profits or bring agricultural land under their control.

Indonesia provides us with another well-documented example of a dual legal system. In the Netherlands East Indies, a sort of "apartheid order" of land rights was developed. The urban centers were usually governed by Dutch law, while the areas inhabited by the local population was governed by a multitude of customary land rights *(adat)*. Non-natives were not allowed to exercise any native land rights (Wertheim, 1958: 56). Though Indonesians were allowed to make use of Dutch private property laws and register their lands, this right was rarely exercised except perhaps by the Chinese minority (Pieters, 1951: 124). Nevertheless, the measurement and registration of land under Western law has increased slowly either in terms of registered area or in its impact or "undermining" of customary land rights (van Vollenhoven 1925: 29).

On the other hand, customary land rights have, in some areas of Indonesia, been more powerful than originally expected and have adapted to the new conditions of urbanization and urban crowding (Evers, 1974).

With the increasing social and economic power of the urban upper class and its speculative endeavors, precapitalist land rights are reduced and consequently the social and economic condition of the peasantry in the rural urban fringe is weakened. A frequent outcome of this development is a mixed urban land tenure system that has no real legal basis:[4] Land is owned by urban absentee landlords, whereas houses are built and "owned" by tenants who pay a nominal land rent to the landowners. This system is described by Clifford Geertz (1965: 31) for Javanese towns (see Table 2). In the *kampong* areas of these towns, a "whole block is owned by one or two people quite commonly but not necessarily one of the people in the stone houses facing the street."

Similar patterns were found in Padang, the provincial capital of West Sumatra (Evers, 1975), and in Singapore (Wong, 1974). As soon as land values rise, these so-called "squatters" are pushed out, very often in circumvention of laws safeguarding the rights of tenants, and are replaced by tenants or owner-occupants of a higher social class. This process is usually termed "urban redevelopment."

This rather summary treatment of a very complex matter is only intended to give a preliminary indication of the problems involved and to draw attention to the need for further detailed studies.

CONCLUSION

In this survey of studies on urban landownership, we found that there is a general lack of empirical research in this area. We have concentrated on the process of urban expansion into rural areas and found that first of all subdivision and land fragmentation take place with possibly short periods of reassembly by land speculators or developers. In this change of the ownership structure, land is eventually developed and its use changes from rural to residential. We have also noted that this trend might be interrupted by land division without development or by "leap-frog" development, whereby large areas remain unused because of land speculation.

With economic development following a capitalist pattern, the urban upper class tends to engage in land speculation due to the lack of other investment opportunities. This speculation may become institutional—that means speculation between speculators—and eventually extend beyond the

TABLE 2
House and House-Land Ownership in Modjokuto

	Own House and Land No. (%)	Own House Rent Land No. (%)	Rent Both No. (%)
Urban (four kampongs)	27 (10.9)	120 (48.6)	100 (40.5)
Semiurban Village	22 (68.9)	7 (21.9)	3 (09.2)
Rural Village	58 (95.8)	3 (04.2)	0 (00.0)

rural-urban fringe into rural areas. Some of the consequences of this process have been pointed out.

Urban expansion does not, however, only take the form of a physical expansion and a change of landownership, but also of an extension of legal concepts that originate from the city center and are historically connected with urbanism and capitalism. Indonesia was used as an example to point to some of the problems and conflicts involved. Also here further studies are necessary to come to a preliminary understanding of the problems of legal change and the ownership of urban property.

NOTES

1. Most examples will be drawn from Southeast Asia, and I might have overlooked or underemphasized available studies from other world regions. A comprehensive bibliography on urban society in Southeast Asia is provided by Cohen (1973).

2. We are, of course, aware of the fact that many other variables should be considered to prove the point. Population density, land use, and nonagricultural employment are some of the factors that would have to be considered. In any case, the data in Table 1 do not contradict my hypothesis.

3. The situation in plantation areas was different but should not concern us here.

4. In Western law, property usually encompasses both land and buildings thereon. Thus, paragraph 94 of the German "Buergerliches Gesetzbuch" stipulates that buildings are an essential part of a plot of land.

REFERENCES

BARRAS, R., A. BROADBENT, and D. MASSEY (1973) "Planning and the public ownership of land." New Society 21 (June): 676-679.

BERRY, B.J.L. and H. SPODEK (1971) "Comparative ecologies of large Indian cities." Economic Geography 47, 2 (Suppl.): 266-285.

BREESE, G. [ed.] (1969) The City in Newly Developing Countries. Englewood Cliffs, N.J.: Prentice-Hall.

COHEN, E. (1973) "Social ecology: a multidimensional approach." Working Paper No. 3, Department of Sociology, University of Singapore.

EVERS, H.-D. (1975) "Changing patterns of urban Minangkabau landownership." Bijdragen tot de Taal- Land-en Volkenkunde 131, 1: 86-110.

——— (1974) "Traditional land tenure in an Indonesian city." LTC Newsletter, Land Tenure Center, University of Wisconsin: 14-19.

——— (1973) "Group conflict and class formation in Southeast Asia," pp. 108-131 in H.-D. Evers (ed.) Modernization in Southeast Asia. London: Oxford Univ. Press.

FELLMANN, J. D. (1957) "Pre-building growth patterns of Chicago." Annals, Association of American Geographers, 47: 59-82.

GAMER, R. E. (1972) The Politics of Urban Development in Singapore. Singapore: Oxford Univ. Press.

GEERTZ, C. (1965) The Social History of an Indonesian Town. Cambridge, Mass.: MIT Press.

GOH, B. L. (1975) "The pattern of landownership in central Georgetown." Universiti Sains Malaysia, Centre for Policy Research monograph series 2.

HENDRY, J. B. (1964) The Small World of Khanh Hau. Chicago: Aldine.

HOFSTEE, E. W. (1972) "Landownership in densely populated and industrialized countries." Sociologia Ruralis 12, 1: 6-26.

Indonesia, Biro Pusat Statistik (1971) Survey Pertanian. Jakarta.

JANSSEN, J. and M. RATZ (1973) Bodenpolitik und Bodenrechts-reform in der BRD. Köln: Pahl-Rugenstein.

KIMANI, S. M. (1972) "The structure of landownership in Nairobi." J. of Eastern African Research and Development 2, 2: 101-124.

LIEBKNECHT, W. (1876) Zur Grund- und Bodenfrage. Leipzig: Genossenschafts-druckerei.

LIM, A.W.G. (1972) "Changing patterns of landownership and social stratification in Singapore—a case study of Upper Orchard Road." Academic Exercise, Department of Sociology, University of Singapore.

LUTHER, H. U. (1970) Reformer gegen Rebellen: Zur Situation der Bauern in Thailand. Hamburg: Mitteilungen des Instituts für Asienkunde, Nr. 32.

McGEE, T. G. (1967) The Southeast Asian City: A Social Geography of the Primate Cities of Southeast Asia. London: G. Bell.

McTAGGART, W. D. (1966) "Private landownership in a colonial town: the case of Noumea, New Caledonia." Economic Geography 42, 3: 189-204.

MAHAJANI, U. (1960) The Role of Indian Minorities in Burma and Malaya. Bombay: Vora.

MARX, K. (1955) "Zur kritik der nationalökonomie. Okonomisch-philosophische manuskripte," in Karl Marx und Friedrich Engels, kleine ökonomische Schriften. Berlin: Dietz Verlag.

MORTIMER, R. (1972) "The Indonesian Communist Party and land reform, 1959-1965." Clayton, Vic.: Monash Papers on Southeast Asia No. 1, Monash University, Centre for Southeast Asian Studies.

OBEYESEKERE, G. (1967) Land Tenure in Village Ceylon: A Sociological and Historical Study. Cambridge, Eng.: Cambridge Univ. Press.

PARSON, J. J. (1972) "Slicing up the open space: subdivision without homes in N. California." Erdkunde 26, 1: 1-8.

PIETERS, J. M. (1951) "Land policy in the Netherlands East Indies before the Second World War," pp. 116-139 in Land Tenure Symposium Amsterdam 1950, organized by the Africa Instituut Leiden. Leiden: Universitaire Pers Leiden.

QUINN, J. A. (1971) Human Ecology. Hamden, Conn.: Archon Books.

SARGENT, C. S. (1972) "Land speculation in Buenos Aires." Economic Geography 28: 358-374.

Singapore Trade and Industry (1973) "Special report on the real estate market." (July): 5-25.

SOJA, E. W. (1971) The Political Organization of Space. Resource Paper No. 8, Washington, D.C.: Commission on College Geography, Association of American Geographers.

SOVANI, N. V. (1969) "The analysis of 'over-urbanization,' " in G. Breese (ed.) The City in Newly Developing Countries. Englewood Cliffs, N.J.: Prentice-Hall.

Thailand, Ministry of National Development (1964) Relationship between Land Tenure and Rice Production in Five Central Provinces, Thailand, 1964. Bangkok: Ministry of National Development.

United Nations (1968) "Urban-rural population distribution and settlement patterns in Asia." International Social Development Rev. No. 1.

U.S. Department of Agriculture (1972) The Agricultural Economy of Thailand. Washington, D.C.

VANCE, J. E., Jr. (1971) "Land assignment in the precapitalist, capitalist, and postcapitalist city." Economic Geography 47, 2 (April): 101-120.

VOLLENHOVEN, C. VAN (1925) "De indonesier en zijn ground," in Een adatwetboekje voor heel Indie. Leiden: E. J. Brill.

WEBER, A. (1904) Uber Bodenrente und Bodenspekulation in der modernen Stadt. Leipzig: Duncker & Humblot.

WEBER, M. (1958) The City. New York: Free Press.

WERTHEIM, W. E. [ed.] (1958) The Indonesian Town: Studies in Urban Sociology. The Hague and Bandung: Van Hoeve.

WHEELWRIGHT, E. L. and B. McFARLANE (1970) The Chinese Road to Socialism. Economics of the Cultural Revolution. New York and London: Monthly Review Press.

WOLFE, H. R. (1967) "A chronology of land tenure, influences on suburban development patterns." Town Planning Rev. 37, 4: 271-290.

WONG, D. (1974) Changing Patterns of Landownership in Singapore: A Case Study of Coronation Road. Singapore: University of Singapore Department of Sociology.

Chapter 5

HOUSING POLICIES AND COMPARATIVE URBAN POLITICS

CORALIE BRYANT
LOUISE G. WHITE

On November 13, 1968, two years after its first showing, "Cathy Come Home" had been viewed by millions of Englishmen. The moving and shocking story of the destitute English family pulled apart by their lack of housing and by the government's housing policy provoked widespread public reaction. It also stimulated the formation of the Squatters movement, a group which translated the concern over housing into political protest and over a period of several years, captured British headlines with its "squatting" activities (Bailey, 1972: 25 f.).

The United States, too, has seen its share of squatters in such large urban areas as New York City. The same cities have also had an array of militant housing organizations, as well as citizen interest groups which have housing as one part of their agenda. Whatever their immediate impact in a given locale, and for the actual participants, none of these organized efforts has had the same impact on the public conscience as have the groups in English cities. This chapter will raise the question of why American urban politics has not witnessed the growth of interest groups which have been as vocal, visible, radical, and effective in mobilizing Americans behind the housing issue as have their counterparts in the United Kingdom.

It is particularly interesting to look at housing policy if one is interested in cities, since so much of the urban landscape is determined by the particular national housing and land-use policies. Since squatters are an ever-present part of the third world urban growth process, their presence in cities in so-called "developed" countries raises additional interesting issues. Unfortunately, space will not permit many of the issues which first and third world squatting have in common, but it is worth remembering that comparative urban politics provides a focus in which to raise the possibility of such comparisons.[1]

Most comparative urban research has sought to explain differences in policies either by the resources of a political system or by its culture. Studies of policy output among the American states have looked at the relative influence of economic and political factors, and have generally concluded that economic variables explain far more of the differences in policies and expenditures than political variables (Dye, 1966; Dawson and Robinson, 1966). Economic indicators do not help us in comparing British and American housing policy, however. As one American housing expert exclaimed,

> How can a country whose national income per capita is about half that of the United States manage to subsidize nearly one third of its people in public housing while we cannot even get up to three percent? How do they manage to get public support to finance such housing? [Niven, 1972: 440]

It is clear that the greater wealth and resources of the United States do not result in greater concern with, or attention to, housing problems of the population. In addition, Robert Salisbury insists that these studies which focus on economic resources essentially beg the more interesting questions.

> While system resources may account for the amount of money that is spent, the active political system continues to be decisive in determining the kind of policy, including the groups that benefit or suffer, the extent of conflict, the ability to innovate, or adapt, and other such questions [Salisbury, 1968: 165; for a related argument, see Heidenheimer, 1973].

Since the issue raised by the Squatters is not only on the absolute amount of housing, but also on who benefits from it, this study will look at several political determinants of housing policy formation.

In contrast to this focus on system resources, most cross-national comparative research has searched in the limitless waters of political culture, and focused on the values inherent in a given culture. Applying this emphasis to housing policy, one would say that the prevailing norms in Britain stipulate public responsibility for housing to a far greater extent than those in the United States. In the latter country, housing is assumed to be appropriately consigned to the private sector, and thus not a legitimate target of public concern. Not the least of the problems with the political culture argument is that it is used to explain everything, and yet results in explaining very little. One cannot but envy the economist, who does not try to explain English interest rates as a function of the English culture, but starts with explicit assumptions and is able to move on to discrete variables. This is not to say that his analysis is not enriched by an awareness of economic and political cultures, but that he does not allow himself to stop with one holistic explanation. The question becomes one of determining what other factors are at work (Przeworski and Teune, 1971: 20-30).

Group activities can also be compared in terms of their available options or strategies. As Kimber and Richardson (1974: 16) put it, explanations of group behavior "must be in terms of the whole strategic situation in which groups are placed." The assumption is that they behave rationally in response to perceived tradeoffs between costs and benefits. It is this explanation which appears most useful in understanding the different degrees of popular concern and activity over the housing issue (see Lipsky, 1968; Alford and diTomasco, 1973). Approached in this way, the resources of the system and the culture become two of a variety of factors which enter into a group's calculus as to which issues to pursue, and by what method.

The specific aspects of the "strategic situation" chosen for study here are three political factors: the extent of a housing constituency, whether or not it is a partisan issue, and the impact of the housing policy. The first factor leads us to ask whether a housing constituency exists or whether it must be mobilized. Obviously, it is far easier to appeal to an existing group of housing policy beneficiaries, as exist in Britain. Similarly, what is the makeup of the groups interested in housing, and the extent of their political clout? Are they heterogeneous groups dispersed throughout the populace, as in Britain, or are they minority groups located in a few areas, as in the United States?

The second factor suggests that the existence of differences among government policy makers offers potential access for interest groups and a reasonable likelihood of gaining attention. More specifically, it was the partisanship over housing in England which provided access for groups to emerge and to perceive payoffs for mobilizing public opinion. In contrast, the consensus between the American parties over housing policy had no natural entree onto the existing political agenda. Riker notes that one aspect of rational choice is the likelihood that one's efforts will be successful (Riker and Ordeshook, 1973: 62 f.). Because of the debate over housing by political elites and the access this provided, British interest groups could estimate a higher probability of success than their American counterparts.

The third political factor is the impact of housing policy, and particularly of housing subsidies. One can best focus on the housing subsidy system directly and ask of each sort of subsidy who is likely to benefit, and hence which sorts of interest groups are likely to perceive it in their interest to organize. When benefits go directly to the consumer, those benefitted may well collectivize for political action to maintain these subsidies. When benefits go initially to developers or builders, middlemen in the subsidy system will organize and dominate in the pressure system. Conceived this way, one can argue that subsides provide "policy opportunities" for a variety of actual and latent groups.[2]

POLICY CONSTITUENCY

The first point of comparison between British and American cities is that because of England's historic commitment to providing housing, a large proportion of residents in any given area live in council housing (Ministry of Housing and Local Government, 1969). About one-third of all the dwelling units in England are owned by public authorities. One result of this sizeable proportion is that council housing tenants are a significant part of any politician's constituency. Their influence obviously varies by locality, but nowhere can they be disregarded. Not only is there a difference in numbers, there is also less social stigma attached to residing in council housing, in part because there is no income limit as a requirement of occupancy in England. (It would, however, be wrong to say that council housing provides *no* social stigma; residents and sociologists continue to argue about how much is 'less.') By contrast, the recipients of public housing in the United States are not only few in number, they are also concentrated in large urban centers, and are in large part composed of either minority groups or the elderly.

This social difference became very important in the respective squatter movements in the two countries. In England, public sympathy was accorded to those squatters who were obviously from working-class families, but was denied when the squatters were students, hippies, or gypsies (Hollister, 1972: 49). The effort in selecting squatters was to find families who would project an image of solidarity and initiative, but who had been unable to find housing or had been otherwise victimized by the system (Bailey, 1972: 40 f.). Whole families with employed fathers were the model squatters. These people could not be dismissed out of hand as counter culture representatives, and by acting wholly within the law, they buttressed their advocacy position.[3] By contrast, in New York City, most of the squatters were blacks or Puerto Ricans, and thus less able to elicit public sympathy. In Washington, D.C., squatters tend not to publicize their activities, for they do not expect to have sympathy on their side. At the same time, squatters are running for, and winning, seats on local councils in England.

A third aspect of the existing housing constituency is also worth noting. In England, local jurisdictions have been given the authority—indeed, the mandate—to provide for anyone without housing in their areas. Given the shortage of council housing, local units have developed a hostel system to provide emergency temporary shelter to those with no place to live. Councils have developed various laws which severely regulate the hostel residents. For example, as described by Ron Bailey, an organizer of the Squatters,

> At 10 Soho Road the Birmingham City Council allowed husbands to visit between 7 p.m. to 8 p.m. weekday evenings only. They met their wives in a communal room, and the children were brought downstairs to see them. Under no circumstances were they allowed up to their wives' rooms. If the women were living on National Assistance the husbands were not allowed to visit them. No pictures, radios, television sets or electric irons were allowed [Bailey, 1972: 14].

The indignities conjured up the world of Dickens, and were effectively publicized by the Squatter groups, in their desire to reach the public conscience. Helping their efforts was the fact that the wretched conditions were the result of government policy. In the United States, by contrast, most of the indignities and indecencies due to the shortage of adequate housing were the result of income inequities, and the lack of government action. It is always easier to mobilize sentiment against the government for doing something wrong than for not doing anything. In the United States, when government politics do result in gross violations of decency, such as the "man in the house" rule and the monstrosities of large public housing projects, most of the controversy has deflected onto the welfare system, rather than the lack of housing. Again, the fact that most public housing residents were from minority groups, and as a constituency were concentrated in a few urban areas further insulated housing from reaching the public agenda.

A final aspect of the housing policy constituency relates to the electoral accountability of the policy makers. The provision of housing in English cities, when not adequately provided in the private sector, is the explicit responsibility of the local government. The central government formulates overall policy, supervises the housing programs on a national scale and, since 1919, has provided funds to subsidize the production of more housing. The local housing authorities must utilize these programs to meet local needs. In direct contrast to the United States, the local housing authorities in England are the elected councils of county boroughs and urban districts (Royal Commission on Local Government in England, 1969). Thus, local as well as national politicians can be, and are, held accountable for the implementation of housing programs. In contrast, in the United States, housing programs are implemented at the local level by appointed local authorities largely isolated from the influence of city politicians. Consequently, one of the reasons for the low profile of housing policy for many Americans is that no local or national elected official can be held accountable for housing shortages. There is some evidence that this political factor is changing as local councils in the United States get increasingly involved in rent control, and as community development provisions of the 1974 housing legislation has its impact. To the extent that political accountability diffuses onto local elected officials, interest groups may perceive it as an opportunity to organize (Alford and diTomasco, 1973).

These factors about the political salience of the housing constituency suggest that in Britain it will be easier to mobilize the public and to get what Kimber and Richardson (1974: 3) refer to as "promotional" as well as "sectional" interest groups. A sectional group is one that exists to promote the particular interests of those in the group. Promotional groups, however, exist to promote causes. Finer suggests that the former usually work through the Executive, and then the legislature, and least frequently make appeals to the public. Promotional groups, by contrast, work in reverse and are most likely to appeal to the public (1958: 130). It was suggested above that groups will form where strategic opportunities exist for them to do so. The very existence of a policy constituency, or a dispersed group of public housing recipients in Great Britain, gives them a greater opportunity, and a more salient issue than exists in the United States.

As noted at the outset of this study, the incidence and success of promotional groups has been much greater in England than in the United States. In England the last five years have witnessed a rapid growth in the number of pressure groups which could be called "promotional." These range from housing associations and societies which help people meet their housing needs either by direct protest or court cases; to the growth of Shelter, a lobbying group dramatizing the needs of many for more adequate housing; to the squatters' groups who are both more angry and more direct in their protests. These latter groups do not follow the usual paths to the executive to make their demands known; they focus on the media, the legislature, and on the courts (Bailey, 1972).

The direct political action of the squatters angered more traditional lobbying groups such as Shelter. The squatters, however, maintained that incremental gains and adjustments were unacceptable, that radical changes needed to be made, and that the only way to affect such changes was to appeal to the public. Ironically, the local boroughs quickly learned that the way to neutralize such appeals was to meet the immediate needs of the actual squatters, thus deflecting demands for radical change (Hollister, 1972; Bailey, 1972). It is worth adding that the local Councils were as apt to destroy such housing by pouring cement in the plumbing, for example, as they were to turn it over to the existing squatting family (Bailey, 1972).

By contrast, in the United States, the predominant pattern of housing interest group activity has been by what Beer would call "producer" groups, or what were called "sectional" groups above. To the extent that lobbying groups have been influential in forming policy, it has been by such groups as NAHB, the National Association of Housing and Redevelopment Officials (Pynoos, Hartman, and Schafer, 1973; Alford and diTomasco, 1973).

In his research on housing interest groups, Harold Wolman demonstrated by interviews with policy makers that it was these producer groups, rather than the broad-scale civil rights groups, which influenced the 1968 Housing Act (1971: 65-69). NAHRO often represented the interests of the poor, insofar as they pushed for public housing, but the poor themselves had no part, and it is not necessarily true that the poor would have always preferred public housing to alternatives such as rent allowances (Pynoos, Hartman, and Schafer, 1973: 17). Pynoos, Hartman, and Schafer note that even where the poor were involved via tenant groups or rent strikes, the demand was for immediate and local payoffs, rather than to follow the English model and make broader public appeals for basic structural changes (1973: 19).

Substantiating the suggestion made here that you need a housing constituency before you can mobilize effective popular action is the fact that the one place where the poor successfully organized to protest housing policy was in St. Louis, where the government itself was the landlord (Pynoos, Hartman, and Schafer, 1973: 20).

THE ROLE OF PARTISANSHIP

A major item on the agenda of both parties in Britain is how the government should fulfill its responsibility to house its people. To pick up the story in 1965, the leading political parties were convinced that changes were needed in housing policy, but they disagreed profoundly over the direction for these changes. The Conservative Party was particularly anxious to move away from public commitments to subsidized construction of council housing. The Labor Party was opposed to any lessening of government's commitment to public housing. By the 1970 general elections, housing was one of the central issues (Scarrow, 1971). The major change proposed by the Conservatives was the sale of council housing to sitting tenants. In addition, they proposed raising council rents, as well as regulating rents in the private sector, and to supplement this with a system of rebates and allowances (Housing Finance Act, 1972; Beer, 1974: 191-192). Labor county councils strongly opposed this legislation.

When the Conservatives came to power in 1972 they introduced legislation which became the Housing Finance Act of 1972. The new rent rebate and rent allowance programs represent a very real change of direction in United Kingdom policies. Under these schemes, payments will be utilized to compensate people in council housing or private housing for costs which exceed prescribed levels of family income. The purpose was to raise rents in council housing and make it more competitive with the private rental market, and to ensure that those families able to afford a market rent would, in fact, pay one. Conservatives spoke of the act as "one small step away from Socialism," and as a way to restrain the public involvement in housing. The unduly long debate in the House of Commons over this legislation was due to the intense Labor Party opposition (Mandelker, 1973: xi-xii). Since this policy had the effect of reducing the total council housing stock, it caused a storm of protest from Laborite housing authorities.[4]

Housing policies in the United States have also undergone great changes within the last several years, but the amount of public attention focused upon this issue has been minimal. Even the Nixon Administration's decision to suspend all housing subsidy programs on January 5, 1973, caused but a brief flurry of outrage in the public arena and received scant recognition from the majority of the electorate. Nowhere did local elections in the fall of 1973 raise the issue of local pressure to counter this moratorium. The administration's House and Community Development Act of 1974 did address the need for additional construction, but much of the argument over the bill was concerned with the House deletion of the controversial sections 235 and 236.[5] But it was not a partisan issue. On the contrary, the House Subcommittee on Housing (largely Democratic) saw itself as allied with the Republican administration's policy in opposition to the Senate Committee's bill. According to one observer, "In America . . . congressional legislation in sensitive fields like housing tends to be the product of a developed consensus" (Mandelker, 1973: 123).

Even so concerned a friend of housing proponents as Congressman Ashley of the Housing Subcommittee (and cosponsor of the Barrett-Ashley Bill)[6] has said of housing policy in the United States, "With all the other domestic needs like health, education, and a cleaner environment, housing simply will not receive a priority claim on the nation's resources" (Washington Post, September 4, 1973). Contrast this with the English position that health policy and housing are interdependent, or contrast it with the current English fiscal commitment to housing. Following the announcement of proposed central government budget cuts of approximately $270 million in 1973, and $1.35 billion in 1974, a staff member of the Ministry of Housing indicated that these cuts would *not result* in any reduction in the amount of funds available to implement the housing program, and, in fact, that additional funds would probably be made available.

There is a reciprocal relationship between the two political variables discussed thus far. The existence of a "policy constituency" provides an "electoral connection" for legislators (Mayhew, 1974). In Britain, this meant that stands on housing could gain votes for the party, and thus the parliamentary parties developed a housing policy as a party issue. Conversely, this partisanship opened up more access points for interest groups, thus making success more likely. The existence of both a concerned public opinion and a partisan issue altered the benefit-cost calculations of interest groups, and hence their decision about whether to organize, and how much to invest in mobilizing public opinion. Returning to the initial point that interest groups form in response to strategic opportunities, the existence of differing policy commitments gives them an entree into the political system. There are public officials who have committed themselves and thus need some support. It also gives them leverage in appealing to public opinion. The interest groups do not have to create an issue or opinion ex nihilo; rather, they can deflect it and mold it to their own purposes.

POLICY IMPACT

A third aspect of the "strategic situation" in which groups find themselves is the political impact of a given policy. Theodore Lowi has argued that policies determine politics. The implication for this study is that the sort of subsidy system a government chooses to implement its housing policies presents opportunities for potential groups. The different subsidy systems create different real and/or potential payoffs for different kinds of interest groups. They organize, mobilize, or go about gaining support as a response to the opportunities which the legislation presents. The pattern of the subsidy in part determines the costs and benefits of political activity for organized as well as latent interest groups.

British housing policies more readily fall into Lowi's distributive or redistributive categories, while U.S. housing policies tend to be distributive and regulatory, with almost none that are redistributive (see Figure 1, based on Lowi, 1972: 298-300, as amended by Salisbury, 1968: 171). In

FIGURE I

IMPACT OF HOUSING POLICY IN THE
UNITED STATES AND THE UNITED KINGDOM

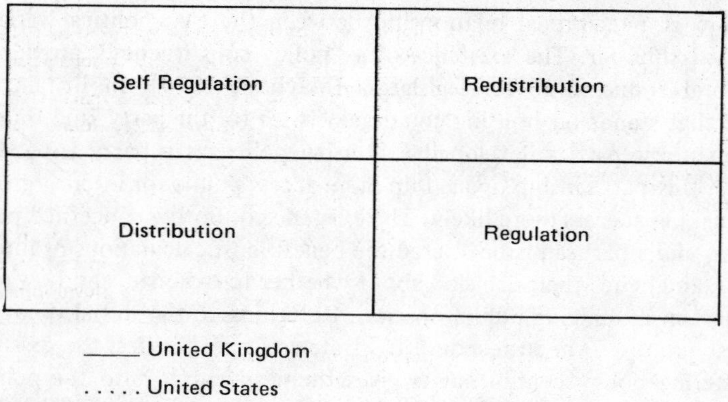

Self Regulation	Redistribution
Distribution	Regulation

———— United Kingdom

. . . . . United States

categorizing policies as Lowi did, the terms distributive and redistributive meant what those terms imply—that is, that distributive policies are those which disperse their benefits to a wide spectrum of groups and classes in the polity while redistributive policies tend to move benefits from one group or class to another. Regulative policies are those which a government may choose to undertake in regard to an industry when distributive policies may be perceived as more costly or politically difficult. Some regulatory policies may very well have distributive effects—a factor frequently mentioned in discussion of Lowi's typology. For example, using zoning at the local level in lieu of a more interventionist land-use planning approach is an example of regulatory policy.

What is there about British housing subsidy systems which reinforces the tendency for this pattern? Or, if policies determine politics—how do Britain's housing polities determine its housing politics? To answer this

FIGURE 2

IMPACT OF HOUSING SUBSIDY SYSTEMS IN
UNITED STATES AND GREAT BRITAIN

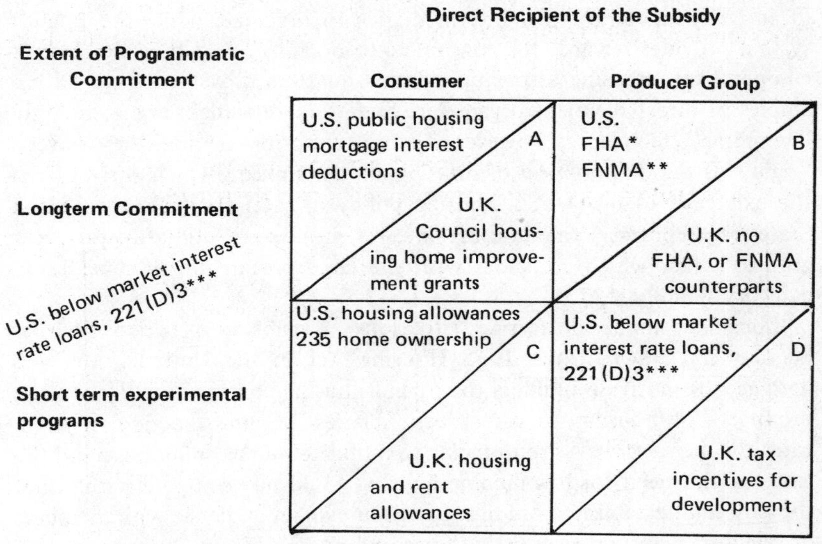

Direct Recipient of the Subsidy

Extent of Programmatic Commitment

	Consumer	Producer Group
Longterm Commitment	U.S. public housing mortgage interest deductions A U.K. Council housing home improvement grants	U.S. FHA* FNMA** B U.K. no FHA, or FNMA counterparts
Short term experimental programs	U.S. housing allowances 235 home ownership C U.K. housing and rent allowances	U.S. below market interest rate loans, 221(D)3*** D U.K. tax incentives for development

*U.S. below market interest rate loans, 221(D)3****

*Federal Housing Administration
**Federal National Mortgage Association
***Below market interest rate program, replaced by Section 236.

question, it is useful to develop a typology of the housing subsidy patterns in the two countries. One dimension of such a classification is the strength of the programmatic commitment. Some programs come and go, and others last forever, or apparently forever. That one can deduct interest paid on mortgages from income tax is a subsidy whose future is not in doubt. Others, however, are experimental and hence somewhat short limit, such as some rent supplement programs for the elderly. The second dimension has to do with who is the direct recipient of the subsidy—the consumer or a middleman such as a developer. Some programs, especially in the United States, go via intermediaries who in turn build houses or finance mortgages (see Figure 2).

The largest part of the United Kingdom housing subsidy systems goes directly to the consumers, while most of U.S. housing policy goes to the consumer only via the housing industry. American policy has derived from the assumption that policy should induce the private market to increase the construction of homes. While the private market is naturally drawn to middle- and upper-income housing, the increased supply will in theory trickle down to meet low-income housing needs. British housing policy, however, concentrated until recently on the direct provision of housing (Solomon, 1972: 443-444). The U.S. subsidy system provides greater incentives and rewards for intermediaries to organize, while the English system provides rewards for consumers to organize. And they do. Tenant co-operatives, housing associations, and squatters movements are all examples of direct recipient organizing. Squatters, one might argue, are only "would-be" recipients; however, their assumption is that they have a "right" to public provision of housing, an assumption which derives from the existence of most U.K. housing policy in category A. In the United States, by contrast, the housing interest groups are primarily producer groups, a fact which coincides with the large proportion of subsidies in category B (Lilly, 1973).

Consider some contrasting situations. A subsidy program such as Section 221 3(A) of the 1968 Housing Act in the United States was designed to motivate builders to expand housing construction. Hence, the producers of housing—as direct beneficiaries—became the fiercest advocates for the section. A group trying to mobilize public opinion around the issue of the need for low-income housing could not compete with either the power of established old-line groups or gain an audience with members of congress who saw very little that could be gained by advocacy for this issue.

A second contrast in the kinds of interest group activity in the two countries derives from the greater incidence of regulatory policies in the United States than in Britain. And regulatory issues easily gravitate to the courts. Groups such as the Chicago-based National Peoples Action on Housing can and do use the courts to gain immediate visibility as well as some immediate payoffs for their supporters. True to their Alinsky-like tradition, court victories are seen as essential in order to mobilize public opinion. The squatters in England also had to win court battles, and they, too, sometimes used them to press public opinion. But, in the main, courts were not perceived as the first place to go to achieve social change. Regulatory politics did not have the same possibilities or potential in England. Labor Party politics was, however, a viable arena for the housing struggle. In contrast, the National Peoples Action on Housing or, more noticeably, the National Welfare Rights Organization found that, after engaging in regulatory politics, further access was greatly constricted by the interparty consensus favoring inactivity and the strong role already played by the National Association of Home Builders and its hold over HUD.

Urban landscapes are determined by these differing political patterns. Cities in the United States will concentrate on policies designed to attract some people back into inner cities and will most likely use regulatory, as well as distributive, policies in their efforts to do so. Cities in England, on the other hand, continue to grapple with housing shortages with a combination of redistributive as well as distributive policies. Urban development patterns will vary in both cases as a reflection of the differing values implemented in these different strategies. While equity might be maximized in England, growth might be maximized in the United States. Thus do political configurations color urban land use and housing patterns.

NOTES

1. U.S. AID has been examining the issue of what third world cities can learn from the U.S. experience in generating citizen participation which they can use in innovative schemes.

2. The authors are grateful to Guy Colarulli for his conceptualization of "policy opportunities," the basis for his forthcoming dissertation.

3. In England, squatting is possible because the legal safeguards to tenancy are relatively strong. A 1331 legal provision, developed in response to crusaders leaving

their lands and squatters moving onto it, was resurrected to help the cause. By contrast, in the United States, squatters have no such legal recourse (Hollister, 1972).

4. Some local councils were so unhappy about the passage of the Housing Finance Act of 1972, that they refused to implement it within their jurisdictions. This action renders all of the councilors liable to be surcharged for the revenue lost the Treasury as a result of not bringing council rents into a competitive position.

5. Both Sections 235 and 236 were established in the Housing and Urban Development Act of 1968. Section 235 was a program of subsidized construction for low, or lower-middle, income homeownership, while section 236 was subsidized rental housing, which was sometimes tied in with a rent subsidy program as well. For the most thorough discussion of these programs, see Anthony Downs (1972).

6. The Barrett-Ashley Bill was enacted as the Housing and Community Development Act of 1974. It was passed in August, 1974, Ninety-Third Congress, Second Session.

REFERENCES

AARON, H. J. (1972) Shelter and Subsidies. Washington, D.C.: Brookings Institution.

ALFORD, R. R. and N. diTOMASCO (1973) "Interest groups and the potential consequences of federal housing subsidies to the states." Washington, D.C.: Department of Housing and Urban Development.

BAILEY, R. (1972) Squatters. London: Penguin.

BEER, S. H. (1974) The British Political System. New York: Random House.

BRYANT, D. and P. HEINAMAN (1974) "Housing policy: some comparative perspectives." Prepared for delivery at the Southern Political Science Association Meeting, New Orleans.

CULLINGWORTH, J. B. (1972) Problems of an Urban Society. London: George Allen & Unwin.

DAWSON, R. E. and J. A. ROBINSON (1966) "The politics of welfare," in H. Jacob and K. Vines (eds.) Politics in the American States. Boston: Little, Brown.

DOWNS, A. (1972) "Federal housing subsidies: how are they working?" Real Estate Research Corporation, October.

DYE, T. (1966) Politics, Economics and the Public. Chicago: Rand McNally.

ELAZAR, D. (1973) "Non-governmental interest groups and potential changes in the organization of federal housing policy." Washington, D.C.: Department of Housing and Urban Development.

FINER, S. E. (1958) "Interest groups and the political process in Great Britain," in H. W. Ehrman, (ed.) Interest Groups on Four Continents. Pittsburgh: University of Pittsburgh Press.

HEIDENHEIMER, A. J. (1973) "The politics of public education, health and welfare in the U.S.A. and Western Europe." British J. of Pol. Sci. (July): 315-340.

HOLLISTER, R. (1972) "The politics of housing: squatters." Transaction Society (July/August).

Housing Finance Act of 1972. London: Her Majesty's Stationery Office.

KIMBER, R. and R. R. RICHARDSON [eds.] (1974) Pressure Groups in Britain. Totowa, N.J.: Rowman & Littlefield.

LILLY, W. (1973) "The homebuilders' lobby," in J. Pynoos et al. (eds.) Housing Urban America. Chicago: Aldine.

LIPSKY, M. (1968) "Protest as a political resource." Amer. Pol. Sci. Rev. (December).

LOWI, T. (1972) "Four systems of policy, politics and choice." Public Administration Rev. (July/August).

MANDELKER, D. (1973) Housing Subsidies in the United States and England. Indianapolis: Bobbs-Merrill.

MAYHEW, D. R. (1974) Congress: The Electoral Connection. New Haven: Yale University Press.

Ministry of Housing and Local Government (1969) Council Housing Purposes, Procedures and Priorities. London: Her Majesty's Stationery Office.

NIVEN, B. (1972) "What can the U.S.A. learn about housing from Britain?" J. of Housing (September).

PRZEWORSKI, A. and H. TEUNE (1971) Logic of Comparative Social Inquiry. New York: John Wiley.

PYNOOS, J., C. H. HARTMAN, and R. SCHAFER [eds.] (1973) Housing and Urban America. Chicago: Adline.

RIKER, W. and P. ORDESHOOK (1973) An Introduction to Positive Political Theory. New Brunswick, N.J.: Prentice-Hall.

Royal Commission on Local Government in England 1966-69. (CMND. 4040).

SALISBURY, H. (1968) "The analysis of public policy: a search for theories and roles" in A. Ranney (ed.) Political Science and Public Policy. Chicago: Markham.

SCARROW, M. (1971) "Policy pressures by British local government: the case of regulation in the 'public interest.' " Comp. Politics (October).

SOLOMON, A. P. (1972) "Housing and public policy analysis." Public Policy (Summer).

WOLMAN, H. (1971) Politics of Federal Housing. New York: Dodd. Mead.

Chapter 6

AUTONOMY AND POLITICAL RESPONSIBILITY
The Enigmatic Verdict of a Cross-National Comparative Study of Community Dynamics

PHILIP JACOB

This article concerns the proposition that political autonomy will engender increased political responsibility at the local level. At issue is a major tenet of democratic theory—that responsible action will flow from the opportunity for responsible participation in the governing process. Evidence bearing on the question is now available from a systematic, comparative cross-national study of political leadership and community activeness in India, Poland, the United States, and Yugoslavia, four countries which differ greatly in the amount of power allocated to local units of government.

What emerges is a strange anomaly. Where there is more autonomy—meaning in this study the opportunity for local institutions to take action on community needs and problems—local leaders *as individuals* aspire for more local responsibility, have a greater sense of personal political efficacy, and set higher standards for the conduct of public office. But there appears to be no carryover into *collective* behavior, either in terms of the actions of local government or socially purposeful activities of the citizenry. The chain of responsibility linked to autonomy somehow breaks between the personal dispositions of leaders and social mobilization in their communities. Thus, the structuring of the political system to spread power in the expectation of increasing responsibility mysteriously loses potency once its influence has been expended on altering the individual

AUTHOR'S NOTE: *An original version of this article was presented at the Eighth World Congress of Sociology, Toronto, Canada, August 19, 1974.*

attitudes of leaders. It is almost as though leadership has siphoned off the full impetus given by autonomy to political responsibility before it has had a chance to reach and affect the community at large.

The data base is the International Studies of Values in Politics, a multidimensional survey of thirty units of local government in each of the four countries (*panchayat samitis* in India, *powiats* in Poland, municipalities in the United States, and *communes* in Yugoslavia.) Interviews with 3,930 local political leaders ascertained attitudes toward and perceptions of autonomy within a framework of personal value-commitments, role expectations, and leadership behavior, as well as leaders' assessments of the political and social climate of their communities. Aggregative data on resource mobilization and popular involvement in community action were secured from government records and on-site inquiry. The formal structure of the local political system, including the scope of local autonomy, was ascertained from relevant legislation and administrative regulations.[1]

The local units in which the studies were conducted were chosen on the basis of a sampling design that controlled for differences in economic level among them, but specifically excluded large metropolitan centers. In India and Yugoslavia, the choice was concentrated in three states or republics respectively that differed in language, ethnic composition, or other regional characteristics; hence, the sample was not representative of the whole country. For Poland and the United States, however, the samples were drawn from the full universe of powiats and cities, within specified limits of size or urban concentration, so nationwide generalizations within these limits are probably justified. In the United States, the sample was structured so as to ensure inclusion of a quota of small towns (25,000-50,000), usually county seats in rural areas, so as to provide some basis for comparison with the predominantly rural or mixed urban/rural units in the other countries. Maximum size of the sample cities was 250,000.

Leaders were selected on the basis of their holding equivalent functional positions across the four countries—mayors, councilmen, or similar elected officials, administrative officials in charge of key community services, party officials, and others who held significant formal positions in the public decision-making processes in the community. A high percentage of the targetted population of leaders was interviewed (99% in India, Poland, and Yugoslavia; 91% in the United States. In effect, the universe of the political "establishment" was covered.[2]

MEASURING AUTONOMY

Autonomy was measured in three respects. *Structurally*, it was defined in terms of legal competence of the local government authority to make decisions on matters directly affecting the life and development of the community, including the raising and disbursement of revenue. *As perceived by local leaders*, it was gauged by their response to the question:

In which of these areas does the local government here lack enough power and autonomy to act effectively? (1) solving housing problems? (2) seeing to it that every man who wants a job gets a job? (3) building schools? (4) providing clinics, dispensaries, health centers? (5) supporting art (painting, music)? (6) providing electricity services? (7) solving problems of youth (juvenile delinquency, vocational guidance)?

The *desirability of autonomy* was assessed by asking the same leaders whether the primary responsibility for action in these seven areas *should* be undertaken by (a) the central or state government, (b) the local government, (c) local nongovernmental institutions, or (d) be left to the people to work out personally.

In choosing these specific functions of local governments as objects for assessment of autonomy, the investigators tried to establish a pool which

TABLE 1
PERCEIVED AUTONOMY

Country	Areas of Community Activity							
	Housing	Jobs	Schools	Clinics	Art & Culture	Electricity	Youth Problems	Mean for all Areas
India	.28	.24	.69	.54	.62	.24	.45	.45
Gujarat	.46	.52	.59	.57	.78	.50	.77	.61
Maharashtra	.14	.08	.70	.48	.50	.11	.17	.31
Uttar Pradesh	.23	.11	.79	.57	.56	.09	.41	.39
Poland	.41	.50	.35	.55	.71	.45	.85	.55
United States	.61	.49	.84	.77	.80	.74	.76	.72
Yugoslavia	.84	.75	.85	.76	.84	.85	.87	.82

NOTE: This table reports the mean response in each country, or state, to the question: "In which of these areas does the local government here lack enough power and autonomy to act effectively?" The question was purposely worded negatively. The scores reported here have been reversed to facilitate interpretation. Maximum score for amount of autonomy perceived is 1.00. (A leader responding to the effect that the local government did have enough power to act effectively in a given functional area would be scored 1.00; he would be scored 0 if he replied to the effect that the government lacked autonomy. Scores were added for all seven functions and divided by 7 to yield the composite score reported in this table.)

would appear relevant to respondents in each country despite the many differences in what local governments customarily undertook to do. It should be emphasized that asking these questions presumed neither identity across countries in the range of local functions nor equivalence in the relative salience of any particular function. The point of the questions was to have political leaders think about autonomy in relation to *specific* areas of actual or potential public service in their communities, rather than to give forth a vague generality in response to a vague and abstract query. Responses (see Table 1) do indicate some significant national differences—and in the case of India, regional differences—in the salience of particular functions. But, for the purpose of this report, it is the overall scope of perceived autonomy and desired autonomy that is of primary interest. The validity of these functional indices is partly sustained by the distribution of responses: No function appeared so irrelevant to leaders in a given country that their answers were meaningless or badly skewed.

STRUCTURAL AUTONOMY

It was evident that Poland clearly maintained the maximum centralization of political authority over local development, both in terms of legal competence, and actual decision-making and execution directed from the center either by government or party.

Its Marxist counterpart Yugoslavia, by contrast, had gone furthest in commitment to decentralization, both ideologically and practically. The commune governs itself under a statute it adopts autonomously in accordance with principles laid down in the Yugoslav Constitution. The statute specifies the mechanism of self-government, the procedures for exercising authority and realizing rights, and the relationship of the commune to larger territorial units such as district and republic. The commune guarantees material conditions for work, protects both socially and privately owned property, and maintains public order. To carry out all these responsibilities, the commune has assumed major fiscal powers. Meanwhile, alongside the territorially defined commune, a parallel system of self-government has been established on a functional basis, with workers' self-management in virtually all productive enterprises and social institutions.

The situation in India is more confused. In an attempt to develop more local responsibility, a three-tiered panchayat system was inaugurated, placing decisions for economic and social development nominally in the hands of elected councils at the village, "block" (*taluk*), and district levels. However, it has operated at different tempos in different states and varies in the tier at which more important decisions are made. In actuality, the really critical decisions over allocation of resources and the strategy of social and economic development are still made either at the center or by the governments of the various states, with the panchayats having sometimes more, sometimes less say about implementation. Furthermore, as one of the principal Indian investigators reports, the intrusion of party control into Panchayati Raj has reinforced the built-in elements of administrative centralization and seriously undercut the intended broadening of the decision-making process. "The *power* of decision remains concentrated and centralized in the political and administrative hierarchies, though in form it seems dispersed through the various organs of local self-government" (International Studies of Values in Politics, hereafter cited as I.S.V.I.P., 1971: 183).

The extent of autonomy in the United States is even more difficult to assess because of the diversity in form and powers of local government that results from each of the fifty states exercising the right to design its own pattern of local government. This right has in turn led to great diversity within some states, as they have differentiated functions and powers according to size and other attributes of municipalities. In general, despite formal dependency on the state and increasing financial dependency on state and federal governments, local political units in the United States appear to have a relatively large amount of autonomy in what they can do and how they can do it. They bear the brunt of supplying services to the population. In addition to traditional service functions of water, sewerage, roads, and education, they have taken to subsidizing museums, theatres and orchestras, owning and operating public utilities, administering massive recreation programs. "What probably prevails in most local governments," concluded the American team, "is a feeling that they have the legal power to deal with problems, but not the capacity to raise the resources in the face of mounting demands" (I.S.V.I.P., 1971: 192).

Putting it all together, the overall conclusion was that the countries probably ranked in order of increasing structural autonomy from Poland to India to the United States to Yugoslavia.[3]

THE MATCH OF PERCEPTION AND STRUCTURE

Turning to autonomy as perceived by local political leaders in these four countries, they tended to agree that autonomy was generally indivisible. If they thought local government had enough power to cope with one function, it was likely they would consider it had been given enough power to cope with others. If they felt they lacked sufficient autonomy in one area, they would feel they lacked it in others. In other words, either you had a whole loaf or you had none at all, measured against problems that typically confront local communities. Only in India did leaders single out an area where they thought local government had more power and autonomy to act effectively than in others—i.e., in building schools. Otherwise, responses to our query concerning the adequacy of autonomy for effective local action were highly intercorrelated across functions.

However, the degree of autonomy that the leaders perceived varied significantly across countries and closely paralleled the amount of autonomy allocated in the political system. Yugoslav leaders perceived the most, followed by the American. Polish and Indian leaders considered their communities had considerably less (see Table 1). But, in India, where the structure was not uniform, there was significant difference in perceived autonomy *between regions*, varying with the amount of power actually exercised by the panchayat samiti in each state.[4]

Thus, manipulating the form of political institutions did appear to affect at least the consciousness of political efficacy. The more power that was allocated, the more the local political leadership felt that they had enough power to deal with the community's problems. Responsibility was there for the taking—*if people chose to exercise it*.

But do they so choose? Does perception of autonomy carry over into action? This study suggests that it does—in the dispositions and behavior of *individual leaders*. But at the point of corporate social action, the chain seems to break. If the measures of community "activeness" developed in this study are valid, the degree of local autonomy as perceived by community leaders influences neither the mobilization of resources for community purposes by local government nor popular involvement in community programs, public or private. We shall return to this puzzling anachronism after citing some of the evidence of autonomy's impact on leadership.

ASPIRATION FOR AUTONOMY

In three of the four countries, leaders who perceived that their communities *had* a large amount of autonomy tended to *want* local government to provide housing, build schools, deal with juvenile delinquency, set up health services, and undertake other activities for the welfare of the community. They shied away from higher levels of government, national or state (see Table 3). One concludes that the more autonomy leaders felt they had, the more they were ready to assume responsibility for governance.

This association between the perception of autonomy and a desire for autonomy was strong even where autonomy ran up against the prevailing political culture, as in India, where far more leaders than elsewhere favored central or state government responsibility (see Table 2). Indian leaders who felt there was at least some measure of autonomy were the ones who believed more strongly that local communities *should* have autonomy. These "autonomists," who broke with the tradition of centralization,

TABLE 2
DESIRED AUTONOMY: WHO SHOULD DO WHAT?

Country	(1) Central or State Government	(2) Local Government	(3) Local Non- Governmental Institutions	(4) Leave to People
India	3.32	2.44	.57	.62
Gujarat	2.85	2.78	.55	.76
Maharashtra	3.80	2.24	.66	.25
Uttar Pradesh	3.30	2.32	.50	.85
Poland	1.47	4.83	.50	.18
United States	1.33	2.96	1.84	.77
Yugoslavia	2.29	3.27	.88	.46

NOTE: This table reports the mean number of functions (out of seven specified) for which respondents considered that primary responsibility should be (1) undertaken by the central or state government, (2) undertaken by local government, (3) undertaken by local nongovernmental institutions (cooperatives, etc.), or (4) left to the people to work out personally. Maximum score: 7.00.

TABLE 3
AUTONOMY: PERCEIVED AND DESIRED

	Preferred Level of Responsibility	
	Central or State Government	Local Government
India	−.577	+.547
Poland	−.030	+.005
United States	−.477	+.369
Yugoslavia	−.486	+.526

NOTE: This table reports correlations between responses to the questions concerning (a) adequacy of local government powers and (b) preferred level of responsibility for action on community problems.

Signs have been adjusted to indicate the direction of association with a high perception of autonomy (leaders stating local government did have adequate powers to act effectively in the seven specified areas).

Correlations reported are between means of community means for leaders' responses to each question in the thirty communities sampled in each country. r = .361 at .05 level of confidence.

tended to be those who believed autonomy was already at hand to some degree.

The exception was Poland. Here, perhaps because the potential range of autonomy was so limited within the givens of the political system, any aspirations that leaders nurtured for greater local powers were completely divorced from their perception of actualities.

AUTONOMY AND SENSE OF POLITICAL EFFICACY

In India and Yugoslavia, leaders who perceived the greatest autonomy in their communities also tended to be those who considered themselves most influential in the widest range of public affairs.

We asked them to identify out of ten areas of community activity those where they felt they had "some" or "great" influence on what was accomplished. The areas included industrial or agricultural development, housing, health, public services and utilities, education and cultural affairs, social welfare, fiscal affairs and political organization activity. There was a highly significant correlation between the amount of personal influence, and the amount of power leaders felt the local government possessed to function effectively in such areas.[5] The greater their estimate of *collective* efficacy, the greater was their sense of *personal* efficacy.

This relationship did not apply to all areas, nor to exactly the same areas in each country. The more autonomy-oriented leaders in India were concentrated among the influentials in housing, health, welfare, finance, and cultural activities. While Yugoslav autonomists were also influential in the areas of housing and health, their other specialties were education, politics, and agricultural development. The link between autonomy and personal efficacy apparently acquires a certain national identity in the specific areas affected, though in terms of overall impact, the association is unmistakable and comparable in both these countries.

The story is different in both the United States and Poland. There was *no* overall relationship between perceived autonomy and the leaders' expressed sense of personal competence. Their judgment about the adequacy of the governing powers of local institutions had no bearing on how influential they themselves felt. Their sense of personal political efficacy somehow evolved independently of the local political system, at least as they perceived it.

On first sight, these findings seem not only illogical, but implausible. How could a *local* leader feel influential in areas of *public* policy and activity at the local level unless such areas were open to at least some local governance?

Conceivably this could occur if the system enabled him to function through an administrative and political hierarchy that controlled from outside and above what went on in the community. This, of course, is exactly the situation that prevailed in Poland.

But, in the United States, the leaders we interviewed were indigenous "locals," not "apparatchiks" of a national governing single-party bureaucracy. On the other hand, they, too, could seek public influence through channels other than local governmental institutions. Note in Table 2 that far more American local readers than those in other countries considered that primary responsibility for dealing with local problems should be undertaken by local *non*governmental institutions, or be left to people to handle personally on their own. Thus, the sense of personal political efficacy might grow from the leader's ability to manipulate action within a totally different framework of autonomy from that of the formal governing structure—for instance, through the complex set-up of local interest groups (often able to press their interests through state or national organizations if local government were unable or unwilling to act effectively).

In any case, it is apparent that, given the American and Polish systems, the dynamics of autonomy function differently than in India and Yugoslavia. The connection is broken between the formal or perceived powers of local governmental institutions and the political responsibility of local leaders because alternative routes to public influence appear more effective. In Poland, the route runs through the structure of a centralized party. In the pluralism of American politics, the influential leader plots a way through the maze of the lobbies.[6]

VALUE COMMITMENTS OF THE AUTONOMISTS

With a heightened consciousness of opportunities for effective action, local political leaders set forth more rigorous standards that they expected leadership to meet. Commitment to principled conduct in public life, as defined in each nation's "political culture," was consistently associated with the perception of local autonomy—except in Poland.

Cross-national measurement and comparison of leaders' value commitments was one of the major contributions of these studies. After two years of intensive joint conceptualization by the collaborators from the four countries, accompanied by a succession of pretests, a survey instrument was constructed including 179 closed-ended questions designed to identify the degree of commitment to nine values considered relevant to political leadership and developmental change at the local level (see Table 4). A common core of these items was identical for all countries. But, in addition, a set of questions was specifically worded to meet peculiarities of language and outlook in each country. Equivalence between the international and nation-specific items was determined by tests of interitem homogeneity, which also served to purify the scales by eliminating those questions that drew inconsistent or ambiguous responses from the leaders. The cross-national equivalence of the scales was then further tested by factor analyses of the entire body of value-items. Five of the value scales were congruent with loadings on specific factors in all four countries and could therefore be considered highly comparable: Participation, National versus Local Orientation, Commitment to Innovative Change, Economic Equality, and "Honesty" (defined for these studies as truthfulness in public conduct). The other four value scales were not as comparable across

TABLE 4
VALUE COMMITMENTS OF LOCAL LEADERS

	India n=946	Poland n=889	U.S. n=905	Yugoslavia n=1178
Economic Development				
Mean	3.64	3.11	2.83	3.45
S.D.	.367	.437	.417	.354
Conflict Avoidance				
Mean	3.13	2.42	2.13	2.85
S.D.	.566	.468	.351	.392
Participation				
Mean	2.13	2.26	2.74	2.74
S.D.	.457	.390	.417	.435
Selflessness				
Mean	3.41	3.23	3.15	3.21
S.D.	.307	.422	.374	.386
National Commitment				
Mean	2.57	2.70	2.29	2.34
S.D.	.604	.382	.346	.383
Action Propensity				
Mean	1.60	2.15	2.48	2.06
S.D.	.469	.393	.407	.357
Honesty (Truthfulness)				
Mean	3.38	3.13	3.28	3.48
S.D.	.466	.351	.374	.322
Change Orientation				
Mean	3.47	3.33	2.83	3.27
S.D.	.420	.386	.388	.375
Economic Equality				
Mean	3.50	2.74	1.72	3.03
S.D.	.429	.463	.428	.496

NOTE: Mean scores are adjusted so that maximum commitment to a value equals 4.00 and the minimum commitment (i.e., maximum rejection) equals 1.00.

all the countries, the Conflict Avoidance scale for instance not being very reliable in Yugoslavia, the Action Propensity scale apparently tapping certain dispositions peculiar to Indian leaders, and the Economic Development scale producing heavily skewed distributions in the less developed countries.[7]

In addition, the survey replicated a portion of the aspirational inquiry developed by Hadley Cantril and Lloyd Free—the portion related to wishes and hopes for the future of the country (Cantril, 1965)—posed an open-ended question about the desirable traits of political leaders; and called for a priority ranking of those values considered most important among the nine that were scaled.

All of this provided a base for assessing in some depth the relationship between leaders' values and the amount of autonomy they perceived or desired. It is clear that "autonomists" in three of the four countries did tend to differ in norms of leadership from those who felt their communities had little autonomy and were content to have it so. For instance, autonomists in India, Yugoslavia, and the United States tended to profess more commitment to such moral standards as truthfulness and concern for public duty over personal interest (see Table 5). In Poland, however,

TABLE 5
PERCEIVED AUTONOMY AND LEADERS' VALUES

	India	United States	Yugoslavia
Commitment to principled conduct in public life[a]	.370	.404	.432
Honesty scale (truthfulness)	.467	.371	———
Selflessness scale	.382	———	.456
National commitment scale	———	———	.417
Action propensity scale	-.511	———	———
Innovative change scale	———	———	.416
Economic equality scale	———	-.548	———
Economic development scale	———	———	.418
Participation in decisionmaking scale	———	———	.448

NOTE: This table reports correlations between community means where probability is at least .05.

In Poland, no correlations between perceived autonomy and leaders' values met the .05 probability criterion, though an association with the participation scale came close (r = .359).

a. This was the first factor in a factor iteration program covering the entire battery of questions designed to scale commitment to nine values, including in addition to those noted in this table, the value of avoiding conflict. Truthfulness and selflessness items formed the core of the first factor which accounted for 10% of variance in India, 18% in the United States, and 13% in Yugoslavia.

leaders' values varied without apparent connection to their perception of autonomy, testifying once again to the paralyzing power of a centralized system on individual political responsibility at the local level.[8]

Aside from their stronger common commitment to personal integrity, autonomists in the other countries demonstrated a higher commitment to values that might be considered distinctive of their own country's peculiar ideology of leadership. Thus, in Yugoslavia, they more than others tended to value wide public participation in decision-making ($r = .448$), economic development goals ($r = .418$), and innovative change ($r = .448$). Furthermore, in Yugoslavia, leaders who felt that local government had the most autonomy tended to be the most strongly committed to *national* goals even if that meant sacrificing local needs. This reflects the fact that autonomy is a cardinal principle of the national political system. A true believer in the official ideology would see autonomy as compatible with rather than opposed to national goals.

In the United States, autonomists more than others *rejected* the value of economic equality ($r = -.548$) in line with but more extreme than the prevailing sentiment expressed by American leaders and strikingly different from the position of leaders interviewed in the other three countries (see Table 4). (Anti-egalitarianism, insofar as steps to minimize differences in wealth and income are concerned, showed up as the most unique hallmark of American local leaders).

In India, those who perceived and valued autonomy most were less inclined than their colleagues to take bold and risky action, more disposed to be deliberate and cautious in making decisions, and more content with existing conditions of life—again in keeping with the prevailing mood, only more so. (The Indian leaders' score on Action Propensity was much the lowest of the four countries [Table 4]; and correlation with perception of autonomy was $-.511$, meaning that autonomists tended to be even less prone to act than the majority.)

DEVELOPMENTAL ORIENTATION

Having discovered a link between autonomy and the operational norms of leadership, the question arises whether greater responsibility for governance also affects the policies that leaders espouse. The data do indicate some such effect in developing countries. In India and Yugoslavia, those leaders more conscious of local autonomy tended to be more developmental oriented. Thus, the Indian autonomists in comparison with others showed more concern over lack of basic physical facilities in their communities (water, roads, sanitation, communication), placed higher importance on economic development in relation to other values, and stressed industrialization more strongly in describing their hopes for the future of the country. In Yugoslavia, industrial development was also a major concern of the more autonomy-minded as they considered the problems facing their communities, and they stood among the most highly committed to national economic development in a country where leaders as a whole were strongly dedicated to this goal.[9]

Autonomists in these two countries split, however, on two very important issues affecting the political dynamics of development. The Indians turned *away from party* and *from nation* as they defined their primary loyalties. Those who perceived more autonomy were *less* likely to state they felt "most strongly committed to advance the interests and welfare" of their political party ($r = -.475$) or of the nation as a whole ($r = -.471$). When asked about their hopes for the future of the country, they expressed far less aspiration for national unity and solidarity than others ($r = -.640$).

On the other hand, the more that Yugoslav leaders felt the reality of autonomy, the *more* they identified with party ($r = .383$) and with nation. Perceived autonomy correlated with scores on the value scale of national commitment at .417, and autonomist leaders tended to rank national interests higher than the other values measured in these studies ($r = .540$).[10] These leaders were also among the more politically active and influential.[11]

Thus in Yugoslavia, autonomy is a solidifying national force, even while local leaders assume and call for ever greater responsibility for governance. But, in India, autonomy strengthens a localist orientation that seems to pull leaders away from the nation, or at least focuses their attention primarily on the needs and problems of their own communities. Furthermore, while Yugoslav autonomists were strongly committed to decisive, innovative social change, Indians tended to tie autonomy to a more traditional perspective, skeptical of "new solutions to problems" and cautious about abandoning settled ways.

For American leaders, however, there is apparently no connection at all between autonomy and either their social goals or political commitments. The link between autonomy and at least some form of political responsibility that prevails among community leaders in countries like India and Yugoslavia that face major problems of economic and social development is not now an attribute of the country that pioneered in local initiative when it was mastering an undeveloped continent. Could it be that a major developmental challenge is needed to make an autonomous political system function? Or, conversely, that autonomy *can* lead to political

THE STRUCTURE OF ACTIVENESS IN FOUR COUNTRIES

India		Poland		United States		Yugoslavia	
1 Chemical fertilizer	RM	1 Local investment	RM	1 Pupil expenditure	RM	1 League of Communists	PI
2 Adults made literate	PI	2 Percentage investment raised locally	RM	2 League of Women Voters	RM	2 Cinema attendance	PI
3 Cattle inoculations	PI	3 Proposals for investment	PI	3 Park and recreation expenditure	PI	3 Library books	RM
4 Sterilizations	PI	4 Local expenditures	RM	4 Library expenditure	RM	4 Percentage investment raised locally	RM
5 Village radios	RM	5 Pathfinder organizations	PI	5 Presidential voting	PI	5 Local investment	RM
6 Smallpox vaccination	PI	6 Local investments in development	RM			6 Voters in communal assembly elections	PI
7 Pumping sets	RM	7 Peasant Party	PI				
8 Artificial insemination	PI	8 Polish United Workers Party	PI				
		9 Union of Rural Youth	PI				
Percentage of total variance explained	23%		29%		12%		18%
Percentage of resource mobilization loadings to total	38.2%		51.9%		63.1%		46.7%
Percentage of popular involvement loadings to total	61.8%		48.1%		36.9%		53.3%

NOTE: This table reports indicators loading above .35 on a factor combining items relevant to "resource mobilization" (RM) and "popular involvement" (PI)—in order of magnitude of the loading.

responsibility under the stress of privation and social upheaval, but loses impetus when life is relatively comfortable and trouble-free? If so, it would turn upside down the easy generalization, so often advanced, that only centralized government can ensure political responsibility in a less developed nation.

COMMUNITY ACTIVENESS—THE CHAIN BREAKS

The problem with such a conclusion is that the impact of autonomy seems to evaporate, even in developing countries, when the line of political responsibility passes from individual leaders to institutional behavior or other forms of collective action at the community level. At least this was the verdict of the International Studies of Values in Politics which undertook an innovative experiment in consructing empirical measures of what they called "community activeness."

Two dimensions of activeness were hypothesized: "resource mobilization" (primarily reflecting decisions of the local government) and "popular involvement" (civic activities demonstrating political or social consciousness). An extensive inventory of relevant data was collected, identical for communities in each country but differing across countries. (Conditions varied so greatly among countries that selection of cross-nationally identical indicators was unrealistic.) The concept of activeness presumed that these dimensions would be *interrelated in an active community: where* local government was vigorously pushing programs of community development, the population would be highly participatory, and vice versa. Factor analyses demonstrated one factor in each country that indeed included indicators of both types of activity—governmental and popular. This was chosen as the principal measure of activeness (see Table 6).

Analysis of the correlates of community activeness was conducted separately, of course, for each country. Given the uniqueness of the indicators, relationships had to be ascertained first within countries. Assuming, however, that we were dealing with a phenomenon common to all these countries (a conclusion that appeared reasonable in light of congruence between the factor structures and the original conceptualization) then comparison across countries of the *patterns of variables* associated with activeness has some validity.

Pursuing this course, leaders' perception of autonomy was found to have *no* statistically significant association with the combined activeness factor in *any* country. Bluntly, this means that even if leaders felt their communities had adequate opportunity to govern themselves, the local government and the local citizenry behaved no differently than in com-

munities where leaders considered they had no such power. An autonomous community (as perceived by its leaders) was just as likely to be
stagnant as one judged to be governed from outside. The autonomous
community was no more likely to show initiative and public vitality than
the dependent one, nor did its agencies of government act more vigorously
or effectively in promoting its welfare.

A remarkable feature of this finding is that it applies equally to the
countries whose political systems tolerate little local autonomy and those
which have gone farthest in decentralizing the powers of government.
Further, national political ideology or culture—be it Marxist or liberal
democrat, "modernizing or traditionalist, Western or Asian—has no bearing
on the failure of autonomy to generate corporate political responsibility.
Nor does the level of the country's economic development.

WHAT IS HAPPENING HERE?

One explanation might be that the measurement of activeness was all
wrong. In candor, the exercise did not come out too well. Many activities
in the original inventory did not survive the factor analysis and enter
significantly into the measure finally used, even though they obviously
were part of the total universe of community dynamics. Important gaps
also occurred because information was not available (as, for instance, in
regard to political participation in India, where statistics were not kept for
talukas' or blocks' which were the units of observation in this study). The
case is not altogether convincing that activeness as measured in one
country was indeed comparable to what was measured in another (the
combinations of indicators were actually so diverse across countries as to
throw doubt on the intriguing theoretical argument for comparability).
Finally, conflicting interpretations of the significance of other factors that
emerged in the activeness analysis were advanced by the principal investigators, some arguing that a "dual pattern" of activeness could be discerned
at least in India and Yugolslavia (I.S.V.I.P., 1971: 403).

On the other hand, the very diversity of the activeness measures argues
for the validity of the finding that perceived autonomy has nowhere
penetrated the processes of social mobilization. It suggests that however
inadequate this particular composite measure may be, the non-relationship
of autonomy to community activeness can hardly be attributed to spurious statistical association. One would reach the same conclusion, dispens-
ing with the composite index altogether, by trying to relate autonomy to
each of the indicators separately.

Of course, the measurement of *perceived autonomy* might be invalid or
inadequate. Aside from internal evidence of the question's reliability,

however, the fact that it brought forth responses that made sense when related to other facets of the inquiry indicates that it is probably not far off base.

Still another possibility, logically, would be that there was insufficient variance among communities either in autonomy or activeness or both to permit statistical demonstration of an assocation. If we had relied solely on structural measures of autonomy, this would indeed have been the case in Poland and Yugoslavia where the amount of formal autonomy in the political system was uniformly prescribed by national law. But the perception of autonomy by local leaders, and their attitude toward the proper scope of local powers varied in all countries, not only among individuals but as between communities (see Table 1). In the United States and India, legal powers of local government also varied. With reference to activeness, the local units varied substantially in all countries, this being corroborated by the many significant associations demonstrated between activeness and other variables. Obviously the study would have collapsed if there had been insufficient variation in the principal dependent variable so the investigators went to great lengths in analyzing the indicators of activeness to make sure that the range of performance was adequate for comparative purposes.

The point has been raised that the break in the impact of autonomy between individual leaders and community activeness might be an artificial effect of trying to relate two different data sets—interviews conducted with individuals and aggregate indices of community behavior. But then why would there be such a raft of strong relationships between other leader attitudes as derived from the interview, and the measures of community activeness? For instance, in Poland the intensity of conflicts perceived by leaders correlates negatively with activeness ($r = -.564$); conflicts between social groups as perceived by American leaders correlate positively with activeness at .411; in India, it is leaders' perception of conflicts between political groups that relate to activeness at .466; while in Yugoslavia leaders of active communities tend more than others to view conflicts as a community problem that interferes with their effectiveness (in this case, leaders were responding to an open-ended question, and the correlation was .445).

Or consider the relationship between leaders' values and activeness. In India, two values as scaled from the interview data were among the strongest predictors of activeness in multiple regression analyses that included both interview data and ecological characteristics such as size, population density, and economic level that were similar in nature to the activeness data set. National Commitment predicted to activeness positively, and Conflict Avoidance negatively. To be sure, there were few of these cross-data relationships that applied consistently across countries. But there were more than fifty instances where major variables measured by the interview data were associated with activeness in one or another of the countries at the .05 level of significance or stronger.

The fact that this analysis attempts to relate data derived at two levels of inquiry does raise the question of whether it has successfully avoided the "ecological fallacy." Are the conclusions undermined by attempting to predict from individual characteristics (perceptions and attitudes) to group behaviors (governmental performance and community participation)? Without debating in this discussion, the merit or general applicability of the ecological fallacy critique, it should be noted that the relationships explored in this article have consistently used the *mean* of responses from leaders of a goven community as the statistic representing leaders' perceptions and attitudes, not only in reference to measuring autonomy but all other leader characteristics derived from the interviews. Thus, individual responses have been aggregated into a group characteristic, just as the figure of membership in a political party or community organization, or an allocation of public funds by local authorities also represent aggregates of individual behaviors and decisions.

In the first part of this article, we used such aggregated responses of the communities' political leadership as a means of measuring degree of autonomy and aspiration for autonomy. We then found relationships between these variables and other characteristics of the leadership groups, also identified by aggregated responses to interview questions. Finally, we sought a relationship between what the leadership group *said* (through the interview) and what it *did* (as reflected in local government decisions in which presumably all or most of these people had participated in some measure); and in turn between what the leadership groups said and what the *public* did in their respective communities. While the data sources were different, the data were used in such a way as to test relationships at a single level—the community.

One problem with relying on overall community means to measure leadership perceptions and attitudes is that it fails to distinguish possible differences within the leadership group, for instance as between those with maximum influence and those with less, or between elected officials and appointed ones. As a matter of fact, there was great variation in responses to the interviews among leaders within the same communities, far greater than variation in the mean responses from community to community. But the variation did not appear to be systematic at least in reference to the two attributes just mentioned. Subset analyses (of the national pools of leaders) revealed little distinction between appointed and elected officials, or between the top level of leadership and others. One could easily be misled by this finding to conclude that there was an official "line" that prevailed throughout the establishment—were it not for unmistakable evidence of substantial diversity *among individuals*. Exploration of other possible bases for this diversity has been reported previously (Jacob, 1971; I.S.V.I.P., 1971: ch. 5).

AUTONOMY—A CLOSED PRESERVE FOR LEADERS ONLY?

The conclusion to which this investigator is pushed is that corporate political responsibility (as expressed through community "activeness") results from an entirely different set of influences than individual political responsibility, and this set simply does not include structural elements, such as local autonomy. Explanations of activeness vary in the four countries, with a major amount of variance in the United States and Yugoslavia accounted for by the economic level of the community, in India by certain values held by leaders (see above) and in Poland by higher-level political decisions to funnel both economic and political resources into particular communities. In Yugoslavia, leaders' education also figures as a stimulus to community mobilization. Except in Poland, manipulation of political structure seems to have little if any effect on what happens collectively in the community, which suggests that only where centralization is extreme and nearly monolithic—extending uniformly throughout a country—is the political system likely to control the pace and direction of public life in a local community.[12]

This leaves to autonomy the genesis of individual political responsibility on the part of local political leaders. In this connection, an insightful study by Leo. A. Hazlewood (1967) of the Indian and American data from I.S.V.I.P. brings out significant causal relationships showing the effect of perceived autonomy to be intermediate between, on one hand, community cleavages (as perceived by their leaders' concern to avoid conflict) and, on the other, the leaders' disposition to act for social change.[13]

Much is still to be learned about the potentialities and limits of autonomy as a determinant of the political dispositions and behavior of individual community leaders. But in regard to the significance of autonomy for collective behavior, these data are sobering to those of us who have thought, and would still like to think, that the opportunity for self-government could transform the political pyramid into a fully responsible community acting cooperatively to promote the common good. We still do not understand why the chain of responsibility has broken.

Maybe the leaders themselves have broken the chain. Enjoying the fruits of autonomy in the exercise of greater personal influence, many are simply not inclined to pass on to others opportunities to participate more actively in the governing process. Something of this mood came out in responses to questions concerned with widening public participation in decision-making. Many were frankly skeptical of such participation, feeling that decisions should be left to experts, to the informed, to "a few trusted and competent leaders."[14]

Thus local elites stand close guard to prevent autonomy from going outside the gates of their own political power.

Does someone have another answer?

NOTES

1. The organization and methodology of the study, and its general findings, are reported by the principal investigators from the four countries in their jointly authored *Values and the Active Community* (International Studies of Values in Politics, 1971).

The original data for India and the United States, and most of the Yugoslav data, have been deposited with the Inter-University Consortium for Political Research, Ann Arbor, Michigan. Polish data are located at the Institute for Philosophy and Sociology, Polish Academy of Sciences, Warsaw, Poland. The analyses on which this article is based were performed at the University of Pennsylvania and the University of Hawaii.

Principal investigators from nine institutions took part in these studies under the general sponsorship of the International Social Science Council: in India, Centre for the Study of Developing Societies (New Delhi), Indian Institute of Technology (Kanpur), and University of Poona; in Poland, Institute of Philosophy and Sociology, Polish Academy of Sciences; in the United States, University of Pennsylvania; in Yugoslavia, Institute of Social Sciences (Belgrade), Institute of Sociology and Philosophy, University of Ljubljana, and Faculty of Political Science, Sarajevo.

2. Though influentials outside the formal structure of political power were admittedly not tapped, several checks indicated that reputational selection would have added at most ten percent to the leadership inventory. However, contact with radical leadership outside normal channels of political representation was obviously missed.

3. The data on structural autonomy are elaborated by V. M. Sirsikar for India, Jerzy Wiatr for Poland, Thomas Watts for the United States, and Anton Vratusa for Yugoslavia in I.S.V.I.P. (1971: ch. 6).

4. The three states examined in this study were among those that had implemented Panchayati Raj to the point of allocating to local councils powers to levy taxes and fees, and receive and disburse grants from the state or central governments.

But they differed in the level at which these powers were effectively exercised, the Zilla Parishad at the district level occupying the key position in Maharashtra, whereas the influence of the middle-level panchayat samiti was greater in Gujarat and Uttar Pradesh. Furthermore, in practice, the panchayats in Gujarat clearly enjoyed (or took) the most initiative and responsibility—and their leaders expressed a significantly higher perception of autonomy.

5. The correlation of community means between total influence scores and perceived autonomy was .513 in India and .491 in Yugoslavia, with $r = .361$ at .05 level of confidence.

Influence scores were computed as follows: 2 = "great influence" in an area, 1 = "some influence," 0 = "no influence." Total maximum score therefore was twenty for the ten areas specified.

6. For calculations of the Polish data related to this and other issues raised in this paper, I am indebted to Dr. Aleksandra Jasinska-Kania, Associate Professor of Sociology at the University of Warsaw. The implications derived from these data, however, are fully my responsibility.

7. The methodology of measuring values in the I.S.V.I.P. and its rationale are fully described in I.S.V.I.P. (1971: ch. 2 and appdx. C.

8. See above, page 0.

These and the following observations concerning aspirations and political orientations of "autonomists" are based on correlational analysis demonstrating an association between responses to attitudinal questions, and opinions expressed on the two autonomy queries previously noted—i.e., the amount of autonomy perceived and the level of government where the leader felt action should be taken in regard to local problems. The strength of association is specifically indicated at various points in the text. All observations reflect a probability of at least .05.

9. See note 8.

10. Furthermore, in tracing the sources of leaders' values, it was discovered that perception of autonomy was characteristic of groups of Yugoslav leaders (but *only* Yugoslavs) whose general value profiles were distinguished by a higher commitment to national goals as against local interests (I.S.V.I.P., 1971: 118, Table 7, "Influence of Leaders' Perceptions on Value Profiles".)

11. Correlation between perceived autonomy and activity in political organization was .501; with influence in such activity, it was .515.

12. Explanations of activeness, as developed from multivariate analyses including various forms of regression analysis, are presented in I.S.V.I.P. (1971: chs. 9 and 10).

13. Using causal modeling as articulated by Herbert Simon and Hubert Blalock, Hazlewood tested five models to link six variables as measured by I.S.V.I.P. data: (1) the value of conflict avoidance, (2) perception of cleavages in the community, (3) perceived autonomy, (4) perceived scope of leader's public activity, (5) perceived scope of leader's public influence, (6) commitment to change (U.S.) or action propensity (India). In the case of the sixth variable, Hazlewood maintains that the change scale in the United States was *functionally* equivalent to action propensity in India and thus he did not enter scores of identical scales for the two countries.

14. Scores on the value scale of participation varied from 2.13 in India to 2.74 in the United States and Yugoslavia (with Poland at 2.26) on a scale of 1.00 to 4.00 with 4.00 representing the maximum possible commitment to participation (see Table 4).

REFERENCES

CANTRIL, H. (1965) The Pattern of Human Concerns. New Brunswick, N.J.: Rutgers Univ. Press.

HAZLEWOOD, L. A. (1967) "Community cleavage and action for change." University of Pennsylvania Political Science Department, Philadelphia. (unpublished)

International Studies of Values in Politics (I.S.V.I.P.) (1971) Values and the Active Community. New York: Free Press.

JACOB, P. E. (1971) "The limits of value consensus." International Studies Q. 15 (June): 203-220.

Chapter 7

URBAN SOCIAL STRUCTURE AND POLITICAL COMPETITION
A Comparative Study of Local Politics in Four European Nations

MICHAEL AIKEN

The purpose of this article is to examine the hypothesis that cleavages and heterogeneity in the social structure of cities is linked to their degree of interparty competition. This hypothesis is tested by carrying out separate analyses among the largest cities in four European nations: France, Belgium, Italy, and the Netherlands. Among other factors, these nations have in common the fact that each has a multiparty system; each is characterized by strong class, religious, and/or ethnic cleavages (Lipset and Rokkan, 1967); each has one or more mass-based socialist or left-oriented, "programmatic" political parties (Lowi, 1967); each uses or has used a system of proportional representation in municipal elections among larger cities;[1] and municipal elections are not held concurrently with legislative or national-level elections, although in one instance they are held concurrently with provincial elections. Such factors make these nations particularly propitious settings for examining this hypothesis.

AUTHOR'S NOTE: *There are a number of people and institutions whose help in assembling these data is greatly appreciated. Hugo van Hassel and Roger Depre of the Management Training Center, Catholic University of Leuven, Belgium, participated in gathering the Belgian data, and the Belgian National Productivity Agency provided the financial resources. Second, I am grateful to Guido Martinotti of the University of Turin, Italy, for permission to use part of the data we have gathered in a joint research project. I am also indebted to the Graduate School, the Western European Area Studies Program, and the Center for Demography and Ecology of the University of Wisconsin for various kinds of financial and other support in carrying out this analysis. Finally, I want to thank John Walton for his helpful comments on an earlier draft of this paper.*

The question about the linkage between the social structure of a collectivity and the nature of its political life has been a topic of considerable research in the past two decades in the United States. Beginning with the study by Eulau (1957) in which he attempted to relate the degree of urbanization to inter-party competition among 88 counties in Ohio, a number of studies addressing this general theme utilizing data on political units in the United States have appeared, often with contradictory findings. Studies using the American states as units of analysis have generally provided support for the Eulau thesis (Dawson and Robinson, 1963; Ranney, 1965; Dawson, 1967), although not fully in all cases (compare Casstevens and Press, 1963). Studies using counties as units of analysis have yielded contradictory results, some supporting the hypothesis (Cutright, 1963; Catlin, 1968) and some providing little or no support (Masters and Wright, 1958; Gold and Schmidhauser, 1960). The most thorough study of this question is that of Bonjean and Lineberry (1970) in which they tested the urbanization-party competition hypothesis among 3,101 American county units and concluded that "the hypothesis, originally formulated by Eulau, that size, density, and heterogeneity are associated with maximal competitiveness does not survive an all-county test" (Bonjean and Lineberry, 1970: 318; compare Franklin, 1971).

Whether counties are the most appropriate units has been questioned by Coulter and Gordon (1968) on the grounds that, in spite of ready availability of data, counties often contain a diversity of ecological units within them. As an alternative, they propose that more homogeneous ecological units such as cities be used as units of analysis in testing this proposition. Of course, this implies a change in the nature of the hypothesis from positing the degree of urbanism-ruralism as a key determinant of political competition to the degree of homogeneity/heterogeneity as the dimension of social structure most crucially linked to the degree of party competition (Coulter and Gordon, 1968). Additionally, this hypothesis would probably receive its best test if an electoral contest were used that was critically linked to local issues—that is, municipal elections. This implies the choosing of a unit of analysis for which the social and political systems are likely to be more tightly interwoven. Of course, to the degree to which local politics is integrated into the national political system, this is less of a problem, but there are clear national and intranational differences in terms of the integration of local political systems with the national political system.

Perhaps because of the inaccessibility of data, the variations in electoral procedures, or perhaps recent disinterest in this hypothesis, there have been few studies of political competition using American cities as units of analysis, and, in the few studies of this kind, electoral contests for higher levels of government have most often been used (Epstein, 1956; Masters and Wright, 1958; Gordon and Coulter, 1969). Gordon and Coulter (1969) found support for their hypothesis of greater competitiveness as cities varied on a continuum from homogeneous rural to heterogeneous urban, but less competitiveness as cities varied from heterogeneous to homogeneous urban.

Likewise, there have been few studies in other nations relating the social structure of cities to the degree of competitiveness. However, there are research findings for the Philippines (Iké, 1969), Korea (Lee, 1971), Mexico (Walton and Sween, 1971), Belgium (Aiken and Van Hassel, 1970), and England (Alt, 1971). While these studies differ in the types of elections examined, measures of political competition, and indicators of social structure, they in general support the generalization that the more heterogeneous and differentiated the social structure of a city, the more politically competitive the city. It is to an examination of this hypothesis in four European nations that we now turn. However, given the complexity of the data used here, we first consider in some detail the nature of the data used in examining this hypothesis.

METHODS AND PROCEDURES

The fact that the data for this study are from four different nations means that while every attempt to obtain comparable data was made, the data are not always exactly comparable, especially for some of the measures of the social structure of cities. This, together with the variations in electoral procedures, number of parties, and other national differences is the reason for carrying out, in effect, four separate analyses. Because of these variations, we shall describe here in some detail the nature of the cities included in the analysis, the data on local elections, the measure of political competition, and the indicators of social structure.

The cities: We include in the analysis here only the very largest cities for each of these four nations, although the lower limit on population size for inclusion in the analysis varies for these four nations.

France: The 154 French cities included in the analysis are cities that had a population size of 30,000 or more in both 1965 and 1971 and which had a population size of at least 9,000 in 1953.[2] Cities having a population size smaller than 30,000 in 1965 and 1971 had different electoral procedures than did those over 30,000, as did those cities having a population of less than 9,000 in 1953. Actually, only one city was excluded because of this latter restriction. There were 159 cities of size 30,000 or more in 1965 and 193 of this size in 1971, but only 158 had 30,000 or more inhabitants at both these points in time.

The three largest cities in France—Paris, Lyon, and Marseilles—are omitted because of special electoral procedures used in these cities in 1965 and 1971. The city of Sarcelles, a suburb of Paris, is also omitted because it had a population size of less than 9,000 in 1953, meaning that it operated under different electoral procedures in that election from the other cities included here, leaving 154 cities. Forty-eight of these cities are located in the region immediately surrounding Paris, while the other 106 are located in provincial France.

Belgium: The 190 Belgian cities are all of the cities of size 10,000 or more on December 31, 1970. While the same electoral procedures apply to all Belgian cities, we limited the analysis here to only the largest cities in an attempt to be somewhat comparable. On the other hand, we include cities in the 10,000-30,000 size range in an attempt to have a sufficiently large number of cities to carry out some regional analyses among the 112 cities in Flanders, the 59 cities in Wallonia, and the 19 cities in the Brussels agglomeration.

Italy: The 263 Italian cities included in the analysis here had a population size of 20,000 or more on October 15, 1961, and were still in existence in 1970. However, the cities located in the five special regions of Italy—Sicilia, Sardegna, Valle d'Aosta, Trentino-Alto Adige, and Friuli-Venezia Giulia—are not included in the analysis. Electoral laws as well as dates of elections varied in some of these special regions for some elections, so they were excluded from the analysis in an attempt to establish greater comparability of the electoral data. Regional analyses are additionally carried out for the 78 cities in the North, the 69 cities in the center, and the 116 cities in the South of Italy.

The Netherlands: The 128 Dutch cities included in the analysis are all of the cities which had a population size of 15,000 or more on May 30, 1960, and which still existed in 1970. Actually, there were 129 cities of size 15,000 or more on May 30, 1960, but one city for which social and economics data were unavailable is excluded. The same electoral procedures apply to all Dutch cities, but we limited the analysis to cities of size 15,000 or more in order to be comparable with the data about the larger cities from the other nations. Had we restricted the analysis to cities of size 20,000 or more, we would only have 93 cities in the analysis. Regional analyses are also carried out for the 20 cities in the provinces of Groningen, Friesland, and Drenthe; 32 cities in the provinces of Overijssel and Gelderland; 43 cities in the provinces of Utrecht, Noord-Holland, and Zuid-Holland; and 33 cities in Zeeland, Noord-Brabant, and Limburg. Fusion of communes during the period under study here presents something of a problem in terms of comparability of units over time. However, less than ten cities included here were affected by fusions. If these cities are omitted and the results recalculated, our substantive conclusions are unaffected.

THE DATA FOR MUNICIPAL ELECTIONS

We include here data about all the local elections held in these four nations during the period 1960 to 1972, inclusive. Actually with the exception of the Netherlands, we include data on all municipal elections held during the twenty-year period 1953 to 1972.[3] There are thus four municipal elections for France, five for Belgium, four for Italy, and three for the Netherlands. The exact nature of these elections is as follows:

France: We include in the analysis the results of the municipal elections of April 26, 1953; March 8, 1959; March 14, 1965; and March 14, 1971—i.e., the date of the first or only ballot for the municipal elections held in these years. Most of the data for these elections was taken from various Parisian newspapers including *Le Monde, Le Figaro, l'Humanité,* and *l'Aurore.* In addition, some electoral results were obtained through correspondence from the office of the mayor of a number of French cities as well as from some prefectures. These procedures were used in cases where the information was either unavailable in these various newspapers (especially in the case of the 1953 election) or where there were major inconsistencies in the newspaper reports. We used these procedures in obtaining electoral results after efforts to obtain this information from the Ministry of the Interior and national archives were unsuccessful.

A complicating factor in analyzing the results of these four French elections is that the electoral procedures in operation for three of these four elections were different. For the election of April 26, 1953, all cities of size 9,000 or more, which includes all 154 cities included here, had a list system of proportional representation with only one ballot, with the splitting of one's votes to candidates from several lists and preferential voting being permitted. The "votes" for each party or list used in the analysis were based on the *suffrages de liste,* which is the total number of votes given to the candidates on each list divided by the number of seats on the city council (*Le Monde,* April 24, 1953, p. 5).

For the election of March 8, 1959, there were different electoral procedures in operation for Paris and the twelve other cities with a population of size 120,000 or more and those having a population size of less than 120,000 (see note 2). For larger cities, the electoral procedure was one of a list system of proportional representation with mandatory voting for the entire list, meaning that no splitting of one's votes, preferential voting, suppression of names on lists, or modifications of lists was permitted in these larger cities. In cities with a population size of less than 120,000 the electoral system was one of *scrutin de liste majoritaire et plurinominal.* For these cities all candidates were elected who received an absolute majority on the first ballot; addition or suppression of names, modification of the order of names, and splitting of one's votes were permitted, but there was no preferential voting (*Le Monde,* March 6, 1959, p. 6).

For the election of March 14, 1965, still another change was made in the electoral procedures. All cities having a population size of 30,000 or more used a system of election by list and absolute majority with two possible ballots. A voter had to vote for an entire list, with no modifications of any kind. If a list obtained the absolute majority of votes on the first ballot (and if this amounted to at least one-fourth of the number of electors on the electoral roll), it was elected and received *all* seats on the city council. If not, there was a second ballot in which the party or list receiving a relative majority of the votes received *all* the seats on the city council. No list receiving less than ten percent of the votes on the first ballot was permitted to participate in the second ballot, and no alliances of first ballot opponents or alterations in the composition of the lists was permitted, but a list could withdraw from participation in the second ballot (*Le Monde,* March 12, 1965, p. 8).

This system, which was also used for the election of March 14, 1971, had a dramatic impact on the electoral behavior in municipal elections. According to Kesselman (1970), this change was a strategy used by the Gaullists to attempt to gain control of the large cities, a strategy which proved to be unsuccessful, although it is by no means the only such example of a party in power manipulating the electoral laws so as to capture or maintain control of cities (Pryce, 1957). However, this change did have the effect of reducing dramatically the number of lists entering these two elections. Approximately 75% of the cities included here had no more than three lists that entered the elections of 1965 and 1971, and these were often coalitions of the left, right, and center (Bon and Ranger, 1972). Naturally, these changes in the electoral procedures had the effect of a striking reduction of the fractionalization scores, as will be shown in a subsequent section.

The Netherlands: The results of three municipal elections for members of the city council *(gemeenteraad)* are included: May 30, 1962; June 1, 1966; and June 3, 1970. Information about the results of these elections was obtained from official publications of the Centraal Bureau Voor de Statistiek of the Netherlands. These data were supplemented with information from the files of the Centraal Bureau Voor de Statistiek in Voorburg as well as from the newspaper *Nieuwe Rotterdamse Courant* for the dates of June 1, 1962; June 2, 1966; and June 4, 1970. In these elections for members of the city council, a list system of proportional representation was employed in all cities (Humes and Martin, 1969).

Belgium: We include in the analysis the results from the five elections for communal councils held in Belgium since World War II—i.e., the elections of November 26, 1946; October 12, 1952; October 12, 1958; October 11, 1964; and October 10, 1970. Most of the information about these election results was taken from the files of the Minister of the Interior in Brussels. However, for the election results of 1946, the information was obtained either from the archives of the various provinces or from officials of the various cities. Belgium employed a list system of proportional representation and the d'Hondt highest average system for allocating seats for these communal elections throughout this period.

Italy: The results of the four administrative (local) elections held between 1956 and 1970 to choose members of the communal council are included. The results of the elections of May 27, 1956; November 6, 1960; November 22, 1964; and June 7, 1970, were taken from official publications of the Ministry of Interior located in the offices of the Province of Milan. Not all these administrative elections were held on these four dates, however. In fact, among the 263 cities, the percentages varied from 79% for the 1970 election to 94% for the 1956 election. In the case that a city did not hold an election on one of these dates, the election held nearest to the date of that administrative election was included.

While there have been some changes in the laws governing local elections in Italy since World War II, a system of proportional representation was used in all the cities included here for each of these four elections (Pryce, 1957; *Corriere della Sera*, 6 November 1960; *Elezioni Amministrative Del 22 November 1964*, Instituto Centrale di Statistica, 1967; *Elezioni Amministrative Del 7 Giugno 1970*, Instituto Centrale di Statistica, 1972). Data for nine cities were unavailable for the 1956 election, so overall fractionalization scores were computed for these cities based on the results for the other three elections.

THE MEASURE OF POLITICAL COMPETITION

A wide variety of measures of interparty competition have been used in the various American studies cited above, and still other refinements have been suggested (Pfeiffer, 1967; Stern, 1972; David, 1972). However, these are generally applicable to two-party, and in some instances three-party, electoral systems, but they are less applicable for multiparty systems such as those included in our analysis.

We employ the Index of Fractionalization as our measure of political cleavage. This measure reflects the probability that two electors chosen by chance would diverge in their electoral choice in the course of a given election (Rae, 1968; Rae and Taylor, 1970). The formula to construct the Index of Fractionalization is:

$$\text{Fractionalization} = 1 - \sum_{i}^{N} p_i^2$$

where p_i is the proportion of votes for the ith party or list and N is the number of parties in that election. Actually, this measure has a long history of use in reflecting social diversity or complexity of social systems (Lieberson, 1969). In general, the more parties or lists entering an election, and the more evenly the votes are distributed among them, the higher the fractionalization score. The upper limit of the fractionalization score is theoretically 1.0, but it varies with the number of parties. For example, if there are two parties in an electoral contest, the upper limit of fractionalization is .500; if there are three parties, the upper limit is .643; if there are four parties, the upper limit is .750; if there are five parties it is

.800; and so on. The upper limit increases quite rapidly up to four or five parties, but then it tends to increase at a decelerating rate as the number of parties increases.

Another index that has been utilized to measure political competition is the Index of Multipartyism (Kesselman, 1966, 1967) which one critic (Wildgen, 1971) has suggested is more sensitive to "hyperfractionalized" electoral systems such as Italy, although there is some disagreement about this contention (Rae, 1971).

This by no means exhausts the kinds of measures that have been proposed to measure interparty competition in multiparty systems, since still other measures have been recently proposed (see, for example, Milder, 1974; Laponce and Uhler, 1974).

Actually we computed and analyzed both the measure of fractionalization and the measure of multipartyism. The correlation coefficients between them was highest in less "fragmented" electoral systems such as France and Belgium, and somewhat lower for more "fragmented" electoral systems such as Italy and the Netherlands, as might be anticipated by Wildgen's remarks. The reason for this is that as the number of parties increases above five or so, the index of fractionalization gives less weight to these smaller, splinter parties, thus accounting for divergence in scores in Italy and the Netherlands. On the other hand, some prior analyses showed that, among Belgian cities, the index of fractionalization provided more conservative relationships than the measure of multipartyism, primarily because of less skewness in the fractionalization measure. In computing correlation coefficients for both measures, we did find some divergences in the magnitude of correlation coefficients between the independent variables and these measures of political competition. In general, the substantive conclusions discussed below obtain, regardless of the measure used. To reduce the amount of data presented here, we included only the results for the index of fractionalization.

To simplify additionally the presentation of findings, we have constructed an average fractionalization score for each city in each of the four nations. The average fractionalization score for each election as well as the standard deviation for each is shown in Table 1, along with the overall average for each nation. The average fractionalization score was thus computed for the four elections in France, the five elections in Belgium, the four elections in Italy, and the three elections in the Netherlands. The correlation coefficients between the fractionalization score for each election for a nation and the overall fractionalization score among the cities in each nation are shown in Table 2.

TABLE 1
Fractionalization Scores for Local Elections
in Four European Nations

	Mean	Standard Deviation
France (n=154)		
April 26, 1953	.6849	.0967
March 8, 1959	.6730	.0964
March 14, 1965	.5344	.1463
March 14, 1971	.5540	.1119
Average	.6116	.0865
Belgium (n=190)		
November 26, 1946	.6119	.0979
October 12, 1952	.5940	.0894
October 12, 1958	.5751	.0803
October 11, 1964	.6444	.0818
October 10, 1970	.6669	.0781
Average	.6179	.0671
Italy (n=263)		
May 27, 1956	.7196	.0542
November 6, 1960	.6983	.0585
November 22, 1964	.7188	.0569
June 7, 1970	.7240	.0578
Average	.7156	.0485
The Netherlands (n=128)		
May 30, 1962	.7177	.0970
June 1, 1966	.7636	.0850
June 3, 1970	.7714	.0745
Average	.7509	.0717

The correlations are .69 or higher; the reason that they are not higher is primarily that there were changes in fractionalization scores over time in three of these four nations, which is discussed in the next section. Because of this there is the possibility that the fractionalization score for a given election might not be related to the measures of social structure in the same way as the average fractionalization score. In those cases where this happened, we indicated it in the discussions of findings.

TABLE 2
Pearsonian Correlation Coefficients
Between the Index of Fractionalization for Each Election
and the Overall Fractionalization Score by Nation

	$p < .001$ Two-tail
France (n=154)	
1953	.74
1959	.79
1965	.82
1971	.69
Belgium (n=190)	
1946	.71
1952	.83
1958	.80
1964	.77
1970	.71
Italy (n=263)	
1956	.80
1960	.88
1964	.90
1970	.84
The Netherlands (n=128)	
1962	.87
1966	.84
1970	.80

MEASURES OF HETEROGENEITY AND DIFFERENTIATION

The various measures of social diversity and heterogeneity are taken, for the most part, from reports of the censuses of population and commerce and industry in each country.

France: The measures of the independent variables are taken from the various volumes of the *Recensement General de la Population de 1962* and the *Recensement General de la Population de 1968.*

Belgium: Measures of the independent variables for Belgium were taken from the various volumes of the *Recensement de la Population 1947, Recensement de la Population 1961,* and *Recensement de l'Industrie et du Commerce de 1961.*

Italy: The data reflecting measures of the social structure of Italian cities were taken in part from the various volumes of the *10e Censimento generale della popolazione, 15 Ottobre 1961.* Other parts of the data were taken (in whole or in part) from data sets initially prepared by the II Mulino Research Group funded by the Twentieth Century Fund and given a new format by the Department of Political Science and Council for European Studies of Yale University.

The Netherlands: The measures of social structure for Dutch cities were taken from a data file on Dutch municipalities assembled by Professor Philip Stouthard of the Institute of Sociology, Higher School of Tilburg, and provided through the Inter-University Consortium for Political Research at the University of Michigan. They are taken for the most part from the various volumes of the *13e Algemene Volkstelling, 30 Mei 1960,* published by the Centraal Bureau Voor de Statistiek.

A COMPARISON OF POLITICAL COMPETITION IN FOUR EUROPEAN NATIONS

In this section, we turn to a comparison of the degree of political fractionalization in local elections among cities in these four European nations. As we indicated at the outset, these nations have certain features in common, such as multiparty system, economic, religious, and/or ethnic cleavages; and one or more mass-based, left-oriented "programmatic" political party. On the other hand, there are great differences in their political, economic, social, and cultural histories that far outweigh these similarities, and in the comparison here we do not intend to minimize these differences.

Two major differences observed here in the local political systems of these four nations are (1) the differences in the degree of political fractionalization in local elections and (2) the changes in the degree of political fractionalization during the past twenty years, but especially during the decade of the 1960s.

The degree of political fractionalization is highest in the Netherlands, followed by Italy, Belgium, and then France, which had the lowest degree of political fractionalization by 1965. This is true whether we examine the average number of parties or lists entering each of the elections included in the analysis (although these data are not shown) or whether we examine the average fractionalization scores plotted in Figure 1 and displayed in Table 1. Some care must be exercised in examining these figures since the

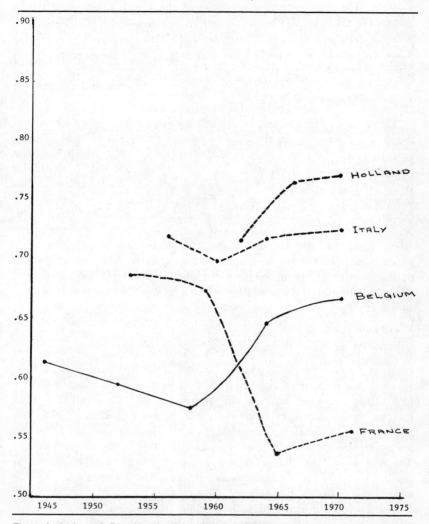

Figure 1: Index of Fractionalization of Local Elections by Year of Election for France, Belgium, Italy, and The Netherlands

lower limit for cities included in the analysis varies from one nation to the next—30,000 for France, 10,000 for Belgium; 20,000 for Italy; and 15,000 for the Netherlands. However, if the analysis is restricted to cities of size 30,000 or more in the four nations, the results are little changed from those shown in Figure 1 although the measures of political competition—both average number of parties or lists entering the elections and average fractionalization scores—increase only slightly for the 54 Dutch and 152 Italian cities of size 30,000 or more, and somewhat more for the 39 Belgian cities of this size. This is because, as we shall show in the next section, political fractionalization tends to vary directly with city size. If we restrict the analysis to large cities, we obviously increase somewhat the degree of political fractionalization.

The second observation to be made from Table 1 and Figure 1 concerns the changes occurring in the degree of fractionalization of local political systems in all the countries with the exception of Italy, which had little change in political fractionalization from 1956 to 1970. In both the Netherlands and Belgium, the degree of political fractionalization has increased in the past decade. In France, however, there has been a dramatic decrease in the degree of political fractionalization since 1959. As described above, there was a system of proportional representation in effect in 1953, which was changed in 1959 for most cities to a plurinominal list system with an absolute majority. This led to a slight decline in the degree of political fractionalization, but the subsequent change in the electoral law in 1964 led to a far more dramatic reduction in the number of lists entering local elections, and, hence, the degree of fractionalization. The effect of these new electoral procedures was to encourage the creation of left, right, and sometimes center coalitions. While in 1959 only 30% of these 154 cities had no more than three lists entering the election, in 1965 85% of these cities had three or fewer lists. In 1971, the number of cities have more than three lists increased slightly (5%), since coalitions broke up in some cities, with the result of a slight increase in the degree of fractionalization between 1965 and 1971 (Bon and Ranger, 1972). Hence, the changes in the electoral laws in France had a significant impact on the level of fractionalization in municipal elections. The reasons for the changes in the degree of political competitiveness at the local level in the Netherlands and Belgium are different and owing to other kinds of causes, however.

The Dutch political and social system has been described by some analysts as a *Verzuiling* system, in which the society is segmented into a number of "pillars" or subcultures. In the Dutch case, these various pillars are both religious—Roman Catholic, Calvinist, etc.—and secular—liberals and socialists (Lijphart, 1974). With each pillar, there are strong mechanisms of social control and social integration; each pillar is likely to have its own political party, labor union, insurance schemes, newspapers, schools, and the like. Hence, there are strong and binding mechanisms of both socialization and social integration within each pillar, but little social intercourse between pillars. In a society organized in this way, one may naturally ask how sufficient political integration occurs to provide for continuity and direction of the polity. The integration of such a society comes about through elite accommodation where the principle of proportionality obtains (Daalder, 1966; Lijphart, 1968).

This type of system has been referred to as a "consociational democracy" (Lijphart, 1969) or one of "segmented pluralism" (Lorwin, 1971), and it has been argued that other societies approximate this model, although the Netherlands is often held out as a particularly clear example of it, at least until the decade of the 1960s. This kind of social and political system in the Netherlands supposedly reached its apogee during the 1950s (Lorwin, 1971), and since then the subcultures have begun to lose their ideological and religious salience, and, hence, their hold on their members. It is generally conceded that this system began to disintegrate during the decade of the 1960s (Lijphart, 1974). It is in this context that increases in the degree of political fractionalization must be understood. As the traditional "pillars" have begun to disintegrate, a variety of splinter political parties have appeared. For example, over the three elections examined here, the number of lists entering the municipal election in Amsterdam increased from eleven in 1962 to twenty in 1970 and from ten to seventeen in Utrecht. Of course, it is precisely this kind of phenomenon that the index of fractionalization was constructed to reflect. No doubt we would see this pattern more clearly if we had data extending back to the 1950s, but unfortunately these data were unavailable at the time this article was written.

The fractionalization scores for Belgium over the period 1946 to 1970 is equally interesting. It might be noted at the outset that it has been argued that Belgium, like the Netherlands, also has a system of *Verzuiling* or segmented pluralism (Urwin, 1970; Lorwin, 1971; Hill, 1974; Heisler, 1974). For example, the major organizational components of the "socialist" pillar in Belgium include a political party, a trade union, a union of mutual health insurance funds, and cooperatives (DeBakker and Claeys-Van Haegendoren, 1973). However, the Belgian system has also been undergoing some changes in recent years (Lorwin, 1971). The degree of political competition was initially high in 1946, with votes going to the three traditional parties—the Catholic (Parti Social Chrétien-Christelijke Volkspartij), the Socialists (Parti Socialiste Belge/Belgische Socialistische Partij), and the Liberals (Parti de la Liberté et du Progrès/Partij van de Vrijheid en Vooruitgang), but also to the Communist Party, which was relatively active in the 1946 election.

In the subsequent twelve years, there were several dramatic events—the "royal question" in 1950, but especially the controversy over state aid to religious schools that led to the school pact of 1958. Since one of the major cleavages in Belgian society is that of religion and since the various political parties are structured to a great extent around this particular cleavage—i.e., the Catholics and the secular socialists and liberals—this controversy had the effect of concentrating votes in two of the traditional parties—the Catholics and socialists—with the consequence that political fractionalization reached its lowest point in the post-World War II years in 1958; in both 1964 and again in 1970, the degree of political competition increased. Lorwin (1971) has argued that 1958 was a turning point in Belgian political life, since the settlement of the school issue took much of the salience out of the religious issue. In the two subsequent elections, there has been a rather significant increase in the degree of political competition, with the high point being reached in 1970. During this period, the linguistic issue and its consequences for fractionalization appeared. In the 1961 legislative elections, regional parties first appeared in Brussels and Wallonia and the Flemish nationalist party reappeared in Flanders. In subsequent local elections as well, regional parties reflecting the linguistic controversy have taken an increasing share and the Socialists and Catholics a decreasing share of the votes, which is reflected in increased fractionalization in 1964 and again in 1970. It might be noted that this pattern also closely resembles the pattern of political fractionalization in post-World War II legislative elections in Belgium, using the thirty electoral arrondissements as units of analysis (Quévit and Aiken, 1975).

In closing this section, we might observe once again that the degree of political competition in local elections in Italian cities has been high and relatively constant over the period 1956 to 1970. This appears to reflect the argument of Sartori (1966) that the Italian political system is one characterized by polarized pluralism. Galli and Prandi (1970) have described how the system revolves around two parties—the Christian Democrats (Democrazia Cristiana—DC) and the Italian Communist Party (Partito Communista Italiano—PCI), and how the system has moved toward greater stability during the 1960s (Capecchi et al., 1968). Analyses of votes by parties not shown here demonstrated that there was indeed great stability in votes for these two parties in both administrative (local) and legislative elections. There were very high correlations between votes for the Communist Party from one administrative as well as legislative election to the next as well as for the Christian Democratic Party among cities in the North and Center, although less so among cities in the South. In this system of polarized pluralism, the nine major parties accounted for over 98% of the votes in 1948 and again in 1968 (Barnes, 1974), again illustrating Sartori's argument. This polarized pluralism at the national level is therefore reflected also at the local level, which provides a background for understanding this pattern of political fractionalization in Italy.

Having examined the context of the electoral systems in these four nations, we turn now to an examination of the hypotheses relating to the diversity and heterogeneity of the social structure of cities and how this is related to political fractionalization.

THE CORRELATES OF POLITICAL
FRACTIONALIZATION

STRUCTURAL DIFFERENTIATION AND
POLITICAL FRACTIONALIZATION

By structural differentiation, we refer to the degree to which the social structure of a city is fragmented into many separate spheres and parts. Our expectation is that more structurally differentiated cities will have higher degrees of political competition since there are more diverse interests generated which, we argue, will be aggregated into political groups. We use population size as a surrogate for the structural differentiation of a city since analyses in both Belgium and Italy for which data were available showed that population size is strongly related to the number of economic establishments. Looking at the relationship between the natural logarithm transformation of the population size of a city and the index of fractionalization, as shown in Table 3, we find that this hypothesis is supported for the cities in three of the four nations; only in the Netherlands is the relationship weak. The zero-order correlations in the other three nations vary between .36 and .38. With a few exceptions—the suburbs of Paris, the nineteen cities in the Brussels agglomeration, and one subset of Dutch cities—we find support for the hypothesis in the various regions of these four nations. It might be noted that the correlation coefficients for three of the four regional subsets in the Netherlands are higher than the all cities category; this latter correlation is low because the relationship reverses among cities located in the southern provinces of Zeeland, Noord Brabant, and Limburg. In part, the reason for this is that, while the traditional parties, especially the Catholic party, have lost considerable votes over this period of time in the larger cities, there has

TABLE 3
Pearson Correlation Coefficients Between Population Size
(natural logarithm transformation)
and Population Density and Average Fractionalization Score
by Region Within Four European Nations

	Number of Cities	Population Size	Population Density
France[a]			
All cities	154	.36	−.15
Paris region	48	.05	.06
Provincial cities	106	.46[g]	.09
Belgium[b]			
All cities	190	.39[g]	.42[g]
Brussels Agglomeration	19	.01	−.16
Wallonia	59	.50[g]	.13
Flanders	112	.31[g]	.37[g]
Italy[c]			
All cities	263	.38[g]	.16[f]
North	78	.51[g]	.22
Center	69	.28[e]	.17
South	116	.32[g]	.11
The Netherlands[d]			
All cities	128	.13	.15
Groningen, Friesland, Drenthe	20	.37	.27
Overijssel and Gelderland	32	.29	−.04
Utrecht, Noord Holland and Zuid Holland	43	.24	.17
Zeeland, Noord Brabant, and Limburg	33	−.31	−.16

NOTES: a - Census of March 1962; b - Census of December 1961; c - Census of
October 1961; d - Census of May 1960.
e. $p < .05$ Two tail; f. $p < .01$ Two-tail; g. $p < .001$ Two-tail.

been and there remains a high proportion of the votes in the traditional
parties, meaning that votes are less dispersed than in some smaller cities,
where votes are often scattered into a variety of nontraditional and local
lists. The consequence of this is that the three largest cities in this regional
subset—Breda, Eindhoven, and Tilburg—have fractionalization scores for
each of these elections which are lower than the averages of the cities in
this subset.

POPULATION DENSITY AND POLITICAL FRACTIONALIZATION

Like population size, population density was included in the original analysis by Eulau (1957). In each instance here, population density is measured by the number of inhabitants per square kilometer. The reason we expect population density to be related to fractionalization is that, in more densely settled cities, pervasive segmentation and divided allegiances are likely to have been generated, consequently causing the emergence of more political groups and giving rise to greater political competition. Hence, we would expect that population density would be positively related to the index of fractionalization. As shown in Table 3, there is support for this hypothesis in only two of the three nations—Belgium and Italy. However, only in the Flanders region of Belgium is there support for the hypothesis among the regional subgroupings. Therefore, we conclude that there is little support for this hypothesis, although this does not mean that density may not be related to the degree of fractionalization, once other factors are controlled.

SOCIAL CLASS AND POLITICAL FRACTIONALIZATION

We have hypothesized that the more socially heterogeneous the city, the more likely it will have a high degree of political competition. Our reasoning is that cities having a large middle class, as reflected in both the occupational and educational structures, are likely to have more differentiated interests, owing to the diverse social milieux and, hence, interests that would be generated by a highly complex division of labor and a highly diverse occupational structure. Similarly, cities with a high proportion of highly educated persons are also likely to be cities in which there is a greater range of ideas, diversity of interests, and, hence, a higher probability of a diversity of political expressions of these diverse interests. Particularly in the European context, where there are multiple parties, we would argue that one of the structural supports for these diverse parties is the availability of a highly educated and occupationally diverse occupational base. Conversely, under the condition that a city is dominated by the working class, it is more likely that the working class is mobilized into one or a few mass-based, left-oriented parties with the effect of reducing the degree of political fractionalization in such cities. Under the condition that the working class is largely mobilized into a mass-based, left-oriented party, the more their votes are likely to be concentrated in only a few parties. Under this circumstance, it would be in the interest of the middle classes to center their political allegiances in only a few political parties or groups. The consequence of this is that votes are likely to be more concentrated in only a few parties, and, hence, there is likely to be less political fractionalization.

By middle-class social status, we normally mean those occupations that in terms of American occupational categories are upper-status and upper and lower white-collar occupations. High educational attainment here

TABLE 4
Pearsonian Correlation Coefficients Between Measures of Social Class and the Average Fractionalization Score by Region Within Four European Nations

	Number of Cities	Percent Middle Class	Percent Working Class	Percent High Education
France[a]				
All cities	154	.38[f]	−.42[f]	e
Paris region	48	.51[f]	−.54[f]	e
Provincial cities	106	.33[f]	−.30[g]	e
Belgium[b]				
All cities	190	.23[g]	−.46[f]	.40[f]
Brussels Agglomeration	19	.44	−.35	.39
Wallonia	59	.49[f]	−.46[f]	.51[f]
Flanders	112	.07	−.34[f]	.25[g]
Italy[c]				
All cities	263	.46[f]	−.46[f]	.51[f]
North	78	.44[f]	−.44[f]	.53[f]
Center	69	.50[f]	−.51[f]	.57[f]
South	116	.46[f]	−.46[f]	.49[f]
The Netherlands[d]				
All cities	128	.24[g]	−.23[h]	.12[h]
Groningen, Friesland, and Drenthe	20	.01	−.06	−.15
Overijssel and Gelderland	32	.16	−.09	.19
Utrecht, Noord Holland, and Zuid Holland	43	.07	−.07	−.02
Zeeland, Noord Brabant, and Limburg	33	.06	−.12	.03

NOTES: a - Census of March 1962; b - Census oı December 1961; c - Census of October 1961; d - Census of May 1960; e - data unavailable.
f. $p < .001$ Two-tail; g. $p < .01$ Two-tail; h. $p < .05$ Two-tail.

normally means the completion of the equivalent of a high school education.[4]

In Table 4, we show the relationships between two measures of middle class—the percentage with higher- or middle-class occupations and the percentage of the adult population with high education as well as a measure of the working-class strength of cities. Because of some differences in the classification of occupations and educational achievement in these four nations, these indicators are not entirely comparable, so the reader should bear this in mind in examining these findings.

We find rather strong support for the hypothesis that cities with a high proportion of middle class have greater political fractionalization. Both the occupational and educational measures of middle-class strength have strong positive relationships with the measure of fractionalization. Similarly, there is strong support for the hypothesis that the greater the preponderance of the working class in a city, the less the degree of fractionalization. These relationships also obtain, with the exception of the Netherlands, under the conditions of regional controls.

These data provide support for our hypothesis that working-class cities have less political fractionalization while middle-class cities have more political fractionalization.

ECONOMIC DIVERSITY AND POLITICAL FRACTIONALIZATION

The degree to which the economic base of a city is diversified is another factor hypothesized to be related to the degree of political competition. To the extent that the economy is diversified across many different kinds of economic activities—i.e., agriculture, various kinds of manufacturing, commerce, transportation, services, and the like—the more likely it is that different configurations of material interest are generated, and the more likely it is that these various interests will coalesce into diversified forms of political expression. To specify this hypothesis even more, we argue that diversified cities are likely to be those in which the economic activities are concentrated in the tertiary sector—transportation, commerce, public administration, and the like. Hence, we would expect that the percentage of the labor force in the tertiary sector would be positively related to political competition, while the percentage in agriculture and manufacturing would be negatively related to political competition.

We constructed an index of economic diversity using a formula suggested by Gibbs and Martin (1962) which is actually the same formula we used in constructing the index of fractionalization. If the labor force is concentrated in one or only a few industries, a city would receive a low score on this measure; if the labor force is dispersed across many industries, a city would receive a high score on this measure. A major problem is the comparability of this index in these four nations, since the number of categories for which economic activity of the labor force is available varies from four categories in the case of Holland to thirty categories in the case of France.[5]

There is some support for the hypothesis that economic diversity is related to political fractionalization, as shown in Table 5, although the hypothesis is most strongly supported in Italy and least supported in the regions of Belgium and the Netherlands. The hypothesis is supported for

TABLE 5
Pearsonion Correlation Coefficients Between the Index of
Economic Diversity and the Average Fractionalization Score
by Region Within Four European Nations

	Number of Cities	Index of Economic Diversity
France[a]		
All cities	154	.25[g]
Paris region	48	−.07
Provincial cities	106	.43[f]
Belgium[b]		
All cities	190	.15[h]
Brussels Agglomeration	19	.05
Wallonia	59	−.01
Flanders	112	.14
Italy[c]		
All cities	263	.30[f]
North	78	.28[h]
Center	69	.25[h]
South	116	.40[f]
The Netherlands[d]		
All cities	128	.26[g]
Groningen, Friesland, and Drenthe	20	.13
Overijssel and Gelderland	32	.12
Utrecht, Noord Holland and Zuid Holland	43	.21
Zeeland, Noord Brabant, and Limburg	33	.17

NOTES: a - Census of March 1962; b - Census of December 1961; c - Census of October 1961; d - Census of May 1960; e - Unavailable.
f. p <.001 Two-tail; g. p <.01 Two-tail; p <.05 Two-tail.

the 106 provincial cities of France, but not among the suburbs surrounding Paris.

Looking at the relationship between the percentage in various sectors of the economy—manufacturing and tertiary—as shown in Table 6, we observe that among all cities in France, Italy, and the Netherlands, the percentage in tertiary is positively related to the degree of fractionalization.[6] Among all cities in France, Belgium, and the Netherlands, the percentage in manufacturing is negatively related to the degree of political fractionalization. As with other variables, the regional analyses yield results that do not always confirm the all cities category in each country. Nevertheless, we conclude that there is some tendency, albeit not an entirely consistent one, for political fractionalization to be positively

TABLE 6
Pearsonian Correlation Coefficients Between Measures of
Economic Activity and the Average Fractionalization Score
by Region Within Four European Nations

	Number of Cities	In Tertiary	Percent in Tertiary
France[a]			
All cities	154	.35[e]	−.29[e]
Paris region	48	.21	−.15
Provincial cities	106	.31[e]	−.21[g]
Belgium[b]			
All cities	190	−.09	−.23[f]
Brussels Agglomeration	19	−.20	−.41
Wallonia	59	−.12	−.20
Flanders	112	−.16	−.12
Italy[c]			
All cities	263	.43[e]	−.04
North	78	.44[e]	−.22[g]
Center	69	.46[e]	−.25[g]
South	116	.41[e]	.11
The Netherlands[d]			
All cities	128	.28[f]	−.30[f]
Groningen, Friesland, and Drenthe	20	.01	−.26
Overijssel and Gelderland	32	.24	−.11
Utrecht, Noord Holland, and Zuid Holland	43	.01	−.10
Zeeland, Noord Brabant, and Limburg	33	.14	−.21

NOTES: a - Census of March 1962; b - Census of December 1961; c - Census of October 1961; d - Census of May 1960.
e. p $<$ .001 Two-tail; f. p $<$ .01 Two-tail; g. p $<$ .05 Two-tail.

related to economic diversity and the percentage in the tertiary sector and negatively related to the percentage in manufacturing. However, there are a number of exceptions to this generalization.

RELIGIOUS DIVERSITY AND POLITICAL FRACTIONALIZATION

We would expect political competition to vary not only with the heterogeneity of the class structure and of the economic base of a city, but also to vary with diversity in other sectors of social life, such as religion. Data on the religious composition of a city's population were available only for the Netherlands, however. Since 1849, the Dutch Central Bureau of Statistics has routinely included questions about religious affiliation in its censuses. In 1960, 40% of the Dutch population were reported Roman Catholics, of which approximately one-half lived in two Southern provinces—Noord Brabant and Limburg, both of which are overwhelmingly Roman Catholic. The largest Protestant denomination is the Dutch Reformed Church which in 1960 included 28% of the total population. The percentage belonging to this denomination was more than one-third in every province in 1960 with the exception of the two Roman Catholic provinces in the South and Noord Holland, a heavily industrialized and de-Christianized province which includes the city of Amsterdam. Thirty-seven percent of the population of this province was reported as belonging to no religious denomination in 1960. As discussed above, different religious affiliations are the basis of some of the "pillars" or subcultures within Holland, although they do not capture them entirely (Lijphart, 1974).

Using the thirteen categories of religious affiliation for which data were available, including a category of no religious affiliation, we constructed an index of religious diversity using the same formula as for the indices of fractionalization and economic diversity and then related this to the index of fractionalization. The previous discussion of "segmented pluralism" in Holland would lead us to predict that the index of religious diversity in a city would be strongly related to the degree of political diversity. The findings support this line of reasoning, as shown by the data in Table 7. The index of religious diversity is related to the index of political fractionalization among all cities and among two of the four regional subsets. The relationship is strongest among the 32 cities in the provinces of Overijssel and Gelderland, but there is no relationship for the three provinces of Groningen, Friesland, and Drenthe and for the 43 cities in three provinces of Utrecht, Noord Holland, and Zuid Holland.

TABLE 7

Pearsonian Correlation Coefficients Between the Index of Religious Diversity
and the Index of Fractionalization in the Netherlands

	Number of Cities	Index of of Religious Diversity
The Netherlands[a]		
All cities	128	.48[b]
Groningen, Friesland and Drenthe	20	−.03
Overijssel and Gelderland	32	.63[b]
Utrecht, Noord Holland, and Zuid Holland	43	.03
Zeeland, Noord Brabant, and Limburg	33	.24

NOTES: a - Census of May, 1960.
b. p < .001 Two-tail; c. p < .05 Two-tail.

Given the earlier discussion of how this *Verzuiling* system has been disintegrating during the decade of the 1960s (Lorwin, 1971; Lijphart, 1974) and our earlier observation about the increase in political fractionalization between 1962 and 1970, it would seem to follow logically that we should expect this relationship between the 1960 measure of religious heterogeneity and the index of fractionalization to decline over the period 1962 to 1970 when political fractionalization was on the increase, and this is indeed the case. The correlation coefficient between the measure of religious diversity and the measure of fractionalization for these three elections declined from .47 in 1962 to .25 in 1970. This pattern was not uniformly true for all regions, however. We draw the conclusion that there is a tendency for religious heterogeneity to be associated with political fractionalization, although there are regional exceptions to this generalization. This generalization, however, must be understood in the specific historical and cultural context of the Netherlands during the decade of the 1960s.

REGRESSION ANALYSES OF FRACTIONALIZATION

Having examined the various zero-order correlates of fractionalization, we now examine the net effects of these measures of urban social structure on the degree of fractionalization in each of the four nations. We include only one of the measures of social class, the percentage of the active labor force in middle-class occupations, since we did not have complete data for education (it was unavailable for France) and since the measure of percentage working class is by and large the obverse of percentage middle class. Five measures of urban social structure are included for France, Belgium, and Italy, but the measure of religious diversity is additionally included for the Netherlands.

Population size is associated with the degree of fractionalization in each nation except the Netherlands, after controlling for the effects of the other variables. In these three nations, the size of the population of a city is associated with greater political fractionalization. Population density is more complex, however. The negative relationship between density and population size remains, and, in fact, increases, after other variables are controlled; the strong relationship between density and fractionalization observed in Belgium remains when controlling for other variables; the relationship between these two variables in Italy goes to zero; and our conclusion that density is unrelated to fractionalization in the Netherlands remains. These results give us little support for the hypothesis relating density to fractionalization.

The positive relationship between middle class and the degree of fractionalization remains strong in three of the four nations. Only in the Netherlands is there no net effect of social class on political competition. In fact, there is no factor among those included here other than religious diversity that is related to political fractionalization. Since the percentage working class is so strongly linked to the percentage middle class, we can conclude that the inverse relationship between working class and fractionalization also remains after controls are made.

TABLE 8
Regression of the Average Index of Fractionalization of Selected City Characteristics in Four European Nations[a]

City Characteristics	France (N=154)	Belgium (N=190)	Italy (N=263)	The Netherlands (N=128)
Population Size (Natural Logarithm Transformation)	.302[c]	.210[c]	.160[c]	−.018
Population Density	−.211[c]	.322[c]	−.011	.088
Percent in middle class occupations	.358[c]	.202[c]	.283[c]	−.147
Index of Economic Diversity	.090	.029	.068	.081
Percent in tertiary Sector	−.016	−.138[c]	.057	.144
Index of Religious Diversity	b	b	b	.441[c]
R^2	.2951	.2782	.2345	.2498

a. The figures in the table are standardized regression or beta coefficients.
b. Data was unavailable
c. The standardized regression (beta) coefficient is more than twice its standard error.

The previously observed relationships between the measure of economic diversity and fractionalization disappear in each of the four nations after other variables are controlled. This is primarily a function of the fact that economic diversity is quite strongly related to the measure of occupational status in each of the four nations and to percentage in the tertiary sector in three of the four nations. Only in Belgium is the measure of percentage in the tertiary sector of the labor force related to fractionalization after controlling for other factors; the previously observed but weak relationship between these two variables increases once other variables are controlled. Neither of these two measures of the economic structure of cities seems to be related as expected to the degree of political fractionalization, once other factors are controlled.

Finally, we examine the measure of religious diversity which, unfortunately, was available only for the Netherlands. Religious diversity is the only factor which has a net effect on fractionalization among Dutch cities; when the other five factors were entered without religious diversity in a regression equation, none of them had a regression coefficient that was twice its standard error. Hence, only this one aspect of the heterogeneity of Dutch cities is related to our degree of political competition. This once again reflects our earlier discussion of the nature of the social structure of Dutch cities and the pervasive influence of the *Verzuiling* system, even though it is alleged to be in decline.

Finally, it should be noted that this set of variables explains from 23% of the variance in fractionalization in Italy to 30% of the variance in this variable in France. While we identify here some of the correlates of political competition, it is clear that there are obviously other factors not included here that undoubtedly have an effect on the degree of political fractionalization among cities in these four European nations. This is not to deny, however, that we have identified some factors that are associated with the degree of fractionalization in local elections. For France, Belgium, and Italy, the most persuasive case can be made for population size and social class. For the Netherlands, the key factor is the degree of religious fragmentation. In Belgium, population density is also important; in France, it is also related to political fractionalization, but opposite from our prediction.

SUMMARY AND CONCLUSIONS

These various findings about the correlates of political fractionalization give us sufficient confidence to conclude that in these four European nations political competition does indeed vary with some aspects of the degree of heterogeneity and diversity of the social structure of cities, although our various hypotheses were not uniformly supported. However, we explain no more than 30% of the variance in any model (in France) and no less than 23% (in Italy) of the variance in the measure of political fractionalization. While this is sufficient to give us some confidence that we have identified some important correlates of political competition, such results merit considerable humility in drawing conclusions. While we were unable to pursue it here, some within-region analyses resulted in considerable variation in the amount of variance explained, as well as in the net effects of various predictors of political fractionalization, being higher in some regions and lower in others. This suggests that regional differences are quite important in these four European nations, and, hence, deserving of greater attention. Additionally, while we were unable to explore it in any detail here, other analyses showed that there were considerable differences in the efficiency of these variables in explaining political fractionalization from one election to the next. By computing an average of political competition over the period, for example, from 1946 to 1970 in Belgium or from 1962 to 1970 in the Netherlands, we ignore some variations in the relationships between correlates of urban social structure and the degree of political fractionalization. In other words, there is a temporal dimension in addition to an areal one which would probably merit additional analysis. These temporal differences are, of course, greatest in those systems undergoing the greatest change, such as Holland and to some extent Belgium, and lowest in stable political systems, such as Italy. In other words, while the method of analysis employed in this paper did not permit us to take these unique historical and contextual factors into full consideration, the reader should be aware of their importance. This, however, raises a more general point about this analysis and these results.

While we found some support for the general hypothesis that more differentiated and heterogeneous cities are more politically fragmented, this should not obscure the fact that there are uniquenesses in local political systems that vary by nation and region, leading to the conclusion that the reasons these hypotheses were supported to the degree they were may vary considerably in each nation and in each region. We suspect that in the various regions of these nations there is often one, sometimes two, dominant parties, the fortunes of which are linked quite strongly to the degree of fractionalization.

For example, in the North of Italy, this is the Christian Democratic Party; in the center of Italy, it is the Communist Party; in the Flanders region of Belgium, it is the Catholic Party; in the Walloon region of Belgium, it is the Socialist Party; and among the cities surrounding Paris, it is clearly the Communist Party. Hence, the major cleavage underlying the workings of local political systems within regions is sometimes class, sometimes religion, and sometimes a mixture of these. Hence, the mobilization of the working classes into left-oriented or Social Democratic, mass-based political parties is a key political process underlying some of these results. Perhaps this is clearest in the case of the suburbs around Paris, cities in the center region of Italy, and the Walloon region of Belgium. In some other regions, however, such as Flanders in Belgium and some parts of the Netherlands, it is undoubtedly religion. What this means is that while the various findings provide some support for the hypotheses stated at the outset of this article, these results must nevertheless be considered as only a first approximation to the understanding of how these local political systems operate. Said differently, the analysis of electoral results such as these reflects in greater or lesser degrees the underlying institutional bases of local political systems nations and regions. These institutional arrangements—the nature of parties, nature of election laws, and the like—vary from one national and sometimes regional setting to the next. Any analysis such as this, which attempts to make comparative statements about some aspect of these institutions, must, we would argue, do so with considerable caution. This, however, raises still another set of questions which returns us to the themes addressed at the outset of the paper.

We observed that the literature about the relationship between characteristics of areal units and political competition carried out in the United States have yielded mixed results. This is due in part to the fact that different units have been included in the analyses, as have different kinds of elections. In this context, the seemingly definitive work of Bonjean and Lineberry (1970) using American counties as units of analysis and national election results should perhaps be reexamined in the context of our findings for European cities. Are they able to draw negative conclusions because of the rather heterogeneous unit of analysis chosen or because they have used electoral results which did not have as its reference issues raised at that level of analysis? Would one find different results if one had used American cities, even taking into consideration the complexities of the type of electoral procedures used in local elections in American cities? We are suspicious that even if this hypothesis were tested under the most optimal conditions among American cities—i.e., cities having partisan elections and using local election results—the results may still show few consistent relationships between elements of urban social structure and the degree of political competition. We observed that in these European nations, two of the most important factors associated with political fractionalization, other than population size, were social class and religion. In each of these nations, one or both of these cleavages are reflected in the party system of cities, and, hence, these cleavages, through the mediation of class-based and/or religiously oriented political parties, contribute to the dispersal or concentration of votes. In other words, it is the institutionalization of these cleavages through the intermediary of political parties that largely accounts for the results shown here. In the absence of political parties oriented around cleavages such as these, we would not expect to find similar results, which is our reason for suggesting that we would not expect to find confirmation for a hypothesis linking urban social structure with the degree of political competition among American cities.

Both Sharpe (1973) and Newton (1974) have recently pointed out some distinctive features of local government in the United States as compared with England. One of the more salient features they have pointed out about local politics in the United States is the absence of a Social Democratic Party which mobilizes class cleavages. This means that political parties here are neither ideologically oriented, in comparison with some parties in the European nations considered here, nor do they have a sustained social program. Crenson (1971) argues that local political parties in American cities serve primarily a brokerage function; they do not aggregate collective interests in a social program that is sustained by an ideology. Lowi (1967) has remarked: "Just as responsible, programmatic parties like Europe's, tend to centralize authority, so programmatic parties tend to democratize regimes by keeping legitimacy and policy in close association." From the perspective here, the consequence of having such programmatic parties which mobilize underlying cleavages of the polity would be a closer association between the nature of the social and political structure of cities; their absence would lead us to expect less articulation between social and political structures. Hence, the results of this study of cities in four European nations may sensitize us to some consequences of the absence of such party structures for democracy as well as for legitimacy and public policy in American cities.

Finally, we end with a question about the central concept of this paper, the measure of competition we have employed, and the results we have observed. We noted that fractionalization was lowest in cities with a strong working class and highest in cities with a strong middle class. But does fractionalization really reflect political competition? If a city's voters are polarized along class lines into a left and a right, is this a less competitive city than one dominated by a middle class that is split into a number of different factions which in most cases will unite against the left when the final choice of who governs is made? Obviously, the methods employed in this paper cannot answer this more subtle and difficult question, but we pose this question to remind the reader and ourselves of the complexity of the concept of political competition.

NOTES

1. The French cities included in this study represent an exception to this generalization that is explained in some detail in the text.

2. The 12 cities with a population size of 120,000 or more were Marseille, Lyon, Toulouse, Bordeaux, Nice, Nantes, Strasbourg, Lille, Saint-Etienne, Toulon, Le Havre, and Nancy. Two of these, Marseille and Lyon, along with Paris, were excluded from the analysis because the electoral procedures in effect in these cities in 1965 and 1971 made analysis of the results of these cities quite difficult to compare with those of the other cities. The remaining 10 cities were retained in the analysis, however, even though the electoral procedures for these 10 cities were different in 1959 from electoral procedures used in the remaining 144 cities. Large cities tend to have greater fractionalization of votes in France, irrespective of the electoral laws. Further, inspection of changes in fractionalization scores for cities in the size range of 100,000 to 120,000 showed no consistent changes in fractionalization scores, even though these cities were no longer in 1959 under electoral procedures of proportional representation. We concluded that it would probably introduce more distortion in the results to exclude these 10 cities than to include them, and, therefore, they were retained in the analysis.

3. It should be noted at the outset that voting was obligatory in Italy and Belgium for all of the elections included here. In the Netherlands, voting was obligatory in the 1962 and 1966 elections, but not in 1970. Voting was not obligatory in any of the French local elections.

4. In France, the following categories were grouped into the middle-class occupational category: industrialists and wholesalers, liberal professionals and higher cadres, and middle-level cadres. Foremen, specialized workers, lower blue-collar, miners, sailors, and fishermen were grouped into the working-class category. Not included in either of these categories were lower white-collar, artisans, small retailers, domestics, other service personnel, salaried agricultural workers, and farmers.

In Belgium, middle-class occupations included liberal professionals, top managers, managers under employment contracts, higher white-collar occupations such as middle managers, priests, professors, judges, and military officers. The working class included the category of workers. Excluded were lower clerks, aides, the unemployed, and the military.

In Italy, the middle-class category included entrepreneurs with at least one non-kin employee with a contract, higher cadres, and liberal professionals or non-self-employed managers and salaried employees. Lower-class occupational categories included wage workers and helpers.

In the Netherlands, middle-class occupations included higher occupational categories and white-collar employees; the working class included the category of workers; helpers and unemployed were not included in either of these two groupings. The publications of the Central Bureau of Statistics gave no categories more discriminating than this.

In Belgium, high educational attainment was defined as persons of age fourteen or older and no longer enrolled in school, who had a high school (lycee) and/or higher diploma or its equivalent.

In Italy, the measure of high educational attainment was the ratio of persons with a high school diploma or its equivalent to the number of males and females age fourteen or older.

In the Netherlands, high educational attainment was based on the "overall level of education" for the population of a city age fourteen or older and no longer enrolled in school. The category which included medium, semi-higher, and higher levels of education was used as the measure of high educational attainment. This was roughly equivalent to high school or more education; approximately eleven percent of the Dutch population of age fourteen or older who were not attending school were included in this category.

5. The French census provides information on thirty labor force sectors. The Belgian and Italian Census of Population provides information about nine labor force sectors. However, only four labor force categories are available for the Netherlands. In each case the labor force residing in the city, not the labor force working in the city, is used.

6. In French cities, the tertiary sector includes the following labor force categories: commerce; banks and insurance; services; water, gas, and electricity; radio and other; and public administration. Among Belgian cities, the tertiary sector includes the following labor force categories: electricity, gas, and water; commerce; banks, insurance, and real estate; transport, storage, and communications; and services. The tertiary sector for Italian cities is approximately the same as for Belgian cities. Finally, the tertiary sector among Dutch cities includes labor force categories other than agriculture and industry.

REFERENCES

AIKEN, M. and H. VAN HASSEL (1970) "De sociale struktuur en het politieke proces." Res Publica 12: 379-425.

ALLUM, P. A. (1973) Italy—Republic Without Government? New York: W. W. Norton.

ALT, J. (1971) "Some social and political correlates of county borough expenditures." British J. of Pol. Sci. 1 (January): 48-62.

BARNES, S. H. (1974) "Italy: religion and class in electoral behavior," pp. 171-225 in R. Rose (ed.) Electoral Behavior: A Comparative Handbook. New York: Free Press.

——— (1966) "Italy: oppositions on left, right, and center," pp. 303-331 in R. A. Dahl (ed.) Political Oppositions in Western Democracies. New Haven: Yale Univ. Press.

BON, F. and J. RANGER (1972) "Bilan des elections municipales de mars 1971 dans les villes de plus de 30,000 habitants." Revue francaise de science politique 22 (April): 213-237.

BONJEAN, C. M. and R. L. LINEBERRY (1970) "The urbanization-party competition hypothesis: a comparison of all United States counties." J. of Politics 32 (May): 305-321.

CAPECCHI, V., V. CIONI POLACCHINI, G. GALLI, and G. SIVINI (1968) Il comportamento elettorale in Italia. Bologna: Il Mulino.

CASSTEVENS, T. W. and C. PRESS (1963) "The context of democratic competition in American state politics." Amer. J. of Sociology 68 (March): 536-543.

CATLIN, D. S. (1968) "Toward a functionalist theory of political parties," pp. 217-246 in W. J. Crotty (ed.) Approaches to the Study of Party Organization. Boston: Allyn & Bacon.

COULTER, P. and G. GORDON (1968) "Urbanization and party competition: critique and redirection of theoretical research." Western Pol. Q. 21 (June): 274-287.

CRAYBECKX, L. (1960) "Problems linguistiques." Socialisme 7 (November): 789-796.

CRENSON, M. A. (1971) The Un-Politics of Air Pollution. Baltimore: Johns Hopkins Press.

CUTRIGHT, P. (1963) "Urbanization and competitive party politics." J. of Politics 25 (August): 552-564.

DAALDER, H. (1966) "The Netherlands: opposition in a segmented society," pp. 188-236 in R. A. Dahl (ed.) Political Oppositions in Western Democracies. New Haven: Yale Univ. Press.

DAVID, P. T. (1972) "How can an index of party competition best be derived?" J. of Politics 34 (May): 632-638.

DAWSON, R. E. (1967) "Social development, party competition and policy," pp. 203-237 in W. N. Chambers and W. D. Burnham (eds.) The American Party System: Stages of Political Development. New York: Oxford Univ. Press.

——— and J. A. ROBINSON (1963) "Inter-party competition, economic variables, and welfare policies in the American states." J. of Politics 25 (May): 265-289.

DeBAKKER, B. and M. CLAEYS-VAN HAEGENDOREN (1973) "The Socialist Party in the party system and in organized socialism in Belgium." Res Publica 15: 237-247.

EPSTEIN, L. D. (1956) "Size of place and the division of the two-party vote in Wisconsin." Western Pol. Q. 9 (1956): 138-150.

EULAU, H. (1957) "The ecological basis of party systems: the case of Ohio." Midwest J. of Pol. Sci. 1 (August): 125-135.

FRANKLIN, B. J. (1971) "Urbanization and party competition: a note on shifting conceptualization and a report of further data." Social Forces 49 (June): 544-548.

GALLI, G. and A. PRANDI (1970) Patterns of Political Participation in Italy. New Haven: Yale Univ. Press.

GATLIN, D. S. (1968) "Toward a functionalist theory of political parties," pp. 217-246 in W. J. Crotty (ed.) Approaches to the Study of Party Organization. Boston: Allyn & Bacon.

GIBBS, J. P. and W. T. MARTIN (1962) "Urbanization, technology, and the division of labor: international patterns." Amer. Soc. Rev. 27 (October).

GOLD, D. and J. R. SCHMIDHAUSER (1960) "Urbanization and party competition: the case of Iowa." Midwest J. of Pol. Sci. 4 (February): 62-75.

GOLEMBIEWSKI, R. T. (1958) "A taxonomic approach to state political party strength." Western Pol. Q. 11 (September): 494-513.

GORDON, G. and P. COULTER (1969) "The sociological bases of party competition: the case of Massachusetts." Soc. Q. 10 (Winter): 84-105.

GROSSER, A. (1966) "France: nothing but opposition," pp. 284-302 in R. A. Dahl (ed.) Political Oppositions in Western Democracies. New Haven: Yale Univ. Press.

HEISLER, M. O. (1974) "Institutionalizing societal cleavages in a cooptive polity: the growing importance of the output side in Belgium," pp. 178-220 in M. O. Heisler (ed.) Politics in Europe: Structures and Processes in some Postindustrial Democracies. New York: David McKay.

HILL, K. (1974) "Belgium: political change in a segmented society," pp. 29-107 in R. Rose (ed.) Electoral Behavior: A Comparative Handbook. New York: Free Press.

HUMES, S. and E. MARTIN (1969) The Structure of Local Government. The Hague: International Union of Local Authorities.

IKE, M. (1969) "Urbanization and political opposition: the Philippines and Japan." Asian Studies 7 (August): 134-141.

KELLY, G. A. (1969) "Belgium: new nationalism in an old world." Comp. Politics 1 (April): 343-365.

KESSELMAN, M. (1970) "Overinstitutionalization and political constraint." Comp. Politics 3 (October): 21-44.

――― (1967) The Ambiguous Consensus: A Study of Local Government in France. New York: Alfred A. Knopf.

――― (1966) French local politics: a statistical examination of grass roots consensus." Amer. Pol. Sci. Rev. 60 (December): 963-973.

LAPONCE, J. A. and R. S. UHLER (1974) "Measuring electoral cleavages in a multiparty system." Comp. Pol. Studies 7 (April): 3-25.

LEE, C. J. (1971) "Urban political competition in a developing nation: the case of Korea." Comp. Pol. Studies 4 (April): 107-115.

LEVY, M. G. (1960) La Querelle du Recensement. Brussels: Institut Belge de Science Politique.

LIEBERSON, S. (1969) "Measuring population diversity." Amer. Soc. Rev. 34 (December): 850-862.

LIJPHART, A. (1974) "The Netherlands: continuity and change in voting behavior," pp. 227-268 in R. Rose (ed.) Electoral Behavior. New York: Free Press.

――― (1969) "Consociational democracy." World Politics 21 (January): 205-227.

――― (1968) The Politics of Accommodations: Pluralism and Democracy in the Netherlands. Berkeley: Univ. of California Press.

LIPSET, S. M. and S. ROKKAN (1967) Party Systems and Voter Alignments. New York: Free Press.

LORWIN, V. R. (1971) "Segmented pluralism: ideological cleavages and political cohesion in the smaller European democracies." Comp. Politics 3 (January): 141-174.

――― (1970) "Linguistic pluralism and political tension in modern Belgium." Canadian J. of History 5 (March): 1-23.

——— (1966) "Belgium: religion, class, and language in national politics," pp. 147-187 in R. A. Dahl (ed.) Political Oppositions in Western Democracies. New Haven: Yale Univ. Press.

LOWI, T. J. (1967) "Party, policy, and constitution in America," pp. 236-276 in W. N. Chambers and W. D. Burnham (eds.) The American Party System: Stages of Political Development. New York: Oxford Univ. Press.

MASTERS, R. A. and D. S. WRIGHT (1958) "Trends and variations in the two-party vote: the case of Michigan." Amer. Pol. Sci. Rev. 52 (December): 1078-1090.

MILDER, N. D. (1974) "Definitions and measures of the degree of macro-level party competition in multiparty systems." Comp. Pol. Studies 6 (January): 431-456.

NEWTON, K. (1974) "Community decision makers and community decision-making in England and the United States," pp. 55-86 in Terry N. Clark (ed.) Comparative Community Politics. New York: Halsted Press. (A Sage Publications Book)

PFEIFFER, D. G. (1967) "The measurement of inter-party competition and systematic stability." Amer. Pol. Sci. Rev. 61 (June): 457-467.

PRYCE, R. (1957) The Italian Local Elections 1956. London: Chatto & Windus.

QUEVIT, M. and M. AIKEN (1975) "La competition politique an sein du systeme politique Belge: 1919-1974." Courrier Hebdomadaire, Centre de Recherche et d' information socio-politiques (24 January): 669-670.

RAE, D. (1971) "Comment on Wildgen's 'The measurement of hyperfractionalization.' " Comp. Pol. Studies 4 (July): 244-245.

——— (1968) "A note on the fractionalization of some European party systems." Comp. Pol. Studies 3 (October): 413-418.

RAE, W. D. and M. TAYLOR (1970) The Analysis of Political Cleavages. New Haven: Yale Univ. Press.

RANNEY, A. (1965) "Parties in state politics," pp. 61-99 in H. Jacobs and K. N. Vines (eds.) Politics in the American States. Boston: Little, Brown.

SARTORI, G. (1966) "European political parties: the case of polarized pluralism," pp. 137-176 in J. LaPalombara and M. Weiner (eds.) Political Parties and Political Development. Princeton: Princeton University Press.

SHARPE, L. J. (1973) "American democracy reconsidered: parts I and II." British J. of Pol. Sci. 3: 1-28, 29-167.

STERN, M. (1972) "Measuring interparty competition: a proposal and a test of a method." J. of Politics 34 (August): 889-904.

URWIN, D. W. (1970) "Social cleavages and political parties in Belgium: problems of institutionalization." Pol. Studies 18 (September): 320-340.

WALTON, J. and J. A. SWEEN (1971) "Urbanization, industrialization and voting in Mexico: a longitudinal analysis of official and opposition party support." Social Sci. Q. 52 (December): 721-745.

WILDGEN, J. K. (1972) "Electoral formulae and the number of parties." J. of Politics 34 (August): 943-949.

——— (1971) "The measurement of hyperfractionalization." Comp. Pol. Studies 4 (July): 233-243.

ZODY, R. E. and N. R. LUTTBEG (1968) "An evaluation of various measures of state party competition." Western Pol. Q. 21: 723-724.

Chapter 8

URBAN ORIGINS AND CONSEQUENCES OF NATIONAL AND LOCAL POLITICAL TRANSFORMATION IN ETHIOPIA

PETER KOEHN

National politics in Ethiopia was radically transformed in 1974 and 1975. Following widespread urban unrest, the constitution and parliament of Ethiopia were suspended, Emperor Haile Selassie was arrested and his property was declared nationalized, and leaders of the armed forces assumed power. Subsequently, members of the ruling elite under Haile Selassie were decimated by execution, and the new military rulers abolished one of the world's oldest monarchies (see Koehn, 1975: 7-14 for details).

The grievances and groups which provoked these radical actions were concentrated in urban Ethiopia. Political change at the national level was secured once the authority of the traditional monarchical regime was challenged by powerful urban collectivities drawn together by the aggravation of economic conditions and shared ideological perspectives.

AUTHOR'S NOTE: *The author gratefully acknowledges support received from the University of Montana Foundation which enabled him to return to Ethiopia during the summer of 1975 and to update and expand upon material contained in an earlier version of this chapter. This chapter is based upon a revision of a paper delivered by the author at the Sixteenth Annual Meeting of the African Studies Association, Syracuse, New York, October 31-November 3, 1973.*

In addition to analysis of the national political roles played by urban-based elites during 1974 and 1975, this chapter contains an assessment of the potential impact of change at the center on municipal government and politics.[1] Of particular interest is whether national political transformation is likely to result in changes at the local level that will improve significantly the quality of life experienced by urban residents.

Contemporary urban politics in Ethiopia has been characterized by widespread suspicion and a high incidence of conflict between central government authorities and urban elites. Yet, pre-coup events in 1974 demonstrated that radical students and military men could coordinate their actions in the pursuit of shared objectives and exercise considerable political power in the process. Subsequently, the rift between central authorities and urban elites has reopened. Continuation of interelite conflict would retard and possibly preclude institutionalization of the radical changes being advanced for the purpose of improving urban living conditions in Ethiopia. Conflict among central and municipal government officials, students, and leaders of selected urban associations thus constitutes a recurring concern of this chapter.

URBANIZATION IN ETHIOPIA

The northernmost provinces of Ethiopia have been the locus of some measures of urban life for at least eighteen centuries (Comhaire, 1967: 28). However, few urban settlements grew up until recently in the southern reaches of the area that makes up the state of Ethiopia today (Howath, 1968: 42) and the history of urbanization in northern Ethiopia has been characterized by abrupt ebbs and flows.[2] Historically, the major factors responsible for expansion of the number of towns and for their growth were the caravan trade, the proliferation of regional capitals ruled by provincial lords, the constant shifting of the location of the capital city of the Empire until the designation of Addis' Ababa as capital by Emperor Menelik in 1887, and the establishment of military garrisons in conquered southern provinces (Comhaire, 1967: 27-29; Pankhurst, 1965: 60-83, 1966: 52; Akalou Wolde-Michael, 1968: 3; Weissleder, 1964: 1). More recently, towns have grown up along the Addis Ababa-Djibouti railway line, in response to the Italian occupation (Howath, 1968: 45-46), and around important natural resource centers. At the western end of the Addis Ababa-Djibouti railway, the towns of Akaki, Debre Zeit, Mojo, and Nazaret form an industrial region with Addis Ababa which contains most of Ethiopia's largest firms.

Although there is a long history of urban settlement in Ethiopia, the country is far from highly urbanized. About 10 percent of the total population live in towns and only 6.5 percent inhabit urban centers that encompass more than 20,000 people.[3] Although the proportion of Ethiopia's total population living in towns is not high, the single city of Addis Ababa (population one million) accounts for one-third of the total town population. Addis Ababa is the most populous city in East and Central Africa; its population is increasing by 7.0 percent annually, while the town population of Ethiopia as a whole is growing at a rate of 6.6 percent per annum (Ethiopia, Central Statistical Office, 1972: 1, 9).

UTILITY OF AN URBAN PERSPECTIVE IN STUDIES OF POLITICAL CHANGE

The major urban centers of Ethiopia represented the most likely geographical loci of political change. Regardless of the relative merits of arguments favoring agricultural or industrial priorities in strategies designed to, foster economic development and independence (see, for instance, United Nations Economic Commission for Africa, 1972: 180; United Nations Food and Agriculture Organization, 1972: 116), decisions concerning the present and future allocation of national resources are made in *urban* areas, by *urban* elites.[4] As Samuel Huntington observes, "The city is still but a small growth in society as a whole, but the groups within the city are able to employ their superior skills, location, and concentration to dominate the politics of the society at the national level" (Huntington, 1968: 74). The African city (particularly the capital city) is where the vital decisions with regard to resource distribution and/ or redistribution are made and, executed (or are not made and remain unexecuted).[5]

Huntington tends to equate revolution with fundamental social transformation. In predominantly rural countries, this, by definition, involves rural peasants. However, social transformation also may be accomplished *for* rural peasants (through the exercise of governmental power by urban elites) rather than *by* peasants.[6] Revolutions initiated *by* peasants require a high level of political consciousness, which generally is absent except when it has been inspired and sustained by a revolutionary (urban-based) government (see Huntington, 1968: 291-301).[7]

In Ethiopia (outside of Eritrea), there was little reason to expect that rural peasants were approaching the requisite revolutionary level of political consciousness in 1974.[8] Urban-rural migration provided a release valve for revolutionary pressures in rural Ethiopia. Thus, those who focused on rural social or political conditions foresaw little prospect of fundamental change on the horizon. In contrast, the urban vantage point turned out to possess considerable utility for explaining the important phenomenon of change in this African country.

MATERIAL CONDITIONS OF LIFE IN URBAN ETHIOPIA

Irrespective of the fact that a preponderance of political power is concentrated in urban jurisdictions, life is difficult for most urban dwellers in Ethiopia. Objective living conditions are deplorable throughout urban Ethiopia (see Koehn, 1973a: 116-125). Capital accumulation in urban areas other than Addis Ababa, Asmara, and Dire Dawa is constrained by the absence of significant industrial development. The vast majority of Ethiopia's towns serve as administrative and educational centers, with small-scale trading constituting the principal commercial activity (Markakis, 1974: 164-167). Underemployment and unemployment are widespread. Most urbanites live in overcrowded and substandard housing units (see Ethiopia, Ministry of Public Works, 1967: 27). Certain densely populated areas of the largest cities are completely inaccessible by road. The inhabitants of such areas are isolated from water outlets, refuse collection and sewage disposal, fire and police protection, and other essential urban services. Sanitary conditions generally are poor in the urban areas of Ethiopia. Outbreaks of communicable diseases, such as typhus, relapsing fever, cholera, and typhoid fever are common. Tuberculosis, microbile and parasitic ailment, worm infestations, trachoma, and venereal diseases infect a large proportion of the urban population. The infant mortality rate is exceptionally high and malnutrition among surviving children is widespread. Professional medical treatment and health education are made available only to a small percentage of those who are in need.

IMPACT OF URBANIZATION

The problems facing urban residents in Ethiopia are being compounded rather than relieved, due to governmental inaction in the face of a high rate of rural-urban migration. As a consequence of rapid urbanization, the demands and problems accompanying modernization tend to cluster and become most urgent and severe in the largest metropolitan areas. Planners must struggle to keep the urban economy growing at a pace commensurate with urban population increases. Urban overcrowding aggravates poor transportation, housing, sanitation, and health conditions. Since it is highly unlikely that the rate of urbanization will be reversed or even reduced in Ethiopia, problems of urban development must be faced directly by responsible municipal and central government officials.

PERFORMANCE OF LOCAL GOVERNMENT
STRUCTURES IN URBAN ETHIOPIA

Ethiopian municipalities are assigned a long list of local functions under national legislation.[9] In practice, even the largest and wealthiest municipal governments find it impossible to perform many of these functions.[10] The major municipalities have not emphasized the provision of public services other than roads. Practically the entire capital expenditure budget of the Municipalities of Addis Ababa and Asmara has been devoted to the construction of monumental projects such as stadiums and office buildings, or to road construction and maintenance. Only token sums have been expended by these municipal governments on social welfare, housing, health, fire protection, and sanitation.

In small towns, municipal offices are often closed and key officials cannot be located. The vast majority of smaller municipalities, and many larger ones, do not yet operate departments responsible for the provision of ·such basic public services as medical treatment, water, and fire protection.

The principal activities carried on by municipalities in Ethiopia are the maintenance of order, tax and revenue collection, and the licensing of businesses. The failure of municipal governments to provide even the most basic human.services is reflected in the fact that in 1963 only 21 of the 210 municipalities had piped water supplies, 6 had fire protection, 5 possessed slaughterhouses, 6 had sanitation facilities, 4 contained parks for recreation, and 57 had electricity schemes. The situation improved only slightly in the next decade (Mesfin Wolde Mariam, 1969: 27; Mohammed Umer, 1972: 120). In short, Ethiopian municipalities have done little to alleviate the unfortunate conditions which surround most dwellers.

They have received little positive assistance at the national level from the Ministry of Interior's Municipalities Department. The Municipalities Department developed grandiose plans for assisting municipal governments in development-oriented projects. In practice, however, the department has offered technical advice and supervision and financial support on an extremely limited basis, principally in the construction of water supply systems, roads, and office buildings, the design of local master plans, the conduct of land surveys, and the administration of financial affairs (Bekele Haile, 1971). The department was sharply criticized on the floor of the

Chamber of Deputies in September of 1974 for wasting money on unful-
filled master plans, for general inaction and for actually retarding development in several towns (Ethiopian Herald, September 5, 1974: 1).

PROSPECTS FOR CHANGE IN MUNICIPAL
GOVERNMENT PERFORMANCE

The obstacles encountered by Ethiopian municipal governments in the
provision of urban social services involve the mobilization of local resources and central government control.

MOBILIZATION OF LOCAL RESOURCES

Large and small municipalities alike have been characterized by failure
to mobilize the resources needed to facilitate the accomplishment of their
legal responsibilities. The dimensions of the resource mobilization failure
are revealed most starkly when municipal revenue accumulations and
collection procedures are investigated. In 1971, 121 of the 210 municipalities in the empire operated with budgets that did not exceed E $25,000
(approximately U.S. $13,000) and 46 of these worked with revenues of
less than E $10,000 (Norris, 1974: 55).

Ethiopian municipalities have been allowed to raise revenues directly by
employing a variety of fees and taxes. Nevertheless, municipal land tax
rates have been uniformly flat rather than progressive and are set at an
extremely low level. The tax on rented property was not fully enforced
because of problems officials experienced when they attempted to distinguish between rented and unrented edifices. In some municipal areas,
local officials have been unable to collect fees for water service from
influential urban dwellers. Even in Addis Ababa, actual municipal revenue
collection consistently has fallen far below the potential level. A 1971
study carried out by the Revenue Department of the Municipality discovered that roughly E $1,000,000 in land and building taxes remained
uncollected each year in *one* of the ten city districts alone, while total land
and building tax revenues actually received by the Municipality in that
year only amounted to E $2,350,000 (Addis Ababa Municipality, 1971:
4-5).

Moreover, Ethiopia is one of the world's poorest nations—and most of
its urban areas are devoid of large-scale economic activity. When it is not
possible to undertake capital-intensive or capital-extensive urban development projects, mobilizing human energies must be relied upon extensively

if programs designed to improve living conditions for large numbers of lower-class urban dwellers are to be carried out (Hunter, 1967: 23). However, the efforts made by municipal governments throughout Ethiopia to involve residents in community improvement projects have not been extensive or intensive in practice, nor particularly impressive in outcome (Koehn and Koehn, 1975).

Finally, most municipal governments have not attracted competent and dedicated staff at higher and lower levels in the administrative hierarchy. As a result, the official energies and skills required for the accomplishment of municipal development projects have not been forthcoming. Municipal personnel serving in outlying towns are particularly poorly qualified to perform development administration roles.[11] A 1971 report by the vice minister in charge of the Municipalities Department of the Ministry of Interior bluntly states that "most chief town officers lack the administrative ability and technical competence to administer their towns" (Bekele Haile, 1971). The failure of local governments to recruit qualified administrative personnel, particularly in technical positions, also extends to the largest municipality in Ethiopia. In 1969, less than thirty percent of the employees of the Addis Ababa Municipality had completed beyond a fourth-grade education (Tadesse Gebu, 1969: 6-8). Many of the technical and supervisory positions in the Municipality of Addis Ababa were filled by persons who had attained, at most, four years of schooling (Public Administration Service, 1970: 40).

Graft is one form of material energy collected in substantial sums by municipal officials (Koehn, 1973a: 174-179).[12] In Ethiopia, wealthy urban landlords, governmental elites, and foreign businessmen have possessed a disproportionate capacity to offer illegal monetary rewards. As a consequence, bribes have induced urban administrators to place priority on elite concerns and have weakened bureaucratic resolve to challenge the local status quo and pursue municipal activities intended for the benefit of low-income urban dwellers. It is significant in this regard that the lord mayors of the two largest Ethipian municipalities (Addis Ababa and Asmara) were among the first officials placed under arrest on charges of corruption and improper use of public money in 1974.

CENTRAL GOVERNMENT CONTROL

Ethiopian municipalities have not only been constrained by their own inability to mobilize financial resources and human energies and skills; their functional performances also have been retarded by central government interference in their affairs. Prior to the coup d'etat of 1974, central government control over municipalities was based upon two normative predispositions which constrained, rather than facilitated, performance at the local level. First, rapid and fundamental urban social, economic, and political change was not valued, and efforts to initiate such change were actively discouraged. And, the devolution of authority to municipal governments was unacceptable to central elites.

Much of the blame for municipal nonperformance in human service areas must be borne by the central government. Emperor Haile Selassie's policy of appointing rivals to contiguous posts in the local government hierarchy and the unintegrated nature of the system ensured that conflict and confusion would characterize urban administration in Ethiopia. As a result, urban living conditions progressively deteriorated while municipal administrators were preoccupied by communication failures and conflicts among themselves and between themselves and provincial and subprovincial governors, central government field officers, and executives of public corporations.

In addition, the central government failed to provide incentives that would encourage the development of human service and popular participation orientations among municipal employees. The monarchical regime of Emperor Haile Selassie I evidenced little interest in norms of efficient administrative behavior and *public* service (Markakis, 1974: 335). Not even *investigative* action was taken against municipal officials who were accused of being corrupt and self-serving.[13] Although only a tiny proportion of Ethiopia's urban populace owned both the home they lived in and the land they dwelled upon and the majority of urbanites owned neither, the central government gave virtually no support to the concept of urban land redistribution or to the construction of low-income housing. At the request of Addis Ababa landowners, in contrast, Emperor Haile Selassie personally intervened in municipal council affairs in 1966 to obtain a delay in increased land tax rates (Amelash Beyene and Markakis, 1966-1967: 35).

Under Haile Selassie, the government was unwilling to implement measures that would generate widespread participation in local political activity and might lead to demands for the redistribution of power and wealth in Ethiopian society. In fact, *all* associations that threatened to engage in overt political acts were deliberately and vigorously suppressed (Markakis, 1974: 331). Since the Emperor ruled by virtue of divine authority invested in him, there was no need to develop institutions specifically designed to organize popular support.

The functional performance of Ethiopian municipalities also has been affected adversely by fiscal constraints imposed at the center and by the national government's unwillingness to delegate authority to cities and towns in the areas of taxation, zoning, and law enforcement (Koehn, 1973a: 170-173, 248-251, 264).[14] As a consequence, municipalities have been beset by chronic shortages of crucial facilitating media—i.e., money and power.

For instance, all revenues collected by a municipality are supposed to be exclusively reserved for the operation of the municipality and the performance of municipal functions. In practice, however, those few municipal governments which have succeeded in raising particularly large amounts of revenues have been kept from spending them by a variety of techniques employed by the Municipalities Department of the Ministry of Interior. First, the budgets of municipalities are not approved by the Municipalities Department until six or seven months *after* the commencement of a new fiscal year. Lengthy delays forced municipal governments to operate for most of the year under the constraints of previous-year figures in the case of recurrent expenditures and to postpone *new capital* investments. As a result, the municipalities found it impossible to expend all collected revenues within the fiscal year on those rare occasions when expenditures for new development were authorized by the Municipalities Department.

Until recently, the Municipalities Department collected all unexpended monies from revenue-rich municipalities at the end of the fiscal year. This money was reissued later as grants or development loans, without interest, usually to poorer municipalities. The most important factors that determined which municipalities obtained these capital improvement loans were the personalities and central political connections of the provincial governor-generals or enderassies, rather than demonstrated need and capacity to utilize the money effectively. This constraining practice was resented by revenue-surplus municipalities—usually the larger towns. The chief town officers of several municipalities decided to refuse to deposit surplus revenues in banks in the name of the Municipalities Department. This strategy enabled them to keep the money on hand for local developmental expenditures. Perhaps in retaliation, the Municipalities Department fails to grant much of the revenue collected from a central government import/export tax that is supposed to be earmarked for distribution to municipalities on a proportional basis.

Progressive municipal officials have encountered great difficulties in increasing local revenues—partly because of extended delay at the central government level in approving and publishing increased municipal tax rates, and partly because municipalities lack power to tax church property, to charge interest on overdue taxes, or to revoke licenses for failure to satisfy municipal requirements. Most significantly, municipalities do not control the police force needed to secure public compliance on tax matters.

The financial position of Ethiopian municipalities deteriorated further following the nationalization of urban land and extra houses by the Derg in August of 1975. Revenue from taxes on urban land and house rentals had made up a major source of income for municipal governments throughout Ethiopia prior to the nationalization action.

PREREQUISITE FOR URBAN CHANGE IN ETHIOPIA

Lack of commitment to change at the center of the Ethiopian political system constituted a pervasive obstacle to social and economic progress in urban settings. The autocratic central government constrained municipal efforts to mobilize revenues for and involve people in urban social service programs and blocked reforms aimed at providing municipalities with greater authority to respond to local problems. Significant improvement in urban living conditions could have been effectuated by Ethiopian municipalities if the central government had taken steps to reshape the unintegrated prefectoral system, revamp the local government bureaucracy at all levels, divert revenues into municipal coffers, grant municipalities increased authority over local affairs, and provide incentives aimed at encouraging a human service orientation among administrators and participation in development projects among urban inhabitants. None of these actions was initiated.

Therefore, *regime change at the center* was an indispensable ingredient in any scenario destined to result in expansion and extension of the urban social services provided by municipal governments. The next section of this chapter analyzes pre-coup urban conditions relevant to prospects for regime change in Ethiopia, employing the concepts *facilitation* and *control*. Values and norms are expected to shape or control behavior, while material resources along with group and individual role actions provide the energy or facilities needed to change (or sustain) a given social or political pattern (Parsons, 1966: 28-29; Scaritt, 1972a, 1972b). Societal conditions in Addis Ababa—the center of national political activity in Ethiopia—constitute the focal point of the following analysis.

BACKGROUND TO POLITICAL CHANGE

Most of the ingredients necessary for political change were in place in Addis Ababa by the early 1970s. Driving energy needed for change was latent in the form of widespread economic dissatisfaction. A clearly defined set of alternative values was articulated by an urban intelligentsia committed to pursuing strategies of rapid and fundamental change. Collectivities (armed forces, labor unions, student organization) which possessed power to effectuate far-reaching changes in the national political system were growing in strength as the power of traditional forces declined in urban areas. The problem remained, however, of linking these disparate change-oriented ingredients into a unified movement. The most serious manifestation of this obstacle to change existed at the collectivity level, where uncoordinated radical political activities could be repressed with facility by the government. Nevertheless, students who had learned the importance of linking deviant value orientations with mass agitation played an instrumental role in promoting political change during this period.

ECONOMIC CONDITIONS: POTENTIAL ENERGY FOR CHANGE

Primarily as a result of inequities in the distribution of material resources, Addis Ababa constituted a capital city largely populated by persons suffering serious economic hardship at the turn of the decade of the 1970s. Industrial growth had been concentrated in the private manufacturing sector rather than among labor-intensive construction activities. And industrial operations and expansion in the capital region was essentially confined to firms owned and managed by expatriates (Duri Mohammed, 1969: 55, 56, 58). Inequities in the accumulation of wealth and material goods were reinforced by elite ownership of land and property, [15] the lack of progressive taxation, and failure of the Addis Ababa Municipality in providing public services. While wealthy urbanites were able to purchase modern services and comforts, such material benefits remained beyond the reach of most urban dwellers in Addis Ababa as long as governmental structures did not provide them. A high rate of inflation exacerbated economic conditions, particularly for poor persons. [16]

The Addis Ababa lumpenproletariat represented a potentially explosive nonelite segment of society in the early 1970s. Belief that there is nothing to lose and everything to gain by revolting against the established structure of society can provoke such a consistently frustrated nonelite group to engage in violent political acts. However, the intellectual elite plays an indispensible role in raising the political consciousness of consistently frustrated groups to a volatile level. Where the material gap between rich and poor is vast and continuing to expand, as in Addis Ababa at the time, the role of intellectuals in raising consciousness of economic exploitation among the mass of under- and unemployed urban residents is made easier.[17] And the collective political and social ideals of Ethiopian students were frustrated consistently after the failure of the 1960 coup d' etat. Later, as an increasing proportion of secondary and university graduates, as well as school leaders, were unable to find urban jobs commensurate with their expectations (Ginzberg and Smith, 1967: 77; Huntington, 1968: 186-187), intellectuals also experienced abrupt frustration of material aspirations for self and family that had been encouraged in the government educational system (Koehn, 1972; Andreas Eshete, 1968: 6-21).

DEVIANT VALUE ORIENTATIONS

The limited modernization measures permitted by Emperor Haile Selassie alienated former supporters of the traditional political system (Huntington, 1968: 188). At the same time, many of those exposed to modern institutions came to reject the traditional authority structure and groups which were denied participation became increasingly aware of and upset by discrimination in official circles. By the mid-1960s, most high school and university students in Addis Ababa adhered to a clearly differentiated set of values calling for radical change in the social, economic, and political status quo. These intellectuals rejected the professed legitimacy of the traditional authority in governmental structures than students from any of the five other African nations included in their sample (Klineberg and Zavalloni, 1969: 222). Orthodox Marxian ideology was espoused by a few student leaders, who tended to be more articulate and radical than the bulk of the membership of the movement. Most politically active students also advocated land redistribution (by force, if necessary) to achieve greater equity in ownership, an end to corruption, and extensive government control of the economy.

Values are important for political change from a second, means-related perspective. Values direct the selection of strategies destined to shape the outcome of political events. The early 1970s marked a significant shift in the means-related values (or norms) directing the Ethiopian student movement. Partly as a result of the frustrations many students experienced during the year they were required to spend in national service in the provinces, the movement's emphasis upon consciousness-raising among rural peasants was gradually abandoned in favor of public demonstrations of solidarity with disaffected urban groups.

Opposition to the autocratic rule and distributive policies of Emperor Haile Selassie I grew more violent in 1971. High school and university students boycotted classes, demonstrated in the streets of Addis Ababa, clashed with police, stoned buses, and protested inflated prices by overturning market stalls. Workers and unemployed urbanites took to the streets and marketplace to join students in protests against higher prices for transporation and food. The armed forces were called upon to restore order. However, they made no overt move to overthrow the monarchy (see Koehn and Hayes, 1973: 23-27).

URBAN COLLECTIVITIES: THE NEED FOR COHESIVE ACTION

The spring crisis of 1971 demonstrated that students possessed the capacity to create urban chaos by linking their ideological and leadership abilities with spontaneous mass protest activity. However, students alone among the organized collectivities of the capital openly engaged in anti-system acts. Other groups, particularly labor unions and progressive units of the armed forces, had to be brought into the political struggle in order to sustain and channel anti-regime predispositions and energies (see Arrighi and Saul, 1973: 84).

PRE-COUP EVENTS OF 1974

Signs of dissatisfaction within the ranks of the military surfaced in early 1974, when mutinies broke out in Neghelli (army) and Debre Zeit (air force) over employment conditions in the armed services and the government's handling of drought relief in Wollo. These revolts coincided with sudden aggravation of already severe inflationary trends in urban areas by extraordinary price increases for fuel and with teacher and parental resentment toward the government's plan to reorient the educational system in rural and vocational directions, limit salary increments for teachers, and restrict growth in secondary school and university enrollments.

Students seized the opportunity provided by the mutinies and public unrest. They initiated demonstrations against higher prices and the government's handling of famine conditions in Wollo and demanded wage increases, free public education, land redistribution, a secular state, and other radical changes. On February 18, a strike by teachers closed public schools throughout the empire. Taxi drivers went on strike in protest against increased gasoline costs. Violent demonstrations broke out in Addis Ababa. During the ten days that followed, student rioters were joined by striking taxi drivers and part of the Addis Ababa lumpenproletariat and were cheered on by parents and teachers. Public transportation in the capital city was brought to a standstill by their actions. Even some private vehicles were attacked.

As in 1971, the military was called upon to restore order. Many demonstrating students were arrested and some were wounded or killed by police. On this occasion, however, the mobilization of the armed forces was accompanied by mutinies within the lower ranks of the army's second division (Asmara), the navy (Massawa), the third army division (Harar), and the air force (Debre Zeit). Finally, rebellion spread to the fourth army division stationed in Addis Ababa.

The government reduced gasoline prices, imposed price controls on all essential goods, and announced a pay increase for privates. These actions were not sufficient to mollify the dissident soldiers, who demanded larger pay increases, the dismissal of the Cabinet of Prime Minister Aklilu Habte Wolde on account of its failure to deal effectively with the problems of drought and inflation, and major social and political reforms. On February 28, the Cabinet resigned and a new government, with Endalkachew Makonnen named as Prime Minister, was appointed by Haile Selassie. After initial hesitation, the Emperor also capitulated to the demands for higher military pay.

For the next six months, reformist elements within the ranks of the military were able to consolidate their power at the expense of the monarchy. Young, educated officers began to organize dissident troops. The Derg, or Provisional Military Administrative Committee,[18] secured one concession after another from the Emperor. Many of the most powerful figures in the previous government, in parliament, and among the landed aristocracy were arrested. The Endalkachew Makonnen cabinet was forced to resign. Finally, the Derg suspended Parliament and the Constitution, disbanded the Emperor's personal military staff, nationalized his palace, and arrested Haile Selassie.

Although the military performed the final acts in this revolutionary drama, the resignation of the Endalkachew Makonnen cabinet and the Emperor's ouster were undeniably hastened by the worker strikes, civil servant work stoppages, and urban unrest sustained by dedicated students which took place concurrently with military pressure during this period. During the intermittent disturbances which plagued Ethiopia from February through September of 1974, students allied themselves with the grievances of teachers, parents, workers, civil servants, Moslems, the unemployed, and peasants experiencing famine conditions in Wollo province. The demonstrations, strikes, and protests which ensued exposed the Endalkachew government's incapacity to resolve the crises it faced and prevented him from consolidating power.

URBAN IMPLICATIONS OF REGIME CHANGE

The removal of the upper nobility—including its reform-oriented element, which assumed power briefly under Endalkachew Makonnen—from positions of political power and social influence represents the first significant political change brought about by the coup instigators. Young men from the middle and lower ranks of the armed forces assumed power, while the upper echelons of the Ethiopian military establishment were depleted by arrest and execution.[19] And the new military rulers quickly demonstrated the seriousness of their commitment to reducing social and economic inequities in Ethiopia.[20]

The refusal of those appointed by the Emperor to positions of power at the center to commit the Haile Selassie government to radical changes constituted a serious obstacle to social and economic progress in Ethiopia at the control level. Thus, the assumption of power by progressive and committed leaders at the central government level constituted an essential initial step in order for fundamental economic, social, and value changes to become institutionalized in urban Ethiopia.

Among the persisting obstacles to further change, two appear to be particularly significant in urban Ethiopia. First, in terms of *control*, the new regime has encountered resistance to its radical-socialist program from local elites with vested interests in preserving traditional private land and property ownership values and bureaucratic privileges, or in promoting capitalist enterprise. Also, at the *facilitation* level, the national government faces serious difficulties in increasing urban resource mobilization and industrial production. Both obstacles must be overcome before most urban residents will experience improved living conditions. And the new government's policy decisions regarding the mobilization and application of power and influence will largely determine whether the obstacles continue to persist, are overcome, or become further entrenched.

The Derg has moved swiftly to introduce economic measures designed to broaden the base of its support in urban areas. Foremost among these measures are price controls, nationalization of the vast urban ownings of the Emperor and the Haile Selassie I Foundation, nationalization of the largest manufacturing and commercial establishments,[21] mandatory rent reductions, and nationalization of all urban land and extra (i.e., rented) houses (Ethiopian Herald, September 13, 1974, July 25, 26, 27, 1975; New York Times, January 2, 1975). Predictably, these radical steps have been favorably received by the poorest urban residents and resented by elites who suffered pecuniary loss in their wake.

It is significant, however, that the Derg has moved less rapidly to introduce *political* changes designed to generate support for its policies at the ideological level and to mobilize human energy for urban development projects. Indeed, the Derg has dismissed parliament, suspended all municipal councils, delayed establishment of the promised single political party organization.

The July 1975 urban land nationalization proclamation did provide for the establishment of small-scale urban cooperatives composed of people living in close geographical proximity. The cooperatives are responsible for collecting house rents of E $100 and less, and for preparing and carrying out community improvement projects. Cooperatives also are intended to constitute the popularly elected base of an urban government system. However, the creation of housing cooperatives was immediately opposed by leaders of traditional urban voluntary associations, such as *edir*. Many leaders of these long-established organizations have been disqualified from holding office in the new bodies for a full year due to their status as landlords. Newly established housing cooperatives are granted a broad mandate to engage in self-help activities that are likely to bring them into further conflict with voluntary associations that only recently were being exhorted by the government to become involved in urban development projects (Fecadu Gedamu, 1974: 74-75) and with municipal government officials who view the new associations as encroaching upon their limited revenue-generating and decision-making authority.

CIVILIAN POLITICAL INSTITUTIONS

As a consequence of the Derg's reluctance to promote civilian political institution-building, the new government has encountered opposition from influential urban groups based upon fundamental differences of attitude over the nature of the political system. Divisions over the right to demonstrate, military versus civilian rule, and the creation of a political party emerged immediately following Haile Selassie's arrest and remain potent. Within days of the arrest of the Emperor, student elation over his ouster was overwhelmed by disappointment over the prospect of continued military rule. In addition, student demands for representation on the constitutional revision commission have been consistently turned aside by the military, and many students have viewed the suspension of classes beyond the tenth-grade level and their assignment to work for two years on rural land reform and literacy programs (zemecha) as a ploy to divert them from participation in Addis Ababa politics. Divisions deepened after students and workers were arrested and shot on orders of the new regime during public demonstrations in September and October of 1974 (New York Times, September 17, 1974, February 25, 1975; London Times, September 24, 1974; Africa Research Bulletin, 1974: 3399; Washington Post, December 21, 22, 1974).

Such cleavages at the ideological level (i.e., over political structure values) are particularly serious, since the government is dependent upon workers and educated urbanites to act as a bridge elite in mobilizing the human energy needed to facilitate urban development schemes. For instance, in August of 1975, approximately 1,400 zemecha students refused to continue registering land and houses and assisting in the formation of new urban associations in Addis Ababa. All of these students were arrested promptly by the Derg, and civil servants and military personnel had to be conspired from various public agencies to replace them.

Urban support also is crucial for achievement of the new government's rural objectives. Students have threatened to leave rural posts, where they have played an instrumental role in the creation of peasant cooperative associations, if their demands are not met. Enforcement of the Derg's radical land policies would be further undermined if renewed urban unrest breaks out at the same time that continued prosecution of the costly armed struggle in Eritrea diverts Ethiopia's limited military resources (see Washington Post, February 16, 1975). Aside from the negative consequences which would result from mass urban alienation, urban elites such as students also could perform vital positive bridge elite roles by virtue of their potential capacity to explain and *influence* persons to accept the Derg's urban and rural transformation programs. The mobilizing political party offers an institutional vehicle with potential to forge a new alliance of urban and rural interests (intelligentsia, workers, lumpenproletariat, peasants), mobilize diffuse (ideological) support of these groups for social and economic changes, provide specific material benefits to members, and generate local enthusiasm for collective involvement in self-help projects.

CENTRAL-LOCAL GOVERNMENT RELATIONS

The national government's efforts to shape and facilitate change in urban Ethiopia also will be greatly affected by the policies pursued in its relations with units of local government. There are two basic structural options open to a new regime that is committed to mobilizing and applying power in a fashion that promotes fundamental social transformation. The first approach emphasizes the centralization of political authority, while the second path stresses the need for popular participation and local self-government. Municipal government officials would be involved in either event; in the first case, they would no longer exercise the degree of independence they have become accustomed to, while a change in the direction of local self-government would focus responsibility for urban service provision on municipal employees.

Strengthened Central Government Control. The Ethiopian system of local government, based upon the unintegrated prefectoral pattern, is not designed in a fashion that allows for unified and effective central control. Under the existing unintegrated prefectoral system, authority is blurred, divided, confused, variable, and shifting. This has permitted local government officials to remain corrupt, inefficient, and responsive only to personal interests and patrons. Most local government officials exercise considerable independence, while eluding responsibility for their actions by referring to the subservient, wholly deconcentrated, legal status of local government units.

Reforms of local government in Ethiopia in terms of making the system more responsive to the values and policies of central government leaders would require major changes that are likely to be resisted by traditional local elites (including many municipal government officials). At a minimum, the unintegrated prefectoral system, which encourages irresponsibility rather than responsiveness at all levels of government, would need to be abandoned. To introduce an effective integrated prefectoral system, firm action must be taken by the new rulers to reduce the division and disunity which presently characterize the *central* government bureaucracy. In addition, attention must be devoted to creating a centralized civil service system with the capacity to train and assign honest municipal government employees who are oriented toward social service needs and are dedicated to changing the local social structure. Job descriptions would need to be prepared so that municipal employees perform standard roles and receive equal pay for equal work. Finally, an incentive structure designed to encourage adherence to central government policies and objectives must be established and put into operation at an early date.

Local Self-Government. The new regime also could approach local government reform by delegating greater authority to popularly elected municipal government bodies. The principal attentions of this option are the prospect it holds out for mobilizing local energies on voluntary collective action schemes and the flexibility it provides for unique responses to local problems.

The devolution of significant powers to municipal government is not likely to occur in Ethiopia as long as the institution is perceived as a barrier to attainment of radical urban social and economic objectives of the new government. Moreover, new regimes tend to be preoccupied in their initial period of governance with securing legitimacy. Military regimes, in particular, prefer to avoid or supress conflict in the pursuit of legitimacy and the appearance of national unity (Welch, 1974: 220-221). Self-government threatens to ignite the volatile divisions which permeate the heterogeneous urban areas of Ethiopia and to unleash massive political demands on the part of workers, students, teachers, civil servants, and unemployed residents (on this point, see Kesselman and Rosenthal, 1974: 30; Clapham, 1975: 81). Self-government involves the risk that local values and policies may arise which the central government has not shaped. Also, emphasis upon local revenue sources may provoke disputes between resource-rich and resource-poor areas.

FUTURE PROSPECTS

For the reasons discussed above, the new military rulers of Ethiopia are likely to initiate local government reform by centralizing authority and substituting standardized local government roles for the unintegrated prefectoral system.[22] To the extent that such reforms lead to more efficient urban service provision, they will generate greater legitimacy and power for the regime and the new local government system. However, the atomized nature of the central government bureaucracy in Ethiopia and the divisions which exist within the military indicate that the new government will find it difficult, if not impossible, to attain the unified central control needed to operate a truly integrated prefectoral system of local government.

As the limits of centralization become increasingly apparent, the self-government alternative may be taken more seriously by the new government as a means of mobilizing popular support and voluntary energies in urban areas. Since power is a non-zero-sum political resource, centralization of the local government administrative structure and certain powers could be accomplished concomitantly with the devolution of authority to local government bodies and the expansion of other powers at the local level (see Walsh, 1969: 179). Such an approach would allow for increases in central government control *and* local facilitation.

The self-government alternative is likely to be considered in the broader context of the transfer of power to a civilian regime. And the Provisional Military Council is likely to become more favorably disposed toward civilian rule if it cannot end the Eritrean conflict, intellectuals and other urban elites committed to modernization continue to oppose military rule, urban agitation spreads, and the technical or political problems of land tenure reform, land redistribution, urban land and house nationalization, and industrialization prove to be insurmountable.

NOTES

1. See Kesselman (1972: 15, 23) on the importance of investigating these relationships and the lack of attention they have received from students of local government and comparative politics.

2. Most recently, growth of the historically important urban administrative centers of Gondar and Harar has slowed to a rate that barely exceeds outmigration (see Comhaire, 1967: 27, 30; also see Gamst, 1970: 380).

3. Urbanization levels vary considerably from province to province, ranging from a low of 2.6 percent in Gemu Gofa in 1967, to highs of 16.6 percent in Eritrea and 21.5 percent in Shoa. The largest city in Ethiopia (Addis Ababa) is found in Shoa and the second largest city (Asmara) is located in Eritrea. These two provinces account for more than half of the total urban population of Ethiopia (Ethiopia, Central Statistical Office, 1968: 1).

4. In fact, the great bulk of the official central government power structure is located in one urban area, Addis Ababa. Assignment outside the capital is viewed as an indication of dimished status.

5. For these reasons, the roots of contemporary Ethiopian political organization and culture are not strictly, or even primarily, rural—as Frederick Gamst (1970: 386, 392) attempts to argue.

6. This is the main basis for the distinction between the revolutionary coup d'etat and guerrilla warfare made by Chalmers Johnson (1966: 151, 155-156, 161).

7. Violent peasant revolutions may be inspired by nonauthoritative revolutionaries (particularly when other potent factors—e.g., nationalism, as described in Fanon's *Wretched of the Earth*—are closely associated with the revolution), but the aims of the revolution are unlikely to be achieved or institutionalized unless and until these goals consistently are supported by the urban-based authorities who dominate central government structures (see Johnson, 1966: 161, 156). A similar view is held by Martin Oppenheimer (1969: 45), who maintains that "the peasants can make a revolution, but they cannot, by their nature, carry it through. This must be done in the cities, by the government. So it is done by the peasants' leaders—and these are seldom if ever peasants (Castro, and so forth); or if they are, they don't remain so."

The emphasis placed upon a long-term urban strategy (through 1960) by Chinese Communist Party leaders for purposes of capturing political power and industrial development is shown by John W. Lewis (1966: 902-903, 908-910).

8. The 1968 peasant revolt in Gojjam Province, for example, was essentially conservative in nature, as evidenced by the major aims of the rebellion (maintenance of the existing pattern of communal land ownership and rejection of increased taxation); (see Schwab, 1970: 250, 253-254; Nega Ayele, 1970: 77-79).

9. The responsibilities assigned to municipalities are set forth in Article 9, Part 74 of the *Administrative Regulations Decree of 1942,* "Decree No. 1," *Negarit Gazeta,* first year, no. 6, March 27, 1942, pp. 51-52 and in the *Municipalities*

Proclamation of 1945; "Proclamation No. 74," *Negarit Gazeta,* fourth yr., no. 7, March 30, 1945, pp. 39-40.

10. The performances of the Addis Ababa Municipality and central government agencies operating programs in the capital city are discussed in Koehn (1973a: 127-157).

11. The social and professional backgrounds of high-level municipal bureaucrats are delineated in Koehn (1973b: 14-19).

12. The separation of urban wealth (largely in the hands of foreigners) and political power (monopolized by Ethiopians) accounts in part for the high incidence of bribery in Addis Ababa—as it does in Nairobi (see Werlin, 1966: 196).

13. This situation changed rapidly as the military began to assume power in Ethiopia. Emperor Haile Selassie was forced to appoint a commission to investigate charges of corruption in March of 1974. In July 1975, four high-ranking officials of the Addis Ababa Municipality including the Vice Mayor for Finance, were detained and charged with "fraudulent practices and negligence which led to the loss of nearly 10.5 million dollars . . . in various uncollected taxes" (Ethiopian Herald, July 5, 1975).

14. In 1967, for instance, the Council of Ministers ruled in favor of the Ministry of Communications in its dispute with large municipalities over the exclusive right to fix the rate and appointment of vehicle registration fees in urban areas.

15. Fully ninety percent of the adult (above nineteen) population of Addis Ababa owned no land in 1961. In 1967, only thirty percent of all occupied private housing units in the capital city were owned by their occupants (Pankhurst, 1966: 154; Addis Ababa Municipality, 1972: 192).

16. The retail prices of food and drink in Addis Ababa increased by 67.5 percent between 1963 and 1971 (U.S. Department of Commerce, 1972: 6).

17. For this reason, gradual degradation in material conditions cannot be treated lightly or excluded from scholarly considerations of revolutionary phenomena. In contrast, see Davies (1972: 68-70, 81).

18. All units of the Ethiopian armed forces (including Territorial Army) have representatives on the eighty-member Derg, which now serves as the chief policy-making body of the new regime.

19. Eighteen officers holding rank of brigadier general or above were executed on November 23, 1974 (New York Times, November 25, 1974: 1).

20. Prior to the events of 1974, Cohen, (1973: 382, 379) argued that the new rulers of Ethiopia would not be committed to land reform because they had been tied into the advantages that accompany extensive government land grants. This conclusion overlooked the possibility that value commitments could prevail over land holdings and failed to consider the prospect that the grievances of lower-level officers might be aggravated by government land grants that were given almost exclusively to upper-level civilian and military elites.

21. The armed forces mutinies in early 1974 also triggered a series of urban strikes that resulted in wage and salary increases in a number of occupations. That these benefits were secured by privileged urbanites at a time of widespread famine and starvation in rural Wollo was the subject of a critical editorial written by Tegagne Yeteshawork in the Ethiopian Herald on March 19, 1974.

22. In fact, the important municipal functions of town planning and road construction, all with all municipal engineers, were brought under the central control of the expanded Ministry of Public Works and Housing in August of 1975.

REFERENCES

Addis Ababa Municipality (1971) Budget for 1964 E.C. (1971-72). Addis Ababa.

——— (1972) "Draft report on housing in Addis Ababa: results from the census of September 1967." (unpublished)

AKALOU WOLDE-MICHAEL (1968) "Some thoughts on the process of urbanization in pre-twentieth century Ethiopia." Prepared for the Second Meeting of Social Research Field Workers in Northeastern Africa, Addis Ababa.

ANDREAS ESHETE (1968) "Some principles of Ethiopian education." Challenge [J. of North Amer. Assn. of Ethiopian Students] 9 (December): 6-21.

ARRIGHI, G. and J. S. SAUL (1973) "Nationalism and revolution in sub-Saharan Africa," in G. Arrighi and J. S. Saul (eds.) Essays on the Political Economy of Africa. New York: Monthly Review Press.

ASMELASH BEYENE and J. MARKAKIS (1966-1967) "Representative institutions inthe political systems of developing societies: the case of Ethiopia. Prepared for the Interdisciplinary Seminar of the Faculties of Arts and Education, Haile Sellassie I University, Addis Ababa.

BEKELE HAILE (1971) "Municipalites Department work report and development plan." Internal memorandum tranalated by Seleshe Sisaye. Addis Ababa: Ministry of Interior.

CLAPHAM, C. (1975) "Centralization and local response in Southern Ethiopia." African Affairs 74 (January): 72-81.

COHEN, J. M. (1973) "Ethiopia after Haile Selassie: the government land factor." African Affairs 72 (October): 365-382.

COMHAIRE, J. (1967) "Urbanization in Ethiopia." Dialogue [Ethiopia] 1 (October): 26-33.

DAVIES, J. C. (1972) "Toward a theory of revolution," in I. Feierabend et al. (eds.) Anger, Violence and Politics: Theory and Research. Englewood Cliffs, N.J.: Prentice-Hall, Inc.

DURI MOHAMMED (1969) "Private foreign investment in Ethiopia." J. of Ethiopian Studies 7 (1969): 53-77.

Ethiopia, Central Statistical Office (1968) Survey of Major Towns in Ethiopia. Statistical Bulletin 1. Addis Ababa.

——— (1972) Urbanization in Ethiopia. Statistical Bulletin 9. Addis Ababa.

Ethiopia, Ministry of Interior, Municipalities Department (1963) "The towns are responsible for their own development." Y'Ager Gizat Minister Mashet 2 (Sene): 24-35.

Ethiopia, Ministry of Public Works (1967) Housing Study. Volume 1. Addis Ababa.

Ethiopian Herald (1974) March 19: September 5, 13.

——— (1975) July 5, 25, 26, 27.

FECADU GADEMU (1974) "Urbanization, polyethnic group voluntary associations and national integration in Ethiopia." Ethiopian J. of Development Research (April): 71-80.

GAMST, F. C. (1970) "Peasantries and elites without urbanism: the civilization of Ethiopia." Comp. Studies in Society and History 12 (October): 373-392.

GINZBERG, E. and H. A. SMITH (1967) Manpower Stragety for Developing Countries: Lessons from Ethiopia. New York: Columbia Univ. Press.

HOWATH, R. J. (1968) "Towns in Ethiopia." Erdkunde [Bonn] 22 (Lfg.): 42-51.

HUNTER, G. (1967 The Best of Both Worlds?. A Challenge on Development Policies in Africa. New York: Oxford Press.

HUNTINGTON, S. P. (1968) Political Order in Changing Societies. New Haven: Yale Univ. Press.

JOHNSON, C. (1966) Revolutionary Change. Boston: Little, Brown.

KESSELMAN, M. (1972) "Research perspectives in comparative local politics: pitfalls and prospects." Urban Research 1 (Spring): 10-30.

——— and D. ROSENTHAL (1974) "Local power and comparative politics." Sage Professional Papers in Comparative Politics 01-049. Beverly Hills, Calif.: Sage Pubns.

KLINEBERG, O. and M. ZAVALLONI (1969) Nationalism and Tribalism Among African Students; A Study of Social Identity. The Hague: Mouton.

KOEHN, E. and P. KOEHN (1975) "Edir as a vehicle for urban development in Addis Ababa." Proceedings of the First United States Conference on Ethiopian Studies. New York: Humanities Press.

KOEHN, P. (1972) "Political socialization and political integration: the impact of the faculty of arts, Haile Sellassie I University." Prepared for the Interdisciplinary Seminar of the Faculties of Arts and Education, Haile Sellassie I University, Addis Ababa.

——— (1973a) "The municipality of Addis Ababa, Ethiopia; performance, mobilization, integration, and change." Ph.D. dissertation. University of Colorado.

——— (1973b) "Urban administrators in Ethiopia: methodological approach and research results." Presented at the 1973 National Conference of the American Society for Public Administration, Los Angeles.

——— (1975) "Ethiopian politics: military intervention and prospects for further change." Africa Today 22 (April/June): 7-21.

——— and L. D. HAYES (1973) "Revolution and protest: a comparative analysis of student anti-system behavior in Ethiopia and Nepal." Presented at the 1973 Western Political Science Association Convention, San Diego.

LEWIS, J. W. (1966) "Political aspects of mobility in China's urban development." Amer. Pol. Sci. Rev. 60 (December): 899-912.

London Times (1974) September 24.

MARKAKIS, J. (1974) Ethiopia: Anatomy of a Traditional Polity. London: Clarendon.

MESFIN WOLDE MARIAM (1969) "Problems of urbanization." Proceedings of the Third International Conference of Ethiopia Studies. Addis Ababa: Haile Sellassie I University, Institute of Ethiopian Studies.

MOHAMMED UMER (1972) "A profile of the bureaucracy of the municipalities central department of the Ministry of Interior (Ethiopia)." B.A. thesis, Haile Sellassie I University, Addis Ababa.

NEGA AYELE (1970) "Centralization versus regionalism in Ethiopia: the case of Gojjam, 1932-1969." B.A. thesis, Haile Sellassie I University, Addis Ababa.

New York Times (1974) September 17; November 25.

——— (1975) January 2; February 25.

OPPENHEIMER, M. (1969) The Urban Guerrilla. Chicago: Quadrangle.

PANKHURST, R. (1965) "Notes on the demographic history of Ethiopian towns and villages." Ethiopia Observer 9 (1): 60-83.

——— (1966) State and Land in Ethiopian History. Monographs in Ethiopian Land Tenure 3. Addis Ababa: Institute of Ethiopian Studies and the Faculty of Law, Haile Sellassie I University.

PARSONS, T. (1966) Societies: Evolutionary and Comparative Perspectives. Engle-wood Cliffs, N.J.: Prentice-Hall.

Public Administration Service (1970) Organization and Management of the City of Addis Ababa, Ethiopia. Chicago.

SCARRITT, J. R. (1972a) "Cultural change theory and the study of African political change: some problems of relevance and research design." African Rev. [Tan-zania] 2, 4: 553-571.

——— (1972b) "Political development and culture change theory: a propositional synthesis with application to Africa." Sage Progressional Papers in Comparative Politics 01-029. Beverly Hills, Calif.: Sage Pubs.

——— (n.d.a) "Elite values, ideology, and power in post-independence Zambia." African Studies Rev. 14 (April): 31-54.

——— (n.d.b) "Control and facilitation: a framework and propositions for the analysis of political change."

SCHWAB, P. (1970) "Rebellion in Gojjam Province, Ethiopia." Canadian J. of African Studies (Spring): 249-256.

TADESSE GEBU (1969) "Problems of personnel administration in the municipality of Addis Ababa." Addis Ababa: Addis Ababa Municipality. (unpublished)

United Nations Economic Commission for Africa (1972) "Industrial development in Africa: problems and prospects," in J. S. Uppal and L. P. Salkeyer (ed.) Africa: Problems in Economic Development. New York: Free Press.

United Nations Food and Agriculture Organization (1972) "The necessity for agricul-tural development in Africa and practical difficulties," in J. S. Uppal and L. P. Salkever (eds.) Africa: Problems in Economic Development. New York: Free Press.

U.S. Department of Commerce (1972) "Foreign economic trends and their implica-tions for the United States: Ethiopia." Publication ET 72-012. Washington, D.C.: Department of Commerce.

WALSH, A. H. (1969) The Urban Challenge to Government: An International Comparison of Thirteen Cities. New York: Frederick A. Praeger.

Washington Post (1974) December 21, 22.

——— (1975) February 16.

WEISSLEDER, W. (1964) "The socio-political character of an historical . . . Ethio-pian capital." Presented at the Makerere Institute of Social Research Conference, Kampala.

WELCH, C. E. (1974) "The dilemmas of military withdrawal from politics: some consideration from Tropical Africa." African Studies Rev. 17 (April): 213-227.

WERLIN, H. A. (1966) "The Nairobi City Council: a study in comparative local government." Comp. Studies in Society and History 8 (January): 181-198.

Chapter 9

SOCIAL CHANGE IN
MOMBASA, KENYA

RONALD S. EDARI

INTRODUCTION

This chapter will look at social change as a continuous sociohistorical process for which an attempt will be made at isolating some of the basic measurable dimensions through principal components analysis and canonical analysis. Before embarking on this brief excursion into the maze of social change, a word of clarification is in order.

Kenya may be said to be "modernizing" to the extent that there has been a progressive application of modern technology toward the solution of various problems of the human condition, such as food, shelter, health, clothing, and the like. The technology employed has come to mean the importation of a number of social and psychological elements of behavior which have tended to make "modernization" synonymous with "Westernization," a term which African leaders regard as pejorative. In any case, it is not uncommon to see a street sweeper in the city of Nairobi dressed in a shabby looking suit and tie, with a soiled newspaper sticking out of his pocket. Whether such self-images are a necessary consequence of "modernization" is not for this paper to discern, sufficing to state that we shall prefer the more comprehensive term "social change," since the multidimensionality of the process of change in Kenya requires a broader definition than that which is implied by the word "modernization."

A major weakness in the studies which have attacked the problem of evaluating the dimensionality and causal antecedents of "modernization" in the developing countries has been their cursory treatment or total

---

AUTHOR'S NOTE: *The word "town" in the title refers to the legal status of Mombasa. Kenya follows the British practice of designating as "cities" only urban centers which are so chartered.*

neglect of the historical factors which have shaped the destinies of the countries or collectivities being studied (see, for example, Inkeles, 1966; Doob, 1967; Kahl, 1968; Schnaiberg, 1970). A good many of these studies have tended to treat the stock of historical knowledge relevant for the study of social change as a summation of the *gemeinschaft* sociocultural elements that hinder rather than promote "modernization." The proto-type of such an approach is to be found in Hoselitz (1963). This type of approach cannot tell us much about why, for example, Ivory Coast and Kenya are "modernizing" faster than Guinea and Tanzania, respectively. Since we have no reason to suppose that the people of Tanzania and Guinea are incorrigibly more conservative than those of Kenya and Ivory Coast, the answer to the question posed above should be sought in the respective colonial experiences of these countries and the type of political leadership which such experiences spawned.

In this chapter, we shall take the urban center of Mombasa as the locus of social change, and isolate some measurable dimensions through a brief historical analysis. The interrelationships among these dimensions will then be clarified through multivariate analysis.

THE SETTING

Mombasa is an urbanized area of 247,073 inhabitants (according to the Kenya Population Census of 1969), located in the East Coast of Africa. It is the second largest urban center of Kenya, and, as a port, it has played a vital role in the economic development of East Africa, comprising Kenya, Uganda, and Tanzania.

The history of Mombasa goes back at least a thousand years ago when the Persians are said to have established a small settlement on the island (de Blij, 1968: 15-18). However, the development of the industrial pat-terns of urbanization in Mombasa can be dated from the commencement of the British colonization of Kenya, which may be said to have begun with the construction of the Kenya-Uganda railway in 1895-1901. Colo-nization brought about the stagnation or decline of a number of the coastal towns such as Gede and Takaungu. Others like Mombasa and Malindi became integrated into the colonial system of production, and, as a consequence, experienced further growth.

SOCIAL CHANGE IN THE COLONIAL PERIOD

The initial presence of the British in what came to be known as "Kenya Colony and Protectorate" in 1920 had very little impact on the African's way of life. In fact, the British had to import indentured laborers from India to work on the railway, since very few Africans offered themselves for wage labor. With the completion of the Kenya-Uganda railway and the subsequent establishment of the white settlers in Kenya Highlands, the labor problem cropped up again in connection with the farm hands for the settlers. Most of the Indians who had come as indentured laborers had returned to India by this time, and the subsequent immigration of Indians into Kenya was dominated by elements whom by their caste division of labor were merchants and artisans rather than farm laborers. In order to meet the demand for labor, it was therefore necessary, from the point of view of the colonial administration, to force the Africans into the colonial system of production through such methods as taxation, described as payable in "cash or kind" (Hailey, 1938: 570), technical violations of the law such as trespassing on the settler lands in the rural areas and vagrancy in the developing towns.

It has been argued that the characteristic labor supply curves of this period were backward-sloping (Berg, 1961: 469-492). It is said that since the African usually worked for a fixed-income target, such as money with which to pay taxes, and quit his job as soon as he realized his objective, labor supply tended to be inversely related to the rate of wages. The major assumption here was that the African had very limited wants for which he needed money income.

Among others, Marvin Miracle has shown on the basis of some historical documents that at least for the Kikuyu laborers, during this early period in Kenya, the assumption of limited wants is not supported by the available data (Miracle, 1974: 9-10). He further states that long before the intro-duction of wage employment, the Kikuyu had been trading in a variety of items including maize, millet, sorghum, beans, cattle, sheep, axes shields, spears, chains, salt, tobacco, ivory, etc. On the basis of the evidence, Miracle concludes that the backward-sloping labor curve was not due to the failure of Africans to respond to economic incentives, but rather due to the costs and disincentives associated with wage employment. Such costs and disincentives included low wages, transportation costs, under-nourishment, diseases, and brutality, which often took the form of flog-ging. Thus, in the final analysis, in these early times the African was better off economically in his rural "non-monetary" sector than in the European sector of the economy, and as such, his behavior was consistent with the model of "the economic man."

Whatever the explanations of the backward-sloping labor curve, the phenomenon did prompt the colonial administration to resort to coercive measures of labor recruitment. Moreover, the pattern of high sex ratios in towns was set by the recruitment process which, with few exceptions, excluded females. This process was facilitated by the so-called Native Registration Ordinance of 1921, which required every male African six-teen years of age and over to carry a registration certificate showing, among other things, his employment history. The pattern of urbanization that began to crystallize from this early colonial period stood in a fairly sharp contrast to the urbanization experiences of a good many of the Western industrial nations. Before we get into some of the specific points of difference, we shall briefly outline the perspective that has been dominant in the study of urbanization in the West.

The dominant urban theory in the West has viewed urban localities in terms of the type of economy they grew to serve. Accordingly, urban areas have been treated as the loci of certain industries and commercial estab-lishments whose growth creates employment opportunities, which in turn stimulate rural to urban migration. The additional inputs of labor and capital lead to further growth in the economy, creating more job oppor-tunities, and encouraging further migration. The outcome of this process of urbanization is a system of spatially integrated urban centers, linked together by communication and transportation networks, with a high degree of functional specialization and interdependence. Within the capi-talist economic framework, the flow of goods and services among centers and their hinterlands is mediated by the market mechanism, resulting in equilibrium, which, when disturbed, sets into motion further readjust-ments which restore the system to equilibrium. One of the major assump-tions in such a model of urbanization is that migrants are sufficiently rational to respond to the income differentials between rural and urban areas.

As applied to Kenya, this theory of urbanization breaks down at a number of points. To begin with, industrial urbanization in Kenya was not a result of indigeneous processes of economic development as was the case in a number of the Western industrial nations. Rather, urbanization has been the consequence of the superimposition of an enclave-type economy, designed to produce raw materials and primary commodities for export. The pattern of economic dependency whose foundation was laid down early in the colonization of Kenya, has continued to the post-colonial period, and has been the main driving force determining the geographical mobility and concentration of capital and labor in two main growth poles, namely Nairobi and Mombasa (in their order of importance). A high primacy index within the urban hierarchy has been one of the archetypal characteristics of this form of dependent development.

Another phenomenon which does not fit in the theoretical framework outlined above is rural to urban migration. As was stated earlier, the migration of Africans into the urban centers was not due to their response to economic opportunities, but to noneconomic coercion on the part of the colonial administration. Also, unlike in the West, where for a long time migration from the rural areas was dominated by females, in Kenya, and indeed in a number of the developing countries, rural to urban migration has been dominated by males. The outcome of this process of migration was a labor force consisting of unskilled men who regarded their sojourn in town as a temporary inconvenience. Clearly, this type of unstable labor force was out of pace with the requirements of a highly organized and rationalized capitalistic system of production. Indeed some of the employers were inclined to vent their frustrations by flogging workers. On the other hand, the African workers were quick to recognize the power of organized protests (see Singh, 1969: ch. 2).

In time, the colonial administration and the European employers came to realize that the only way they could stabilize labor supply was by improving the working conditions and welfare of the African workers. Employers were therefore urged by the government to provide housing or housing allowances for their workers, and other basic necessities such as *posho* (food rations). These measures did have the intended effect, especially considering the fact that the wages paid to the Africans could hardly provide for their means of subsistence, as well as meet their tax obligations. Also, the increase in the demand for skilled workers did create a basis for occupational mobility for those who had mastered some skills, and those who had managed to receive an education of some sort. Thus, by participating in the colonial economic system, the African had come to be related to the world economy and its international division of labor. The town of Mombasa with its port facilities at Kilindini harbor became the cornerstone of the colonial economy of Kenya, geared primarily toward production for export to the "mother country" Britain.

As the economy picked up pace, population movements among Africans assumed even greater proportions. It was no longer necessary for the colonial government to employ coercive labor recruitment tactics, for by now the Africans were responding to "economic forces" such as the relative scarcity of arable land and the demand for industrial goods such as bicycles, clothes, pots, cutlery, and the like. Consequently, migrant workers in search of employment began trickling into the colonial plantations and towns. These movements and their attendant consequences are among the most profound changes which affected the African peoples.

CONCEPTUALIZATION OF SOCIAL CHANGE

From the foregoing account, we can isolate three basic dimensions, which are strategic in analyzing African social change. These are (1) migration, (2) socioeconomic differentiation, and (3) social interaction across ethnic lines. A brief discussion of these dimensions and their translation into measurable variables follows below.

(1) Migration. Among others, Samir Amin (1974: 67-69) has outlined a useful scheme for classifying labor migrations in Africa, which is based on the following considerations: the place of origin and destination, the duration of migration, distance, and the qualification of migrants.

The criterion of place of origin and destination is broken further into rural to rural, rural to urban, urban to rural, and urban to urban migrations. With respect to Kenya, we may view these subtypes as corresponding roughly to the developmental stages of the nation as a whole. The initial phase of development was marked by the forced migration of workers from one part of the rural area to another, depending upon the labor requirements of the plantation economy of the time. The growth of the major colonial towns, whose main economic functions were packaging and transmission of the surplus appropriated from the rural areas, and distributing manufactured goods from the "mother country," led to the forced migration of labor from rural to urban areas. This was complemented by the reverse process of urban to rural migration, a phenomenon associated with the so-called backward-sloping labor curve. The process of urban to urban migration is still insignificant in Kenya. The dominant pattern of migration has been the movement from rural to urban areas, in which economic exigencies have replaced coercion as a determinant of migration flow.

Closely associated with the criterion of place of origin and destination is the criterion of the duration of migration. Since the costs and disincentives of working for Europeans were rather high, as noted by Miracle (1974), the initial duration of migration tended to be short. This situation came to change to the degree that there was an improvement in working conditions, housing, and payment in cash or kind. The change was initiated by both the struggles waged by the African workers and employers' interest in a stable labor force. This meant a gradual translation of the labor supply curve to a new position with a positive slope. It also meant a decline in the rate of urban to rural migration, which had been characteristic of the backward-sloping labor curve situation.

The criterion of distance has not been an important consideration in the study of migration in Kenya. However, the criterion of the qualifications of workers has assumed even greater significance as a result of the increase in the demand for skilled and managerial workers.

We may add another criterion for classifying labor migrations, which is the classification of migration according to ascribed characteristics, particularly ethnicity. Apart from ethnicity, migration is also selective in terms of age and sex. The salience of each of these ascribed attributes is not only dependent upon the nature of the labor market at the point of destination, but also upon the differential responses to the objective conditions prevailing in the area of origin. Thus, the expropriation of the Kikuyu land by white settlers in the Kenya Highlands set the stage for the migration of young, male Kikuyu workers into the city of Nairobi, while many others were reduced into "squatters" in the rural areas.

In the present chapter, we have chosen to focus on urbanization as an integral part of the process of migration. A strategic variable for measuring the degree of urbanization at the individual level is the length of stay in an urban area. Since a persons' age increases also with his continued sojourn in town, it was thought to be advisable to include age among the measures of urbanism. This, of course, introduces the well-known problem of multicollinearity between age and length of stay in town. However, for our purposes, this is not an insurmountable problem, since the two variables are treated as surrogates for the same latent dimension—namely, urbanism. Furthermore, age and length of stay in town are used to derive another variable, which has to do with the proportion of lifetime spent in an urban area. This variable is included because of the fact that a young person may spend less time in town than an older person, and yet in the extreme case in which such a young person was born in town, the years spent in this locality would be the same as his age.

The significance of the length of time spent in town as a dimension of African urbanization becomes apparent when we realize that the longer a person stays in town the weaker the social bonds binding him to his kinsmen and tribe tend to be and, by corollary, the greater his integration into the urban socioeconomic environment (Wilson, 1941).

(2) Socioeconomic Differentiation. As Africans participated in the colonial system of production they came to be differentiated in terms of occupation, education literacy skills, and income. This was a function of two main factors, the desire of the Africans to improve their standards of living and the demand for skilled labor on the part of the employers.

Despite the rhetoric of some African leaders, who have tended to deny the existence of socioeconomic strata, a chant that has been echoed by some American social scientists (see, for example Grundy, 1964), a number of researchers have demonstrated the increasing significance of socioeconomic differentiation along the lines outlined above, (Mitchell 1959; Lloyd, 1966; Clignet and Foster, 1966; Caldwell, 1968). In fact, in publicly owned companies such as the Railway Corporation in Kenya, Uganda, and Tanzanis, the British instituted an elaborate system of occupational ranking which has persisted with only one profound modification— namely, the elimination of the practice of job reservation according to three racial categories: European, Asian and African.

(3) Interaction Among Ethnic Groups. As a consequence of migration into towns, increase in the length of stay in town and participation in multiethnic socioeconomic subenvironments, the frequency, duration, and intensity of social interaction among African ethnic groups increased considerably. Among other things, the stage for this development was set by the British colonial policy of encouraging employers to provide housing for their employees. It has already been stated that this move was motivated by the need for stabilization of labor supply by providing the necessary minimum housing for the African workers. In time, multiethnic housing "compounds" came to be part of the colonial urban scene.

All told, the above were the basic dimensions of social change which the author was interested in—namely urbanism as measured by the length of stay in town, socioeconomic differentiation and social interaction across ethnic lines. These three dimensions are regarded as strategic in coming to terms with emergent social structures as well as in assessing the prospects for national integration as manifested in microcosm by the urban social space. To get around some possible non-linearities inherent in the scaling of a number of the above variables, we performed a logarithmic transformation of the form $Log_{10} X_i \rightarrow X_i$, whereby each variable, with the exception of the dummy variables, was replaced by its common logarithm.

THE SAMPLE

The sample space was restricted to the employees of the Railways Corporation from the four largest ethnic groups of Kenya, who constitute the bulk of the employees of the corporation in Mombasa. A stratified sample of 240 respondents was drawn systematically from a universe of about 2,400 names. Four field assistants from the respective ethnic groups above conducted interviews in their own vernaculars, Swahili or English, as the case might have been, but in each case they had to record the answers in structured questionnaires written in English. The simplicity of the question- naire and its short length were among the strategies adopted to minimize the loss of information due to translation. The entire questionnaire and its format need not concern us here.

A PRINCIPAL COMPONENT ANALYSIS OF
TEN MEASURES OF SOCIAL CHANGE

The program used for principal component analysis was MESA 1, of Northwestern Program Library. This program performs rotation according to Kaiser's algorithm, which simplifies column vectors (factors) rather than row vectors (variables). In line with our conceptualization, the maximum number of factors to rotate was placed at three. The results of the analysis are shown in Table 1 and a scheme of interpretation is offered in Table 2.

As it can be seen in Table 2, Factor I was identified as Socioeconomic Status, Factor II as Urbanism, and Factor III as (Informal) Interethnic Interaction. Rather suggestive in the outcome of this anlysis as indicated in Table 1 is the fact that the variables subsumed under Factor II (Urbanism) show negative loadings for the other two factors. Even though these loadings are rather low, which is partly a consequence of orthogonal rotation, we can take their negative loadings to imply that urbanism as a component of social change seems to be related rather negatively to the other two components, socioeconomic status and interethnic interaction.

TABLE 1
PRINCIPAL COMPONENT ANALYSIS OF
TEN MEASURES OF SOCIAL CHANGE

		Rotated Factors		
		I	II	III
Eigenvalue		3.530	1.733	.925
Percentage Communality		57.0	28.0	15.0
		Factor Loadings		
No.	Variable	I	II	III
1	AGE	−.139	.618	−.245
2	YRSTWN	−.034	.913	−.067
3	RURURB	−.010	.720	.083
4	LITRCY	.817	−.203	.351
5	EDUCAT	.782	−.238	.241
6	OCCPTN	.918	−.006	.093
7	INCOME	.884	.092	.088
8	NOACTY	.148	−.169	.362
9	VISITS	.139	.061	.701
10	VBLCOM	.100	−.046	.666

This is further corroborated by the fact that the latter are themselves negatively loaded on urbanism. In order to make this rather anomalous finding more explicit, a canonical analysis of the ten measures of social change was carried out.

A CANONICAL ANALYSIS OF TEN MEASURES

Canonical analysis is essentially a generalization of multiple regression and correlation analysis, and it is a particularly useful search procedure when we have multiple criteria and predictors and seek to clarify their interrelationships.

The results of canonical analysis are given in Tables 3, 4, and 5. These are based on the output of the program WISE* CANONX of the Wisconsin Information Systems for Education, University of Wisconsin, Madison. For the purposes of this chapter, the three measures of urbanism were treated as predictors and the remaining seven measures as criteria. This order of input. variables was reversed by the program for computational expediency, a process which does not affect the outcome.

Table 3 shows only one significant root, the square root of which yields a canonical correlation of .47 between the three predictors and the seven criteria.

TABLE 2
A SCHEME OF INTERPRETATION OF
THREE ROTATED FACTORS

Factor I: Socioeconomic Status (SES)

Variable	Loading
Literacy (LITRCY)	.817
Education (EDUCAT)	.782
Occupation (OCCPTN)	.918
Income (INCOME)	.884

Factor II: Urbanism

Variable	Loading
Age (AGE)	.618
Length of Stay in Town (YRSTWN)	.913
Place spent most life time (RURURB)	.720

Factor III: Inter-ethnic Interaction

Variable	Loading
Activities with outgroups (NOACTY)	.362
Frequency of visiting outgroups (VISITS)	.701
Frequency of communication with outgroups (VBLCOM)	.666

The canonical weights in Table 4 indicate that age (AGE) and length of stay in town (YRSTWN) are the main predictor variables contributing to the canonical correlation. The nature of this association is apparent in Table 5, which shows that the predictors are, generally speaking, negatively associated with the criteria.

INTERPRETATION AND DISCUSSION

The results of principal component analysis show that, while urbanism may be regarded as occupying the same common factor-space as socio-

TABLE 3
THE TESTS OF SIGNIFICANCE FOR LATENT ROOTS (λ_i)

Latent Root	Canonical Correlation	Chi-Square	D.F.	P
.2219	.47	52.5763	9	< .005
.0351	.19	7.4764	7	> .05
.0080	.09	1.6883	5	> .05

TABLE 4
CANONICAL WEIGHTS FOR THE SIGNIFICANT ROOT

Predictors	Criteria
.69 (AGE)	−.33 (LITRCY)
.69 (YRSTWN)	−.37 (EDUCAT)
−.23 (RURURB)	−.26 (OCCPTN)
	.67 (INCOME)
	−.31 (NOACTY)
	.27 (VISITS)
	−.26 (VBLCOM)

TABLE 5
THE CORRELATION BETWEEN ORIGINAL SCORES
AND THE CANONICAL (PREDICTED) SCORES

Predictors	Criteria
.94 (AGE)	−.64 (LITRCY)
.85 (YRSTWN)	−.68 (EDUCAT)
.40 (RURURB)	−.25 (OCCPTN)
	−.07 (INCOME)
	−.59 (NOACTY)
	−.14 (VISITS)
	−.36 (VBLCOM)

economic status and interethnic interaction, its coexistence with the latter dimensions seems to be negative, a fact which is corroborated by the results of canonical analysis. To explain this finding, we have to take a hindsight look at the history of colonial labor migrations and the characteristics of the early migrants into town.

A good many of these early migrants came into town as unskilled laborers, and their continued sojourn in town did not lead to some commensurate change in socioeconomic status. In contrast to this cohort of migrants, more recent migration into Kenya urban centers and the subsequent probability of finding employment, manifests selectivity in favor of younger males with considerably more education than their counterparts in the colonial era. We therefore find that if we took measurements of social change at a fixed point in time we would likely find urbanism (as measured by length of stay in town) to be negatively related to socioeconomic status, since we would be looking at the results of a trend in which each successive wave of inmigrants consisted of young males with more education and better equipped to develop skills in their respective occupations.

The negative association between urbanism and SES should be expected to hold out only for the short run, since the demand for skilled, white-collar, and professional/managerial workers will tend to create a new group of workers whose skills will be "locked in," so to say, with the urban socioeconomic system. This trend is well under way in Kenya, and it has produced a generation of youth who were born, reared, and educated in urban areas such as Mombasa, Nairobi, and Nakuru.

The point of entry of African inmigrants into the urban colonial system of production also explains the negative association between urbanism and frequency of interethnic interaction. The early migrants were not only illiterate and unskilled, but were also highly tribal in the objective sense of having been well-integrated participants in their respective cultures and characteristic ecological circumstances. When these elements moved into town, they tended to form ethnic "pockets," as a result of which there was a relatively low degree of interethnic interaction outside the formal setting of the various colonial industrial situations. What the present study demonstrates is the persistence of such patterns of interaction in the case of the older town dwellers.

Historically, such urban ethnic linkages have served the function of providing material aid and psychological support, especially in crisis moments. However, the increase in socioeconomic differentiation has tended to create a process of selective interaction in which persons with a high socioeconomic status have tended to minimize their contacts with those with lower socioeconomic status, regardless of ethnic affiliation. This has, of course, been a protective device against the prospect of exchanging unequal benefits in the course of social interaction.

The remarks in the preceding paragraph need to be qualified in light of the increased competition for job opportunities, which has resulted in a rather sharp increase in mutual antipathies between certain ethnic groups. However, even in such instances, the motive force at work is economic rather than cultural in a primordial sense.

In conclusion, it should be reiterated that the purpose of this chapter has been to isolate some basic dimensions of social change in Mombasa, Kenya, through historical analysis, beyond which we have sought to clarify the empirical content of the dimensions and their interrelationships by use of principal component analysis and canonical analysis. The results of statistical analysis show that the measures of social change relative to the setting under consideration do not covary positively, as might have been expected. This is shown by further historical analysis to be due to the peculiarities of the colonial labor migrations. While the study is of a rather limited scope, it nevertheless points to the crucial linkage between the type of economic system responsible for the modernization of Kenya, and the sociological consequences of change for the African ethnic groups. This change has been closely associated with urbanization as an integral part of the general process of spatial development. What needs to be examined further is the linkage between the emergence of a national bourgeoisie and the type of socioeconomic policies which have resulted in specific forms of urbanization. For this purpose, what is needed is a broader theoretical framework which takes into account the different types of dependence relations and their impact on urbanization.

REFERENCES

ANDERSON, T. W. (1958) An Introduction to Multivariate Statistical Analysis. New York: John Wiley.

BARTLETT, M. S. (1941) "The statistical significance of canonical correlation." Biometrika 32: 29-38.

BERG, E. (1961) "Backward-sloping labor functions in dual economies: the Africa case." Q. J. of Economics 75: 488-492.

CALDWELL, J. C. (1968) Population Growth and Family Change in Africa: The New Urban Elite in Ghana. Canberra: Australian National Univ. Press.

CLIGNET, R. and P. FOSTER (1966) The Fortunate Few: A Study of Secondary Schools and Students in the Ivory Coast. Evanston: Northwestern Univ. Press.

DE BLIJ, H. J. (1968) Mombasa: An African City. Evanston: Northwestern Univ. Press.

DOOB, L. (1967) "Scales for assaying psychological modernization in Africa." Public Opinion Q. (Fall): 414-421.

EDARI, R. S. (1971) "Ethnic relations and prospects for national integration in Kenya." Ph.D. dissertation. Northwestern University.

GRUNDY, K. W. (1964) "The class struggle in Africa: an examination of conflicting theories." J. of Modern African Studies 3: 379-394.

HAILEY, W. M. (1938) An African Survey. London: Oxford Univ. Press.

HORST, P. (1961) "Relations among m sets of variates." Psychometrika 26: 129-149.

HOSELITZ, B. F. (1963) "Main concepts in the analysis of the social implications of technical change," pp. 11-31 in B. F. Hoselitz and W. E. Moore (eds.) Industrialization and Society. New York: Humanities Press.

HOTELLING, H. (1936) "Relations between two sets of variates." Biometrika 28: 321-377.

INKELES, A. (1966) "The modernization of man," pp. 138-150 in M. Weiner (ed.) Modernization. New York: Basic Books.

KAHL, J. A. (1968) The Measurement of Modernism: A Study of Values in Brazil and Mexico. Austin: Univ. of Texas Press.

LLOYD, P. C. (1966) "Introduction," pp. 1-85 in P. C. Lloyd (ed.) The New Elites of Tropical Africa. London: Oxford Univ. Press.

Ministry of Finance and Economic Planning, Republic of Kenya (1969) Kenya Population Census, Volume II, Data on Urban Population.

MIRACLE, M. P. (1974) "Myths about the behavior of Kikuyu laborers in the early colonial period." Institute for Development Studies, University of Nairobi, Working Paper 57.

MITCHELL, J. D. (1959) "Causes of labour migration." International Labour Institute Bull. 6: 12-46.

SCHNAIBERG, A. (1970) "Measuring modernism: theoretical and empirical explorations." Amer. J. of Sociology 76: 399-425.

SINGH, M. (1969) Kenya's Trade Union Movement to 1952. Nairobi: East African Publishing House.

WILSON, G. (1941) An Essay on the Economics of Detribalization in Northern Rhodesia. Livingston, Northern Rhodesia: The Rhode-Livingston Institute Papers, Part I.

Chapter 10

ACCOUNTING FOR BEHAVIORAL DIFFERENCES
Three Political Systems and the Responses of Squatters in Brazil, Peru, and Chile

ANTHONY LEEDS
ELIZABETH LEEDS

Our problem in this chapter is to account for the variation in forms of behavior of residents of squatter settlements and closely related types of urban occupation,[1] individually and collectively, in Brazil, Perú, and Chile in confronting the political systems of those countries, given their interest in extracting goods and services from the polity. We observe variations in their ways of dealing with, manipulating, resisting, and otherwise coping with the political system external to themselves which have previously been explained largely in terms of *immanent* characteristics of the populations themselves. In these explanations, the immanent characteristics vary from country to country in a way which has, up to now, itself been left unexplained. We argue that the differentiated forms of behavior are accounted for effectively in terms of the variation in the forms of the political systems which the squatter populations confront and that it is quite unnecessary to appeal to immanent characteristics as a mode of explanation.

AUTHORS' NOTE: *We wish to thank Professor Ernst Halperin, Department of Political Science, Boston University for his helpful comments and particularly Shirley Darwin, formerly of the Methodist Mission in Chile for her detailed comments on squatter settlements based on her lengthy, intense experience working and living in them.*

The problem emerged when we encountered contradictions to assertions in the existing literature during observations carried on, first, in extensive field work in favelas of Rio de Janeiro and, later, in prolonged visits in barriadas of Lima and shorter visits to the squatter settlements of Caracas, San Juan (Puerto Rico), and in Brazil, Curitiba, São Paulo, and Salvador.[2]

The general argument of the paper is that the political action of any given agent or actor is conditioned, constrained, and even perhaps determined by a wide range of external variables of the inclusive polity. The description and understanding, or predicting back, of the behavior of any such actor in a polity requires specification of the variables operating as constraints on and/or options available to that actor—that is, a description of the order *external* to the actor chosen for study—in our case, the squatters of Brazil, Perú and Chile. Without a thorough discussion of the variables of the inclusive polity, the behavior of actors such as squatters tends to be viewed, as will be shown below, in terms of stereotypes and ethnocentrisms very prevalent in the existing literature written largely by North Americans or by representatives of classes of the society in consideration who are, in effect, also foreigners to the settlements concerned.

Here, we define 'political' as including any action, interest articulation, or attempt by an actor to maneuver public or private bodies which is aimed at extracting goods and services from a given system by other than standardized exchanges of value, usually be means of money. In the cases under consideration, such an attempt may be by informal, individualistic ties with politicians, by intentional withdrawal from participation in formal political processes in order to retain bargaining power by remaining outside the formal political commitments, or through participation in formal political channels, including the bureaucracy, or combinations of these varying according to conditions.

A "HOLISTIC" METHODOLOGY AND MODEL: "CONTEXT" AS VARIABLES DETERMINING ACTION

The reader will detect in the preceding a certain orientation, with its terminology, which we wish to discuss briefly before proceeding, since philosophically and methodologically it underlies our approach to understanding our subject matter[3] and leads to certain conclusions about the results of prior studies.

Our paper is built on two interlocked methods: the understanding of our cases by means of a specific form of holism, general systems analysis, and a comparison of cases. These cases are chosen not merely because of some accident of having two or three units of study with which we happen to have become familiar, but on the basis of some attempt to use criteria of comparability to select them. Though the selection procedure is admittedly still crude, it is far from purely ad hoc and represents a step in the direction of a proper comparative method whether for political, social, or other analyses. This is discussed further below.

Holism has for a very long time been a methodological model especially for anthropology, largely for history, and notably for certain kinds of political economy, especially Marxism. It asserts, in essence, that for any subject matter to be studied, it is essential to understand its setting, its surroundings, the scene in which that subject matter is observed and therefore some description of the context is needed. Conversely, the subject matter of study does not stand alone, is not self-contained, but is, in some significant way, related to context whose specification illuminates our understanding of the subject matter. Context also supplies grounds for judgment in interpreting the meaning of the subject matter—it is a kind of control. What the "understanding" of context actually entails has not been clearly set forth philosophically in the holistically-oriented disciplines or sub-disciplines, but it is taken—virtually as an act of faith and of aesthetic sense—that it is essential. In practical effect, this means that an anthropologist or a political economist gets to know more and more aspects of "his culture" or "his society" (i.e., the socio-cultural "entity" under consideration) intimately until, ideally, he knows them all and sees them all interrelated and interpenetrating. Whether "his culture" is needed a proper whole at all has never been much questioned—this is taken (erroneously in our view) as axiomatically self-evident, also an act of faith. Finally, what the efficacy of a holistic treatment is is not clearly explicated philosophically, but rather perceived esthetically, and hence also an act of faith.

We wish to suggest some ideas on this matter in setting forth the method underlying our study. "Context" has traditionally been thought of, essentially, as "the rest of culture" or "society" (other than what one is focusing on in the study) acting for one's subject matter as a constant ground or stage on which its role is played.[4] It is treated rather as a unitary Thing standing over against the subject matter of study.

We reject the view of an unmoving context. Rather than seeing "it" as a Thing, we treat context as a set of variables in a system of variables, in the general systems theory use of these terms. Each variable or "element" directly or indirectly interacts—has an active role—with and affects every other, of which our subject matter of study is simply one or a set which we have chosen, on various grounds, for special attention. Thus, rather than our model's consisting of a two-bodied structure of a variable subject matter of study and a constant ground or set of conditions called "context," it is seen, holistically, as a multibodied entity (if, indeed, it is an entity at all, other than as a mental construct in a theoretical model) consisting of elements called variables, known, ideally, by direct observation and measures of a quantitative sort, all interacting on each other in greater or lesser degree, sometimes directly and sometimes indirectly through other variables. In this conception, context as a conceptual Thing disappears; one is left with a subject matter of study with respect to which actions—"forces," pressures, etc.—and constraints are occurring from sources outside itself upon which it, in turn, exercises action and constraint.

Before detailing other aspects of a systems approach, let us consider how our subject matter has usually been treated. Until recently, most of the literature on squatter and squatter settlements treated them essentially in isolation, as self-contained entities (e.g., "rural enclaves in the city," Bonilla, 1961) whose supposed characteristics are explicable in terms of their immanent attributes or essences. In the more extreme version, virtually nothing of the ground or context is even set forth (ibid.; DESAL, 1965; Lewis, 1959, 1961, 1965-1966, etc.; Mangin, 1967a, 1967b, Pearse, 1956, 1959; Portes, 1971; Turner, 1963, 1966, 1968, 1969). As the literature evolved, and particularly as the political scientists began to take an interest in the squatter settlements, more attention was paid to the context but essentially in a passive way. Thus, squatters as individuals or collectivities were seen as behaving or not behaving in the political sphere (mainly conceived in terms of elections), a fact that necessitates the specification of the context in terms of parties, elections, and the like (see Goldrich, Schuller, and Pratt, 1967-1968; Goldrich, 1970; Portes, 1970, 1972) or the legal system (e.g., Conn. 1969). The reverse is also true: the study of the political system with respect to squatters, but treating the latter rather as a passive ground (Collier, 1971; Leeds and Leeds, 1972; Medina, 1964).

The systems view of holism, essentially rejecting context as a passive ground, requires that one specify both the subject matter of interest and appropriate aspects of the ground as "actors," or variables in the system. Looked at from the point of view of the squatter actors as variables, we are obliged to see how external variables (in this case, the political system broadly understood) actively interrelate with squatters as individuals and collectivities—*and* to see how squatters interrelate with the external political variables. Our phrasing, here, simplifies the picture because it makes unitary categories out of squatters and the political system—a sort of two-body model—whereas, in fact, in a fuller analysis, we would argue that differential consideration would have to be given to residents of *"poblaciones," "campamentos,"* "popular" (i.e., working class) housing schemes, squatter settlements, and even various kinds of squatter settlements, etc., which are differentiated by secondary variables of the larger system (see A. Leeds, 1969). Further, we should have to include in our fuller account more detailed differential accounts of the unions, the party system, the bureaucracy, the legislative, the executive, and, often, the military and the church. In any case, putting the matter in other words, the general systems model *requires* us to examine how the variables act on each other in a system of mutual causation—a causation of degree, not of absolute determinacy.

The conception of mutual causation has the profoundest implications for systems involving human populations because human beings appraise not only situations and trends, but, above all, each other's acts and then govern their own actions accordingly. This appraisal effect on the behavior of elements—our "actors" or variables—of a system is technically called feedback. Feedback is of the essence in human interaction since all actors involved in the system are involved in feedback circuits and constantly adapt behavior to changes in behavior of variables (actors, including agencies, institutions, conditions) outside themselves, as well as to their own changed behavior. Methodologically, this means that the treatment of any group as a self-contained entity is inherently misrepresentational and can only be made on the basis of implicit and rather preposterous but nonetheless very widely-held assumptions, e.g., that a population locked into a political situation can somehow be "depoliticized."[5] Such an assumption leads one *away* from research on appraisal, assessment, cognition, conation, action—with the resultant mythic pictures which have been presented to us about squatters (see below).

The fact of feedback in human populations has further implications of great interest for political (and other) analysis. Because people appraise and govern their behavior accordingly, the possibility of feedback constitutes a constraint on any given variable: the feedback limits its range of variation. In the political terms, with reference to squatters, this means that a political actor, such as a party needing an electorate which does not produce a reward for its electorate—such as an infra-structural improvement in the squatter settlement—stands to lose its electorate. It is, therefore, constrained—it *must* produce something if there are competing parties around. From the point of view of squatters, the absence of competing parties or the inaccessibility of the party system constitute constraints on their possibilities of action, unless, for example, the parties are in competition with the bureaucracy or the executive for constituencies, or unless there are other routes to pressuring parties or government to produce goods and services, e.g., through the syndicates.

Our holistic treatment, then, dissolves "context" into active variables importantly related, directly or indirectly, to the system variable, also active, that we have chosen to focus on. Ideally, one describes the *system of interaction* of the variables specified as delineating the system. This description obliges us to describe for human populations not only the organization of the actors ("structures of the variables") but also their appraisal procedures, the feedback mechanisms, and the system of mutual constraints operating—that is, the limitations on actors which exist for each actor on the stage, whether individual or collectivity. We are methodologically *bound* to avoid the traditional procedure of isolating some subject matter of study for purely unique internal examination based on the assumption that the internal structure is self-generating. Rather, we assume that internal structure is a product of the interaction of both internal process and external action. We are obligated to avoid searches for essences. If an internal structure be self-generating or has some sort of an "essence," this must be *empirically demonstrated*, not taken as axiomatic.

We may spell out the relevance of these considerations for our problem more fully. First, action of any actor is constrained by the usefulness or uselessness of his acts in achieving ends. Some acts that can be imagined are impracticable because, for example, of their undesirable feedback effects (so that, like nasty revenges, we usually remand them to fantasy). Put another way, for any given system, the ranges of useful action are limited and such limits must be described—empirically.

Second, within these limited ranges, for any given action the range of political action is still more constrained by virtue of the political responses that the actor may envision other actors as producing. An envisioned political reaction might be one that occurs actually or only potentially, is purely postulated as a possibility, is one that is imputed to the other party or is anticipated from it. It need not ever materialize in actual behavior to operate as a constraint on the actions of any actor. The proposition holds for all actors in principle. In essence, the game of politics for any given actor consists of his minimizing constraints on his action and maximizing the constraints he can exercise over others.

Third, the description and understanding of, and the possibility of predicting back, the behavior of any actor in a polity from the model of it that is constructed requires the inclusion of descriptions of the various constraints and of a model of their interaction. This means specifying also, the options available to the actors. All in all, these various requirements mean a description and modelling of the larger systems of variables—both the orders external to the actor chosen for study and the actor himself.[6]

THE POLITICIZATION LITERATURE:
ALLEGATIONS OF NON-POLITICALNESS OF SQUATTERS

The recent literature dealing with Latin American urban proletariats exemplifies clearly some of the methodological problems just discussed. It combines the fundamental error of taking units of analysis out of context, isolating the phenomena being studied—in this case, modes of political organization and articulation. The subject matter is approached with strong ethnocentrism, largely based on assumptions of Anglo-American socio-political analysis, but also sometimes, on the implicit class-generated assumptions of Latin American observers from the intelligentsia—essentially members of the elites or their American congeners (e.g., Collier, 1971; the DESAL group, see DESAL, 1965, 1966; Medina, 1964; Portes, 1970, 1971; Schmitter, 1971; some of the dependency literature). Though taking the subject matter out of context and ethnocentrism are not inherently linked, isolating the political behavior from its political context permitted erroneous, ethnocentric interpretations to flourish because the observers were blind to the characteristic constraints operating in each country and hence failed to see the rationales for the observed behaviors of their squatter actors (assuming the observations to have been correct).

The literature has tended to view the kinds of populations we are concerned with almost entirely in terms of "political socialization," marginality," "integration," "politicization," and similar notions essentially growing out of the thinking committed to the idea of development and appearing to think that political life is a recent invention in cultural evolution. The notions are so defined that they fit only that kind of central orientation.[7] What is meant by these terms is that some population of persons, individually or collectively, goes through a process whereby they learn to "participate" in the "political process" and in "political institutions" as ethnocentrically conceived by the observing social scientist who assumes that the population was *not* politically involved, if in a different way, before. These concepts carry with them the assumptions that to be politicized, to participate, to be integrated into Anglo-American forms of political organization are more "rational," more "politically mature," more "stable"—hence, also "better" and demonstrative of "progress" and "development"—than the "more traditional" forms of behavior so often actually observed. The latter are looked at context-free, hence undetermined, and are, therefore, not understood, while the irrelevance of the Anglo-American models to the contexts into which they would be fitted escapes these observers entirely.

Characteristic of such analyses, since the notions of "underdevelopment," "emerging nations," "third world areas," and similar ideas became fashionable in the late 1950s and early 1960s, is the expectation that "developing" countries will naturally and necessarily evolve or adopt certain political practices and that their populations will adopt certain attitudes as such countries reach the exalted levels of Western European or American "development" (see a like assumption in Leeds, 1964a). These political practices, processes, and attitudes will, given the unilinear evolutionistic principle underlying such thought, be homologues of those of the "highly-developed countries." The forms of political articulation other than those conceived by such writers seem to them either irrelevant or suggest a low degree of politicization or political "socialization" for these rural and urban proletarian (and other) populations.

The American political scientist Goldrich, in particular, dealt with political socialization of residents of squatter settlements and of low-income government housing projects in Lima and Santiago in the context of a unilinear conception of development. this development should progress through a determinate sequence, which begins with "nonawareness of government" (one wonders where in human history this has ever occurred!) and then procedes to the following stages: "awareness of government," "perceptions of the government's utility," "realization of its manipulability," "development of a political preference," "an appraisal of one's probable effectiveness," "calculations of gains and costs of action," and, finally, the "making of demands." Another American political scientist (S. Powell, 1970) considers political participation of Lima barriada residents primarily and narrowly in terms of voting behavior, again a western, and particularly, Anglo-American, way of viewing political behavior. A British sociologist (Bamberger, 1968) is perhaps most guilty of developmentalist thinking in his discussions of political integration in the "unstable" barrios of Venezuela whose conditions "make it difficult to achieve the political integration essential to a functioning democracy." Ray (1969) echoes this attitude in milder form throughout his book.

What is objectionable in this literature is, first, the normative assumption that a given population should necessarily achieve a particular type of politicization or socialization. Such an assumption, on one hand, imposes a set of political values on a population, the historical context and sociopolitical structure of which might indicate quite different forms of political behavior. It has been found in Brazil, for example, that the "variable" 'political efficacy,' a variable often employed by the politicization writers, was inappropriate in the Brazilian context for the study of political attitudes among favela residents of Rio. "The favela resident who says he can do something to influence the government is not more efficacious, more modern, or more competent as a citizen, but simply more deceived by the rhetoric of the government—less in touch with reality. It is a tribute to the favela resident's common sense that this group is in the minority" (Perlman, 1971: 383).

Second, the imposition of normative assumptions prejudges certain types of political behavior as being "underdeveloped" when, in the perspective of the methodology discussed above, this behavior appears to be the most expedient and effective mode, given a certain set of structural limitations imposed by political conditions and actions external to the actors in question. For example, the "personalistic" *patron* or *patrão* relationship common particularly in Venezuela, Brazil, and elsewhere, has been characterized as contributing to the "immaturity" of barrio political life (Bamberger, 1968). Another form of political behavior, withdrawal from active associational participation is seen as a process of "depoliticization" by Goldrich (1970) and would occupy a low spot on his politicization scale. We would assert that under certain conditions it can be shown that this is a rational and politically expedient decision on the part of squatment residents. We intend to show that such kinds of political behavior as patron-client relationships or withdrawal from overt political association, rather than being indicators of political under-development as is so often alleged, are, in fact, adaptive, rational, and *strategic political* responses to structural conditions external to our actors in the polity at large.

Still another problem with the literature on the urban proletariat is the assumption that the relationship between a given proletarian population and the external polity is necessarily one of one-sided exploitation on the part of the external actors. The picture of the poor, unsophisticated rural migrant, at the mercy of demagogic politicians, is given in descriptions of squatter settlements in Brazil, Venezuela, and Chile. Although one point that we shall make is that a series of controls and constraints exist which severely limit the channels through which squatter populations may extract goods and services from the larger system, nevertheless, within that set of controls (see E. Leeds, 1972: ch. 2, "Games Favelas Play"; Uzzell, 1972: ch. 6, "Play Lexicons and *Chollo* Self-Creation"). In the case of Brazil, for example, the favela association or president uses the politician or government administrator, public or private welfare agency, Peace Corps Volunteer, or similar potential provider, fully as much as the favela is used by external agents for electoral or other constituency support. To call the relationship one of one-sided exploitation is, in the first place, to fail to see this game at all (as so many observers have failed to do, e.g., Collier, 1971) or, in the second, seeing the game, is to fail to understand the game being played as a *necessary* response to the political actors of the larger system, given the constraints the latter have thrown up.

As stressed before, the absence of adequate descriptions of the external polity and its relationship with proletarian bodies such as squatter settlements is a major objection to most of the literature dealing with political behavior of these groups. The existing literature tends to treat the populations of squatter settlements, or low-income groups generally, in isolation, rather than in the contexts of the wider political structures in which they in fact do operate.

To reiterate, we shall argue that any analysis of political behavior or organization among such a population as an urban proletariat must include an extensive discussion of the channels available for such a population to operate through, the pressures and constraints upon the population which limit its operation and give form to its attitudes and behavior, and further, policy with regard to such a population on the part of the external governing bodies which ultimately close or open or shift the channels. After a brief discussion of our reasons for choosing Brazil, Perú, and Chile, we turn to descriptions of these features for these countries and to the squatter's response to them.

THE THREE POLITIES—BASES OF SELECTION

The three countries we have chosen are societies with several roughly comparable aspects. First, all three have clear multi-party political systems, with at least three or more, competing independent parties playing important roles in the national political game. All three countries have large, complex bureaucratic structures with evolved welfare mechanisms which have existed for some decades as have specialized agencies dealing with housing and settlement. Further, all three have long histories of extensive syndical organization,[8] though the unions' degree of autonomy from the governmental structure varies considerably—itself an important determinant of political behavior. Fourth, all are at least one multimillion person city and several other large cities as well. They all, thus, have large, sophisticated urban populations with proletariats which have existed now for a very considerable time especially in the urban metropolises. Finally, each of the countries has long had a substantial industry, especially in the main cities, a fact related to proletarianization and to urban mass settlement and politics. Though a country like Mexico fits most of these characteristics, its highly divergent party-structure changes the political variables of our model so much that, in the absence of the formulation of more generic models, we do not know what to predict from this divergence in terms of the effect on political life of the actors we are concerned with. Other countries, chiefly Venezuela, would have fitted our criteria, but the descriptive material needed was inadequate.

The three polities vary in a way which can be neatly ordered logically, a fact which provides the central structure of our argument.[9] In one, none of the parties has (or had) a mass base, however much masses of votes may have been mobilized in Brazilian elections. The essential organization, personnel choices, and interest articulations were all intra-elite. In the second, Peru, only one party (APRA) has (or had) a mass base, primarily in both rural and urban labor unions. In the third, Chile, several parties have a mass base, that is, have operating subsidiary units within the popular masses which function politically, make local choices of personnel, articulate local interests up the party hierarchy. The game of politics in the three polities, we argue, varies for all social levels and sectors of the society, according to the variation in party systems and according to party interaction with bureaucracies, syndicates and various branches of government, especially the executive and the military.

BRAZIL

The Polity. Brazil presents a picture of channels for demand-making and interest articulation very different from those of Perú or Chile which are described below. Essentially, the *formal* political system for the distribution of the rewards, goods, and services of society is devoid of any mass base. Consequently, as we shall show, the responses on the part of the proletariat to this distinctive structure of reward redistribution must necessarily be quite different. To expect to find electoral forms of political organization such as those observed in Chile would be delusional and to judge those of Brazil as "immature," "depoliticized," etc., is not only to fail as a political analyst but also to put oneself in a dubious ethnical position.

In contrast to those of Chile and Perú, none of the Brazilian parties had a mass base. The one party which, in name, appeared to have been intended as a party of the people—the Partido Trabalhista Brasileiro—was, in fact, created by President Getúlio Vargas in 1943 in order to form a manipulable, controllable, mass following which he could, essentially, direct in the anticipated political play which was to emerge with the elections that had been promised for 1945 and the thus necessary end of his dictatorial status. The PTB was constructed of a coalition of labor unions completely under the domination of the government and of other "progressive" forces which supported programs of industrialization, nationalization, and social welfarism—programs intended, on their purely political side, increasingly to strengthen the power of one of the major elite factions of Brazilian society (see Leeds, 1975). The PTB was aimed, then, at capturing as a corral of votes (*curral eleitoral*) the urban populations which had vastly increased during the Vargas dictatorship with the rapid growth of industry, especially in São Paulo. Basically, they were a relatively new phenomenon in Brazilian society which had to be accounted for in the political strategies of various actors in the polity trying to get access to power or accumulate more power. At the time of the largest initial growth of these urban populations, Vargas was the only one in a political position to incorporate them into a political strategy, while all the other parties remained elitist in constituency and control, even though the Partido Social Democrático (PSD—neither social nor democratic) often tapped the mass electoral corral of the PTB at national elections when they worked in coalition. It is to be noted, in passing, that even this mass following did not exist for the PTB in all parts of the country—in a number of the overwhelmingly agrarian Northeastern states, the PTB had no following in the mass at all; its electorates, directorates, and orientations served the landed aristocracies entirely and it behaved in a manner almost identical to the right-wing União Democrática Nacional (UND, even less democratic than the PAD) state organizations in the southern half of the country.

The one other party that had a wide popular backing, largely among the working classes both urban and rural, was the Partido Communista, PC, which, however, existed as a legal party for only a few years before the establishment of the Estado Novo in 1937 and for about two years between the end of the so-called dictatorship in 1945 and its renewed suppression after its strong electoral successes in 1947. It continued as a substantial more or less underground influence for perhaps a score of years, maintaining members in elected, appointive and other (such as union) posts and still is of importance as a highly clandestine organization. today. But *because* it was operating underground, subject to repression and harassment, it did not function very successfully as a channel for political manuever to get goods and services for proletarian populations such as the majority of squatters.

Thus, in Brazil, are found an array of parties, none of which has a mass base in the sense of effective, formally organized, local, self-expressive constituencies acting within the operational norms of the party.[10] All the parties both intentionally and unintentionally (perhaps!) follow policies, make choices, and act in such a way that such a mass base cannot or will not develop. Specifically, whether deliberately or not, they act to maintain links to the constituencies through patronal ties alone and even encourage their clients in the masses to operate as lower level or sub-patrons to *their* clients, voters in general. Collusion among such party sub-patrons occurs frequently as informally organized networks—cliques—which control the goods channelled through them from above to the voting masses, but control them in significant degree, in their own interest unconstrained by formal responsibility to an association of voters. The voters' interests, ultimately, are largely in the pay-offs they can command, but only peripherally, at best, in the party as such. The voters' strategy is to wrest goods from as many party sub-patrons as possible.

This structure of party organization, of course, defines the rules of the game that must be played *among* parties. For example, aside from each party's elite-class interest *not* to allow an organized mass-base to develop, it is also *constrained* from organizing such a base (which, in the ideal, it could hopefully keep under control) by the threat of the other parties' also organizing a mass base—indeed, by the threat of creating a Chilean kind of party situation, a quite intolerable idea in Brazil. The peculiar congeries of circumstances which, in Perú, allowed an APRA to spring up as a unique mass-based party did not occur in Brazil. Preventive action (e.g., such as after the coup of 1964, the military's smashing the unions, low-ranking military, student, and left-wing clerical movements) is taken expeditiously when such a set of circumstances seems to be developing—usually by a broad elite-party coalition of peculiar bed-fellows who fall out with each other shortly afterwards. Brazil, then, from the point of view of elite-bounded parties, is characterized by a pulsating tension between controlledly mobilizing for votes a mass excluded from real participation and intensifying its exclusion sometimes to the point of almost universal repression. One major feature of the procedure is the maintenance of that fragile bond, the paternalistic politician, who can so easily, too, be withdrawn as a contact route for the proletariats.

In view of this party organization, there have never been for the proletariats, for squatters who are largely proletarian, Brazilian political parties regularly usable as means of channelling demands and pressures on a day to day basis. No *formal* structure of responsiveness to local social or political conditions has ever been constructed that such populations may use—other than, even after 1964, the periodic national and state elections (really the only level of electoral political expression for the masses, especially the urban, since *municipios* (largely rural) were mainly controlled by local elite cliques). But even the national and state elections could not inspire confidence since (a) they existed only from 1945 till, effectively, 1965 (by which time many elected officials of wide proletarian popularity—like Miguel Arraes, Governor of Pernambuco—had already been violently removed by the military and popular candidates declared ineligible to run), and, (b), they had repeatedly been threatened by intervention or military coup (e.g. 1954, 1955, 1961, and, effectively, 1964; see Leeds, 1975).

Although Vargas made great overtures, especially to the urban proletariat, neither the PTB nor the PSD ever created a continuing grass-roots party structure based on such bodies as formally organized ward committees, party precinct organizations, or the like. It is striking that in the nearly 250 favelas existing in Rio de Janeiro before 1968, with a combined (substantially literate) population of nearly twenty percent of the city, to our knowledge no local party commissions (like the Peruvian *comités*) or other local formal organization has existed nor has there been a single successful grass-roots candidate for local office from a favela. Though one occasionally found a building used as a campaign headquarters for a specific candidate, the candidate, despite an explicitly identified party affiliation, made his presentation primarily in his own name.

We do not intend to suggest by this that parties have no meaning or continuity in Brazil or that *personalismo* is the only significant mode of political interaction. On the contrary, the parties have been quite consistent ideologically and in personnel. However, for present purposes, what we wish to stress is that parties, and especially the PTB, made use of the personalistic, paternalistic *form* of organization in attempts to maintain an underlying continuity of policy and ideology while stifling any moves at independence or initiative on the part of the proletariats or their squatter sub-segments. This political mode of operation is intimately connected with elite-class self-maintenance in a society with extremely limited upward mobility (see Hutchinson, 1960; A. Leeds, 1964a, 1964b; 1973a; Leeds and Leeds, 1970), however, much the occupational diversity within classes has increased in the past three or four decades.

Though all the significant parties made use of paternalistic political procedures, the use is most significant in the case of the PTB, the party supposedly aimed at the toiling masses and the one that became the primary heir of "Cetulista" policies, welfarism, and controls over the labor movement—its major bases of inter-elite power negotiation, coalition (with the PSD), and power politics (as in the "spontaneous" strikes of the summer of 1962: see Leeds, 1975). Any politician who was of the PTB whether in office or campaigning for election could and did call on the name of "Pai Gége" or "o grande Presidente Vargas" to sanctify some measure he was preparing or to indicate his closeness to the social and ideological aims of Vargas that were of interest to a proletariat. Many favela informants have said that in the past elections almost any candidate appearing and supporting the Vargas regime, invoking Vargas's name in any manner, or simply being a member of the now ex-PTB, stood a firm change to win. As one shrewd political figure said several years ago, "todos os candidatos que vem em frente, nas costas, ou atrás dele vencem. Todos os outros perdem." ('All the candidates who come in front of him, on his shoulders, or behind him win: all the others lose'). The contact, however, remains controlled and paternalistic.

Getúlio Vargas's name and image, so long as they continued politically lucrative, were used by politicians—but could be used only by PTB or left-wing PSD politicians, be it noted—to show solidarity with "o povo" ('the people'). This solidarity rarely, however, extended beyond the election time—a *structural* fact made possible by the paternalistic form of linking mass voting to elite control of the parties, which is fostered assiduously by *all* the parties. No formal obligations continue beyond election time.

A concomitant of this characteristic mode of elite handling of the parties is, of course, their deliberate avoidance of creating or allowing to be created, overt, public, formal organizations for political ends at the local level. The Peruvian type of party *comité* headquarters building, like the shacks with the star of APRA in so many of the barriadas of Lima which are outnumbered by the headquarters of other parties, are notable by their total absence in Rio's *favelas, vilas, parques proletários*, and *subúrbios*. One only discovers the local political organizations after much intimate participant observation and after having developed close personal friendships in favelas—from both of which sources information as to the fact that such—highly informal—bodies exist and who their personnel is can be gleaned. Put in other words, the local political groups are almost exclusively informal cliques (whose membership is stable over long periods), without organized constituencies. Their rewards consist primarily of private and personal pay-offs from the party organization or its particular representatives, the *políticos*. Their job, in turn, is to create an ambience of pro-party feeling which will produce votes but *not* to create an organization which might have an independent basis of power and negotiation. Attempts to create or seize such (e.g., by using an intra-favela bureaucratic body, such as the Guanabara State Electricity Commission's favela light committees as a front organization) are either discouraged or fought by the other actors from outside the favela and the proletariat.

The lack of grass-roots party activity contrasts sharply with the party participation in squatter settlements of Perú and Chile as described below. There, the parties are involved in promoting formal party affiliation, a pursuit which entails lively organizational activity and exchanges of favors in times other than election periods, and, thus, provides formally effective channels through which squatter settlements may make representation and may receive goods and services from the inclusive socio-economic system. From the active presence of one or more parties, opportunities to negotiate goods and services exist in squatter settlements in Peru and Chile which are lacking in Brazil.

It is not accidental, but an inherent aspect of the elite character of Brazilian politics and political history that the proletariats, squatters, and other interest groups do not find alternative channels of interest articulation in the labor unions or the bureaucracy.

Labor unions in Brazil have never been independent bargaining agents since their inception in the first Vargas regime in the 1930s. Conceived partly as an effort by Vargas to increase direct federal contact at local levels and, thus, to undermine the power bases of the State governors which had been characteristic of Brazilian politics before 1930 (Skidmore, 1967: 34), the unions were and have always been, whatever the government, almost entirely controlled at, or creatures of, the federal level through the Ministry of Labor acting for the Presidency, even though their inclination has consistently been towards the PTB. It was during the last two years of the first Vargas regime in particular, 1943-1945, that control was broadened over the unions in an effort to pre-empt the increasing left-wing tendencies of the mid-forties, especially the influence of the Communist Party. Federal control over the unions was accomplished, first, by recognizing as legal only those unions which were approved by the Ministry of Labor. Second, the political party coalition in power (after 1945 till 1964 almost exclusively PTB-PSD), but mainly the PTB, achieved control by playing agents, known in Brazil as *pelegos* ('henchmen'), through the intermediacy of the Ministry of Labor, into key positions of leadership in the unions. By this means, dissident elements were eliminated from positions of influence and control was exercised over the rank and file. Third, the Federal Government instituted compulsory labor union dues which were redistributed through the Ministry of Labor to the union leaders of the legally recognized unions whose positions therefore depended on the top political officials of the country.

Following Vargas's overthrow in 1945, the administration of General Dutra continued the policies of labor control and, in fact, actively purged the unions of Communist and other left-wing elements in 1947, the year the Communist Party enjoyed its greatest electoral support. In short, Vargas's original labor structure, slightly modified by Dutra, has not changed significantly in thirty or more years.

Suffice it, here, to say that, until the present, labor unions have remained essentially an instrument of the Ministry of Labor and have rarely been able to present an independent base from which any portion of the proletariat or middle class could effectively press demands upon, or even significantly articulate interests to, the government.

Still another potential channel for proletarian (especially urban) demands on the larger social and political system—the administrative and bureaucratic structure dealing with policy regarding favelas and low-income populations generally—has remained unresponsive and essentially elite-controlled. A brief look at the history of social policy regarding favelas over the past forty years would show a history of some support but also of much repression of positive development in favelas as well as a repression of any moves towards independence or initiative shown on the part of favela residents, whether as individuals or as a group (see Leeds and Leeds, 1972).

Consistent in government policy over the last forty years has been the theme of erradication of a social ill, the removal from society, and especially the visible society of Rio de Janeiro's elite and tourist-filled South Zone, of the "pathological, cancerous growth ruining the tropical landscape" (see Leeds and Leeds, 1972, for detailed history and quotations). The few attempts during this period of forty years to enact policy of a nature to provide a base for positive improvement of favelas or to provide a base for independence or initiative of favela populations have always been met with either direct contravention of that policy in subsequent administrations or simply the ignoring or non-recognition of that policy by those charged with its enactment. The most recent and blatant example of the theme of erradication of a "social ill" has been the wholesale removal of favelas—especially in the South Zone of Rio—to outlying regions devoid of labor markets, often of transportation, and generally of the urban ambience which the former favela residents were integrated into (see Leeds and Leeds, 1972). Erradicated, in effect, along with the physical squatter settlements was (by police action) the state-wide Federation of Favela Associations whose actions and analyses of the relationship between the urban proletariat and the national economy, explicitly in class terms, were seen as a direct threat by the military dictatorship (see A. Leeds, 1973b).

The absence of party, labor union, and bureaucratic (including military) channels for squatters to extract rewards, goods, and services out of the system both limits and determines, in large part, the kinds of options open to Brazilian squatter settlement residents and the ways most effectively to take advantage of these options—to which we now turn.

The Favela Response. Given this sketchy picture of the national political order within the structure of which the urban proletariat is forced to operate—or, perhaps more accurately, is prevented from operating—one can better understand its forms of response to the aspect of the polity external to the favela segment of the proletariat. These responses are dictated in large part by the nature of the system through which rewards, goods, and services are distributed and by the very limited means of access to the external polity. Faced with the kinds of barriers discussed above, favela populations have been forced to operate in modes and through channels which will permit them most effectively to gather what few rewards they can.[11]

Brazilian politics generally, and favela politics in particular, may be characterized by the oft-used phrase "*troca de interêsses*" ('exchange of interests'). This mode of political behavior characterized both formal and informal interactions. Whether the exchange is between a legal favela residents' association and a politician looking for votes or a member of the state bureaucratic structure, or an individual resident and a politician or bureaucrat—the mode is the same—a bargain is struck. the rewards being promises of votes (always a risk for the politician) or other electoral support at some future date, on one side, and, on the other, urban services, employment, monetary rewards, housing placement, or personalty, and so on (an equivalent risk for the favela personnel).

From the point of view of the favela resident, the double game that is being played, in addition to acting as a means for gaining goods and services, also serves to assure some power to the favela by means of such sanctions as electoral opposition (when elections are operative). In calculating what their political gains may be, favela residents are aware that a large number of pre-election "benefactors" who visit favelas, describing impressive-sounding plans for favela improvement, will never return. In these circumstances, playing one candidate against another is a common tactic (often developed to a fine art) involving promises to vote or round up the votes of others in exchange for, if possible, immediate small- or large-scale goods and services—and delivering perhaps nothing.

Although playing one political party off against another (note the difference from Brazil: *party* rather than candidate!) is a tactic in Chile and Perú as well, the key difference there is that the other alternatives such as unions or, in Perú, a military in search of a constituency, are almost invariably absent in Brazil. The absence in Brazil of recruitment into parties to which the proletariat are wooed for votes but not for participation, also keeps them from access routes to rewards, goods, and services. Thus, as will be shown below, the sum total of rewards accessible from external public or private sector sources is much greater in Perú and Chile where more viable alternatives exist.

At the same time, a built-in limit exists to what the Brazilian politician can offer in terms of urban services for a favela—for he must be careful not to give too much. His relationship with any given proletarian population can be maintained only so long as its need for external goods, support, or aid continues. If the conditions he is ostensibly trying to improve are in fact improved "too much," he will have lost his raison d'être in the favela and, consequently, will have lost a significant portion of his power base. Thus, the politician's interest must be fundamentally one of perpetuating the system in which he operates. It is not surprising that criteria for politicization such as Goldrich uses for Perú and Chile, if applied to Brazil, would, by Goldrich's assumptions, yield an image of a most "unpoliticized" population, but at the same time, these criteria would entirely fail to describe political realities within which that population must operate.

Given the general lack of positive government response, given the fact that parties and unions do not serve as effective channels for voicing pressures—in short, given the extremity of constraints on effective political expression—favela residents have been forced to continue to seek their betterment through the paternalistic, individualistic channels of favors and exchanges of interest, although they do make use of other channels—the vote, bureaucratic support, the Church, even labor union support—at the infrequent moments they are available. Acting thus is, in fact, not only politic, but also highly political—in the only important mode of political action that is really available. When attempts at mass interest articulation are systematically and violently repressed, personal or group advancement must be carried out in ways not threatening to the governmental structure until such time as the removal of barriers or a cumulative organization base permits a flow of communication and demands about values, choices, and needs and a counter-flow of recognition, goods, and services.

PERÚ

The Polity. The Peruvian polity is one having a multi-party system with a mass base in only one party, the Alianza Popular Revolucionaria Americana (known as APRA; its members as Apristas). The other parties, with the possible exception of the Communist party, are all either more or less established representatives of long-term elite cliques or rather personalistically oriented parties of exiguous viability (like Belaúnde's Acción Popular, or AP). The Communist party appears to have a genuine popular following, especially among the urban industrial workers, but has never figured significantly as an electoral power like APRA, nor has it ever had the latter's scale of mass backing.

The fact of the mass base in a single party is the *key* element in inter-party politics in Perú. In any open election, APRA or one of its front parties, alone or in coalition, can almost always win major victories out of hand and, indeed, often did. The mass base and APRA's vote-getting capacities mean that, if other parties or political actors are to remain viable competitors in the political arena, they must operate in relation to APRA's popular following in a way that successfully competes with APRA policy, whether or not that policy has ever been formally implemented.

APRA'a tightly-knit party structure long aimed, first, at achieving power, and, then, having taken over government, at, minimally, reforming the Peruvian socio-political system or, more radically, revolutionarily reconstructing it from top to bottom. This party organization reached into most popular spheres of the society,[12] but especially into the labor unions and the agrarian labor sector, although it had also had considerable influence in squatter settlements, as well, a point we return to below. APRA's main power—its mass base—has long lain primarily in its close association with the Peruvian industrial syndical movement including the large rural-labor syndicates in the sugar-raising coastal north where APRA had its origins. Though APRA has relatively less extensive influence in the ever-increasing barriada populations than among rural laborers or than other parties based in the barriadas, we nevertheless observed its presence more or less ubiquitously in the squatter settlements—identified by its starred emblem on the local headquarters buildings.

APRA's mass base which has existed now for well over forty years[13] is *the* salient feature of Peruvian politics. All political action whether undertaken by any of the other parties, by coalitions, by the bureaucracy, by the executive or legislative branches of government, by the military (even today), or by the established Church have had to cope with the fact that APRA could and would (and wanted) to take over the government completely. Every party, short- or long-lived, swirling in and out of coalitions, has had to work out strategies and tactics of survival in view of APRA's vote command, whenever there were open elections, or, lacking open election, in view of APRA's covert organizational links in the bureaucracy, the military, the legislature and elsewhere. Basic to this situation, too, is the fact that all the other parties have tended to have absolutely no, or very small, popular bases. (Note that the total electorate in 1945 was only 450,000, of which perhaps half or so were the APRA's "mass" base and all the rest largely middle- and upper-class voters!; Pike, 1967: 280) The only one that has developed a considerable popular following is the Union Nacional Odrista (UNO; and possibly also the AP)—chiefly in the barriadas (see below). However, the Odristas and all the other parties, except APRA, are essentially parties of elite factions, representing fairly consistent interests and ideologies, though organized, usually, about a single person like Odría, Prado or Belaunde (for a fuller discussion of this type of party, see the preceding section on Brazil).

It is inherent in this structure that the strategies and tactics of the non-mass-based elite parties—when they did not actively either set aside elections or their results by mobilizing military intervention—required large-scale cooptational efforts either to dampen electoral enthusiasm (which they could generally expect to be APRA-oriented) or to shift the vote to other parties than APRA in order to keep the presidency in the hands of one of the elite parties or coalitions and the legislature much splintered among many parties. A more vigorous tactic was, periodically, to declare APRA illegal, although doing so never stifled its activities. Still another tactic, several times successful, was to seek APRA's coalitional support against other party groupings in an attempt both to defeat the latter and to coopt APRA (*not* successful, since APRA was always seeking its own ends, although its original "revolutionary" ends became more and more rhetorical as it adopted means of operating and short-term ends characteristic also of the other parties).

Government action with regard to squatter settlements must also be seen largely as a response to the policies and actions of APRA which, although never having been in executive power has, through its own programs and its electoral coalitions with elite parties, forced action by competing parties. APRA's very presence and periodic control of substantial national power have been a key factor in the proliferation and development of, and attention paid to, squatter settlements by the national government.

Thus, from the point of view of an electorate, particularly the ever-increasing squatter populations, the party sector of the formal political organization has presented a highly unpredictable order of things: sometimes responsive, sometimes evanescent, sometimes flourishing, sometimes repressed but functioning, sometimes virtually non-existing. The very unpredictability of the party system means the electorates have had to work out alternative political strategies to get the rewards they wanted. One set of strategies made use of any incumbent government; another set manipulated the relatively stable bureaucracies; still other sets worked through the military, the Church, autonomous agencies, and the unions. In what follows, we shall try to map out what is involved by means of a brief historical recital of the shifting political arrangements which presented a moving framework or set of parameters for squatter action, each phase involving a different structure of options in regard to the usable channels of squatter response.

Although barriadas had existed for decades, the rapid increase in Peruvian squatter settlement formation started in 1945 at the time that APRA, after a period of illegality during President Manuel Prado's first regime (1939-1945), regained legal status and sought formally to re-enter the political arena in the elections of 1945.[14] Collier (1971: 60) suggests that APRA's great congressional electoral successes and its consequent access to government resources permitted it actively to attempt to broaden its party and union base, especially by means of its involvement in land invasions which constituted one of the means it used to establish that base.

In President Bustamente's administration (1945-1948), the then Minister of Government, General Manuel Odría, in an attempt to discredit the APRA, became actively engaged in countering APRA's growing popular appeal. Odria, like APRA, took measures which included protection of squatters against eviction by the police.

> Odría's appeal to the settlements was made necessary and relevant by the fact that the re-emergence of APRA had made this a period in which military leaders who wished to gain political power had to make some attempt to get popular support. Hence, the re-emergence of APRA is a crucial immediate cause of the increase in the rate of formation [of barriadas] regardless of the exact proportion of the invasions in which they were involved [Collier, 1971: 61].

One should note the role of the military indicated in this passage—it is a repeated theme in Peruvian politics and one especially marked in recent years. The military government which entered in 1968 has, until today, given a great measure of support to what it renamed the "*puebles jóvenes*."

APRA's abortive coup of 1948 was followed by Odría's successful one, toppling Bustamente's coalition government. Paternalistic and co-optative politics with respect to squatter settlements were to characterize not only his whole regime (1948-1956), but also the second Prado administration (1956-1962) and the present military regime (1968-). The politics of these three periods may best be seen as responses to APRA's attempt to promote an independent mass-base in both the barriadas and the labor unions. Whereas the aim of APRA's action was to corporativize and institutionalize both the barriadas and the unions, the counter-aim of Odría's and, later, Prado's and the present military's policy has been to maintain as tight a control as possible over the two often over-lapping groups essentially by dividing them, by linking them to different agencies, by paternalistic and dependency relationships, or sometimes merely by defusing them or trying to mobilize them in new directions (especially since 1968).

Attempts at co-optation are in large part recognized as such by barriada residents who then correspondingly formulate their own counter-plays so as to use the co-optational plays for their own purposes. In other words, they play at being co-opted as long as something can be gained from the game. Such plays will be discussed below. What is important to note at the present is the contrast between the kind of relationship established between the squatment and the polities of Chile and Perú. Whereas a key focus of contact between the polity and the squatment in Chile lies in the competing, formally-organized bases—the parties, the contact in Perú has quite frequently taken the form of brokerage ties and "paternalistic" exchanges.

Examples of the governmental paternalism are plentiful. Odría's above-mentioned attempt to destroy APRA was accompanied by his attempt to destroy the unions with which APRA was closely associated. The effort to substitute direct patronal ties in place of an institutional structure is described by Payne (1965: 51):

> While on the one hand he gave employers what amounted to complete liberty to destroy the unions in their shops, he would give startling wage and social benefits to the workers. He decreed, for example, seven blanket wage increases while in power.... Odría's labor policy was, in an elephantine manner, paternalistic. Smashing or incapacitating worker organizations, but using government power to make employers deliver his presents to the workers, he practically destroyed what little existed in the way of conflict-resolving processes.

Odría's active promotion of squatter settlement formation and the involvement of his wife, a la Eva Peron, in making good-will trips to barriadas was accompanied by the promotion of Odrista-oriented residents' associations.[16] While "paternalism" remained a key characteristic of the Odría regime, from the point of view of the barriada residents, substantial concessions were being made and gains being won. Seen in the perspective of a twenty-five year trajectory, these concessions and gains functioned in such a way—a kind of positive feedback—as to establish firmly the phenomenon of squatter settlements as a viable form of urban housing and their residents as a political force in their own right.

Just as the Odría regime had been concerned with countering the mass-base appeal of APRA, the second Prado regime (1956-1962) was also concerned with establishing its own support base among the proletariats,[17] partly because of the need politically to counter Odría's influence. Although promoting invasions was a tactic used also by Prado, the more characteristic feature of his administration was the attempt to institutionalize channels for barriada demand-making and to establish a formal administrative apparatus for dealing with the phenomenon of squatments. The two administrations, viewed together, exemplify the process described at the outset of this paper—that of two different parties both competing for mass support—and in this case both operating in relation to APRA's mass-base. The result of the competition was to multiply the forms of action and organization available for manipulation by the barriada residents—another positive feedback phenomenon, both increasing the absolute and relative size of the barriadas and strengthening their political position.

Though the forms of action and organization available to Peruvian and Chilean squatters are probably about the same in number, their arrangement is quite different. As we shall show in detail below, Chile's appear to occur simultaneously and consistently, because of the consistency (until recently) of party politics, while Perú's occur in a sequential manner, entailing for the squatter residents a continual shift in the weighting of forms used while keeping all the forms accessible concurrently. Although some of the options lie dormant at any given moment, they must be kept ready for mobilization as the political order of the State varies in response to the interplay among parties, military, bureaucracy, government, and unions—an interplay whose structure is governed by the basic relationship to APRA as it moves through its periodic repression and irregular electoral victories.[18]

The bureaucratic and legislative concern with barriadas in the Prade years may be seen as the first overt governmental institutional support of squatments. It culminated in the all-important Ley de Barries Marginales (Law No. 13517) of 1961, fostered by Senator Alberte Arca-Parró (an economist, one-time director of Perú's National Statistic Service and organizer of censuses for several Latin American countries), which established the channels through which existing barriadas could be legalized and rebuilt, and elevated the earlier Corporacion Nacional de la Vivienda into, first, the Institute and, shortly thereafter, the Junta Nacional de Vivienda to promote more controlled types of settlement called *urbanizaciones* (see Leeds, 1973a, 1974) and to help with squatment "urbanization" (rebuilding them to appropriate urban specifications).

The Prado years were also ones of extensive publication of governmental studies on barriadas.[19] Perhaps the most important of all was the *Informe sobre la Vivienda* (1957) produced by Prado's special Comision para la Reforma Agraria y la Vivienda which had been organized in 1956 under his finance minister, the economist Pedro Beltran (a strongly anti-APRA figure and owner of the influential newspaper, *La Prensa).* This report was a major influence in creating the Ley de Barrios Marginales of 1961.

Furthermore, the Prado government was willing to try innovative experiments. For example, it acceded to the architect and urban planner John Turner's suggestions and request to turn over a sum of money, with no strings attached, to be used for housing and infrastructural improvement by a barriada directorate as it saw fit. The idea was both revolutionary and shocking to many people who were certain that the poor either could not handle money at all or would surely embezzle it. In fact, the barriada, Huascaran, with the money channelled to it through, we believe, the Instituto Nacional de la Vivienda, did an excellent and economic job of reconstruction, with great probity.

By the end of the Prado regime, barriadas were an integral part of Limeño and Peruvian life, "recognized"[20] (where fitting the law) by the government, and understood by it as a necessary form of urban housing and settlement under the regnant socio-economic conditions of the country. There is considerable evidence that all this had its effect on the electorates in the barriadas, many of which still support Pradista politics.

The short military interregnum of 1962-1963 and the Belaúnde period represent a break in the paternalistic and openly co-optative policies of the prior regimes. Belaúnde gave little heed to barriadas but turned his attention, on one hand, to large scale building of middle and upper income housing and generally supporting the construction industry which he, as an architect, was connected with[21] and, on the other hand, to the development of the interior of the country. This development had a co-optative aspect about it, too, in the form of Cooperacíon Popular—a sort of community development arm of Belaúnde's more or less personal political party, the AP. It is hard to demonstrate, but it would appear that Cooperacíon Popular was to be seen as rendering services, helping the poor to help themselves, and the like. Cooperacíon Popular had little contact with the barriadas which were left increasingly unsupported throughout the regime as funds for the Junta Nacional de la Vivienda and other urban

agencies steadily shrank while opposition parties blocked legislation that
would help barriada residents because they did not want to give anything
away that would redound to Belaúnde's credit (Collier, 1971: 85-86).

Although the period was one of relative openness politically, one with
open elections and freedom of action for Apristas, Odristas, and others,
squatters found themselves forced to work as much as possible through the
bureaucratic agencies (which, indeed, continued rather supportive, when
they could, despite shortage of funds—as in giving squatter settlement
invaders planning assistance for settlement layout) and through the
Church. This is the period of the greatest activity and influence of the
more left-wing Church and especially of the "Bishop of the Barriadas"
Monseñor Lúis Bambarén, who developed Pueblos Jóvenes (ONDEPUJOP).
Numerous other Church organizations from many countries also flourished
in the barriadas in this epoch, providing, most notably, health and education
services.

Barriada residents also significantly manipulated elected officials by
means of the paternalistic form of political operation. An example is the
mutual use of each other by the alcalde of San Martín de Porras (an
all-barriada municipality of Lima), interested in his own political aggran-
dizement by mobilizing a constituency, and the residents of that barriada,
interested in security of tenure on their plots. The alcalde "mobilized"
them—and they allowed themselves "to be mobilized"—into a march
which moved towards Belaúnde's presidential palace to demand the issuing
of titles. Belaúnde, rather than have a possibly dangerous public demonstration, as he saw it, acceded to the request by promising that titles
would be issued. This promise of mid-1968 was an important politico-
administrative commitment (by an elected executive) for the residents of
Lima's barriadas who acted very widely on it in terms of investment in
building. It is interesting to note that the co-optating alcalde, receiving a
pittance of votes, was defeated at an election that took place shortly
thereafter.

Again, the irregularity of sequence in Peruvian politics has led to
extensive readjustment and flexibility of response in the squatters' political adaptation to the external political conditions.

The policies of the present military regime with regard to squatments
must be seen in the light of the foregoing discussion of competing political
parties and other bodies, for it, too, must compete for the support of a
constituency. It came into power with virtually none. One of the first
major steps taken was, at least rhetorically, to remove the stigma of
marginality from the barriadas and to adopt, officially, the name "*pueblos
jóvenes*" ('new towns') for the settlements.[22] Shortly thereafter,

ONDEPUJOP was established as the official national office to deal with squatments.

Although some people thought that the move was intended as a rather demagogic gesture to bring the squatter populations directly within the sphere of governmental attention and thus, on one hand, remove feelings of alienation and potential dissidence and, on the other, to try to co-opt a support base, the actual rewards distributed in the process of incorporation have nonetheless been substantial. Urban services continue to be provided and the squatments consolidated as permanent parts of the urban structure (see note 16).

The military regime's goals of control and of linking barriada residents to various agencies are clearly seen in the establishment of the Sistema Nacional de Apoyo a la Movilizacíon Social (SINAMOS) in 1970 whose aim is to prepare the masses for the coming "social democracy with full participation" (*Latin America,* 1973, 7(9): 65). The Oficina Nacional de Cooperativas (ONDECOOP), also involved with barriadas, became a subsidiary of SINAMOS. As will be seen in the following section, the responses of the masses to such mobilizing attempts vary with the situational context—that is, with the external variables. If it is to their advantage to be mobilized, they allow themselves to be mobilized; if it is not, they forcefully refuse to be mobilized. We turn next to these responses.

THE POLITICAL RESPONSES OF SQUATTER
SETTLEMENT RESIDENTS IN PERÚ

The relationship between the Peruvian barriadas or "pueblos jóvenes" and the political order external to them has tended more and more to focus on an increasingly diversified bureaucratic structure rather than to deal with competing parties because the latter compete so undependably. Because a complex administrative apparatus has been set up to deal with settlements over the past fifteen or more years, the means for getting rewards tend to be seen as associated more with the bureaucratic establishment than even with any incumbent government, except when very clear electoral possibilities are opened at national, departmental, or municipal levels (the latter appeared for the first time as part of Belaúnde's co-optative experiments). The very diversity of agencies and semi-official or semi-private associations (like the churches), operating in parallel with relatively reduced communication among them permits a wide ground for maneuver to barriada residents who could play them off against each other.

In part this possibility appears to be rooted in the needs of the bureaucracies (as well as of the parties), to have constituencies to represent before the executive or the legislative as allocators of resources. The bureaucracies make such representation in their own interest as well as in the interest of the political parties which may control them (often by generating votes from the constituencies in anticipation of elections). They may also represent various interest groups which influence the bureaucracies through controls over key bureaucrats exercized by various means (e.g., bribery, network linkages) or through other forms of interest articulation. The interest groups may be served, for example, by the bureaucracy by allocation of resources to the constituencies. Thus, if the Junta Nacional de la Vivienda urbanizes a barriada, resources are used which benefit the construction industry while creating a double support for the Junta bureaucrats. The interest group may, in turn, lobby for the bureaucracies in the legislative or executive branches or with the other bureaucracies.[23]

As in the Chilean squatments, barriada associations often started as outgrowths of initial invasion committees. As basic invasion priorities are met and needs change more to neighborhood, family, or personal sorts (educating one's children, putting in a local water system, etc.) as opposed to tasks requiring the aid of the community at large (installing the electric system, the sewer system, etc.) the formal barriada associations often cease to exist altogether, lie dormant, or divide into block organizations to handle problems on a more local level, a process described by Mangin (1967a) for Lima in the early 1960s.

But, as in the Chilean case, when a collective cause arises that requires mobilization and joint appeal, an entire barriada can be quickly mobilized to take action (this happens, of course, also in Brazil, but more rarely). Innumerable examples may be cited such as the march described above, but a recent one will suffice here. In October of 1972, 1000 families from a squatment along the Rimac River wrote an open letter to the newspaper, Expreso, in Lima, accusing the local SINAMOS office of siding with the alleged owners of the land who wished to evict the invaders. The offer by the government to move the squatters to a new settlement five miles to the south of Lima was rejected by the squatters who instead demanded recognition of their right to the land on the river's bank and called upon others in unstable land-tenure situations along the bank to act with them.

By calling for urban reform, expropriation of building land and the abolition of long-term rents, all in the uncompromising language of class struggle, the squatters' leaders have challenged not only the government's urban policies— founded on encouragement of savings and loans societies and self-help individual ownership, and presided over by reassuringly conservative admirals who have repeatedly promised the nervous private sector that there will be no urban reform—but also the whole basis of its social mobilization policies. In effect, they are telling SINAMOS that they do not need outsiders' support to get them mobilized [*Latin America*, 7(9): 66, 1973].

Further, squatters have proved adept at maneuvering desired values from another set of external agencies, merely mentioned above, which also conceive of their aim as "mobilizing" the squatters. These agencies often turn out to be as valuable to squatter settlements as competing political parties and bureaucratic channels. We refer to numerous and diverse private, semi-private, and religious bodies[24] such as Acción, Peace Corps, Oblate Fathers, Fé y Alegría, to name a few which, in the past ten to fifteen years have attempted their own kind of invastion—of the squatments. Each external benefactor group usually brings with it a set of resources—such as American religious charity funds, American and Peruvian industrial contributions (e.g., te Acción), American AID funds, labor services of the American Peace Corpsmen or the British International Volunteers, and the like. That many of these groups, like the Peace Corps and Acción operate under the direct or implicit sanction of the government is itself a resource for the barriadas since it legitimates then and thereby also give added political protection and visibility.

There develops, between the "benefactor" agent and the squatment leaders an exchange relationship—the squatment leaders find the agency useful for whatever materials, services, and often contacts (such as job placements, bureaucratic pleas, legal services, etc.) it can offer, while the benefactor needs the cooperation of the squatment leaders for the success of its program which provides the overt rationale for its being there. The game is sometimes expanded by the squatters to create competition among benefactor groups if the squatment is large enough. This relationship is quite like the Brazilian "mutual exchange of interests" (see above) between favela residents and external politicians, as will be seen below.

The actions of benefactor groups has been analyzed as being fundamentally co-optative. Rodrigues, Riofrío, and Welsh (1972) see the presence of the benefactors as masking such fundamental issues as the distribution of wealth in the society at large behind the immediate "problems" of installing urban services and establishing social clubs. The criticism levelled against the benefactor agents is similar to that made by Collier (1971) with regard to the Odría and Prado administrations and by Cotler (1969) with respect to the present military regime. Such analyses, accurate as they may be with regard to the intentions of the governments or the private benefactors, tend to neglect those on the receiving end of the offers made or treat them as passive, totally manipulated subjects. What is neglected is the fact that squatment residents usually recognize the co-optation attempts and skillfully go along with the game as long as it is profitable to do so, and within the limited advantages represented by the offers. The result is the continuous flow of goods, services, and other resources which has led barriadas to become "pueblos jóvenes" and pueblos jóvenes" gradually to become fully incorporated into the city and the State both in physical terms and in politico-administrative terms as municipios with full jural functions. Such incorporation has occurred neither in Brazil nor in Chile.

CHILE

THE POLITY

Chile (see footnote 9) is our case of a multi-party system with a mass base in several parties and a syndical movement which has displayed a considerable independence and dynamism for well over half a century. The parties with mass bases range from the Christian Democrats (the PDC), through the Communists (the PC), to the Socialists (the PS) and their semi-independent subdivisions the Movimiento Izquierda Revolucionaria (the MIR), and even include one or two of the right wing parties. Also, Chile, until recently, had regular and effective elections for forty or more years.[25]

In such a case, one would expect to find that the political actions and appeals of any one party must be carried out in the recognition that, since the other parties likewise have mass bases in varying degree, they, too, can accumulate support in the form of both individual and corporate (e.g., squatter settlement) actors and incorporate such actors into the active structure of the party—if the party produces rewards and services for them. Each of the parties *must* produce for its constituencies, for if it fails to do so, the other parties stand quite ready to capture their mass support through more effective appeals and action. The parties of Chile, therefore, continuously want, *need*, and must regenerate their mass bases and have evolved mechanisms for working with them. Further, since all the major parties have played a significant role in various spheres of government, each also has important sources of resources to distribute as goods, services, and other rewards to its constituencies, actual or potential. Party competition also resulted in widespread interlocking between parties and unions. Indeed, much union strategy is strongly influenced by party policies (Angell, 1972).

Given this structure, the parties are concerned about variations in their accumulated electoral power or other forms of constituency action such as shows of strength like *tomas* ('land seizures' or 'invasions'). This concern leads parties to attempt to maximize the accumulation of electoral or other organizational power by differentiating rates at which rewards, goods, and services may be given and significant participation for squatter actors afforded or elicited. The parties try to mobilize potential supporters using a variety of means and a variety of rationales. It is to be emphasized that the parties operate with the means, appeals, and rationales *within* the mass bases in both their geographical and social loci (for example, squatter settlements and unions respectively). However, the articulation of the central party organizations and the mass bases may involve quite different internal controls over the mass base within the party hierarchy as well as quite diverse goals of the central party powers.

In what follows, the distinctions among various types of settlement mentioned early in this paper must be reitereated since the various types show different behaviors in the context of the Chilean multi-party structure. It will be noted that *callampas* are squatter settlements usually established by accretitive occupation of a piece of land, while *campamentos,* as their name suggests, are squatter settlements ordinarily established by an instantaneous swooping in on the piece of land by an organized mass—the *toma,* or invasion (see Handelman, 1975: 65, fn. 8; Castells, 1974: 250-262). *Mejoras* and *poblaciones* refer to settlements either established in various forms, or improved by government action, although the term 'población' is also used generically to refer to any sort of settlements. We use it in the former sense only.

The nature of the party competition at the locality level varies with the type of settlement in which the parties are acting. For the callampa, lacking a history of unified socio-political movement in its own creation (see below), the competing parties present alternative channels which the callampas can play against each other or through which they can operate to extract goods and services and other values from the upper levels of the political system. The play is not restricted to parties but may be extended through patronal ties to bureaucracies and other external agents such as unions (see various passages in Castells, 1974, e.g., p. 248-b, 259-260, 264ff; Handelman, 1975: 58-63, passim).

There is some evidence that the *poblaciones* also relate to the party system in this way (see Vaughan, 1968, Castells, ibid.). Generally, the poblaciones, or popular housing projects, are first constructed as physical places either in the form of sites-and-services infrastructures or of the infrastructure with minimum housing. Then a more or less heterogeneous population, derived, for example, from a callampa or several callampas and from the *conventillos* of the inner city slums, is moved by the government rather than by a party trying to create a new branch of its own organization. Any given government is, of course, largely, though not exclusively, controlled by a party or a coalition and takes such action as supplying housing to a poorly housed population with the idea of capturing a constituency. Even though clearly inadequate in any absolute sense, the government has some resources to use in this sort of co-optative effort which are not available to individual parties not represented in the government. The relationship established with the poblacion, then, is a bureaucratic one in so far as the government is concerned, thus opening the possibility of patronal as well as party ties for the residents.

Callampa and poblacion affiliations tend to be rather heterogeneous in contrast to those of the campamentos. The callampas' political games are accordingly, played differently (see below). According to Handelman (1975: 55), the callampa populations tend to be different from those of the campamentos—the former consist more markedly of "lumpenproletariats" and the latter of industrial workers or proletariats.[26] We suspect that the distinction is meaningless and hides alternative strategies not only of political action and of land invasion seen in a political context, but also of coping with the constraints of the labor market. We return to this problem below.

Campamentos are almost invariably engendered or led by a party or by political groups like the MIR or possibly the Movimiento de Acción Popular Unitaria (MAPU). Having been established in a single swoop on some piece of land, they *start* as highly organized and unified bodies, although it is not clear from our sources what the mechanisms for aggregating such a body prior to the invasion is.[27] In Chile, this organized body is in fact very often, if not always, a part of, or directly attached to, the party organization: the toma has been fostered by a party and organized by its leaders, sometimes with and sometimes without leaders from among those mobilized. One carried out, the invasion is fostered and protected by the party. In a real way, the campamento, both in its internal leadership and in its response to the party structure outside the locality, represents a branch and a client of the party. At the same time, the party needs the branch as a significant source of power both for electoral and for collective action.

Thus, the competing parties represent something quite different to the campamentos and to the callampas. Campamento interest—and external party interest—rests on maintaining party organization and discipline as well as internal discipline related to the party. It is important to note, however, that this parallel aim does *not* thereby mean that the interests of the campamento and the external party leadership are identical. The latter, whether it be the PDC, the PC, the PS, the MIR, or another party or group, is acting in the national political sphere trying to control or accumulate power. It does So by a variety of means of which fostering campamentos is only one—and one which may be *not* desirable in the *long* run since it may create a very strong, independent political groups with a social organization not directly under the party's control. The PDC, for example, though it may occasionally have suggested an invasion, especially in the last years of President Eduardo Frei's regime (1964-1970) when it was competing sharply with Salvador Allende's Unidad Popular (UP), tried to avoid them by creating poblaciones and developing mejoras. If the central party organization's aim is mainly to achieve and control power, as in the case of President Frei's PDC, the campamento can be seen as a *tactical* vehicle for the short run, its power later to be eroded or rendered rhetorical rather than real. If the party's aim is social mobilization, especially with extensive reform or revolution with total seizure of power in mind, as in the case of the MIR, the campamento can be seen as a *strategic* vehicle for both short and long runs, one which would require ideological training in addition to organization so that the long-run adherence to, and control by, the central party structure and its interests might be guaranteed. There may also be parties, party segments, or individual leaders who encourage campamento formation in the interest of squatter betterment as an end in itself as a reflection of their strong ideological commitment. The recent support given to campamentos by UP is useful politically as well as socially beneficial both in the sense of providing housing possibilities to squatters through self-help where formal dwelling construction by government cannot be provided and, from the point of view of UP, in the sense of broadening social participation in the political processes and in the general social welfare. These varying party interests, programs, and strategies are clearly reflected in the data on squatter settlements in Chile, which we give in greater detail below.

Either form of squatment, from its point of view, is concerned with extracting goods and services or redistributing wealth from the inclusive society. However, given Chile's several mass-based parties with quite divergent policies, all linked into government with greater or lesser efficacy and all operating (until 1973) in a predictable and effective electoral system, different response patterns would necessarily be expected. Yet, given the degree of salience of the parties in the political life of all sectors and strata of Chilean society, one would expect that the coupling of the squatments with the parties would be much tighter than in Brazil and Peru: that much more of the action to extract goods, services, and other rewards would be carried out through the party relations than through other means such as direct patronal ties with bureaucracies. Indeed, one would expect the patronal ties to be aspects of the intra-party relationship, [28] with relatively few possibilities of independent patronal ties outside the party system.

In view of the preceding and the known range of party characteristics, we should expect a distribution of squatter settlement response ranging from a virtual identity of action between party and settlement, through various gradations and even mixed relations, to a relatively reduced number of cases in which the squatter settlement is coupled to external agents—party, bureaucracy, or some other—by patronal ties while maintaining a certain independence of parties. With the increasing importance of the mobilization of mass bases by the left-wing parties, generated from the 1950s on by interparty competition, we would expect a gradual shift towards the first end of the range. The two ends of the scale correspond more or less with what have been designated campamentos and callampas.

In respect to these expectations, note Handleman's summary (1975: 44) of the research findings of the Centro de Desarrollo Urbano y Regional (CIDU) respecting "outside leadership" in the squatter settlements:

> On one end of the spectrum were organizers representing legitimate political parties wishing to establish a patron-client relationship between their own party and their campamento. Communities with such leaders might solicit specific services from the political system in return for the promise of electoral support. At the other end of the political spectrum were highly radical campamento organizers who saw the urban squatter movement as a means of creating revolutionary consciousness among the masses and challenging the existing political order. They were less interested in instrumental, pragmatic goals.

Finally, we shall argue that the structure of more or less exclusive action through the parties *reduces* the long-term strategic advantage for squatters because it reduces their operational alternatives and the ambiguity that such alternatives present to the party leaderships in a functioning electoral system. The Chilean data appear to confirm these expectations in detail.[29]

The action of competing political parties with respect to proletarian settlements may best be seen by examples from the last ten years, although one could cite innumerable cases extending back to the early 1950s. The kinds of "interventions" practiced by parties range, as noted, from fomenting and organizing invasions and directing the *juntas de vecinos* ('community councils') and, beginning in the Frei period and flourishing in the Allende regime, a number of other kinds of groups in the settlements, once established, to merely founding a *comité* ('ward committee') in a given settlement.

Such interventions must be seen in the context of government action to accumulate mass political support by producing goods and services—action not, of course, divorced from political party interests of incumbent elective officials, but channelled through government-supported official and bureaucratic bodies instead of through the parties in order (among other ends) to strengthen the party holding the chief governmental positions. One may interpret in this way the housing policies of President Frei's Christian Democratic government, most notably Operación Sitio and the Planes de Ahorro Popular (PAP).[30]

The party in power has a distinct advantage with regard to mobilizing and maintaining popular support by virtue of its control of the State bureaucratic apparatus. Examples are Frei's Operación Sitio and the PAP mentioned above and Allende's Operación Invierno, a measure taken to avoid the usual problems occurring in winter such as flooding and shortage of shelter, or holding the resources actually to carry out material improvements, grant titles, issue decrees, and the like, which are at hand for the government and its bureaucracy.

The Ley de Junta Vecinos[31] of 1968 put forth by the Christian Democrats was seen by competing parties as much as an attempt to mobilize electoral support of settlers as it was a political concession to the settlements allowing them to establish a channel for making social demands. As a plan to "legalize" or create settlement organizations, the project received unanimous approval of competing Congressional parties. The parties objected, however, to the PDC's additional measure of placing the *juntas* under the authority of the Consejária Nacional de Promoción Popular on the grounds that the PDC wished to "penetrate the settlements and channel, for its own advantage, support and votes of the populare urban sector." Promoción Popular was defeated and the settlement organizations were attached in a diffused manner more accessible to all the party participants (including the right wing parties which also voted against it) in the bureaucracy (Vanderschueren, 1971b: 73 and 68).

The case of Promoción provides an example of a point made above— namely, that the four or five main competing parties (especially before the coalition of UP[32] are acutely aware of the potential electoral support stemming from the action of the others—a variable which, to a considerable extent, determines their action. They are unwilling to allow actions of a support-mobilizing nature without an attempt to counter or match that action. The countering actions cannot involve, for example, a total blockage of a proposal that would aid settlers because, the parties doing the blocking would lose their own support or potential new support; the action must therefore be one which defuses the opposing party, as in the Promocion case, or tries to attract new supporters as by directing a land invasion or establishing a comite inside a settlement. The counter-attack must be positive, a striking feature of the Chilean situation.

Thus, the governmental-bureaucratic programs mentioned above were countered, in terms of mobilizing popular support, by a number of invasions directed by parties, especially the MIR, the extreme left wing of the PS. An example is the invasion of the campamento, La Victoria, in Santiago in 1965, directed by the PC. As the election year of 1970 approached, the number of illegal tomas, many fomented by the MIR, increased sharply, as can be seen in the following figures (Informe de la Direccion General de Carabineros del Senado, reported in CIDU, 1972b: 56)

Invasions of Urban Lands

1966	1967	1968	1969	1970	1971	Total
?	?	8	23	220	175*	426

*first six months, only; estimate for year 350 or more

MIR's actions both just before and in the election year had the effect of forcing the PDC government, then in power, not only to refrain from taking repressive action against what in previous years had been cause for such action—the illegal invasions, but even to incorporate the process of illegal tomas into its own political action in order to maintain or increase support among the settlers. While, just after the elections of 1970, President Salvador Allende's UP coalition was attempting to slow down the invasion process, the Christian Democrats, in an attempt to recuperate from its electoral losses, increased its participation in invasions of land and extended its action to recently constructed, non-inhabited houses (CIDU, 1972b: 56).

The PDC's increasing involvement in invasions was complemented by the MIR's political aim of pushing a much earlier and more drastic revolutionary change than Allende appeared prepared to develop, a top-level inter-party conflict to which much squatter settlement behavior adapted. The MIR, as part of its political strategy both to accumulate more power in the Chilean polity and to push Allende into much more deeply revolutionary action, rapidly expanded its fomenting of campamento invasions, while both evolving a more explicit revolutionary socio-political and ideological organization in its campamentos and even, reportedly, helping arm many of them. The PDC and MIR pressure forced Allende to go to much greater lengths in taking action in squatter settlements than, presumably, he had wanted to (since he wanted to slow the rates of invasion), although he undoubtedly sympathized with and supported most of the social and welfare aims of the far left. Thus, from 1970 to 1973 when the military coup cut all this off, we see a picture of several major parties and party coalitions operating in sharp competition with very different programs and strategies to capture constituencies constituting a very large segment (perhaps 30-40%) of the urban population. In this sense, the 1970-1973 period is continuous with the previous decades, though a rather exacerbated version of the earlier times. The details of party strategies, given above, strongly confirm our general argument.

All the principles of party action discussed in the previous paragraphs are well illustrated by the extraordinary array of organizations and activities, fostered by all the major political parties, that arose after Allende came to power in 1970.[33] During the Allende years, inflation and other economic difficulties brought about major problems in the distribution of foods and other necessities, especially during the period of increasing scarcities in 1972-1973. The competing parties proposed different policies in their efforts to appeal to the larger publics, but all wished to dominate through the distribution system. For example, the MAPU favored public rationing cards. The PC favored the Juntas de Abastecimientos y Precios (JAPs) and price controls. Socialists, the MIR, and the Izquierda Cristiana favored the "Canasta Popular," i.e., regular allotments per family of staple items (beans, oil, sugar, rice, coffee, tea, etc.). The major form of organization to emerge was the JAPs which became increasingly active and decisive, determining the access of squatters and pobladores to food, kerosene, and other needed items. Distribution was carried out according to levels of participation. This system, as might be expected, "was fought over tooth and nail." However, in the year before the coup, all systems were functioning at the same time. Because of the growing black market, the control over prices and delivery of goods through the JAP had decreased greatly. Canasta Popular was the only sure way to get family necessities unless one had—and most settlers did not—networks into, and money for, the black market, i.e., were a member of the upper classes. Supply and distribution problems were thus capitalized on for purposes of building party support with the MIR increasingly advantaged.

The formal organizations with the campamentos and poblaciones ranged from the juntas de vecinos (mentioned above as having been fomented by government action during Frei's regime and after), to sports clubs to which large numbers of young men belonged. The sports clubs

often responded to mobilization on community issues as well as to
political parties within the settlements. Another set of organizations was
the Comandos de Pobladores Sin Casa (Castells calls them Comités Sin
Casa; 1975, e.g., p. 273, 280), highly militant organizations dominated by
the MIR and the Socialists. The Comandos, by their militancy and extensive membership among settlers and pobladores, were able to accomplish
ever more for the latter, especially in the Ministries of Housing and
Urbanism and of Labor. The parties, through the Comandos, dealt with
unemployment in the settlements by presenting lists of the workless to the
Labor Ministry so that many found jobs, especially in the construction
industry during the Allende government. Further, the Centros de Madres,
initiated under the Frei government, were very important in organizing
women—at first around "typical" women's activities, but, under Allende,
around women's political education and as channels for UP mobilization.

We see in the preceding account the complex interplay among parties,
the bureaucracy, the executive, specially developed associations, and the
squatter settlements, linked through externally fostered, intra-squatter
settlement formal organization. This process has only the barest parallel in
Brazil and is not extensively developed in Perú. As noted above, leadership
in Chile is largely externally generated, contrasting with both Brazil and
Perú where leadership tends largely to emanate from the squatments
themselves—and to remain within them.

The array of organizations and activities generated reflects the sharpen-
ing conflicts among the parties in the context of the unique situation
where an assertedly Marxist party had come into office in an open
election. From the point of view of squatters, responding to such an array
could only be a viable political behavior in the very peculiar context of the
national political system of Chile of that time.

The political system was patently in a certain disorder, unable to
resolve major economic problems, and confronted major political resistance and retaliation from electively still potent center and right-wing
parties occupying various national offices, especially in the Congress, the
military, and the bureaucracies. It also was confronting increasingly mobilized extra-legal right-wing violence and was clearly unable to excercise
control over such developing extra-legal institutions as the black market.

THE RESPONSE OF SQUATTERS AND POBLADORES

We shall argue that, though the unique ferment and political openness
of the times made a great array of squatter response possible, nonetheless,
in view of the political confusion, the viability of the responses was

variously assessed. Different segments of the squatter population inter-preted the potentialities of that political situation differently and cor-respondingly took different forms of political action: some, like the callampas, more cautious, guarded, and self-protective; others, like the campamentos, more directly committed, more open, and—as it was to turn out [34] more exposed. The populations on the receiving end of party actions to mobilize support—the squatters in callampas and in cam-pamentos and the pobladores in poblaciones—developed various forms of internal organization and external dealings and manipulations which, in the context of the politically ambiguous situation, they saw as best taking advantage of the party maneuvers to "co-opt" them, win their votes, or mobilize them for seizures of goods, services, and wealth. They adapt these forms to the external political organization and their maneuvers in order to maximize their own gains. In Chile, these external organizations and maneuvers, despite their rhetorical clarity in the 1970-1973 period, were quite ambiguous with respect to where power actually lay and what the possible political outcomes might be. The squatter response varied accordingly.

First, it is most striking that the interlacing between intra-squatment political life and the external polity is much tighter from an organizational point of view in Chile than in Brazil and Perú. In terms of organization, as we understand the data sources, it often seems very difficult to separate the external political system from the internal political response (or, even, sometimes, vice versa) except at the end of the range of response variants we have attributed to callampas, the settlements mostly established by accretion. Clearly, given the multi-mass-based party system with stable elections, a high frequency of squatter participation in the polity by direct ties and shared action is to be expected—and, indeed, is found as the data given above and reported in the literature demonstrate (see Goldrich, 1970; Goldrich, et al., 1967-1968; Portes, 1970, 1971, 1972; CIDU, 1972a; CIDU, 1972b; Rodríquez, et al., 1972; Vanderschueren, 1971a, 1971b; Castells, 1974; Handelman, 1975). What is not developed in the sources, especially in the recent ones, is the incidence—apparently with a relatively low frequency but nevertheless there—of squatters who avoid such participation by developing indirect patronal connections and some who use mixed strategies combining direct participation and various forms of patronal manipulation. These types of squatters are adverted to here and there (see Handelman, 1975) but no recent systematic survey or interview work and no intensive ethnographic work whatsoever has been done with them (however, see DESAL, 1965, 1966; Vaughan, 1968). The absence of any systematic, co-residential, participant-observational ethnog-

raphy applied also to the directly participating squatters and their settlements—the campamentos—so that we do not in fact know whether
alternatives to direct party affiliation and direct political participation are
or are not present in these places and available as tactical procedures for
the squatters. However, the oblique indications are sufficient, along with
Darwin's information (personal communication), to suggest some observations on squatter responses.

In a población or callampa, given the presence of two or more formally
organized *comités* of national parties, each competing for members, individual actors remain free to move back and forth among parties and their
comités if the party to which they verbally pledge their allegiance does not
produce (Vaughan, 1968). The same argument applies where two or more
national parties or party groups are operating by means of *any* organized
modality as the case of the JAPs cited above clearly indicates. One would
suspect that where Centros de Madres and sports clubs existed equivalent
competitions for their affiliation would occur, leaving the associations and
their individual members the option to play parties (or ministries) off
against each other; for this, however, we have no evidence. That the tactic
was in fact used is, however, evidenced by the cases given above.

The fact that there have been competitive elections whose results have
been honored for forty years or more and parties have competed within
the settlements means that, for the settlers and pobladores, there necessarily always exists a viable and mobilizable contact point to reach the
higher party levels. That several contact points exist in competition means
that the opportunity for exerting pressure for and maneuvering goods and
services remains a possibility even if one contact point were to cease
operating—an unlikely event since it would entail political suicide (as the
election results of 1973 seem to suggest, especially in the sharp decline of
the conservative Radical Party and the increased strength of the Socialist-
MIR group (see *Latin America*, 7(10): 73).

The kind of associational life found in any one settlement of the sort
we are considering no doubt reflects the history of the settlement, for
example, the organizational character of its formation. Yet, too, it undoubtedly reflects choices made by residents among different response
options. The forms of associational life found in the poblaciónes and
squatments varies considerably with regard to degree of participation of
the residents, kind of leadership, and ideological orientation of the junta
de vecinos (if any). The variation appears (that is the most that can be said
given the paucity of published data) to be determined in part by the kinds
of problems and issues faced by the settlement collective and by its
members individually, in part by its location, in part, as said, by its

history, and possibly also by other variables such as direct external pressure. In the absence of sufficient data to sort out what variables and variable states govern the variations, we can only point to the very striking diversity to be observed, suggesting that the diversity indicates both broad squatter experimentation with respect to externalities as well as different analyses of strategic possibilities and advantages from a largely instrumental viewpoint.

Variation is illustrated in many ways. For example, leadership may be *organizaciones de masa, comités políticos de caudillo* (CIDU, 1972b: 69), university students, party hacks, individual patrons, and so on (see, also, Handelman, 1975: 43-45). The internal organization of settlements is marked by a rich inventory of associations for diverse purposes—juntas de vecino, centros de madres, centros de padres (a kind of PTA), sports clubs, youth groups such as the Juventud Socialista, the Juventud Comunista, etc. All of these are, assertedly, directly linked to outside bodies. The sports clubs, for example, have links to the Ministry of Culture, while the juntas de vecinos maintain formal representation to the Ministry of Housing and Urbanism. Whether groups similar to some of these but *not* linked to the outside exist is not reported, but that this occurs would appear to be the case from the brief comments on the patronally-organized callampas (see also quotations from Portes below).

Whatever the incidence of the latter, striking is the marked degree to which residents of settlements in Chile, in partial contrast, under specifiable external conditions, to Perú and in sharpest contrast, as a rule, with Brazil, are organized into formal community assocations. It is consistently reported—with a few oblique exceptions in the recent literature but more frequently in the older—that *the* body to negotiate with the external polity is the community association rather than an individual or private group of people operating in a brokerage or patronal relationship, as is almost invariably the case in Brazil and occurs fairly consistently in certain kinds of relationships, notably with the bureaucracy, in Perú.

However, a somewhat different light is shed on the variation by Portes, reporting on his study (by survey) of four Santiago settlements in which he finds participation to be very much a "function of rational-utilitarian consideration . . ."—a view which supports the interpretation we are arguing. He says:

> taking part in meetings and social activities consumes time and effort; its utility, hence, must be evaluated against the economic or psychological profits derived from other activities such as work, home improvement, family life, interaction with friends.

He goes on to say,

> utilitarian considerations dictate that when problems which require communal actions become relevant, participation in voluntary communal associations increases. On the other hand, solution of problems, fulfillment of aspirations, and absence in general of socially relevant issues result in decreasing participation. Organizations at such times lie dormant. They remain, however, latent as potential instruments to be employed in future confrontations. From the point of view of the slum inhabitants, the communal assocation is not an artificial group to be maintained for its own sake, but an instrumental tool to be employed when necessary [Portes, 1972: 273].

For purposes of our present argument, the significance of Portes's findings lies in the notion of a community organization's being "an *instrumental tool* to be employed when necessary" (emphasis ours)—a tool to negotiate in the interest of the community of residents.

The instrumental ability to negotiate with the external polity is also seen as crucial by the CIDU team (1972b: 60) who find that

> la directiva es el elemento decisivo del campamento, pero no lo es tanto por su propio carácter, sino por ser el vínculo de relación entre los agentes externos (aparato del Estado y sobre todo, organizaciones políticas) y el tratamiento de los problemas concretos del campamento.

As has been seen in the foregoing, the problem of negotiating with the external polity and the ability to do so are key features of squatter settlement politics in all three countries under discussion. What varies in the three cases is the external political structure so that the options for and channels to negotiation—and, thus, the kinds of organization and behavior used in negotiation *must* vary correspondingly. Hence, it is not surprising that Goldrich found, in his comparison of politicization in settlements of Santiago and Lima, that residents of Chilean settlements tended to score "higher" than the Peruvians on tests of "awareness of government," "perception of the government's utility," "realization of its manipulability," "development of political preference," "appraisal of one's probable effectiveness," "calculations of gains and costs of action," and "the making of demands" (Goldrich, et al., 1967-1968: 14). We assert that all this is meaningless. The higher score for the Santiago residents does not mean that they are more politically socialized—as Goldrich concludes and Handelman, eight years later, appears to reiterate (1975: 59, speaking of Perú) but that the Peruvian and Brazilian political structures, under specified political conditions, permit fewer options and channels for negotiation of the Chilean sorts, while having evolved their own possibilities and routes.

Most writers on Chile before 1973 did not foresee a major military coup, or, if they thought a coup possible, saw it in terms of the continuity of a society operating with a stable electoral system. The possibility of a coup is not foreseen in the Chilean squatter literature we have read, let alone foreseeing the violent extremes to which the 1973 coup went. Had they entertained such a possibility, their political analyses of squatter articulations might have been rather different. What the post-1973 political conditions of Chile indicate is that a structure of formal linkages such as we have described above which is pervasive and almost exclusive (technically a tightly-coupled system), also may prove highly rigid and unadaptive under changing circumstances. By contrast, the combination of patronal ties which both link and separate, often combined with other modalities of reward extraction, provides a much greater degree of flexibility. In the perspective of the Brazilian and Peruvian situations, the incidence of cases in Chile in which callampas are reported to have operated through patronal types of relationships suggests an interpretation at variance with both that of the developmentalists like Goldrich et al., and Handelman and the ideological Marxists like Castells and the CIDU personnel who were looking at the Chilean situation from a MIRist viewpoint. For different reasons and in different ways, both see patronal structures as backward, conservative, and politically undeveloped.

We present the alternative interpretation that patronal structures, especially when used in conjunction with other forms of linkage, as in Perú, represent, first, a recognition of *very* real constraints on action; second, a cumulative, historical recognition of how in the class system users of patronal structures are locked into works in political practice; and, third, an astute assessment of stratagems and instrumentalities used for the individual and collective interest. Patronal ties constitute a structure in which a buffer exists between the externalities and the squatter populations; a certain degree of severability from external ties is restained.[35] The severability has a number of advantages: (1) the population becomes the object of various efforts at "co-optation" and "mobilization," hence maximizes its possibilities of extracting goods, services, and other rewards from the external system under conditions of substantial constraint; (2) severability leaves the population free to shift patrons when no rewards are forthcoming, or, in fact, to play several patrons off against each other or to have several at once; the threat of such severance itself exerts pressure for continuing flow; (3) the severability maximizes survivability under severe class constraints such as repressive situations following coups d'etat like those in Brazil, 1964, Peru, 1968, and Chile, 1973.

One implication of this interpretation is that, if settlements are predominantly tied to the external polity by formal links, with formal internal organization, and are directly involved in political action or events, they become extremely vulnerable to loss of property or life if a sudden change in the national political order take place. Conversely, if settlements have multiplied their ties and depend to a considerable extent on shiftable patronal ties, they reduce vulnerability as reflected in retention or increase of property, relative safety of life, and the locational stability of the settlement. The Chilean and Peruvian cases illustrate these two poles clearly.[36]

CONCLUSIONS

We claim to have shown that the *forms* of political responses of squatters and related populations are predictable given (a) the sorts of interests and needs which they confront in daily life and articulate politically and (b) the states of a system external to themselves and of its variables which are the diverse elements of institutional politics of the society—political parties, the incumbent government, bureaucracies, the military, labor unions, the churches. The interests and needs of the population we have treated are, to most intents and purposes, common: decent food and clothing, housing, security of residence, water, light, and, just as immediate in pressure but more remote in expectation, better incomes. What varies in our sample is the structuring of the larger system, the polity. In essence we examined the interaction of the squatter subsystems which start with largely common physical characteristics and needs and the variable states of the hierarchically inclusive systems—the polities. We show that the interaction between the variant polities and their changing states and the squatter settlements predicts in high degree the behavior of the latter. Indeed, we argue, given the initial conditions of both sets of actors, that the interaction *generates* the behavior, though a varying degree of freedom exists from case to case. We assert that one need postulate no cultural, moral, personal, psychological, or racial—or other such variables—to account for the behaviors.

A few generalizations of interest emerge:

(a) The more undependable the operation of any one variable of the higher level system or of the collective variables of that system, the more options for response are the populations concerned likely to develop.

(b) The more operational options, the greater the rewards extractable.

(c) The greater the number of options and the greater the rewards extractable for the collectivity, the greater the cumulative, long-run political bargaining power in the polity for the coup concerned.

The interpretation or model used has much wider application than to squatter settlements alone. Rather, from this point of view, one can look at the political action of *all* local level political units (the lower order systems in the kinds of hierarchical systems we are here concerned with) in confrontation with the political action of supra-local political units (the higher order systems of the hierarchy) in terms of the definition of appropriate variables, the weighted effects of the variables, the mutual constraints they exercise, the options open, and the behavior thus determined. From another point of view—more general still—the model applies to *all* political action in confrontation with other political action, *regardless* of hierarchy or level (see Leeds, 1973a, 1973c).

NOTES

1. "Related types of urban occupation" refers to the fact that the analytic distinction between squatter settlements and other types of housing-residential areas often relate to only one aspect of the very many which characterize these places. Thus, for example in Chile, it is misleading to talk about one kind of settlement where, over the past twenty years or so, different kinds of groupings known variously as *callampas, mejoras, poblaciones* (of various types), and *campamentos* have evolved in response to varying socio-political conditions and government action. A thorough description of the different types of settlement in Chile up to 1965 is given in DESAL, 1965. More recent developments are discussed in Cuellar, et al., 1971; CIDU, 1972b. "Experiencias . . ."; Castells, 1974; and Handelman, 1975. Nevertheless, these four types have in common that they are geographical units, each composed of low-income populations in more or less substandard (if occasionally considerably improved) conditions, each with a vested interest in their settlement as such. Parallels to these types are found in Perú in (a) *barriadas tugurisadas* (see Delgado, 1968), (b) what are now called *pueblos jóvenes* (those two categories subdivided by their status as being "recognized" or "not recognized" by the Junta Nacional de la Vivienda), (c) the multi-house low-income housing development, (d) *corralones,* and possibly, (e) the *unidades vecinales.* Brazilian parallels would be (a) the *favelas,* (b) the *villas,* and (c) the *parques proletarios* (see Leeds and Leeds, 1970; A. Leeds, 1974a). The absence of a full range of parallels in Brazil is clearly related to the nature of political policy and action and to the political structure as set forth in the text. Because of the common features of these various types and the numerical dominance, on the whole, of squatters and squatter settlements, as well as the fact that some of the other types partially involve squatting and invasion, we have used the term squatter settlements generally for all of them in the paper, recognizing that some variations in political behavior is thereby, inevitably glossed over. The differents among them seem most significant in Chile.

2. In addition to our own research and our visits, we have read the literature on squatter settlements and related low-income housing (see Leeds and Leeds, in preparation), particularly that having to do with politics and social organization not only for Perú, Brazil, and Chile, which are best documented, but also for Venezuela,

Colombia, Guatemala, Nicaragua, and Mexico which follow in quality of materials. To this may be added comparative literature on Hong Kong, Delhi, Lusaka, Lisbon, and Manila.

3. The awkward phrase 'subject matter' or 'subject matter of study' is used in order to avoid 'subject' or 'object' (of study) with their complex and entangling philosophical implications, expecially in the Hegelian and Marxian traditions, on one hand, and, on the other in their adjectival forms, 'subjective' and 'objective' in the British positivist tradition. We also avoid 'entity' or 'thing' since both often involve reifications based on built-in, unexplicit axioms (see Leeds, 1974b).

4. The ground is seen as constant in both passive and active ways, sometimes in a peculiarly contradictory manner. The passive view sees the ground, say, as an environment which, to all intents and purposes, is fixed or so macrocosmic that its variations are trivial and purely local. This view was (and largely still is) pervasive in approaches to understanding the individual in society or culture or, very frequently also, in ecological studies where the natural environment (even with seasonal or other variability) has been taken simply as an external given with which humans must deal. The more active view of this ground involves its conception as *determining* human action—humans, essentially, as the pawns of physical or social environments acting on them. Yet these environments are still, in these views, treated as essentially fixed and external, not themselves acted upon, shaped, and formed by individual, group, or aggregate human action. At the same time, the focus of study is human *action* and *activity* so that the ground, though determining, is still seen as curiously passive, while, since they are determined, humans are seen as peculiarly passive though in fact constantly acting. We find these views inherently contradictory, built into the metaphysics of categories and causal conceptions in inherited social science wisdom. We suggest that the general systems view resolves the problem.

5. It has endlessly been repeated in political science literature that people living under heavy-handed dictatorships are "depoliticized" since they "lack" practice in politics (i.e., electoral practice). They fail to see that exactly these conditions sharpen political strategic sense and analysis and strengthen organization—as the recent history of Portugal after a 50-year totalitarian regime and the continuing anti-authoritarian political events of Portugal and Spain respectively should once and for all indicate.

6. It is interesting to note that the utility and efficacy of psychological, including motivational, explanations of social phenomena, are reduced to an extremely peripheral role in a world that is seen in the manner described above. Perhaps the single basic assumption of a psychological sort that one need make is that, however much people may also act altruistically, they basically behave in terms of individual and collective self-interest. We would like to avoid the value reaction that that assumption always seems to elicit by pointing out that self-interest is not necessarily malign but can be, and perhaps usually is, benign and in fact makes altruism possible: one who has not adapted to a real world with some form of self-interest cannot also be altruistic.

7. The notion of 'integration', for example, means *only* the linking of populations of various sorts into the kind of political and social participation and organization characterized by western politics. That other forms of integration are equally valid, viable, and valued is excluded from further scientific consideration by definition with the result that especially the political science observers have been unable to see alternative modes of integration. However, see Payne (1965) and J. Powell (1970),

who are both clear on alternatives, that is, not boxed in by a tautological definition.

8. It is interesting to note the importance, too, of anarcho-syndicalist influence in the syndical or union movements at least of Brazil and Chile around the turn of the century, and afterwards, for nearly twenty years.

9. Recent political events in each of the three countries (Brazil, 1964; Perú, 1968; Chile, 1973) have changed some of the structures discussed in varying degrees.

After the elections of 1965 which, especially in Rio de Janeiro, went quite against it, the Brazilian military government which had entered with the coup d'etat of 1964, decreed a two-party system, though the old parties persisted "clandestinely" in various ways for several years afterwards (if not till today). Brazil does, in fact, have an operating three (or more) party system—the government party, Arena; the opposition Movimento Democrático Brasileiro, or MDB, and at least one highly constrained, underground communist party. Given the erraticness of electoral politics in 40 or so years preceding the military coup of 1964 and the structure of political strategies open to squatters under such conditions, the post-1964 conditions represent a continuity of one extreme of a familiar pattern.

In Perú, the 1968 coup d'état left the APRA and communist parties, as well as the small elite parties, essentially intact while trying to undercut their power by creating new constituencies in part drawn from the old parties. But this is, in fact, a standard political pattern for Perú so that our description applies continuously (including its applicability to the strong unions which have, in fact, continued to hold much power across the structural divide represented by the entrance to power of the present military regime).

In Chile, the multi-party system still exists despite extreme constraint from the repressive military regime. In fact, the pre- and post-Allende government coalitions persist today (in part underground, in part in exile; see Engler Perez, 1975). Both parties and coalitions still attempt to maintain political organization and mobilize action against the present government. Our description, however, is mainly restricted to the 40-year period up to 1973 characterized by "stable" electoral politics which, it was assumed, would continue indefinitely into the future.

It is important to note that neither author has, effectively, been in Chile. All our information comes from published sources or occasional personal communications. The ethnographic literature on Chilean (i.e., mainly Santiago) squatter settlements or other forms of proletarian settlement is almost entirely from recent times, the most thorough being post-Allende. Neither the time depth nor the richness of ethnographic detail that we have for Rio, Lima, or San Juan is available. Much of the data from DESAL, later from Portes's studies, and even from the Castells-CIDU research is essentially more or less detailed survey work and interviewing, rather than intensive, resident and participant-observational ethnographic work. The Castells-CIDU research is also, in our opinion, heavily freighted with *a priori* assumptions about class and ideology typical of French Marxism which prefigure their interpretations (see detailed summary of the latter in Handelman, 1975). We excluded Venezuela as an example, although it fits the comparative criteria, because the sources (e.g., Karst, Schwartz, and Schwartz, 1973) are too scattered over different cities and sites) to permit adequate analysis. Also the period of its multi-party organization has been rather short.

The reader will bear with our treatment of the Chilean case, recognizing that it is provisional until more ethnographic materials such as that gathered, but not published, by James Clifton becomes available.

10. We wish to emphasize that we are *not* asserting that "effective organized constituencies" necessarily get terribly much (however that be measured) from the external sources via the party structure but that, of what they *do* get, the bulk is gotten more efficiently through the party structure than through other channels. In fact, the Brazilian squatters' combined party-electoral, bureaucratic-personalistic, Church-patronal, and other minor options appear, at times, to have won almost as much as in Perú and Chile, with two notable differences. First, the Brazilian results are more irregular and unpredictable (see Leeds and Leeds, 1972); they do not have the kind of evolutionary direction which appears to be the case for Perú and, until recently, for Chile; second, the goods and services are not, on the whole, cumulative for the collectivities individually or as a category—a process most marked in Perú with the increasing rates of regularization, legalizing of titles, and municipalization of barriadas now ideologically raised to the status of "new towns" (*'pueblos jovenes'*). In this sense, squatters and squatter settlements of Peru, by combining purely-electoral, bureaucratic-personalistic, syndical, military-patronal, and economic-associational operations (e.g., using the vast sums of savings collected in popular housing cooperatives) appear to have extracted more goods and services out of the polity than either of the other systems.

11. One fundamental difference between the settlement pattern of squatments in the three countries should be noted here. Favelas are, for the most part, settled accretatively, with almost no pre-organization of the invasion. To our knowledge, only one favela in Rio has been settled in a manner even vaguely resembling an organized invasion, and the period of invasion stretched over a year, unlike the overnight process described for about half of the settlements of Lima and many of those of Santiago. For descriptions of invasions in Lima, see Mangin, 1963; Collier, 1971; Dietz, 1969; for Santiago, Giusti, 1971; Castells, 1974. The high frequency of the occurrence of such overnight invasions has, in Lima and Santiago, significance in its effect of making solidary invasion participants who then act in a relatively unified manner to secure and improve their holdings, at least until basic priorities are met. This opportunity for unification, then, is largely absent in Rio.

12. APRA's Lima headquarters was organized into divisions which would be ministries if APRA took over the government; among these divisions was a secretariat of barriadas.

13. Actually, APRA continues to exist till today (see *Latin America*, 9(43): 343, 1975) as a power in the politics of Perú—almost 50 years since its founding. Its original founder and ideologue, Haya de la Torre, is also still alive.

14. It was in Prado's first presidency that APRA was declared illegal, an act indicative of APRA's being seen as a threat to the status quo or at least to the control of power by the old elites.

15. It should not be understood that Odría reacted positively to all invasions. In the first two years of his regime, when he was dependent on conservative members of the coup coalition, he successfully evicted a little less than a third of all invasions. This contrasts with no evictions in the remaining six years (Collier, 1971: 69).

16. Of the many squatter settlements established during the Odría period, one was called Tarma Chica (after Odría's birthplace) and the other "27th of October," the anniversary of Odría's coup. Still others were named after his wife and the wife of a close associate (Collier, 1971: 64).

17. Collier (1971: 71-72) says: "Odría had used squatter settlements so success-fully that any politician who wished to oppose him not only had to devote a great

deal of attention to problems of housing, but was inevitably tempted to get directly involved with settlement formation as well. . . . It is therefore not surprising to find that political opponents of Odría made a calculated appeal to squatter settlements for political support, even political opponents on the right. What Collier does *not* see is how successful a political game the *residents of barriadas* had played.

18. It is interesting to note that of Collier's classification of six types of political involvement in settlement formation, out of a sample of 62 settlements, only four involved intervention by a non-presidential political party (p. 38). This also suggests that the simultaneous party competition predominant in Chile becomes, in Perú, a less sharply defined, more diffuse competition.

19. Leeds and Leeds, in preparation, list no less than twenty government reports in studies carried out from 1958 to 1962.

20. Under certain conditions, the Junta Nacional de la Vivienda "recognized" barriadas, that is, listed them as having an official status as urbanizable or otherwise formally under the supervision and physical support of the JNV.

21. There are other circumstantial chains of connection to the construction industry. Belaúnde promoted the peripheral highway along the lowlands at the base of the eastern Andes—to be built by Brown and Roote, the giant Texas construction firm. Belaund is a graduate of the University of Texas's school of architecture. In the American system of states having "sister countries," Texas's sister country is Perú through an organization called Texas Partners for Perú whose director was one of President Johnson's chief public relations men. Belaúnde and Johnson of course knew each other reasonably well.

22. At the inauguration of an electrical switching station in the pueblo joven, Comas (see A. Leeds, 1973b), one of the speakers, a minister of State, said "todo el Perú es un pueblo joven!"—i.e., all Perú is in the same condition as you are; we are all in this together without distinction.

23. As far as we are aware there is no systematic theory of the nature of politics in states lacking an electoral system or other local-level interest articulation mechanisms. Presumably this would include a theory of constituency interest aggregation articulated through bureaucracies, conflict being channelled among, and within factions of, bureaucratic agencies.

24. These sorts of groups no doubt exist in Chile, although they are unrecorded in the literature we have seen.

25. Since the Chilean case is our third paradigm, we use the present tense when referring to its paradigmatic character. In recounting historical events we use the past. That the paradigm no longer exists in actuality does not affect our usage.

26. The term is not usefully defined in these works. We find it a virtually useless term generally—even for the Europe for which is was originated—and specifically *not* useful for Latin America where it fails, in our empirical experience in Brazil and Perú (and probably in the United States as well) to distinguish systematically any two populations. We consider the concept one which reflects the class bias of the observers (much like the 'culture of poverty' notion)—all solid middle class (or, in the rhetoric, "bourgeois") from Marx and Engels on. The class bias is also a methodological one because of the failure actually to understand the options and strategies for living of the poor and relatively poor under severe constraints in the labor market. Such understanding requires intensive, participant observational, co-residential ethnographic work which *none* of the users of the term has done. They have failed, therefore, to see how persons confronted by labor market constraints strategize to

use various parts of the labor market in some maximizing or at least optimizing way (see Gianella, 1970; Hart, 1973; Machado, 1971; Mayhew, 1849-1850, 1861-1862; Peattie, 1975; Uzzell, 1972). They have failed, therefore, to discover that persons—given individuals—may operate in two or more sectors of the labor market concurrently as an optimizing-maximizing strategy, i.e., the same persons are industrial workers, or proletarians, and petty street sellers or odd-jobbers, or lumpenproletarians, at the same time. The two concepts, we hold, do not distinguish any valid categories of actors or of structures in the societies under discussion; the concept of lumpenproletariat is fundamentally rhetorical and class-based and should be dropped.

27. The mechanism is much better known for Perú—the invasion groups utilized personal networks of kin, neighbors, and home-town ties and associations to create the organized body of invaders. The networks not only recruited the personnel but also served as the information channels, e.g., to establish the place, date, and time of invasion and instructions for tactics and materiel needed for potential defense against police efforts to remove them. These invasions often had party sanctions as mentioned in the text, but were not as such organized by parties but by the invaders through their social ties. This was true also in the case where an invasion was encouraged by private persons (e.g., a land-owner whose land lay between the city and the proposed invasion spot so that, in the Peruvian context, it would appreciate as an urban instead of a rural land value) or possibly by a bureaucratic agency such as the Junta Nacional de la Vivienda.

28. This sort of organization is reported for the Italian political party system including the CP—and constitutes the characteristic mode of internal control over the party by the leadershop. Darwin (personal communication, 1975) provides a number of passages which suggest parallels in the Chilean organization of internal party controls although her intent is not that at all. "Squatter settlements in Chile are developed by a party. The toma is set up by X party. "The negotiating for titulos, infrastructure and community organizations: juntas de vecinos, centros de madres, etc., is handled by the party with government offices—Minesterio de la Vivienda, etc." "In most cases, the settlements continue under the domination of the founding party and its reps. in the sq. settlement." "During last years, 1971-1973, of Allende, the JAPs became more and more active and decisive . . . determining, according to level of organization and activity, the access of pobladores to food kerosene, etc. . . . according to participation levels."

29. Note that Talton Ray (1969) in effect describes these two orientations for the squatter settlements of Venezuela without understanding their implications. He bemoans the fact that some of the settlements do not participate more fully in the democratic process by becoming more attached to party politics and election. On the other hand, he points out that it is precisely the squatter settlements which are not so committed—as contrasted with those directly attached, in the original invasion and subsequent political life to a particular party—which get the greater rewards from the external political system.

30. Operación Sitio, advertized as the "solucion habitacional" of the Frei government, allowed persons to opt for a semi-urbanized 'sitio' which was paid for in monthly installments. PAP is a savings and credit scheme for families wishing to have either a semi-urbanized lot or a finished house. President Allende's Unidad Popular retained this scheme and modified it only slightly.

31. Ley 16,880 passed by the Chilean Congress on November 4, 1968.

32. The pre-1970 main independent parties—the PDC (Christina Democrats), PC,

PS, Partido Radical, and Partido Nacional were, in the elections of March, 1973, lined up as follows: CODE (Confederación Democratica), a coalition of Christian Democrats and the Partido Nacional and the Partido de Izquierda Radical (PIR); Unidad Popular, coalition of Communists, Socialists, Radicals, and Organizacion de Izquierda Christiana (OIC), Acción Popular Independiente (API), and the MAPU.

33. Much of what follows including the section on responses was supplied by the kindness of Shirley Darwin (personal communication, 1975) and in some passages constitutes a loose paraphrase of her statement. Hers is the nearest to ethnographic data we have encountered and we wish to thank her for letting us use it.

34. In the period immediately after the coup, it was reported in many sources that many mass shootings occurred especially in shantytowns or squatter settlements controlled by the left, that is, in campamentos, where oppositional organization might be supposed by the military to be high. See for example, the report of strafing "shantytowns in the *National Guardian*, Nov. 7, 1973, p. 14, by M. Mann.

35. We are speaking of patronal ties in urban situations. Such ties in the relative isolation of rural areas is quite another matter, since, in the absence of supportive political structures, no alternatives are available.

36. Given this hypothesis, it would be interesting to compare the degree of vulnerability and consequent loss of options after the Brazilian coup of 1964, the Peruvian coup of 1968, and that of Chile in 1973. We would predict that Brazilian and Peruvian settlements and their leaders suffered less overt repression and loss of options than their Chilean counterparts. We know of no parallels to the strafing mentioned in fn 34, nor with the mass shootings reported for squatments, especially those closely associated with the left, the MIR in particular. We were in Brazil each year from 1965 to 1969; each year saw major institutional and military acts of repression—against unions, students, the Church, etc., but only very limitedly against the favelas. We also went briefly to Perú in 1968, 1969, and 1970. Nothing remotely comparable to the Pinochetazo was reported from there either. Only in the great squatter invasion of 1971, were there some deaths when the thousands of invaders were removed. It is to be noted that these same invaders were immediately given another area to settle, somewhat further from Lima but still quite accessible. This was essentially a local event. The barriada residents are still a powerful political constituency to be coped with by the government.

REFERENCES

ANGELL, A. (1972) Politics and the Labor Movement in Chile. London: Oxford University Press.

BAMBERGER, M. (1968) "A problem of political integration in Latin America: the barrios of Venezuela." International Affairs 44, 4: 709-719. (London)

BONILLA, F. (1961) "Rio's favelas: the rural slum within the city." Reports Services 8, 3: 1-5 (East Coast South American Series). New York: American Universities Field Staff.

CASTELLS, M. (1974) La lucha de clases en Chile. México, Madrid, Buenos Aires: Siglo XXI.

CIDU (1972a) "Pobladores y administración de justicia." EURE 2, 5: 135-151. (Santiago)

——— (1972b) "Reivindicación urbana y lucha política: los campamentos de pobladores en Santiago de Chile." EURE 2, 6: 55-79. (Santiago)

COLLIER, D. (1971) "Squatter-settlement formation and the politics of co-optation in Perú." Ph. D. dissertation. University of Chicago.

CONN, S. (1969) The Squatters' Rights of Favelados. CIDOC Cuaderno No. 32. Cuernavaca: Centro Intercultural de Documentación.

COTLER, J. (1969) El Populismo militar como modelo de desarrolio militar, el caso peruano. Serie: Estudos Políticos 2. Lima: Instituto de Estudos Peruanos.

CUELLAR, O., R. CHEETHAM, S. QUEVEDO, J. ROJAS, and F. VANDER-SCHUEREN (1971) "Experiencias de justicia popular en poblaciones." Cuadernos de la Realidad Nacional 8: 157-172.

DARWIN, S. (1975) Personal communication. April 28.

DELGADO, C. (1968) Tres Planteamientos en Torno a la Problema de Urbanización Accelerado en Areas Metropolitanas: El Caso de Lima. Lima: Oficina Nacional de Planificación Urbana, PLANDEMET (Plan de Desarrollo Metropolitana).

DESAL (1965) Poblaciones Marginales: Un jemplo latinoamericano: Chile. Santiago: DESAL.

——— (1966) Antecedentes para el Estudio de la Marginalidad en Chile. Santiago: DESAL.

DIETZ, H. (1969) "Urban squatter settlements in Perú: a case history and analysis." Journal of Inter-American Studies 11, 3: 353-370.

ENGLER PEREZ, L. (1975) "Two years after coup: Chile struggle growing." National Guardian (October 8): 16.

GIANELLA, J. (1970) Marginalidad en Lima Metropolitana (una investigación exploratoria). Cuadernos Desco A8. Lima: Centro de Estudios y Promoción del Desarrollo.

GIUSTI, J. (1971) "Organizational characteristics of the Latin American urban marginal settler." International Journal of Politics 1, 1: 54-89.

GOLDRICH, D. (1970) "Political organization and the politicization of the poblador." Comparative Political Studies 3, 2: 176-202.

———, R. B. PRATT, and C. R. SCHULLER (1967-1968) "The political integration of lower-class urban settlements in Chile and Perú." Studies in Comparative International Development 3, 1. St. Louis: Washington Universify, Social Science Institute.

HANDELMAN, H. (1975) "The political mobilization of urban squatter settlements: Santiago's recent experience and its implications for urban research." Latin American Research Review 10, 2: 35-72.

HART, K. (1973) "Informal income opportunities and urban employment in Ghana." Journal of Modern African Studies 11: 61-89.

HUTCHINSON, B. (1960) Mobilidade e Trabalho: um estudo na cidade de São Paulo. Rio de Janeiro: Centro Brasileiro de Pesquisas Educacionais, Instituto Nacional de Estudos Pedagógicos, Ministério de Educacao e Cultura.

KARST, K. L., M. L. SCHWARTZ, and A. J. SCHWARTZ (1973) The Evolution of Law in the Barrios of Caracas. Los Angeles: University of California, Latin American Center. Latin America (periodical). London: Latin American Newsletters, 1966ff.

LEEDS, A. (1957) Economic 'Cycles in Brazil: The Persistence of a Total Culture Pattern: Cacao and Other Cases. Ann Arbor: University of Microfilms.

——— (1964a) "Brazilian careers and social structure: an evolutionary model and case history." American Anthropologist 66, 6: 1321-1347.

——— (1964b) "Brazil and the myth of Francisco Julião," pp. 190-204, 244-247 in J. Maier and R. W. Weatherhead, (eds.) Politics of Change in Latin America. New York: Praeger.

——— (1969) "The significant variables determining the character of squatter settlements." America Latina 12, 3: 44-86.

——— (1971) "The culture of poverty concept: conceptual, logical, and empirical problems, with perspectives from Brazil and Perú," pp. 226-284 in E. Leacock (ed.) The Culture of Poverty: A Critique. New York: Simon & Schuster.

——— (1973a) "Locality power vs. supra-local power institutions," pp. 15-41 in A. Southall (ed.) Urban Anthropology, Cross-Cultural Studies of Urbanization. New York: Oxford University Press (written 1964).

——— (1973b) "Political, economic, and social effects of producer and consumer orientations toward housing in Brazil and Perú: a systems analysis," pp. 181-211 in F. Rabinovitz and F. Trueblood (eds.) Latin American Urban Research, Vol. 3.

——— (1973c) "Economic-social changes and the future of the middle class," pp. 48-72 in Proceedings of the Experts Conference on Latin America and the Future of the Jewish Communities. London: Institute of Jewish Affairs.

——— (1974a) "Housing-settlement types, arrangements for living, proletarianization and the social structure of the city," pp. 67-99 in W. Cornelius and F. Trueblood (eds.) Latin American Urban Research, Vol. 4. Beverly Hills: Sage Publications.

——— (1974b) "Subjective' and 'objective' in social anthropological epistemology," pp. 349-361 in R. J. Seeger and R. S. Cohen (eds.) Philosophical Foundations of Science . . . Vol. 11, Boston Studies in the Philosophy of Science. Dordrecht, Boston: D. Reidel.

——— (1975) "Brazil: a systems analysis," Ms. (original version: "Investment in Brazil: the political climate: the opposition and security." In Brazil [mimeo]. London: Focus Research Inc.)

——— and E. LEEDS (1970) "Brazil and the myth of urban rurality: urban experience, work and values in squatments of Rio de Janeiro and Lima," pp. 229-272, 277-285 in A. J. Field (ed.) City and Country in the Third World . . . Cambridge: Schenkman.

——— (forthcoming) A Bibliography of the Sociology of Urban Low-Income Housing-Settlement Types in Latin America. Los Angeles: University of California, Latin American Center.

LEEDS, E. (1972) "Forms of 'squatment' political organization: the politics of control in Brazil." M.A. thesis. University of Texas.

——— and A. LEEDS (1972) Favelas and Polity, the Continuity of the Structure of Social Control in Brazil. LADAC Occasional Papers, Series 2, No. 5. Austin: University of Texas, Institute of Latin American Studies.

LEWIS, O. (1959) Five Families: Mexican Case Studies in the Culture of Poverty. New York: Basic Books.

——— (1961) The Children of Sanchez. New York: Random House.

——— (1965-1966) La Vida: A Puerto Rican Family in the Culture of Poverty—San Juan and New York. New York: Random House.

MACHADO DE SILVA, L. A. (1971) "Mercados Metropolitanos de Trabalho Manual e Marginalidad. M.A. thesis. Rio de Janeiro: Universidade Federal de Rio de Janeiro, Programa de Pos-Graduacãoem . . . Antropologia Social.

MANGIN, W. (1963) "Urbanization case history in Perú." Architectural Design (August): 365-370. (London)

——— (1967a) "Squatter settlements." Scientific American 217, 4: 21-29.

——— (1967b) "Latin American squatter settlements: a problem and a solution." Latin American Research Review No. 3: 65-98.

MANN, M. (1973) "Seeing the coup from Santiago." National Guardian (November 7): 14. (New York)

MAYHEW, H. (1849-1850) London Labor and the London Poor. 4 vols. New York: Dover (1968; first published in book form in London, 1861-62).

MEDINA, C. A. de (1964) A favela e o demagogo. Sao Paulo: Editora Martins.

PAYNE, J. L. (1965) Labor and Politics in Perú: the System of Political Bargaining. New Haven and London: Yale Univ. Press.

PEATTIE, L. (1975) "Living poor: a view from the bottom." Paper for the Colloquim on "Urban Poverty: A Comparison of the Latin American and the United States Experience." Los Angeles: University of California, Comparative Urban Group and Institute for Social Science Research.

PEARSE, A. (1957) "Integraçhão social das fámilias de favelados." Eduçacão e Ciencias Sociais 2, 6: 245-277. (Rio de Janeiro)

——— (1958) "Notas sobre a organizacão social de uma favela do Rio de Janeiro." Educacao e Ciencias Sociais 3, 7: 9-32.

PERLMAN, J. (1971) "The Fate of Migrants in Rio's Favelas: The Myth of Marginality." Ph.D. dissertation. Massachusetts Institute of Technology.

PERU (1957) Informe Sobre la Vivienda. Lima: Comision para la Reforma Agraria y la Vivienda.

PORTES, A. (1970) "El Proceso de urbanizacion y su impacto en la modernizacion de las instituciones politicas locales." Revista de la Sociedad Interamericana de Planificacion 4, 12-14: 5-21.

——— (1971a) "Urbanization and politics in Latin America." Social Science Quarterly 50: 697-720.

——— (1971b) "Political primitivism, differential socialization, and lower-class leftist radicalism." American Sociological Review 36: 820-835.

——— (1972) "Rationality in the slum: an essay in interpretative sociology." Comparative Studies in Society and History (July): 268-286.

POWELL, J. D. (1970) "Peasant society and clientist politics." American Political Science Review 64, 2: 411-425.

POWELL, S. (1970) "Political participation in the barriadas: a case study." Comparative Political Studies 2: 195-215.

QUIJANO, A. (1972) "La constitucion del "mundo" de la marginalidad urbana." EURE 2, 5: 89-106. (Santiago).

RAY, T. F. (1969) The Politics of the Barrios of Venezuela. Los Angeles: University of California.

RODRIGUES, A., G. RIOFRIO and E. WELSH (1972) "De invasores a invadidos." EURE 2, 4: 101-142. (Santiago).

SABLE, M. H. (1971) Latin American Urbanization: a Guide to the Literature and Personnel. Metuchen, N.J.

SCHMITTER, P. C. (1971) Interest Conflict and Political Change in Brazil. Stanford: Stanford University Press.

SKIDMORE, T. (1967) Politics in Brazil, 1930-1964: an Experiment in Democracy. New York: Oxford.

TURNER, J. F. C. (1963) "Dwelling resources in South America: Lima barriadas today: the unaided self-help solution . . ." Architectural Design: 360-393. (London)

––– (1966) "Asentamientos urbanos no reglados." Cuadernos de la Sociedad Venezolana de Plantificacion, No. 36. Caracas: Sociedad Venezolana de Planificacion.

––– (1968) "Uncontrolled urban settlement: problems and policies." International Social Development Review 1: 107-130.

––– (1969) "Cuevas, El Ermitaño, El Agustino, Mendocita, Mariano Melgar," pp. 131-214 in H. Caminos, J. F. C. Turner, and J. A. Steffian, Urban Dwelling Environments, an Elementary Survey of Settlements for the Study of Design Determinants. Massachusetts Institute of Technology Report No. 16. Cambridge: MIT Press.

UZZELL, J. D. (1972) "Bound for places I'm not known to: adaptation of migrants and residents in four irregular settlements in Lima, Perú." Ph.D. dissertation. University of Texas.

VANDERSCHUEREN, F. (1971a) "Pobladores y conciencia social." EURE 1, 3: 95-123. (Santiago).

––– (1971b) "Significado política las juntas de vecinos en poblaciones de Santiago." EURE 1, 2: 67-90. (Santiago).

VAUGHAN, D. (1968) "Links between peripheral income residential areas and political parties in a Latin American city." Austin: University of Texas, Anthropology Department. (ms.)

ABBREVIATIONS

AP	Acción Popular (Perú)
API	Accion Popular Independiente (Chile)
APRA	Alianza Popular Revolucionaria Americana (Peru)
ARENA	Alianca Renovadora Nacional (Brazil)
CIDU	Centro de Desarrollo Urbano y Regional (Chile)
CODE	Confedaracion Democrática (Chile)
DESAL	Desarrollo Económico-Social de America Latina (a research group at the Catholic University, Santiago, Chile)
EURE	Estudios Urbanos, Regionales, y Económicos (journal, Santiago, Chile)
JAP	Junta de Abastecimientos y Precios (Chile)
JNV	Junta Nacional de la Vivienda (Perú)
MAPU	Movimiento de Acción Popular Unitaria (Chile)
MDB	Movimiento Democrático Brasileiro (Brazil)
MIR	Movimiento Izquierda Revolucionaria (Chile)
OIC	Organización de Izquierda Cristiana (Chile)
ONDECOOP	Oficina Nacional de Cooperativas (Perú)
ONDEPUJOP	Oficina Nacional de Pueblos Jóvenes (Perú)
PAP	Plan de Ahorro Popular (Chile)
PC	Partido Comunista (Brazil, Chile)
PDC	Partido Democrata Cristiano (Chile)
PIR	Partido de Izquierda Radical (Chile)

PS   Partido Socialista (Chile)
PSD   Partido Social Democrático (Brazil)
PTB   Partido Trabalhista Brasileiro (Brazil)
PUJOP   Pueblos Jovenes (a barriada service organization, Peru)
SINAMOS   Sistema Nacional de Movilizacion Social (Peru)
UDN   Unian Democrática Nacional (Brazil)
UNO   Union Nacional Odrista (Peru)
UP   Unidad Popular (Chile)

Chapter 11

THE IMPACT OF CITYWARD MIGRATION ON URBAN LAND AND HOUSING MARKETS
Problems and Policy Alternatives in Mexico City

WAYNE A. CORNELIUS

Among the most visible and enduring consequences of large-scale rural-to-urban migration in Third World countries in recent decades are the changes it has brought about in urban settlement and landholding patterns. Coinciding with a period of rapid population growth due to natural increase, in-migration from the countryside has exerted extreme pressure on supplies of land and conventional housing, sharply increasing land prices and providing unprecedented opportunities for land speculation by urban elites and middle-class city dwellers, which has artifically driven up land and housing prices even further. Incoming migrants and the native-born urban poor have found themselves increasingly priced out of the conventional land and housing markets, leading to the formation of alternative, illegal or quasi-legal markets which respond primarily to mass demands for low-cost

AUTHOR'S NOTE: *For their very helpful comments on an earlier version of this paper I wish to thank John Walton, Alejandro Portes, James W. White, and other participants in the Conference on the Urban Impact of Internal Migration, held at the University of North Caroline, Chapel Hill, September 18-20, 1975, at which the paper was originally presented. Financial support for the larger study of migrants in Mexico City from which this paper grows was provided by the Danforth Foundation, the Foreign Area Fellowship Program of the Social Science Research Council and American Council of Learned Societies, the National Science Foundation (Grant GS-2738), and the Ford and Rockefeller Foundations' Program in Support of Social Science Research on Population Policy (Grant RF-73070).*

housing rather than the profit-making and capital accumulation goals of urban elites. At the same time, political conflict within large cities stems increasingly from the struggle for control of land, pitting the land-seeking poor against government officials and planners, large private landowners, speculators, unscrupulous subdividers, and even poor small farmers on the urban periphery whose land is increasingly coveted both by the poor and elite speculators.

Unfortunately, the social science literature on urbanization and the city in Third World countries is quite deficient in empirical studies of urban land tenure and land markets, which seriously hampers any effort at systematic, comparative analysis of the problems just described.[1] This paper is an attempt to expand the data base for such a future analysis, by focusing on the evolution of land and housing markets in the Mexico City metropolitan area since 1940. In addition to the studies cited below, data have been drawn from my comparative study of six predominantly low-income neighborhoods on the periphery of the city (Cornelius, 1975a), fieldwork for which was done in the 1970-1972 period, and from documentary research and personal interviews with government officials concerned with low-income housing problems conducted during the past year.[2] I begin with a brief survey of patterns of migration to metropolitan Mexico City, and the ways in which urban land and housing markets and government interventions in them have determined housing alternatives for migrants and the urban poor in general. The middle section of the paper deals in greater detail with problems of urban land speculation and the increasing penetration of the informal land and housing markets by elements of the formal, capitalist markets. Finally, I will review and evaluate some of the major public policy alternatives available to governments seeking to ameliorate these problems.

MIGRATION TO METROPOLITAN MEXICO CITY[3]

The mobility of the Mexican population has increased dramatically since 1940, to the point where in 1970 more than fifteen percent of the people—or 7.4 million out of 48.4 million—had lived in at least one state other than the one in which they were censused. It has been estimated that between 1950 and 1970 approximately 4.5 million persons migrated from rural to urban localities (Unikel et al., 1973: 24). Small and medium-sized cities have been bypassed by the majority of those leaving the countryside, whose preferred destinations are large metropolitan areas, especially the national capital. More than forty-three percent of the growth of the

Mexico City urban area during the 1960s was due to migration—about 1.8 million migrants in that decade alone (Unikel, 1972: 24). By 1970 the population of the capital's urban area—including the old urban core (Ciudad de Mexico), the Federal District surrounding it, and contiguous *municipios* (counties) in the state of Mexico—had reached 8.4 million, as compared with about 1.5 million in 1940. The figure approached 12 million in 1975, and is expected to reach 14.4 million by 1980. Projections by Luis Unikel and his associates at El Colegio de Mexico indicate an urban area population of 20.8 million by 1990, making Mexico City the third largest conurbation in the world, after Tokyo and New York.

During the 1950-1960 period the Mexico City metropolitan area grew at an average annual rate of 5.4 percent; in 1960-70 the rate rose to 5.7 percent; and from 1970 to 1975 it has been about 5.5 percent (Unikel et al., 1975). At the present time Mexico City's population is increasing by an estimated 1,650 inhabitants per day, of whom nearly half are newly arriving migrants from rural villages and small towns. The proportion of Mexico's total population residing in the capital has risen continuously, from 7.9 percent in 1940 to 17 percent in 1970 and an estimated 25 percent in 1980.

URBAN HOUSING ALTERNATIVES FOR THE MIGRANT POOR

At a time of sharply increasing demand for low-cost housing, the supply of conventional housing units for Mexico City's poor has been declining. The city's stock of low-rent housing has been depleted as centrally located tenement slums (*vecindades*) deteriorate and are replaced by commercial structures and high-rise middle-and upper-income apartment buildings. Very few housing opportunities remain in the surviving vecindades, whose populations tend to be highly stable, kept there largely by the extremely low, controlled rents in many vecindades. Rent controls, initially applied in 1942 to vecindad housing with a rent below 300 pesos per month and maintained ever since, have hastened the decline of the central-city tenements, whose owners have little incentive to invest in their upkeep. Many vecindades have already deteriorated to the point of physical collapse, forcing their residents to seek housing in squatter settlements or low-income subdivisions on the periphery of the city. This is reflected in the fact that the proportion of renters occupying rent-controlled housing in the central city has declined by more than fifty percent since rent controls were first imposed. The more fortunate residents of rent-controlled vecindades which are still structurally sound pay rents of 15 to 60 pesos (U.S.

$1.20 to $4.80) per month for their one- or two-room dwelling units. Those seeking housing in non-rent-controlled vecindades, whose primary advantage is their proximity to sources of low-skilled employment in the central city, must often pay rents 1,000 to 2,000 percent higher than those charged for rent-controlled vecindad units (Turner, 1971: II-6).

Housing opportunities in another basic type of centrally located low-income settlement, the *ciudad perdida* ("lost city"), have also declined substantially in the past two decades. Ciudades perdidas are tiny, very densely populated shantytowns, usually occupying the interior of a central-city block and completely surrounded by commercial or industrial structures. Most residents—whose incomes are among the lowest in the city—rent their plots of land from private owners and occupy self-built shacks of *lamina de carton* (a corrugated mixture of wastepaper and petroleum byproducts) and scrap materials. Many of these settlements sprang up in the 1945-1955 period when space in the central-city vecindades began to run out. In the past two decades they have become the most frequent target of "urban renewal" projects, which usually consist of demolishing the shacks of the poor and clearing the land for commercial developments, upper-income housing, or large public works. Emulating the example of its recent predecessors, the current Mexican government has triumphantly announced that between January 1971 and February 1975 it succeeded in "eradicating" a total of 157 ciudades perdidas and 62 vecindades in central Mexico City, as part of its "urban housing program." Many of the families forcibly evicted were subsequently relocated in government housing projects, in housing which they could not afford and soon abandoned, making way for more affluent working-class and middle-class families.

As mentioned above, earlier low-income migrants entering Mexico City usually settled in vecindades and ciudades perdidas in the old urban core; then, when finances permitted, they moved toward the periphery, where land was available for squatting or purchase at relatively low cost, and single-family dwellings could be built. Those arriving during the past two decades have found it necessary to pursue other types of housing alternatives on the urban periphery. Not only was the supply of housing in the urban core much depleted, but the dwelling units still available there (e.g., in non-rent-controlled vecindades) were often prohibitively expensive. Moreover, certain advantages afforded by residence in a peripheral settlement (savings on rent, the possibility of eventually owning a plot of land, isolation from the noise and pollution of the central city, a better environment for raising children, proximity to relatives who preceded them in migration to the city, and the replication of some aspects of rural life—

open space, tranquility, small-scale vegetable and livestock raising) made such settlements particularly attractive to recently arrived migrants.

The increased settlement of newly arriving migrants on the urban periphery, together with the continuing displacement of established migrants and the native-born poor from the central city, have fundamentally altered Mexico City's pattern of growth. According to one estimate, about 750,000 persons abandoned the central city during the 1960s, whereas the peripheral *colonias* (neighborhoods) gained about 2.4 million residents (Bataillon and Rivierde d'Arc, 1973: 42). By far the most explosive growth has been occurring in four municipios located in the State of Mexico, adjoining the Federal District: Ecatepec, Tlalnepantla, Naucalpan, and Metzahualcoyotl. Ecatepec and Netzahualcoyotl more than quadrupled their populations between the 1960 and 1970 censuses, and the other two municipios either doubled or tripled their populations. All four zones are now fully integrated into the Mexico City metropolitan area, and contain hundreds of low-income settlements.

Among the peripheral *colonias,* the prospective low-income settler may choose from two basic types, the squatter settlement and the low-income subdivision. Squatter settlements (*colonias paracaidistas*) have been formed through illegal occupation of public or privately owned land, usually in areas which have been left undeveloped because of highly irregular topography or unstable subsoil conditions. For example, on the western edge of the urban area, there are numerous steep ravines formed by small rivers flowing toward the city; and the extreme irregularity of the topography makes street construction in nearby areas very difficult. The bottoms of the ravines often contain sandpits exploited by commercial mining firms. When the sand mines are exhausted (sometimes even before they are completely worked out) the land they occupy is invaded by squatters. Similarly, ancient lava flows in the area known as the Pedregal in the southern part of the urban area have left large tracts of land with highly irregular topography, which is unsuitable for most conventional uses without a very large investment in urban infrastructure. These zones, too, have been occupied by squatters in large numbers. Other kinds of land bordering the urban area, such as the communally owned agricultural zones (*ejidos*) established during the agrarian reforms of the 1930s, have also been invaded by squatters, especially those lands unfit for cultivation or abandoned for some other reason by the *ejidatarios* (holders of ejidal land). Although invasions of this type of land have sometimes provoked violent clashes between ejidatarios and would-be squatters, many ejidatarios have actually encouraged squatting on some of their land, in hopes of receiving payments from the invasion organizers or indemnification from the government (in the event that the resulting squatter settlement is legalized by the government).

In some cases, squatter invasions take the form of a rapid, highly organized occupation; in others, a much more gradual and more or less unorganized occupation occurs over a period of several months or years. Since the early 1950s, when *paracaidismo* (squatting, but literally "para-chuting") became frequent within the Federal District, most land invasions have been resisted by government authorities, sometimes using riot police and sometimes even bulldozers. The amount of resistance encountered has usually been proportional to the number of squatters involved in an invasion and/or the political influence of the owner of the invaded land. Invasions of land in the public domain have generally met with less resistance from the authorities. In any event, government eviction attempts are rarely effective in the long run, since the invaded land is soon reoccupied, either by those who participated in the initial invasion or by another group of squatters.

The members of the invasion groups are typically families who began their urban careers as renters in established squatter settlements or other types of low-income neighborhoods on the urban periphery. The earliest invasion groups, in the 1950s, tended to be more heterogeneous and were recruited from the residents of vecindades and ciudades perdidas widely dispersed through the central city, often through work-place ties. Most of these "pioneer" squatters had accumulated considerable experience in Mexico City prior to joining an invasion group. During the past decade, however, participation in land invasions has been influenced most strongly by geographic proximity to the invasion sites: most of the initial residents of these more recently formed settlements had lived in rented housing in adjacent low-income neighborhoods, or were living with relatives (as "*arrimados*") in these same neighborhoods.[4] Peter Ward (1975: 23) has observed this recruitment pattern in a large squatter settlement, Santo Domingo de los Reyes, invaded in 1971:

> Immediately after the invasion of the first few hundred families, [migrants living with kin in adjacent neighborhoods] quickly realized the implications of such a move and joined in. The pressures to do so would probably be considerable; they would be urged on both by the desire to live apart and get a foothold in the land market . . . as well as being encouraged by their successful squatter relatives, with the proviso that they could always return if the invasion failed. . . . The rapidity and "fait accompli" that [the invasion of] Santo Domingo de los Reyes demonstrated was a result of the highly mobile supply of householders that surrounding squatter settlements were able to provide.

Thus, while it is still true that few incoming migrants participate in squatter invasions to solve their immediate housing problem, they are doing so after an increasingly brief period of cohabitation and urban orientation with relatives. Ward's data from Santo Domingo de los Reyes and several other older squatter settlements included in his study clearly indicate that the period of urban residence for migrants prior to their arrival in squatter settlements is declining. My own data from three additional squatter settlements formed during the 1950-1968 period reveal a similar trend. This reflects not only the higher incidence of kin-mediated migration to the periphery of the city in recent years, which places higher proportions of newly arrived migrants in closer proximity to potential invasion sites, but also the increasingly severe shortage of conventional (legal) housing alternatives for the poor.

The perceived legitimacy of squatting as a housing solution among low-income sectors of the population has increased dramatically during the past two decades. My interviews with migrants living in three squatter settlements revealed that virtually all of those who participated in the initial invasions through which these settlements were formed were acutely aware of the illegal character of their actions and of the danger of reprisals by landowners or government authorities. Yet they also felt strongly that the land affected had not been fulfilling any useful social purpose, having been abandoned or left undeveloped by its legal owners; and economic necessity compelled them to assume the risks and take advantage of the opportunity for a homesite afforded by the land invasion.

Even among the poor in Mexico City who have never participated in a squatter invasion, there appears to be much sympathy and understanding for those who have done so. To illustrate, migrants interviewed in my six research communities—only half of whom were residents of squatter settlements—were asked the following question:

> Now I would like to know *how right or wrong* you think different kinds of actions are. For example, most people think that something like murder is very wrong, while something like bragging may seem only a little bit wrong or not wrong at all. Here is another example: A man recently arrived from the countryside invades a piece of land when he has trouble finding a place to live in the city. Would you say that this is not wrong, that it is only a little wrong, or that it is very wrong?

Thirty percent of the total sample of migrant respondents believed that squatting in such a case would be "only a little wrong," and an additional thirty-three percent felt it would not be wrong at all. As might be expected, about eighty percent of migrants living in the two most recently formed squatter settlements included in my study expressed approval or only mild disapproval of squatting. Clearly, a conception of private land-holding rights quite different from that shared by the majority of low-income city dwellers prior to the 1950s has taken root among this sector of the urban population.

The Mexican government itself was, however unwittingly, one of the chief instigators of this change of attitude. Squatting became widespread in the Mexico City urban area only in the mid- and late 1950s, after a ban was imposed on the establishment of new residential subdivisions within the Federal District. During the 1952-1970 period this ban was selectively enforced by the head of the Department of the Federal District (the principal organ of local government for Mexico City and the surrounding Federal District) in a crude attempt to discourage further in-migration by preventing the subdivision of land for settlement by low-income families. However, many new upper- and middle-class subdivisions were opened up within the Federal District during this same period. The government's restriction of new conventional housing opportunities for the poor in the Federal District, at a time when the city's population was growing (mainly due to in-migration) at an unprecedented rate, had two principal conse-quences. First, land invasions became endemic in the Federal District. The incidence of squatting rose continuously during the 1950-70 period, de-spite vigorous repression by Federal District authorities and a policy of denying basic urban services and land tenure rights to any squatter settle-ments which survived government eviction attempts. Squatters often suc-ceeded in providing themselves with electricity by illegally tapping power poles and transformers in nearby areas with regular electrical service; but most other improvements and government recognition of land tenure rights had to be sought through protracted and difficult negotiations with Federal District authorities, most of which were unproductive until a new Federal District governor more favorably disposed to legalization and extension of basic services to existing squatter settlements was appointed in 1966.

The second major consequence of the Federal District's restriction of low-cost housing opportunities was the rapid expansion of the Mexico City metropolitan area into the eight State of Mexico municipios bordering the subdivisions by private developers. The number of government-authorized subdivisions in these municipios grew from 10 in 1957 to 125 in 1968, and today the total is well above 200. This proliferation of subdivisions in the State of Mexico, together with the expansion of industrial employment opportunities in such municipios as Tlalnepantla and Ecatepec (partly in response to the State of Mexico's tax exemption policy for new industries), produced a major demographic shift within the metropolitan area during the 1960-1970 period. In 1960, ninety-four percent of the metropolitan population lived in the Federal District, while only six percent resided in the State of Mexico; by 1970 the State of Mexico's share of the metropolitan area population had risen to twenty-one percent (see Table 1).

Initially, the land used for low-income subdivisions was among the least valuable property in the metropolitan area. Most of it, especially the immense, almost dry Texcoco lakebed extending east of the international airport, was not suitable either for agriculture (because of high soil salinity and seasonal flooding) or industrial use (having no convenient sources of water and electricity). It had been bought up in the 1940s for a few *centavos* per square hectare by a handful of entrepreneurs—including some army generals—who were later to become millionaires from their miniscule investment.

Among the rapidly proliferating low-income subdivisions in the State of Mexico, the 56 subdivisions established in the *municipio* of Ciudad Netzahualcoyotl experienced the most explosive population growth. Netzahualcoyotl's population grew from about 65,000 in 1960 to 650,000 in 1970 and about 1.3 million by 1975, rendering it the third largest urban zone in the nation, exceeded only by Mexico City (the old central core plus contiguous urbanized areas of the Federal District) and Guadalajara. During the 1950s and most of the 1960s, land in the Netzahualcoyotl subdivisions and many others within the State of Mexico was generally

TABLE 1
METROPOLITAN MEXICO CITY:
POPULATION GROWTH AND PHYSICAL EXPANSION, 1900-1970

Year	Total		Federal District		State of Mexico	
	Population (millions)	Area (sq. km.)	Population (millions)	Area (sq. km.)	Population (millions)	Area (sq. km.)
1900	541,000	27,137	541,000	27,137	--	--
1910	721,000	40,100	721,000	40,100	--	--
1920	906,000	46,375	906,000	46,375	--	--
1930	1,229,600	86,087	1,229,600	86,087	--	--
1940	1,757,500	117,537	1,757,500	117,537	--	--
1950	3,480,000	240,587	3,480,000	240,587	--	--
1960	5,086,900	342,750	4,870,900	333,000	216,000	9,750
1970	8,634,000	526,500	6,874,200	413,000	1,760,000	113,500

SOURCE: Bazant (1975: 10).

within the reach of families with very limited means, since the promoters offered very small individual lots, low down payments (often as low as 50 pesos, or U.S.$4), and extended payment terms (usually 7-10 years). Settlers were also lured by promises of "complete" urban services and improvements, to be provided by the subdividers. However, virtually all of the subdividers of land for low-income settlement defaulted on their promises of urban services, leaving the residents themselves to install whatever provisional improvements they could finance, unassisted by the State or municipal governments.

Following the enactment of a 1958 law by the legislature of the State of Mexico, individuals or companies subdividing a tract of land into lots to be sold on the public market were obligated to install certain basic services (piped water, sewage systems, and electricity), to pave the streets, to install curbs and sidewalks, and to set aside a certain amount of land within the subdivision for schools, public markets, parks, and other community facilities. Those who had secured government authorization to subdivide before 1958 were not legally obligated to contribute anything to the improvement of their subdivisions, since the legislation was not retroactive. The 1958 law was almost totally ignored by subdividers, and their violations went unpunished. As a result, their contribution to the "urbanization" of low-income subdivisions has consisted of little more than the creation of a more or less regular layout of unpaved streets to provide access to the lots being sold off.

Even more serious abuses were committed by the scores of subdividers who failed to obtain any sort of government authorization for their activities, resulting in completely illegal, unserviced subdivisions (*fraccionamientos clandestinos*). Many of these "clandestine" subdividers even lacked clear title to the land they were selling, and thousands of poor families who purchased lots from them have found their tenure threatened when the subdivider's claim to the land was successfully challenged. Of course, most low-income purchasers of land in unauthorized subdivisions have not been aware of their illegal status, at least at the outset. The magnitude of land fraud committed in this way since the early 1950s has reached into the billions of pesos. The proliferation of clandestine commercial subdivisions has not been limited, of course, to the State of Mexico; hundreds of them emerged simultaneously with squatter settlements within the Federal District, whose authorities made no serious attempts to control unscrupulous promoters or to deal with the problems left in their wake until after 1970.

This failure is not too surprising, in light of the fact that many of the most "successful" subdividers were themselves middle- and upper-echelon government officials, politicians, and army officers, or had close personal contacts with those in authority. One of the most striking examples of the political influence commanded by the subdividers is provided by the recent experience of Ciudad Netzahualcóyotl, where the federal government finally intervened in 1974 to "regularize" the land tenure situation in unauhorized subdivisions and provide basic urban services to these as well as the officially authorized subdivisions which had been left unimproved by their subdividers. The government's "solution" to these problems took the form of a special agency (Fideicomiso Netzahualcoyotl) empowered to collect payments totalling 13,200 pesos (110 pesos monthly) from each lotholder for regularization of tenure rights and introduction of basic services, services for which they have already paid (to the subdividers as well as the municipal government) but have never received. Incredibly, the subdividers are to receive forty percent of all funds collected by the agency. The government's intervention in Netzahualcóyotl occurred only after fifteen years of sustained protest by the residents and, most recently, a residents' moratorium on all outstanding lot payments owed to the subdividers. The latter now seem assured of reaping an even more handsome return on their "investment."

The third type of housing alternative which is theoretically available to low-income families seeking housing on the urban periphery is the government housing project. In recent years such projects have taken two principal forms: the "conventional" public housing project, in which residents purchase government-built row houses or units in multifamily buildings, located in more-or-less fully serviced areas; and "site-and-services" projects, in which settlers purchase a small lot and build their own houses, sometimes with government technical assistance and low-cost building materials purchased through official agencies. Basic services and urban improvements in "site-and-services" projects may be nonexistent at the outset, but they are usually installed over a period of several years as the population density in project zones increases. The settlers make installment payments to the government to cover the cost of their plot of land, basic urban services, and any construction materials purchased from government agencies.

Both types of public housing projects have been designated by the government as reception areas for families evicted from vecindades, ciudades perdidas, or squatter settlements to make way for public works and "urban renewal" projects, although the majority of these settling in them had not been displaced in this way. A large proportion of public housing has been offered initially to lower-level government employees (including bureaucrats, police, army personnel, and school teachers) or unionized industrial workers affiliated with the official political party (PRI). Many other upper-low and middle-class families have purchased houses or land in such projects from poorer families who had been among the original settlers, but who lacked the resources to make regular install-ment payments on their lots or houses or to pay for urban services—even though virtually all of these property transfers are illegal under govern-ment regulations for public housing projects. In fact, most housing in government projects is not accessible to the poorest forty percent of the city's population, for both political and financial reasons. By early 1970, only 500,000 people—or 6 percent of the metropolitan area population—lived in public housing (Turner, 1973: 240), and this proportion has not increased appreciably in the past five years.

THE DYNAMICS OF LOW-COST URBAN LAND
AND HOUSING MARKETS

A formidable array of political, economic, and demographic forces have combined in recent decades to restrict housing opportunities for the poor in Mexico City while creating unprecedented opportunities for profit-making and capital accumulation among a limited sector of the city's population. It is clear that the sheer volume of in-migration from the countryside, coupled with a rate of natural population increase ranging between 3.0 and 3.5 percent in recent years, has been the principal factor responsible for rapid expansion of demand for low-cost housing. At the same time, government interventions such as central-city rent controls and restrictions on the subdivision of land for settlement by the poor have had a negative impact on the supply of conventional low-cost dwelling units, leaving the poor to find their own solutions to the housing problem—solutions embodied in the explosive growth of squatter settlements, unauthorized subdivisions, and other types of "non-planned" or "spon-taneous" urban settlements.

Yet these distortions in urban land and housing markets are not by themselves sufficient to explain the slow rate at which new housing assessible to low-income migrants and other elements of the urban poor have been created in recent decades. Other factors—a private real estate and housing construction industry geared primarily to the creation of housing opportunities for upper-income families in "luxury" subdivisions, rampant land speculation, and the very limited amount of credit made available to would-be low-income land purchasers or home builders—have also contributed powerfully to the acute shortage of conventional low-cost housing opportunities.

Investment in unimproved urban land as a source of prestige and a shelter against inflation and unstable currencies has been practiced extensively by elites in Mexico and other Latin American countries since the early colonial period (see Portes and Walton, 1975: ch. 2). It is a form of investment which requires little specialized knowledge, returns a quick profit, and entails little risk, certainly as compared with most alternative investment opportunities. Although the most important speculators in urban land are large real estate firms, consortia, and individual members of the political and commerical-industrial elites, who buy up large tracts of land for future subdivision, initially low lot prices in unimproved subdivisions have made it possible for many middle and lower-middle income families to engage in speculative land investment.

Returns on investments in urban land have been impressively high, especially in land on the periphery of the capital city, where land values have been increasing at annual rates of fifteen to fifty percent, as compared with eight to twelve percent per year in more centrally located zones (Turner, 1971: IV-11; Ward, 1975: 27, note 3; Bazant, 1975: 75). Such rates are well in excess of the rate of inflation in the general price index in Mexico, even during the period of double-digit inflation experienced since 1970. In the peripheral low-income subdivision included in my study, lot prices had risen from five pesos per square meter in 1951 to 320 pesos per square meter in 1970, when the last of the 3,200 lots in the subdivision were sold. About 500 of the lots remained undeveloped, the majority of them held by nonresident land speculators. In more recently established subdivisions, the proportion of speculative lot holding is much higher, and increases in land values up to forty percent during the first two or three years following the opening of a subdivision are not uncommon. Speculative investment has affected property values to such an extent that low-income families are increasingly finding lots in officially authorized subdivisions beyond their reach.

The flow of domestic capital into the urban land market has had serious negative consequences for the rate of investment in productive (and job-creating) enterprises. As the industrial sector has come increasingly under the control of foreign corporations, it has become highly capital-intensive, and in recent years the rate of job creation in Mexico City has declined significantly, at a time when the age structure of the population and rates of in-migration and natural population growth all dictate that many more jobs are needed if disastrously high unemployment and under-employment rates are to be avoided (Contreras, 1972: Muñoz, et al., 1972;

López Rosado, 1975; Robles Quintero, 1975). By 1974 an estimated 5.7 percent of Mexico City's economically active population were unemployed (6.3 percent in the Ciudad Netzahualcóyotl section), and 35.3 percent were underemployed (Excéisior, 21 June 1975: 10A; Manuel Gollas, quoted in Moiron, 1975: 7). To the extent that the opportunities available to the low-income population for obtaining stable and reasonably well-paid employment are declining, their chances of competing successfully in the land, housing, and credit markets are greatly reduced. Speculative investment in urban land by upper- and middle-class elements of the population is likely to continue at a high level, as long as such investment is less risky and more profitable than investment in productive enterprises, and direct government intervention in the land market remains negligible.

Recent years have also brought an increase in the incidence of "urban *latifundismo*"—the holding of vast tracts of unimproved land, especially on the urban periphery, usually for speculative purposes. Under existing market conditions, it is clearly more profitable to engage in large-scale, speculative land acquisition than to invest in housing construction, especially the construction of low-cost housing units for rental or sale. Although there are legal limitations on the size of handholdings in rural areas, specified in Mexico's agrarian reform code, no such restrictions apply in the urban sector. In May 1975, the Department of the Federal District announced that it had identified more than eight thousand land parcels within the Federal District having a value in excess of 20 million pesos each. However, government officials refused to publicly identify any of their owners (since it is not illegal to possess large unimproved landholdings within the city), and they readily admitted that the actual number of such large holdings is undoubtedly much larger than the announced figure due to the frequent practice of registering several smaller but contiguous parcels of land under the names of relatives and/or private organizations and holding companies, usually for purposes of property tax evasion (Excéisior, 8 May 1975: 1A, 11A, 15A).[5]

Large landholdings can be amassed by purchasing tracts of unimproved agricultural land bordering the urbanized area, either from private landowners or *ejidatarios* (even though the sale, rental or mortgaging of ejidal land is explicitly prohibited by agrarian reform legislation). However, they can also be assembled by buying up numerous lots in low-income subdivisions, squatter settlements, or even public housing projects. The sellers are often the poorest residents of these settlements, who are compelled to secure quick cash to meet some family emergency (illness, loss of job by the family head, etc.), or who simply find it too difficult to resist the offers of affluent land-seekers. Many of the poor families who transfer their property in this way are soon forced back into the illegal land and housing markets, participating in squatter invasions or buying new lots in recently established clandestine subdivisions.

The severe limitations on credit available to low-income families through public and private lending institutions represent yet another major constraint on low-cost housing opportunities in Mexico City. The vast majority of poor city dwellers do not qualify for bank loans due to their low and unstable incomes, and even those with higher incomes are often ineligible for home building or home improvement loans because, as residents of clandestine subdivisions or "non-regularized" squatter settlements, they lack legal title to the land they occupy. In any event, most sources of credit would prefer to serve the more lucrative, lower-risk upper-income market. As in many cities in the United States, financial institutions in Mexico City are usually unwilling to provide the low-income home-seeker with mortgage credit except through the intermediary of the speculative developer, i.e., they prefer to finance the speculator rather than the prospective homeowner directly. "The financial institutions, by denying funds to certain groups in particular areas and channeling investment to preferred speculative borrowers, created a decision context in which speculative activity was almost bound to succeed" (Harvey, 1975: 146). Government institutions have done little to expand the amount of credit available to the neediest residents of the city, preferring to channel their funds primarily to unionized industrial workers, government employees, and other more favorably situated in the socio-political hierarchy.

Students of urbanization in Third World countries have frequently observed that, unable to compete successfully in conventional urban land, housing and credit markets, the poor have increasingly tended to bypass these markets entirely by occupying land in illegal or quasi-legal settlement zones, resulting in "the forced partition of the system of urban land allocation into a dual structure: one formal and governed by capitalist market forces, the other informal and ruled by popular demand" (Portes and Walton, 1975: ch. 2). In Mexico and several other Latin American countries, however, the "informal" (illegal or quasi-legal) markets have become increasingly penetrated by elements of the conventional, capitalist markets. Clandestine subdivisions are often established by speculative developers who also own one or more government-authorized subdivisions; squatter invasions are increasingly led by "professional" invasion organizers, acting either individually or as agents of speculative developers, politicians, *ejido* leaders *(comisarios ejidales),* and others whose motives are identical to those who operate in the conventional urban land market.[6] Traffic in land within squatter settlements and clandestine subdivisions is

usually an exceedingly lucrative business, even though the property transfers have no legal standing, and the settler's tenure rights may be challenged by the government or private landowners at any moment (see
Cornelius, 1975a: ch. 6).

A resident of an unauthorized subdivision may also be arbitrarily
dispossessed by the clandestine subdivider himself or a local leader acting
at his behest; the subdivider may then proceed to resell the lot, at a price
considerably higher than the original purchase price. Numerous lots in an
illegal settlement may be "repossessed" and resold in this manner up to six
times during a period of ten to fifteen years. Of course, the settlers evicted
have no legal recourse due to the irregular tenure situation of the settlement or subdivision. In those cases where the government finally intervenes to halt illegal land transfers and regularize the tenure situation,
settlers must pay again for the land they occupy—this time to the government—at a price which often reflects the inflation of land values in the
subdivision during the period since it was established. Of course, much of
this increase in land values results from the settlers' own investments in
permanent housing construction and provisional urban services.

POLICY ALTERNATIVES AND CONSTRAINTS

The dismal performance of Mexico City's conventional land and housing markets in meeting the demand of low-income migrants and native-
born city dwellers for basic shelter and landownership opportunities has
prompted a steady stream of policy recommendations from concerned
urbanists and planners. Among other steps, they have called for large-scale
expropriation (with indemnification) or purchase of privately owned land
within the metropolitan area and bordering it by the national government,
with redistribution of the expropriated land in the form of lots in "site-
and-services" projects, or simply as "sites-without-services"; the designation
of large tracts of undeveloped, publicly owned land in the metropolitan area
for settlement by low-income families; and legalization of most already
established squatter settlements and clandestine subdivision. The overall
objectives of such policies would be to increase the supply of "secure" land
available for self-built housing for the urban poor, and halt the anarchic,
horizontal expansion of the city through greater government control over
land use.

Unfortunately, the existing configuration of economic interests and
political power within the Mexican system raises grave questions about the
political feasibility of any of the proposed schemes for "urban land

reform." The political influence enjoyed by real estate interests, professional speculators, the construction industry, and their allies within the official party-government apparatus is such that most policy initiatives in this area can be blocked, or their implementation subverted in such a way as to greatly weaken their impact. Sweeping urban reforms such as that implemented in Cuba since 1959 (see Acosta and Hardoy, 1973), involving such measures as complete socialization of the housing construction industry and strict controls on the transfer of land through sale or inheritance, run so strongly against existing economic and political currents that they are not even seriously proposed.

The vociferous reaction of the landed elite to a recent government initiative in the area of urban property taxation is indicative of the basic problem confronting would-be urban reformers. It is clear that the lack of an effective or substantial tax on urban land, particularly unimproved parcels, has been one of the most important factors encouraging land speculation during the past three decades. Only in 1975 did the Department of the Federal District begin enforcing urban property tax reforms which substitute a system of progressive tax rates based on size of landholdings for the uniform rate in effect until January 1, 1975. The reforms also specify an immediate 20 percent increase in tax rates for unimproved landholdings. The response of the wealthiest landholders was to block collection of their new tax assessments through court injunctions (*amparos*) (El Día, Mexico City, 16 July 1975: 13; 23 July 1975: 13). In any event, the impact of the tax reforms on urban land and housing markets is likely to be rather limited, due to the evasion strategies available to large landholders (e.g., registration of parcels under the names of various relatives or holding companies, hiring "squatters" to erect temporary dwellings on unimproved land, etc.), and because they do not affect landholdings in those portions of the metropolitan area located in the State of Mexico—precisely the areas in which land speculation is now most intense.

The experience of many Third World and advanced industrial countries with urban property taxation suggests that this policy instrument is rarely sufficient by itself to halt land speculation and make land available in adequate quantity at reasonable prices to both public agencies and low-income individuals (see, for example, Mohan, 1974). To achieve these goals it is necessary to "disinflate" the cost of urban land, preferably through large-scale government acquisition of privately held land and subdivision of land already within the public domain for residential use. Direct State participation in urban land markets has resulted in significant declines in land prices in some countries (Hardoy, 1972a: 38); but massive interventions of this sort are also the least likely to be attempted because of the high political costs they entail.

Given the existing tightness of fit between the distribution of political power and the distribution of wealth in countries like Mexico, even the more limited policies and programs which are likely to be implemented in this problem area seem destined to benefit the already privileged sectors of the population. While a more extensive program of legalizing and up-grading established squatter settlements and clandestine sub-divisions would undoubtedly deal more effectively and economically with the low-cost housing shortage than an "urban renewal" program involving eradication of illegal settlements and transfer of their residents to public housing projects, most governments have opted for the latter approach. Of course, large-scale destruction of spontaneous low-income settlements has the effect of only further depleting a city's stock of potentially usable housing for the poor. Almost invariably, the land made available by such eradication schemes is quickly occupied by middle- and upper-class hous-ing or high-rise commercial developments. But the interests of the banks, real estate firms, and construction companies are well served.[7]

The continued flow of government resources into conventional public housing projects represents another kind of subsidy to the already privi-leged. In Mexico City and virtually all other major Latin American cities for which data are available, the principal beneficiaries of government-constructed housing have been lower-middle and middle-income families, even in projects supposedly destined for occupancy by the neediest. Although corrupt or inefficient administration of the projects during the period since they were completed is partly to blame, the basic problem has been that only the more affluent working-class families with stable in-comes can afford such housing. Despite this dismal record, no fewer than twelve different federal and state government agencies operating in the Mexico City metropolitan area continue to build conventional public housing. The cost of such housing to the government limits construction to a few thousand dwellings per year.[8]

What seems essential to any effective strategy for increasing the housing opportunities available to low-income city dwellers in Mexico City and other Latin American cities is a greatly expanded governmental presence in both the formal (legal) and informal (illegal or quasi-legal) urban land market. As Hardoy (9172a: 38) has argued, without greater public control of land allocation and land values, "there is no solution to the present situation, much less to that of the future." In most Latin American countries, such control would represent a drastic reorientation of public policy in this area. In these countries, "the dominant role of contemporary public institutions has not been to prevent capitalist distortions of urban development but rather to adapt the city, as well as possible, to the new and difficult conditions. It has been, by and large, an alleviating, 'patching up' function, not a regulatory or preventive one" (Portes and Walton, 1975: ch. 2).

All available evidence from Mexico City and other major cities in the region indicates that a shift to a more active, regulatory and preventive role for government in urban land and housing markets is imperative if the worst excesses of capitalist market forces are to be curbed and the position of the materially disadvantaged in the struggle for urban housing opportunities is to be improved significantly. Unfortunately, the prospects for such a shift are not bright.[9] In its absence, the poor will continue to provide easy sources of profits for unscrupulous land invasion organizers, speculative subdividers, and indigenous leaders of spontaneous settlements.

NOTES

1. The only recent cross-cultural analysis of which I am aware is Evers (1975), which concentrates on Southeast Asian cases. Portes (in Portes and Walton, 1975: ch. 2) has provided a valuable historical analysis of the dynamics of urban land markets in Latin America, and Vance (1971) gives additional historical perspective on the issues involved. For a comparative study of government intervention in urban land markets in the United States and several West European countries, see Heidenheimer et al. (1975: ch. 4). Papers addressed to specific cities include Kimani (1972), on Nairobi, and Sargent (1972), on Buenos Aires. There is also a small (largely perscriptive) literature on urban land policies in developing countries; see especially Mabogunje (1972), on Nigeria; Keles (1972), on Turkey; Mohan (1974), on India; Hardoy (1972a, 1972b) and Acosta and Hardoy (1973), on Cuba and other Latin American countries. The extensive literature on squatter settlements and other types of "uncontrolled" urban settlements in Third World cities is also suggestive of important insights, but is not generally addressed to the structural conditions and institutional forces which determine lower-class housing alternatives. Among the notable exceptions are Leeds (1969, 1973, 1974), Peattie (1974), and Portes (1971).

2. The six neighborhoods studied include three squatter settlements of different types of origin and at different levels of development, a low-income, commercially promoted subdivision, a government "site-and-services" project, and a conventional public housing project. The research sites are widely dispersed around the periphery of the Mexico City metropolitan area; no central-city slum was studied, due to the lesser and constantly declining importance of these zones as receiving areas or ultimate residential locations for low-income migrants from the countryside. Further criteria for site selection as well as a complete description of the research design and data-gathering techniques are provided in Cornelius (1975a: ch. 1 and Appendix D).

3. Portions of this and the following section are drawn from Cornelius (1975a: ch. 2). In this paper I concentrate on the political-economic aspects of the various

types of settlements in which most migrants to the Mexico City metropolitan area in recent decades have settled. For a more detailed description of the physical and developmental characteristics of these settlement types, see Cornelius (1975a: chs. 2, 5, 6).

4. Most of the older squatter settlements and low-income commercially promoted subdivisions on the urban periphery contain a certain amount of rental housing, most frequently in small vecindades constructed on single lots by the lotholders. In addition, it is increasingly common to find two or even three kin-related households occupying separate dwellings on a single subdivision lot or parcel of land within a squatter settlement (see Ward, 1975: 23; Lomnitz, 1974, 1975). Such lot-sharing apparently facilitates the functioning of informal mutual-assistance networks which help their members to cope with periods of unemployment and other temporary family crisis.

5. Such practices are also widespread in Mexico's rural sector, where multiple registrations of single large landholdings are used to evade agrarian reform restrictions. These holdings are often denounced by groups of landless peasants as *"lati-fundios simulados"* (disguised latifundios).

6. The collusion of politicians and government bureaucrats in squatter invasions and in the activities of clandestine subdividers appears to be widespread in the Mexico City metropolitan area, and is frequently the object of public protests by defrauded settlers and ejidatarios whose land is invaded.

7. This phenomenon has been observed in a number of Latin American countries, but particularly in Brazil. See Leeds (1973: 199 ff.) and Harrigan (1975: 217).

8. Nationally, the Mexican government built approximately 56,000 dwelling units in 1975. The national housing demand (including accumulated deficit) has been estimated conservatively at 350,000 units per year. The government is currently (1974-1975) investing about 7,900,000,000 pesos annually in public housing, which at recent rates of construction averages out to 100,000 to 150,000 pesos (U.S. $8,000-$12,000) per dwelling unit.

9. Two new laws sent to the Congress by President Luis Echeverria in late 1975—the General Law of Human Settlements and the Law of Urban Development of the Federal District—provide for a more active role for the federal government in urban development planning, including government purchases of urban land to be held in reserve for future residential use. While the impact of these new laws on land and housing markets in the Mexico City metropolitan area is potentially very important, this impact will depend on the strength of the political and financial commitments which the incoming administration of Jose Lopez Portille is willing to make to ensure full implementations of the legislation. Organized opposition from private sector interests has not materialized as of this writing (February 1976), but this condition is not likely to persist should the new administration decide to proceed seriously with implementation.

REFERENCES

ACOSTA, M. and J. E. HARDOY (1973) Urban Reform in Revolutionary Cuba. New Haven: Yale University.

BATAILLON, C. and H. RIVIERE d'ARC (1973) La Ciudad de México. Mexico City: Sep/Setentas.

BAZANT, J. (1975) Economic Characteristics of Urban Dwelling Environments in Mexico City. Cambridge, Mass.: MIT Press.

CONTRERAS SUAREZ, E. (1972) "Migración interna y oportunidades de empleo en la Ciudad de México," pp. 359-418 in J. Martínez Ríos et al., El Perfil de México en 1980. Mexico City: Siglo Veintiuno.

CORNELIUS, W. A. (1975a) Politics and the Migrant Poor in Mexico City. Stanford, Calif.: Stanford University Press.

——— (1975b) Urbanization and Inequality: The Political Economy of Urban and Rural Development in Latin America (Latin American Urban Research, Vol. 5). Beverly Hills: Sage Publications.

EVERS, H. D. (1975) "Urban expansion and landownership in underdeveloped societies." Urban Affairs Quarterly 11, 1: 117-129.

HARDOY, J. E. (1972a) "Urbanization policies and urban reform in Latin America," pp. 19-44 in G. Geisse and J. Hardoy (eds.) Regional and Urban Development Policies: A Latin American Perspective. Beverly Hills: Sage Publications.

——— (1972b) Las Ciudades en America Latina. Buenos Aires: Paidos.

HARRIGAN, J. J. (1975) "Political economy and the management of urban development in Brazil," pp. 207-220 in W. A. Cornelius and F. M. Trueblood (eds.) Urbanization and Inequality: The Political Economy of Urban and Rural Development in Latin America (Latin American Urban Research, Vol. 5). Beverly Hills: Sage Publications.

HARVEY, D. (1975) "The political economy of urbanization in advanced capitalist societies: the case of the United States," pp. 119-163 in G. Gappert and H. M. Rose (eds.) The Social Economy of Cities. Beverly Hills: Sage Publications.

HEIDENHEIMER, A. J., H. HECLO, and C. T. ADAMS (1975) Comparative Public Policy: The Politics of Social Choice in Europe and America. New York: St. Martin's Press.

KELES, R. (1972) "Urbanization policy in Turkey." Studies in Comparative Local Government 6 (Summer): 27-39.

KIMANI, S. M. (1972) "The structure of landownership in Nairobi." Journal of Eastern African Research and Development 2, 2: 101-124.

LEEDS, A. (1974) "Housing-settlement types, arrangements for living, proletarianization, and the social structure of the city," pp. 67-99 in W. A. Cornelius and F. M. Trueblood (eds.) Anthropological Perspectives on Latin American Urbanization (Latin American Urban Research, Vol. 4) Beverly Hills: Sage Publications.

——— (1973) "Political, economic, and social effects of producer and consumer orientations toward housing in Brazil and Perú: A systems analysis," pp. 181-215 in F. F. Rabinovitz and F. M. Trueblood (eds.). (Latin American Urban Research, Vol. 3). Beverly Hills: Sage Publications.

——— (1969) "The significant variables determining the character of squatter settlements." America Latina 12, 3: 44-86.

LOMNITZ, L. (1975) Como sobreviven los marginados. Mexico City: Siglo Veintiuno.

——— (1974) "The social and economic organization of a Mexican shantytown," pp. 135-155 in W. A. Cornelius and F. M. Trueblood (eds.) Anthropological Perspectives on Latin American Urbanization (Latin American Urban Research, Vol. 4) Beverly Hills: Sage Publications.

LOPEZ ROSADO, D. (1975) El costo de la vida en la Ciudad de México. Mexico City: Departamento del Distrito Federal.

MABOGUNJE, A. L. (1972) "Urban land policy and population growth in Nigeria," pp. 235-242 in S. M. Ominde and C. N. Ejiogu (eds.) Population Growth and Economic Development in Africa. London: Heineman.

MOHAN, R. (1974) "Indian thinking and practice with urban property taxation and land policies: a critical view." Department of Economics, Princeton University. (unpublished)

MOIRON, S. (1975) "El desempleo: un problema creciente y poco estudiado." Diorama de la Cultura, Excélsior (Mexico City) 18 May: 6-7.

MUNOZ, H., O. de OLIVEIRA, and C. STERN (1972) "Migración y marginalidid ocupacional en la Ciudad de Mexico," pp. 325-353 in J. Martinez Rios, et al., El perfil de México en 1980. Mexico City: Siglo Veintiuno.

PEATTIE, L. R. (1974) "The concept of 'marginality' as applied to squatter settlements," pp. 101-109 in W. A. Cornelius and F. M. Trueblood (eds.) Anthropological Perspectives on Latin American Urbanization (Latin American Urban Research, Vol. 4). Beverly Hills: Sage Publications.

PORTES, A. (1971) "The urban slum in Chile: types and correlates." Land Economics 47, 3: 235-248.

PORTES, A. and J. WALTON (1975) Urban Latin America: The Political Condition from Above and Below. Austin: University of Texas Press.

ROBLES QUINTERO, S. (1975) "Análisis de la economía mexicana." El Día (Mexico City) 9 June: 18; 10 June: 15.

SARGENT, C. S. (1972) "Land speculation in Buenos Aires." Economic Geography 28: 258-174.

TURNER, J.F.C. (1973) "Análisis, diagnóstico y evaluación del sistema general de vivienda de los sectores de escasos resursos y sus subsistemas específicos en el área metropolitana de la Ciudad de México." Department of Urban Studies and Planning, MIT, and Oficina del Plano Regulador, Departamento del Distrito Federal (Mexico). (unpublished)

––– (1971) "Notes for a housing policy with special reference to low income housing systems in metropolitan Mexico." Department of Urban Studies and Planning, MIT, and Instituto AURIS (Mexico). (unpublished)

UNIKEL, L. (1972) La dinámica del crecimiento de la Ciudad de México. Mexico City: Fundación para Estudios de la Población, A. C.

UNIKEL, L., G. GARZA, and C. CRESCENCIO RUIZ (1975) El desarrollo urbano de México: Diagnóstico e implicaciones futuras. Mexico City: El Colegio de México.

––– (1973) "Factores de rechazo en la migracion rural en México, 1950-1960." Demografía y Economía 7, 1: 24-57.

VANCE, J. E., Jr. (1971) "Land assignment in the precapitalist, capitalist, and postcapitalist city." Economic Geography 47 (April): 101-120.

WARD, P. M. (1975) "Intra-city migration to squatter settlements in Mexico City." Department of Geography, University College London. (unpublished)

Chapter 12

HOUSING: REPRODUCTION OF CAPITAL AND REPRODUCTION OF LABOUR POWER
Some Recent French Work

C. G. PICKVANCE

In this chapter our aim is to indicate some elements of a Marxist approach to the analysis of housing in capitalist societies. This will be done by examining the main arguments in three recent French studies of various aspects of housing: owner-occupation; state housing and land policy; the emergence of public housing legislation at the turn of the century in France; and the creation of a particular type of housing, the *'grands ensembles'* (large developments comprising blocks of flats and a varying range of shopping, educational, and other facilities.)[1]

These three studies, which were all produced within the same research centre, are notable for their attempt to marry theoretical and concrete analyses. Furthermore, as well as sharing a Marxist perspective, they all take for granted a particular development within Marxist theory—namely, the theory of state monopoly capitalism.

In this introductory section, we shall give a very brief outline of relevant aspects of the theory of state monopoly capitalism and then present some of the ideas about the role of housing in the capitalist mode of production common to all three studies.

In succeeding sections, we shall discuss and (where appropriate) raise questions about the arguments in the three studies concerned. Needless to say, our reading of the studies is selective, but, we hope, in a fruitful way.

THE THEORY OF STATE MONOPOLY CAPITALISM

The main feature of the theory of state monopoly capitalism, as developed within the French Communist Party, concerns the growing role of the state in the economy. State monopoly capitalism, which is seen as developing from simple monopoly capitalism in the early years of the twentieth century, is characterized by the combination of the power of the monopolies and that of the state into a 'single mechanism' in order to save capitalism. A central role in the theory is played by the 'capital' advanced by the state at a nil or below-average rate of profit. This capital is described as (completely or partially) *'devalorized,'* i.e., not seeking its own self-expansion.

The term devalorized capital does not appear in Marx's writings, but is seen as arising out of his discussion of overaccumulation of capital and responses to it, where he uses phrases such as capital lying 'completely or partially idle' and capital having to 'give up its characteristic quality as capital' (Marx, 1971: 250-259). The theory of state monopoly capitalism argues that state intervention is a means of counteracting the falling tendency of the rate of profit and the tendency toward overaccumulation. This it does by advancing devalorized capital in various sectors of the economy (such as the building industry, to be discussed below) so that the average rate of profit is higher than it would otherwise be for capital seeking profit. However, since the state and monopoly capital are seen as combined in a 'single mechanism' (though the state—and its policies—are not 'above' the class struggle but reflect the relative strength of the dominated classes), it follows that state policy on the whole serves the long-run interests of monopoly capital. In particular, devalorized capital has an unequal effect on the capitals engaged in self-expansion; it will tend to raise the rate of profit of monopoly capital relative to that of non-monopoly capital.[2]

HOUSING IN THE CAPITALIST MODE OF PRODUCTION

The starting point of any analysis of housing in capitalist societies must be the dual relation of housing to the capitalist production process. On the one hand, housing is a commodity produced by a particular sector of production, the building industry; on the other hand, adequate housing is a prerequisite of the capitalist production process in general since it is necessary for the reproduction of labour power,[3] the source of value in that process. In this respect, housing is unusual in that it is a commodity which must not only be sold, but also consumed for capital accumulation to take place.[4]

This dual relation of housing to the capitalist production process indicates a first contradiction concerning housing—namely, that between capital engaged in the building industry,[5] and industrial capital in general. The former has an interest in a high selling price for housing, to increase its profits, whereas the latter has an interest in low housing costs since housing is a subsistence commodity whose cost enters the determination of wage levels. Higher housing costs may thus lead to pressure for higher wages and hence lower profits for industrial capital in general.

It is necessary to describe this contradiction in slightly more detail since capital engaged in the building industry (which will be referred to in aggregate as building industry capital) is in fact of two kinds, industrial capital and circulation capital. The products of the building industry have a long production period and a long circulation period. The long circulation period is related on the one hand to the durability of housing—i.e., it yields use-values over a long period, and on the other to the disproportion between workers' wages and the selling price of housing which means that only the fortuned few can buy housing outright.[6]

In order to speed up the rotation of industrial capital in this industry, a specialized circulation capital intervenes which purchases (at below their value) the products of industrial capital (namely, housing and property generally) and takes charge of their sale to final users. Now this circulation capital, which is usually termed property capital (or real-estate capital), requires the backing of extensive credit facilities to enable it to mediate between the (low) ability to pay of final users, and the (high) cost of the product. (These credit facilities are provided by a 'loan capital' whose function is to collect savings together—under either 'private' or 'public' sector auspices—and direct them to the property sector.)

Now property capital, like all capitals, constantly seeks to increase its productivity by speeding up its rotation, and one way of doing this is to increase the share of wages devoted to housing (whether in the form of house rent or mortgage repayments.) Thus, the contradiction between capital engaged in the building industry and industrial capital in general has sources in both the attempts of the industrial capital and the circulation capital engaged in that industry to increase their productivity. This contradiction is expressed in struggles over rent levels, for example. Pressure for greater profits in the building industry creates upward pressure on rents and thereby reduces the share of wages available for other reproduction costs—e.g., food and clothing. In turn, this creates pressure for higher wages, which cut into the profits of industrial capital in general.

Conversely, rent freezes effectively restrict the profitability of the building industry to the advantage of industrial capital as a whole. Thus, the peculiar role of the commodity housing gives rise to a conflict of interest among the supports of industrial capital.

The second contradiction concerning housing derives from the fact that housing cannot be built without land. While the precise role of land in this respect is currently the object of some debate,[7] it is agreed that it is not the need of housing for land as such which is the source of a contradiction but rather the existence of the institution of landed property, or private ownership of land.

Marx's own analysis of landed property in the capitalist mode of production focuses on three agents: the landowner, the capitalist farmer, and the labourer. As compared with previous forms of landed property, that 'corresponding to the requirements of the capitalist mode of production' was one in which landed property was divorced from 'relations of domination and servitude' and from 'land as an instrument of production.' Land became for the landowner simply a source of ground-rent 'which he collects by virtue of his monopoly from the industrial capitalist, the capitalist farmer' (Marx, 1971: 617-618), or, by extension, from the tenant who leases urban land. The contradiction in this system was that 'the improvements incorporated in the soil [by the capitalist farmer] become the property of the land-owner'; hence, the leasehold system was 'one of the greatest obstacles to a rational development of agriculture' (Marx, 1971: 619-620).

On this argument, the distinction between landed property and industrial capital persists in the capitalist mode of production and gives rise to a conflict over the share of surplus-value taking the form of ground-rent (accruing to landed property) and the share taking the form of profit (accruing to capital engaged in the building industry, in the case of land leased for building).[8] Thus, there is a contradiction between the interest of landed property in high ground-rents, and that of capital engaged in the building industry in low ground-rents (and thus greater profit).

What then are the implications of the common practice of developers today to *purchase* land (directly, or through the intermediary of the state) for building rather than to lease it? Is the obstacle of ground-rent thereby removed[9] and the 'rational development' of urban land permitted?

First, the function of landed property persists as long as private ownership of land persists. The sale of land by one agent to another may change the distribution of landownership and indeed may be part of a process by which landownership becomes concentrated in the hands of monopoly financial groups, but it does not change the institution of private property in land. All that happens in the case of the developer who purchases land for building is that the *function* of landed property (and its economic expression, ground-rent) and the *function* of (circulation) capital engaged in the building industry are combined by a single *agent*.

Second, the 'rational development' of urban land does not occur through the combination of these two functions by a single agent precisely because 'rational development' of urban land and the 'capital considerations' referred to by Marx are incompatible. As Lojkine notes, referring to Lenin's (1970: 65) comment about the merger of the 'monopoly of the banks' with the 'monopoly of ground rent' in the simple monopoly stage of capitalism, this merger

> far from eliminating the contradiction between capital and ground rent, may on the contrary develop it by linking it with the wider contradiction between the parasitic, speculative tendencies of capital and its tendency to increase the role of surplus value by increased investment in production.

> The monopolistic appropriation of ground rent . . . is above all a structural obstacle to all real urban planning; collectivization of the use of urban land in fact clashes much less with small private property which the new arsenal of laws allows to be expropriated very 'efficiently,' than with monopolist private property whose elimination presupposes the abolition of the capitalist mode of production itself [Lojkine, 1976].

In sum, the fact that housing needs land, and that land is subject to the institution of private property gives rise to a contradiction between landed property and building industry capital, which is not removed by the combining of the two functions in the case of developers purchasing rather than leasing building land.

TOPALOV ON OWNER-OCCUPATION AND STATE LAND AND HOUSING POLICY

Having sketched in the theory of state monopoly capitalism and examined the contradictory relations between housing, building industry capital, and landed property, we are now in a position to turn to the first of the studies to be considered here, Topalov's *Capital et Propriété Foncière* [Capital and Landed Property].

This study is in two parts: the first concerns owner-occupation and is based on both theoretical and concrete analyses; the second, concerning state land and housing policy, is purely theoretical.

OWNER-OCCUPATION

Historically, owner-occupation in France has developed in two main phases. In the 1780-1880 period, historical studies of property left in estates reveal a substantial shift in property-ownership away from the artisans and small independent producers (who formed the main part of urban populations in the early part of thy period) and the nobility, to the industrial, commercial, and rentier bourgeoisie which had come to own the major share of urban property by 1880. This period, then, saw a process of massive dispossession among the small independent producers which Topalov attributes to the emergence of industrial capitalism with its effects of pauperization and proletarianization on this social category. The economic significance of this dispossession process was that by destroying the previous mode of consumption of housing, user-ownership, or owner-occupation, it created the conditions for the emergence of building as a sector in which capitalist production could develop.

Since 1880, and especially since 1920, there has been a phase of rapid spread of owner-occupation.

Topalov's main aim here is to understand the economic function of this spread of owner-occupation.

His starting-point is to reject the popular interpretation of homeowner-ship as ownership of capital and to insist that owner-occupiers own a use-value, not a capital. As Engels (1969: 330-331) pointed out,

> Capital is the command over the unpaid labour of others. The little house of the worker can therefore become capital only if he rents it to a third person and appropriates a part of the labour product of this third person in the form of rent. But the [owner-occupied] house is prevented from becoming capital precisely by the fact that the worker lives in it himself.

Housing owned and subsequently rented is capital; housing owned and occupied is not.[10] The fact that owner-occupied housing becomes an exchange-value when it is sold does not alter this, according to Topalov, since owner-occupiers have to buy new houses subsequently: likewise any 'differential profit' (i.e., due to price differences between regions) on a transaction is incidental.

First, we shall look at owner-occupation in relation to the reproduction of capital, and second in relation to the reproduction of labour power.

From the point of view of reproduction of capital, owner-occupation is a 'particular form of circulation.' The durability and high cost of housing in relation to wage-levels mean that payment has to be spread out; in this respect, renting and owner-occupation are identical. However, this extended period of realization of housing in its money-form increases the share of total capital engaged (unproductively) in circulation, and thereby tends to reduce the general rate of profit. Now while the pressure thus exerted on the average rate of profit is not of concern to property capital and loan capital engaged in the circulation of housing, and whose profits derive precisely from this phase, it is of concern to industrial capital in general and hence the object of counteracting measures.

According to Topalov, one such measure is to reduce the share of the housing stock functioning as capital. This may be done either (1) by devalorizing circulation capital—e.g., by public housing or rent control; or (2) by increasing owner-occupation which gradually removes housing from the capital cycle. Both alternatives increase the average rate of profit, but each has a different effect on the profitability of *monopoly* capital. Devalorized circulation capital has two disadvantages for monopoly capital: It reduces profitable investment opportunities in the housing sector, and reduces the flow of savings available to finance the operations of monopoly capital. The second alternative, the spread of owner-occupation, on the other hand, opens up a new field of activity for monopoly bank capital.[11] though devalorized capital usually intervenes here too (e.g., via subsidized house-purchase loans). Topalov points out that the two periods of rapid spread of owner-occupation (1950-1963) and slower spread (since 1963) are correlated with major and minor roles, respectively, of devalorized loan capital.

Owner-occupation may also be related to the process of reproduction of labour power.

As we have seen, owner-occupied housing is not capital. On the contrary, the initial deposit required may absorb capital acquired by inheritance, for example—and which otherwise might have functioned as such.

Now unlike renting, owner-occupation involves repayments over a fixed period, say twenty years, during which the worker's labour power is fully exploited. The effect of these repayments is to reduce income available for consumption of other goods, and increase the number of household members working. Topalov suggests that these effects are likely to prevail over a third possible effect—namely, pressure for higher wages to restore expenditure on non-housing goods. This is because housing costs vary considerably within a given occupation, and wages are aligned on the *lowest* housing costs for that occupation, whereas owner-occupied housing usually involves the *highest* costs.

At the end of the loan repayment period, the household benefits from free housing. By this stage, household members will usually be retired, and the effect of owner-occupation here is to reduce reproduction costs, and to lower pension levels and overall wage levels.

Topalov would be the first to admit that the above arguments are formal and deductive in character, although in part they are based on analysis of the French experience. In my opinion, however, they are valuable in indicating a style of analysis in relation to housing which appears very promising and worthy of application elsewhere.[12]

STATE LAND AND HOUSING POLICY

The second part of Topalov's study, concerning land and housing policy, is purely theoretical and is presented as a preliminary to concrete analyses in these fields.

The questions posed are what housing and land policy the state adopts in the face of the contradictions discussed at the start of this article: namely, between industrial capital in general and building industry capital over house prices; and between landed property and building industry capital over ground rent?

Before answering these questions, Topalov analyses in greater detail the role of landed property in the capitalist mode of production.

Landed property in an economic sense (as opposed to ideological or legal-political senses) may refer to three types of relation. A relation of production—i.e., the effective power to determine whether or not land is used productively by capital seeking profit; a relation of distribution—i.e., concerning the distribution of surplus-value as for example between capital and landed property; and a relation of consumption—i.e., the use of land by landowners for purposes other than the fructification of capital—e.g., for the reproduction of their own labour power.

If the capitalist mode of production is defined, following Balibar, by the fact that it is *capital* which has both the capacity to set means of production to work and the power to control their use and appropriate the product, then it follows that landed property under this mode of production cannot be a relation of production. Its sole capacity is to demand a price (e.g., ground-rent) for the lease of the land to the capitalist who does use it in a production process he organizes and controls. It is thus capital which has effective power: "Landed property is transformed into nothing but a relation of distribution" (Topalov, 1973: 224). The class of landowners becomes a 'survival' without any role in the organization of production.[13]

Topalov distinguishes two types of contradiction between landed property and capital in the capitalist mode of production. The first, which is '*internal*' to it, is that just described: the struggle over the share of surplus-value accruing to each. The second contradiction, which is '*external*' to the capitalist mode of production, is between capital seeking control over the production process, and outdated, 'inappropriate' forms of landed property—e.g., that of peasants, artisans, shopkeepers, and homeowners.

We now return to the question of the state housing and land policies adopted in the face of the contradictions mentioned earlier.

In the *period of transition to capitalism*, Topalov identifies three policies which may be followed. The first, the use of the pre-existing housing stock, is restricted to those cases where industrialization takes place in existing settlements. Since such housing was not produced under capitalist conditions—i.e., is not capital seeking a share of the surplus product—this policy increases the general rate of profit in the capitalist sector of the economy. A second policy is the use of rural labour, whose reproduction costs are lower since they possess a dwelling and land for cultivation.[14] A third policy is 'self-housing' (as in the shantytowns of today) which also reduces the value of labour power since only the materials are purchased; labour is provided free.

Finally, in *monopoly capitalism*, Topalov identifies three possible state policies in relation to land and housing. The first, already mentioned, is the provision of devalorized circulation capital in order to raise the average rate of profit of building industry capital. This policy may involve a variety of schemes for directing credit into the housing sector through the aggregation of savings by new credit institutions or the use of state tax revenues. The second policy is to reduce the value of housing (in the interests of industrial capital as a whole), for example, by increasing productivity in the building industry.[15]

The third policy affects landed property directly: namely, the restriction or transfer of ground-rent. *Restriction of ground-rent* reduces the regulating price of housing and thus of labour power, thereby increasing the general rate of profit. It may take any of the following forms: encouragement of owner-occupation—i.e., prevention of part of the housing stock from becoming capital; devalorization of property capital with a consequential reduction in ground-rent; state ownership of land when this is accompanied by a restriction of the profitability of capital invested in public land;[16] and finally the state could act directly to reduce differential rents by controlling the location of investments so as to 'homogenise' space.

The alternative state policy of *transferring ground-rent* from landed property to other capitalist agents may take two forms, according to

Topalov: restriction of the transformation of local surplus profits into ground-rent—i.e., the transfer of rent to property capital at the expense of landed property; and the direct levying of ground-rent by the state in order to assist the financing of monopolistic accumulation.

Clearly, these various policies are not like so many books on a book-shelf waiting to be taken down according to arbitrary decision. Rather, each policy advances certain interests and hinders others, and the particu-lar policy chosen will reflect the current state of forces between the various interests involved. The state is not an entity 'above contradictions,' but 'actively reflects' them, to use Lojkine's (1972: 8-9) phrase. Hence 'state intervention,' in Preteceille's (1973: 88) felicitous phrase, "is not a response to the contradiction as such but a *contradictory response* to the terms of the contradiction." This is why, as Engels noted, state policy simply shifts problems around without resolving them. State policy is not. independent of the determinations which give rise to the problem or contradiction in the first place.

It is perhaps unfortunate that the studies being discussed here do not deal in detail with the political struggles preceding the particular policies implemented. Certainly the importance of this type of analysis is accepted (Preteceille, 1973: 87, 113-114; Magri, 1972: 16, 25, 95, 161-162 Topa-lov, 1973: 192-193), but its absence is perhaps the price to be paid for research contracted directly by state agencies.

MAGRI ON THE EMERGENCE OF CHEAP HOUSING LEGISLATION

We now turn to Magri's study of the emergence of cheap housing legislation in France at the turn of the century. This study shares the same theoretical framework as Topalov's study, but places greater emphasis on housing as a use-value, and therefore its role in the reproduction of labour power. Conventional studies of housing as a use-value relate it to the 'satisfaction of human needs.' Magri argues that this paradigm is invalid since the rise and fall in the production of housing, or the more or less adequate provision of housing, would have to be explained by changes in the level of needs. In fact, she suggests, it is the laws of capitalist production which determine the availability of this commodity, and these laws must have a central place in any theoretical framework in this field.

Thus Magri starts from the contradictory function of housing noted in the introduction—i.e., as both a use-value in the reproduction of labour power, and as a commodity whose production is governed by the laws of capitalism. Her thesis is that "capitalist production is structurally 'incapable' of ensuring, except in special cases, the reproduction of necessary labour power" (Magri, 1972: 22), and that this can be demonstrated in concrete cases, as she seeks to do for the Paris region at the turn of the century. In particular, the number, size, cost, and location of dwellings (i.e., location in relation to work-places, facilities, etc.) available is not adequate to that required. Furthermore, she argues that in each phase of the capitalist mode of production there is a characteristic relationship between the economic and the political. In the phase she analyses, it is the attempt by the state to *manage* the process of reproduction of labour power. In the case of housing, this takes the form of providing devalorized capital for the building industry, attempting to control the availability of land, and controlling the use-value of housing (e.g., by setting space and amenity standards).

Magri's analysis of the emergence of cheap housing legislation proceeds in two stages: (a) a description of conditions influencing the reproduction of labour powers; (b) an analysis of state legislation.

The context is the rapid demographic and geographical growth of the Paris agglomeration throughout the nineteenth century. This was associated with economic change. Whereas prior to 1850 the Parisian economy was similar to that of London in the late Victorian period (Jones, 1971: ch. 1)—i.e., characterized by small shops and workshops in which craft production was carried on, factories being restricted to provincial towns— the post-1880 period saw the first phase of industrialization take place in the Paris region. Engineering and chemical factories developed in the suburbs, unskilled labour being supplied by provincial and rural immigrants. Wage levels in Paris remained higher than those in the provinces throughout the nineteenth century, though the cost of living was also higher.

The major theme of Magri's analysis here is the effect of the slowing down of immigration, or 'stabilization' of the migrant labour force. This, she argues, produced a crisis in the process of reproduction of labour power. On the one hand, the costs of reproducing migrant labour now had to be paid entirely out of wages, rather than being supplemented by goods and services available to the migrant in his place of origin;[17] on the other hand, the post-1880 period was one of housing crisis—characterized by high rent levels, overcrowding, increasing shares of wages being spent on housing, low levels of new house construction, and limited family formation. Those hit hardest were the unskilled labourers employed in suburban factories, who, in addition, had to accept housing which was badly placed in relation to the workplace, had very poor transport facilities, etc. Thus, the stabilization of migrant labour placed new demands on already inadequate housing and facilities.

It is in this period of housing crisis that the first attempts are made by the state to provide cheap housing for the workers.

The legislation of 1894, 1906, and 1908, which Magri describes as the first phase, gave favourable tax treatment to private firms building cheap single-family dwellings, provided local authorities with certain powers to assist them, and channelled state-subsidized loan capital to the building firms mentioned and to house purchasers. Homeownership, it was thought, would lead to the social and moral improvement of the working-class. In fact, according to Magri, the result of this legislation was the building of houses which were beyond the means of most workers. In relation to the real problem, this legislation was an 'ideological response,' which had the effect of relaunching investment in the building industry.

Only with the 1912 legislation does Magri describe state intervention as a 'concrete response' to the housing problem. This legislation gave local authorities powers to set up agencies to build cheap housing (individual houses, or blocks of flats), and in particular housing for large families whose rents could be subsidized (a measure which is alleged to have increased the frequency of large families). They could also now have some control over the location, price, and size of such housing. An important aim of this policy was the constitution of stable family units, now necessary for the reproduction of labour power.

The 1912-1930 period saw three changes. An increasing role was given to local authority cheap housing agencies which were now enabled to receive devalorized loan capital, whereas previously it had gone only to their private sector counterparts. Local authority power increased—e.g., over land allocation, the amount of cheap housing built, and the balance between owner-occupation and renting. Second, rents of pre-1914 dwellings were frozen or allowed to rise only gradually, and the rights of landlords were reduced; the housing share of budgets fell, though housing conditions themselves did not change much, and owner-occupation of cheap housing was made easier financially. Third, standards were set concerning the space and provision of amenities inside the dwelling and in the immediate neighbourhood. These standards allowed space only for essential household activities and assumed a single-family household, thus reflecting, according to Magri, the function of housing in this period and for this category of the labour force: namely, provision of the minimum needs of reproduction of labour power, and the constitution of single-family units.

Magri concludes by showing that, while cheap housing legislation can be analysed as a response to the contradictions underlying the housing problem, it does not fundamentally affect these contradictions. This is apparent, she argues, from the limited number of cheap dwellings built in relation to the total. (The necessity of this limited response is not, however, demonstrated.)

Thus the two stages of Magri's argument are,

(a) delineation of a contradiction between the effects of the system of house production, and the requirements of industrial capital for the reproduction of labour power in Paris at the turn of the century;
(b) description of state cheap housing legislation as a response to this.

However, she does not conceive state intervention as being a direct response to the contradiction but rather a *mediated* response reflecting power relations (a) among the dominant classes, of which the predominant class or class fraction will affect the type of legislation, and (b) between the dominant and dominated classes, insofar as the contradiction has an effect on the latter. Thus the change she identifies from an 'ideological response' to a 'concrete response' on the part of the state is attributed to the increasing strength of the dominated classes.

One problem with this type of argument regarding state intervention is the danger of circularity. It is taken as an axiom that state policy reflects the balance of social forces, and inferred that policy favouring the working class is the result of the increased strength of this class as against other classes. The danger lies, in my view, in leaving this inference as a formal argument, rather than supporting it with evidence about the relative strength of different classes at the time of the intervention in question. This danger is particularly real in studies such as those being discussed here which do not deal in detail with the political processes involved in the formulation of legislation, but rather focus on the economic conditions preceding it, and economic (and political) effects resulting.[18]

A further difficulty emerges in Magri's analysis which is general to analyses which emphasize contradiction relating to the process of reproduction of labour power. The problem is to determine whether labour power is being adequately reproduced. Two approaches would appear possible. First, an 'indirect' approach—which is the one Magri adopts—and in which one provides evidence of deteriorating housing conditions (overcrowding, lack of amenities, etc.), high rents, and inadequate transport and other facilities and infers from this that labour power is not being adequately reproduced. Second, a 'direct' approach, which is based on the fact that labour power is reproduced *for* a certain purpose: production. While the relevant historical data may have been unavailable to Magri, it would seem more appropriate to judge the adequacy of the process of reproduction of labour power by its *effects within the workplace.* This would suggest examination of information on worker turnover, absenteeism, sickness, productivity, etc. (insofar as they arise from the reproduction process rather than from the production process—admittedly something difficult to establish in the absence of controlled experiment) and responses to these (e.g., provision of housing and other facilities) directly by employers, rather than indirectly by state provision. In brief, the 'indirect' approach risks focussing on the *means* of reproduction of labour power rather than on the *end* to which this process is directed. Admittedly, there may be disagreement as to what types of phenomena within the workplace indicate non-reproduction, or inadequate reproduction, but on theoretical grounds this would seem to be the correct place to start to tackle the question.

PRETECEILLE ON THE PRODUCTION
OF THE 'GRANDS ENSEMBLES'

The third and final study to be discussed shares the same analytical framework as the studies discussed previously. Thus, Preteceille's study of the grands ensembles—perhaps the most visually distinctive feature of the French housing scene in the post-war period—deliberately eschews questions such as whether the residents are 'satisfied,' a question posed within the paradigm of 'need satisfaction.' Similarly, the conception of buildings as in expression of the architect's intentions, or the more 'sociological' conception which sees them as the outcome of the strategies of various 'actors,' are both rejected. Such conceptions give priority to the actor(s) rather than to the conditions under which they act.

Preteceille is concerned with the processes which go into the *production* of the grands ensembles, and his aim is to show how the characteristics of the latter are shaped by these processes. The study is based on interviews with those concerned in six such developments in the Paris region.

The argument is as follows. The various components of the grands ensembles (blocks of flats, shops, roads, etc.) are in the main produced under the capitalist mode of production. The capital involved is a combination of productive capital and circulation capital, under the relative domination of the latter. Circulation capital can be subdivided, as we saw earlier, into property capital, which may be private (monopoly or non-monopoly) or state devalorised capital, and loan capital which may be remunerated at the normal rate of interest (bank loan capital) or below this rate (devalorized loan capital). Preteceille's fundamental thesis is that the character of a given grand ensemble derives from the types of capital involved in its creation, and their 'rules of operation.'

We shall examine in turn the two main types of capital, private and devalorized, and the effects of their rules of operation.

First, *private capital*, which is guided by the rule of profit. The primary sources of profit in a grand ensemble are the construction of dwellings and of 'private' facilities such as shops, cafes, and cinemas. As far as dwellings are concerned, the use of private capital is reflected in a concern for marketability. This has effects as follows. Each operation is split into phases each of which is relatively independent so that dwellings in the first phase can be sold or let before those in the second phase are completed. This also enables modifications to be incorporated—e.g., if there is difficulty in marketing dwellings in the first phase. Since 'status' is an important selling point, the areas chosen for the construction of grands ensembles by private capital will be high-prestige areas, and efforts will be made to differentiate them from H.L.M. (low-cost government-subsidized housing) by superficial additions to the otherwise uniform design. As regards shops, the profit rule demands that an adequate clientele be available before shops are opened. This explains the lag between the construction of dwellings and the opening of shops.

Second, *devalorized circulation capital*, which is subject to more political rules of operation. This type of capital has certain broad effects independent of the whether the support is, for example, the central state or the local state—a source of differences we shall discuss later. As regards housing, this type of capital is involved primarily in the provision of cheap housing, and since there is an excess demand for this, marketability is a less important influence on the product. In fact, Preteceille uses the phrase 'conditioned freedom' in relation to the design of such housing. In other words, while certain limits are set (e.g., minimum standards regarding space, lighting, and amenities, and cost-ceilings), the scale of the operation, its location and possibly some internal characteristics may reflect political factors. And whereas private capital pays little attention to subsequent maintenance costs, devalorized capital attempts to reduce these in order to facilitate housing management.

The public facilities of grands ensembles produced by devalorized capital also reflect certain of its characteristics. First, the limited quantity of such capital available may be reflected in the limited provision, delayed provision, or even complete absence of certain types of facility. Second, the fragmentation of this capital among a variety of supports (see below) makes it difficult to mobilize, and reinforces the effects just mentioned. Finally, the differing rules of operation or policies of these supports (e.g., different government departments, local authorities, etc.) may hinder the adequate provision of facilities—e.g., the railway network is planned at a regional level and investment in a new line or new station to serve a grand ensemble may not fit in with railway policy.

The tendencies outlined above are strengthened by the use made of devalorized loan capital—to which all developers, private or otherwise, have recourse.

Finally, certain differences may be noted according to whether devalorized capital is provided by the central, state, or a local authority.

Devalorized capital controlled by the central state is, first, usually restricted in total amount, leading to the slower than forecast realization of operations: residents of grands ensembles thus often find themselves living on a permanent building site. Second, it is divided into 'specialized fractions'—e.g., with different government departments as supports, with little possibility of switching funds from one use to another. This leads to the construction of collective facilities lagging behind that of housing. Third, each 'specialized fraction' operates according to its own rules, with predictable consequences when cooperation is required. Preteceille gives an example of the failure to construct an administrative centre which was to house a social security office, a post office, a clinic, etc., due to the differing norms of each department concerning the population size to be served by such facilities—the result was a large empty space in the centre of the complex.

Devalorized capital controlled by local authorities is also in limited supply, and generally has the effect of slowing down the provision of facilities in grands ensembles. Centrally provided funds are deliberately restricted in quantity, and local authorities' own ability to raise funds is strictly limited. The grands ensembles themselves are not large tax bases, since they are largely residential, and are exempted from certain taxes for a period. And there are severe political limits to the extent that facilities in grands ensembles can be financed out of taxes from residents living elsewhere in the area: Preteceille notes that in none of the six cases he studied was a grand ensemble project initiated by a local authority.

In these ways, then, the particular supports of the devalorized capital involved in the construction of the grands ensembles have specific effects on their characteristics.

Preteceille's (1973: 6) study adopts a problematic which is radically different from those normally used in studies of housing. Rather than interviewing the residents and collecting 'the everyday ideology diffused by the information media,' he is interested in the processes by which the features of grands ensembles, to which the residents respond, are themselves produced.

Once again, the study is 'economic' in nature. The 'rules of operation' of devalorized capital, which reflect the policies of the supports concerned, are taken as given: the process of policy formation is not investigated.

In conclusion, the three studies discussed here seem to me to open up important new directions in housing research. They do so by relating housing to the capitalist production process—as a product of a particular industry, as a user of land, and as an element in the reproduction of labour power—rather than treating it in isolation. This new approach is of broader significance insofar as 'urban studies,' whether within the disciplines of geography, economics, sociology, or politics, tend to deemphasize the link between the residential function and the economic system in general.

Clearly, much more work needs to be done to exploit the possibilities of this approach. In particular, comparative studies are essential in order to establish whether effects deduced from the theory of the capitalist mode of production are peculiar to it or whether they also exist in societies where other modes of production predominate.

NOTES

1. The three studies are Magri (1972); Topalov (1973); Preteceille (1973). Publications of the Centre de Sociologie Urbaine, may be obtained directly from the Centre at 118 rue de la Tombe-Issoire, Paris 14e.

2. The theory is expounded in *Le Capitalisme Monopoliste d'Etat: Traite Marxiste d'Economie Politique*, (2 vols.) Editions Sociales, Paris, 1971, and in Boccara (1974). Marxists in the urban field working with this theory include the authors of the three studies discussed here, Jean Lojkine, etc.

3. Labour power refers to the worker's work capacity. Strictly speaking, it is this rather than 'labour' which is sold to the capitalist in return for wages. Labour power together with means of production and relations of production are the three conditions which must be reproduced for the capitalist mode of production to persist.

4. The same is true of other subsistence commodities, of course. However, it does not follow that the arguments outlined below with regard to housing can also be applied to, say, food expenditure, since housing, as will be seen, has additional peculiarities.

5. Housing is only one product of the building industry; a more complete

analysis would take into account the production of commerical, industrial and other types of property.

6. Magri (1972: 10) argues that when landowners provided land for the construction of houses, and used their fortunes to purchase them, the conflict between productive capital and circulation capital did not exist, and that it only emerged when wage-labour became the source of effective demand.

7. This is due primarily to problems in extending Marx's analyses regarding agricultural land to urban land see Alquier, 1971; Lojkine, 1971; Harvey, 1974; Edel, 1975.

8. Strictly speaking only a part of the 'lease-money' received by the landowner is ground-rent (see Marx; 1971: 619-633).

9. This could be inferred from Marx's statement: "when the landlord is himself a capitalist, or the capitalist himself is a landlord . . . landed property does not constitute an obstacle to the investment of capital. He can . . . therefore be guided solely by considerations of expansion of his capital, by capitalist considerations" (1971: 751).

10. This is in fact the major point made by Haddon in the debate about 'housing classes' in British urban sociology (see Rex and Moore, 1967; Rex, 1971; Haddon, 1970: 124-133).

11. The parallels and differences with the British system of financing construction and homeownership require detailed analysis.

12. Topalov does present some concrete analyses concerning trends in owner-occupation in France in the 1954-1968 period. For example, he shows the heterogeneity of owner-occupiers (as regards their incomes, their socioeconomic categories, and the use-value of their houses), their differential sensitivity to credit restrictions (e.g., managers and professionals are shielded to some extent by their inherited money or ability to save out of income), the concentration of credit for the purchase of new houses, the decreasing attraction of owner-occupation due to the partial withdrawal of devalorized loan capital, etc.

13. While this might be true if landowners never combined any other function, when developers, builders, or bankers are also landowners, a different conclusion would seem in order. See our earlier discussion and also Lojkine (1975: 18-40).

14. This point will be returned to below in our discussion of Magri's argument concerning immigrants to the Paris area. The role of rural labour in urbanization processes in predominantly capitalist societies is not unimportant (see Castells and Godard, 1974: ch. 4, pp. 178, 183, 202, 229).

15. This was one of the aims of the 'grands ensembles' construction policy, which involved large programmes planned several years ahead and mass production by industrialized techniques (see Preteceille, 1973: 29-31).

16. If, conversely, it is associated with a restriction of rents paid by capitalist users of land, a *transfer* of surplus profits to the latter is involved.

17. For a more extended analysis of the role of immigrant labour, emphasizing both the economic advantages (i.e., reduced reproduction costs) and political advantages (i.e., via fragmentation of the working-class) it represents for capital, see Castells (forthcoming).

18. In Lojkine's (1975) most recent discussion of urban policy, he distinguishes between policy orientations which are a direct response to working-class pressure, and those involving the 'anticipation' by the political authorities of a reaction on the part of the dominated classes. The notion of 'anticipation' implies a concept of the

state as capable of learning, which is surely undeniable. However, such a notion makes it more difficult still to avoid the danger of circular argument mentioned above.

REFERENCES

ALQUIER, F. (1971) "Contribution a l'etude de la rent fonciere sur les terrains urbains." Espaces et Societes 2: 75-87.

BOCCARA, P. (1974) Etudes sur le Capitalisme Monopoliste d'Etat sa Crise et son Issue. Paris: Editions Sociales.

CASTELLS, M. (forthcoming) "Immigrant workers and class struggles in advanced capitalism: the Western European experience." Politics and Society.

——— and F. GODARD (1974) Monopolville. Paris: Mouton.

EDEL, M. (1975) "Marx's theory of rent: urban applications." Birkbeck College (London) Discussion Paper 38.

ENGELS, F. (1969) "The housing question," in Volume 2 of K. Marx and F. Engels, Selected Works. Moscow: Progress.

HADDON, R. (1970) "A minority in a welfare state society: the location of West Indians in the London housing market." New Atlantis 1: 80-133.

HARVEY, D. (1974) "Class-monopoly rent, finance capital and the urban revolution." Regional Studies 8: 239-255.

JONES, G. S. (1971) Outcast London. London: Oxford Univ. Press.

LENIN, V. I. (1970) Imperialism: The Highest Stage of Capitalism. Peking: Foreign Languages Press.

LOJKINE, J. (1971) "Y a-t-il une rente fonciere urbaine?" Espaces et Societes 2: 89-94.

——— (1972) La Politiqye Urbaine dans la Region Parisienne 1945-1972. Paris: Mouton.

——— (1975) "Strategies des grandes enterprises, politiques urbaines et mouvements sociaux urbains." Sociologie du Travail 1. (English translation to appear in 1976 in M. Harloe, ed., Captive Cities. New York: John Wiley.)

——— (1976) "Contribution to a Marxist theory of capitalist urbanization," in C. G. Pickvance (ed.) Urban Sociology: Critical Essays. London: Methuen.

MAGRI, S. (1972) Politique du Logement et Besoins en Main-d'oeuvre: Introduction a l'etude de l'intervention de l'Etat. Paris: Centre de Sociologie Urbaine.

MARX, K. (1971) Capital. Volume III. Moscow: Progress.

PRETECEILLE, E. (1973) La Production des Grands Ensembles. Paris: Mouton.

REX, J. (1971) "The concept of housing class and the sociology of race relations." Race 12: 293-301.

——— and R. MOORE (1967) Race, Community and Conflict. London: Oxford Univ. Press.

TOPALOV, C. (1973) Capital et Propriete Fonciere: Introduction a l'etude des politiques foncieres urbaines. Paris: Centre de Sociologie Urbaine.

Chapter 13

URBAN SOCIOLOGY AND URBAN POLITICS
From a Critique to New Trends of Research

MANUEL CASTELLS

We start with a paradox: While urban problems are more and more considered as priorities in political programs and in the daily lives of people, urban sociology seems more and more incapable of providing scientific answers to these problems. That is, it can describe problems, but it seems incapable of *explaining* the processes at work. We can agree on the fact that even though empirical research is an indispensable moment in any demonstration, it is hardly sufficient. Research data, to be something other than simply a photograph of reality at a precise point in time (and, hence, *depasse* since reality is always changing) must be used to verify hypotheses which themselves have to be integrated into a cumulative, evolving body of knowledge. Of course, the metaphysical lucubrations associated with the search for a "Grand Theory" have taught researchers to distrust abstract constructions that become only formal games. Yet this distrust should not lead researchers to abandon the search for an understanding of the relationship between empirical observation and explanatory theoretical schemes; such a relationship constitutes the only means for social scientists to understand social action beyond specific concrete situations.

Moreover, this observation is particularly important given the fact that certain fields of sociology, such as the sociology of organizations, the sociology of social mobility, the sociology of development, and the like

AUTHOR'S NOTE: *This is a revised version of article published in Comparative Urban Research, 1975.*

have made considerable progress in strictly scientific terms in recent years. While there is not a unified and undisputed overarching theory, there are the beginnings of some relatively circumscribed fields of knowledge which now permit exchanges and some progress in common despite their very different starting points. Such is not the case, it seems to me, for urban sociology, in America as well as in Europe, even though it is one of the oldest branches of sociology.

Our hypothesis is that such a situation is essentially due to the fact that urban sociology is not a scientific domain, nor a field for observation, but rather an ideological artifact. That is, its existence, as it was constituted historically, is justified less by the effects of the knowledge it produces than by its ideological impact on social relations (see Castells, 1975). Let us explain.

A scientific discipline is built either by a certain conceptual cutting up of reality—i.e., through the definition of a *scientific object*—or by a specific field of observation—i.e., through the choice of a *real object*. Most of the specific fields of sociology (industrial, political, medical, etc.) are established by applying general sociological theories to a particular sphere. In other cases, it is a *social process*, abstracted in theoretical terms, which constitutes a special area of sociology: for instance, social mobility is a field of study which corresponds to a certain problematic which cuts across all of social reality.

However, *urban phenomenon* or *urbanization* is neither a specific real object nor a scientific object. Indeed, what is the urban phenomenon? What is relevant to cities that is not relevant to the countryside? Is an urban phenomenon something that is not rural? But, what is rural? Is it a phenomenon that is non-urban? Is it a certain organization of the economy, defined by the nature of industry or by the division of labor? But then, why call it "urban"? In this sense, most of what is going on in our societies is urban since the city is the major scene of action. Yet, if we consider as "urban problems" transportation and criminality, housing and political cliques, racial tensions and green areas, educational infracture and leisure activities, it seems that we are far from the specificity of an observed, concrete reality. Of course, we may call "modern" society an "urban" society, but this caprice of terminology is not without its consequences, both theoretical and ideological.

While we mean by urban a certain style of society (whose description strangely resembles either American or Western European society), we also mean by this term a certain social organization of space characterized by the concentration and interpenetration of people and their activities. But if this space is the arena of a given sociological inquiry (in contrast to space which is "rural"), it is because we embody within it certain *social* properties. Otherwise, we would consider this space as a factor contributing to the social activity which we study, in much the same way as if we were to consider the mineralogical structure of the land upon which a school is built as influencing its pedagogical system which we are studying.

In reality, it is this implicit, obvious, almost natural association between a certain type of space and a certain type of society which defines the possibility and utility of an urban sociology. The best attempt to provide a conceptual basis for this discipline was that of Wirth and the Chicago school, who tried to define urbanism as a specific cultural system (basically, the liberal capitalist society).[1] It was called urban because it was produced by certain specific qualities of the spatial organization of the human species: density, size, and heterogeneity of urban agglomerations. In this sense, urban sociology is not an empirical or conceptual specification, but its very definition implicitly assumes an entire "theory" of society: The forms of space produce social relations and the physical characteristics of human territorial collectivities determine their cultural models of behavior. This is, in fact, one of the most advanced versions of naturalism and of the organicism of the beginnings of functionalism. Such a "theory" is extremely useful to ruling political elites inasmuch as it conceptualizes social organization as depending less on social data, in particular class relations, than on natural, spatial, technical, and biological data.

As a consequence any action for reform or any action for control is examined using the objective technical terminology of the organization of space. Hence, urban planning by technocrats replaces the political debates between social groups.

On the other hand, since urbanization is a natural consequence of human evolution and since it necessarily produces certain social effects—that is, the "Western" cultural model—human history is in fact predetermined, and all countries may be ordered in terms of more or less proximity to "urban" or "modern" society (in effect, this means an advanced industrial society of the American type). This type of society is considered as the historical model with which we can judge the degree of progress or backwardness of other countries. Besides, did Toynbee hesitate to assimilate the terms "urbanization" and "westernization"? (see, for a systematic discussion of the whole problem, Castells, 1972; see also Castells, 1976.)

We would be wrong to underestimate the importance of this debate by dismissing it as a purely epistemological problem. The theses of "urban sociology," which are the basis of urban sociology, are also the basis for extremely important daily ideologies, such as, for example, the explanation of criminality by the size of cities or of political radicalism by the level of urbanization. All of these analyses are based on spurious correlations because, if we control for the "social" variables, *spatial variables product different effects, depending on the circumstances*. But it is easier to put the responsibility for criminality on "the monstrous huge city" than to introduce into the explanation variables such as the growth of unemployment among ethnic minorities evicted from the South by the mechanization of agriculture.

Most of the works in urban sociology are influenced, implicitly, by such a perspective, or they are descriptive empirical investigations. In neither case is it possible to explain the observed phenomena, especially since the so-called urban perspective has progressively moved from themes of social integration and the acculturation of migrants to themes of urban politics or of social conflict over issues such as some aspect of a city's infrastructure. For it is, in fact, this social evolution which explains the decreasing capacity of the old functionalist schemes to be credible and the increasing demand for a new type of "urban sociology."

The transformations which are at the root of an increasing, politically important new urban perspective may be summarized as follows (Harvey, 1973: 50-120):

(a) On the one hand, the economy of advanced capitalist societies rests more and more on the process of consumption; that is, the key problems are located at the level of the realization of surplus-value, or, if one prefers, on the extension of the market.

(b) The accelerated social and spatial concentration of the means of production and of management units also determines a concentration and growing interdependency between the processes of consumption and distribution. Consequently, there is more and more of a concentration of the organization and management of the means of consumption such as housing, schools, health services, commerce, leisure, etc. The concentration is not necessarily realized in the same space, however, although it is articulated around a system which is increasingly centralized from a functional point of view. So consumption processes are more and more organized on the basis of the equipment of collective consumption which determines the structure of residential space, and, hence, of urban units (Harvey, 1973).

(c) Thus, a series of new social contradictions emerge at the level of consumption processes, and especially at the level of processes of collective consumption in correspondence with the displacement of economic contradictions toward the sphere of consumption (Gartner and Riessman, 1974). The urban social movements which result from this contradiction are a new datum which directly affects the dynamics of the transformation of advanced societies to the extent that they affect those social strata (such as the middle class) which until this moment have remained outside of social conflicts (see Castells, forthcoming).

(d) Finally, to the extent that these means of collective consumption are generally managed by public authorities (the state at its different levels—national, regional, and local), the entire urban perspective becomes politicized, since the organization of hospitals, schools, housing, and transportation are at the same time fundamental determinants of everyday life, tightly linked and interdependent networks, and political options linked to class interests which form the social structure. Consequently, the state becomes through its arrangement of space the real manager of everyday life (O'Connor, 1973). But, on the other hand, the politicization of the urban question also politicizes the consequent social conflicts; urban movements become one of the axes of social change in advanced societies (Castells, 1973).

This increasing politicization of urban affairs has rendered even more decrepit an urban sociology based on the perspective of social integration and the adaptation of migrants of rural origins to the urban culture of modern society. This is why political science has increasingly taken the lead in urban research, in particular in the study of the power processes in the studies of communities. Urban problems have ceased to be the natural consequence of modernization. Such urban problems are inserted into a web of social and political strategies and are redefined and transformed according to power relations. Urban political studies of a liberal[2] bent (from Robert Dahl to Terry Clark, including Nelson Polsby and Edward Banfield) accomplished a genuine change of perspective and opened the way to *social* analysis of urban contradictions. But these studies remained enclosed within an individualist and social-psychological approach to power which impeded them to probe the questions more deeply. The central object of such analysis has been the network of strategies among *actors*, each one of whom is defined by the attempt to maximize power and gains. Thus, trade unions, the press, or businessmen are considered as being on the same level, and power is viewed as an end in itself which each tries to monopolize, with the relative equilibrium of forces always forcing compromises. Such a perspective, even though it has permitted very fine descriptions of concrete situations, has been able to generalize its discoveries only through the use of highly formalistic perspectives—for example, the search for determinants of a centralized or decentralized power structure, of a unitary or pluralist network of power, etc. But it has not accounted for the relations between political processes, urban contradictions, and general social interests—i.e. the economic, political, and ideological interests of the social classes which form the totality of a society. This has occurred for two reasons:

First, such studies usually remain at the level of a local community, while urban problems—even those which appear at the local level—are determined by general social forces and structures (see Hill, 1974). Of course, this determination of urban problems by social structures is expressed in a specific way in each case. But such specific traits cannot be the beginning of research. On the contrary, in order to understand the logic of these specific traits, we must locate them within their general determinants.

Second, one cannot analyze a social or political process independently from its structural context and from the web of structural interests which determine it (see Alford and Friedland, 1975; also see Cloward and Piven, 1974). Consequently, we cannot base urban research on the analysis of actors and of their strategies without first analyzing urban issues and the contradictions in the social structure which these issues express. These contradictions will objectively define the social interests at stake and will allow an understanding of the unfolding of the political process, which possesses relative autonomy vis-à-vis the socioeconomic structure, but which becomes a pure formal game, coupled with a utilitarian metaphysic, if it is not studied starting from class relations (see Molenpkoff, 1975).

This perspective on urban research has been developed in France and in other European countries by a more and more influential wave of urban research which has been forcefully developed since 1968 (and it is not without reason that it has dated from that year). The central interest of this wave of research is that, even though it attempts to pose problems theoretically starting from an analysis of the class structure, it advances only through *empirical research* which simultaneously attempts to understand certain urban political problems as they exist as well as to verify some more general hypotheses about the nature of emerging contradictions in advanced societies.

The result is represented by more than a hundred pieces of empirical research in urban sociology carried out in France in the last five years; if these works do not provide definitive solutions to problems, at least they open the way to new theoretical and methodological perspectives toward the problems which have been posed.[3]

These research results attempt simultaneously to recognize the new importance of urban contradictions, trying to give them a precise place within the social structure, and to develop, starting from there, a theoretical and empirical analysis of the political processes which seem to us to be at the heart of the question. It is normal that such an ambitious attempt is still in its infancy, but it tries to confront real social and theoretical problems in a spirit which is both scientific and socially engaged.

It seems evident that a dialogue between this intellectual effort and some new emerging trends within American sociology might be extremely fruitful. While French and European researchers know quite well the evolution of American research, in general, the inverse is not true. Of course, there are the barriers of language which exist, and it will be necessary to solve them by less ethnocentric publication policies. But before this technical obstacle is overcome, there is a more important cultural obstacle to be surmounted. It is difficult to change one's perspective and to accept, even tentatively, the consideration of another point of view, another way of asking questions about reality. One's curiosity must first be aroused. Before any start toward genuine scientific discussions (which can only be based on concrete research results and specific problems) can begin, it is necessary to be ready to bring into question one's accepted approaches to problems in order for one to realize intellectual progress relative to the new questions which we have asked here.

Such is the goal, modest and limited though it may be, of these few questions which we have addressed to urban sociology: to open an exchange of experiences between the different approaches that try to answer questions about the political implications of the urban crisis and which try to understand, little by little, how mankind builds his cities, and, hence, how mankind makes his history.

NOTES

1. In fact, the Wirth theory is still underlying the best theoretical attempts to ground urban sociology from an idealistic perspective. See, in particular Claude S. Fischer, "Towards a Subcultural Theory of Urbanism" American Journal of Sociology, Vol. 80, Number 6, May, 1975.

2. By "liberal" we refer to the *theory* underlying the analyses and not to the political attitudes that are extremely diversified among this group of urban political scientists ranging from rightist conservatism to radical liberalism.

3. See the bibliographical Appendix.

REFERENCES

ALFORD, R. and R. FRIEDLAND (1975) "Political participation." Annual Rev. of Sociology.

CASTELLS, M. (forthcoming) "Recent experiences of urban social movements in Western Europe." Social Policy.

––– (1976) "Advanced capitalism, collective consumption and urban contradictions," in L. Kindberg (ed.) The Politics of Post-Industrial Society. Lexington, Mass.: D. C. Heath.

––– (1975) "Theory and ideology in urban sociology," in C. Pickvance (ed.) Critical Essays in Urban Sociology. London: Methuen.

––– (1973) Luttes Urbaines. Paris: Maspero.

––– (1972) La Question Urbaine. Paris: Maspero. (English edition in 1976, London: Edward Arnold Press.)

CLOWARD, R. A. and F. F. PIVEN (1974) The Politics of Turmoil. New York: Pantheon.

GARTNER, A. and F. RIESSMAN (1974) The Service Society and the Consumer Vanguard. New York: Harper & Row.

HARVEY, D. (1973) Social Justice and the City. Baltimore: Johns Hopkins Press.

HILL, R. (1974) "Separate and unequal: governmental inequality in the metropolis." Amer. Pol. Sci. Rev. (December).

MOLENPKOFF, J. (1975) "The post-war politics of urban development." Politics and Society 2.

O'CONNOR, J. (1973) The Fiscal Crisis of the State. New York: St. Martin's Press.

APPENDIX

Some *selected* references on recent urban research in France and Italy:

1. Chris Pickvance, "On the Study of Urban Social Movements", *The Sociological Review,* Vol. 23, n 1, Feb. 1975.

2. Chris Pickvance, "Housing and Class: some recent Frenchwork", *Antipole,* 1975.

3. Christian Topalov, *Les Promoteurs Immobiliers,* Mouton, Paris, 1974.

4. Christian Topalov, *Capital et Propriété Foncière,* Centre de Sociologie Urbaine, Paris, 1973.

5. Francois Ascher et Chantal Lucas, *Analyse des conditions de production du cadre bati,* 3 volumes, UER-Urbanisation, Grenoble, 1972.

6. Francois Ascher et Daniel Levy, "Logement et Construction", *Economie et Politique,* mai 1973; Francois Ascher et Chantral Lucas, "L'industrie du batiment: des forces productives à libérer", *Economie et Politique,* mars 1974.

7. Denis Duclos, *Propriété foncière et processus d'urbanisation,* C.S.U., Paris 1973.

8. Edmond Preteceille, *La production des grands ensembles,* Mouton, Paris, 1973.

9. Brunot Theret et Migeul Dechervois, *Contribution à l'étudé de la rente* fonciere capitaliste, Mouton, Paris 1975. Alain Lipietz, *Le tribut foncier urbain,* Maspero, Paris, 1974.

10. Claude Pottier, *La logique du financement public de l'urbanisation,* Mouton, Paris, 1975.

11. Edmond Preteceille, *Critique des Jeux Urbains: jeux, modeles et* simulation., Mouton, Paris, 1974.

12. Alain Cotterean, articles in *Sociologie du Travail,* 4, 1969 and *Sociologie du Travail,* 4, 1970.

13. Jean Lojkine, *La politique urbaine dans la région parisienne,* 1945-1972, Mouton, Paris, 1973; Jean Lojkine, *La politique urbaine dans la région lyonnaise,* 1945-1972, Mouton, Paris, 1974 il faut aussi signaler des contributions théoriques plus générales, très importantes de Jean Lojkine sur les thèmes de l'urbanisation: "Contribution à une théorie marxiste de l'urbanisation capitaliste", *Cahiers Internationaux de Sociologie,* 1, 1973; et "Urban Policies and Urban Social Movements", in Michael Harloe (editor), *Captive Cities,* John Wiley, London, 1976.

14. Francis Godard and alter, *La Renovation Urbaine à Paris.* Structure urbaine et logique de classes, Mouton, Paris, 1973.

15. Sylvie Biarez and alter, *Institution Communale et Pouvoir Politique.* Les cas de Roanne, Mouton, Paris, 1974.

16. M. Castells et F. Godard, *Monopolville,* Mouton, Paris 1974.

17. Michel Amiot et autres, *Politique municipale et équipements culturels,* Ministère de l'Equipement, Paris 1972.

18. Jacques Ion et autres, *Les équipements socio-culturels et la ville,* Ministère de l'Equipement, Paris, 1973.

19. Manuel Castells, Eddy Cherki, Francis Godard, Dominique Mehl, *Sociologie des Mouvements sociaux urbains. Enquete sur la région parisienne.* Volume 1: *CRise du logement et mouvements sociaux,* Mouton, Paris, 1976; une enquête est en cours sur les mouvements sociaux liés aux transports urbains; une enquête a aussi été realisee sur les luttes urbains en Europe, en 1974-75.

20. Armel Huet et autres, *Le role ideologique et politique des comités de quartier,* Ministère de l'Equipement, Paris, 1973.

21. Henri Lefebvre, *La production de l'espace,* Anthropos, Paris, 1974.

22. Henri Lefebvre, *La persee marxiste et la ville,* Castermann, Paris, 1972.

23. En particulier, CERFI, *Les equipements collectifs,* numéro spécial de

Recherches Paris, 1973?

24. Alain Medam, *La Ville-censure*, Anthropos, Paris, 1972; et, surtout, sa thèse en cours de publication, *Les sens de la ville*.

25. Raymond Ledrut, *Les images de la ville*, Anthropos, Paris, 1973.

26. Jean-Claude Thoenig, *L'ère des technocrates*, Dunod, Paris, 1974.

27. Jean Remy et Liliane Voye, *La Villè et l'urbanisation*, Duculot, Bruxelles, 1974.

28. Andreina Daolio (sous la direction de), *Le lotte per la casa in Italia*, Feltrinelli, Milano, 1974.

29. Giuliano della Pergola, *Diritto alla citta e lotte urbane*, Feltrinelli, Milano 1974.

30. Enzo Mingione, "Sociological approach to regional and urban development: some theoretical and methodological issues" in M. Harloe (editor) *Captive Cities*, John Wiley, London, 1976.

31. M. Boffi, S. Cofini, A Giasanti, E Mingione, *Citta e conflitto sociale*, Feltrinelli, Milano 1972.

32. Marcella della Donne, *La questione edilizia*, De Donato, Bari, 1973.

33. Franco Ferrarotti, *Roma, da capitale a periferia*, Laterza, Bari, 1971; Franco Ferrarotti, *Vita dei Baraccati*, Roma 1974.

The most important journals publishing research material on urban studies within a new theoretical perspective are, for France, *Espaces et Societes* (Anthropos, Paris) and for Italy *Archivio di Studi Urbani e Regionali* (Marsilio, Venezia)

Some of the most well known research centers developing this kind of research are:

—Centre de Sociologie Urbaine, Paris

—Centre d'Etude des Mouvements Sociaux, Ecole des Hautes Etudes en Sciences Sociales, Paris

—Instituto di Economia Regionale, Facolta di Architectura, Universita di Venezia

—Instituto di Sociologia, Universita di Roma

—Instituto Nazionale di Urbanistica (INU), Roma

Chapter 14

POLITICAL ECONOMY OF WORLD URBAN SYSTEMS
Directions for Comparative Research

JOHN WALTON

Although it may appear commonplace, we should begin with the observation that there exists no distinctive field of comparative urban research, that is, no corpus of empirical research that proceeds from a general paradigm or a limited set of competing theories. Rather, the "field" presents us with investigations of a wide variety of phenomena broached typically from a number of more or less encapsulated disciplinary orientations.

At least two explanations can be advanced for the extreme fragmentation of comparative urban research. On the one hand there is little agreement on what is "comparative" the term being applied to everything from research done in some "foreign" or non-native setting to carefully controlled field experiments or stratified case comparisons. Whereas the logic of genuinely comparative research has been developed in several places (Abu-Lughod, this volume; Armer and Grimshaw, 1973; Marsh, 1967; Prezworski and Teune, 1970; Walton, 1973) the application of the term has not been restricted to these strategies.

On the other hand consensus, or even concern, about what is "urban" has been lacking. Typically this research deals with certain general social processes with the urban setting serving merely as a locale for their convenient observation (Walton, 1975). For example, one central preoccupation of comparative urban research has been migration. Although urban migrants may be studied at the point of destination, the migration process is clearly a societal or systemic matter involving rural conditions that may initiate it, step migration from smaller to larger towns, and return migration from city to countryside (Balan et al., 1973). In short, there is no principaled connection between the urban setting and the object of analysis, the process. The same could be said of most research generally referred to as comparative urban. Space does not allow elaboration of the argument, but consider another cornerstone of comparative urban research, the social ecology of cities. Essentially this important work deals with the connection between land use and social organization. But the use of space is a general social process; uses of urban space depend upon uses of rural space, vice versa, and both depend on larger forces of production and accumulation (Evers, this volume).

In summary comparative urban research is a loosely defined and somewhat specious rubric that includes all manner of investigations whose common denominator is the fact that they take place in cities and towns. In Castells' (this volume) words this work lacks a "theoretical object," that is, from a theoretical standpoint there is no unique comparative urban field.

In this volume we have tried to render some order to the confused state of comparative urban research by organizing these essays around a set of developing perspectives. Each section, we believe, provides some strong indications of where the field is moving, some sense of a theoretical foundation that will lend coherence to a variety of urban concerns. The purpose of this essay is to draw out these indications, to introduce some new thinking about the nature of urbanism, and to trace its theoretical implications for comparative research. Stated differently, this essay is a modest attempt at providing a theoretical basis for comparative urban studies and characterizing the kind of research that would follow from such a formulation.

Recent years have seen the emergence on an international basis of a new school of urban social science. This approach has been described in terms that vary by national setting. In France and Italy it is referred to as Marxist or neo-Marxist (e.g., Castells, 1973; Lojkine, 1972), while some of the British prefer the term "structuralist" approaches (e.g., Pickvance, 1974 and 1976; Harloe, 1976), the North Americans "political economy" (Harvey, 1973 and 1975; Sawyers and Tabb, 1976; Hill, 1976; Gordon, 1971), and the Latin Americans "dependent urbanism" (Castells, 1972). Despite the several labels, these developments have enough in common to constitute a general theoretical paradigm. For example, they agree that urban social science founders in confusion due to the absence of a theoretical perspective that would justify the analysis of the city as a "focus" rather than merely a "locus"; that is, theoretical perspectives that would explain the distinctive characteristics of urbanism and urbanization as social processes. Second, they are heavily influenced by Marxist theory, yet endeavor to extend this mode of analysis in the direction of a materialist explanation of urbanism; a topic which, it is generally conceded, Marx did not give systematic attention. Third, and by implication, the approach attempts to develop the historical and economic foundations of urbanism and urbanization; to account for various urban forms by reference to changing modes of production and accumulation. Fourth, many of these authors move on to deal with urban socio-spatial organization (e.g., Harvey, 1975), politics (Hill, 1976; Mollenkopf, 1976), and social movements (Castells et al., 1976) as these grow out of particular forms of economic integration. While historical materialism provides the general theoretical orientation, the approach is empirically grounded seeking non-stereotyped answers to contemporary puzzles.

Whatever one's theoretical tastes or predelections, it would appear that at least the first point joining exponents of this critical school is valid. What we must ask, therefore, is where the approach takes us; how well does it succeed in developing a theoretical foundation for comparative urban research that would organize disparate knowledge and suggest new and fertile fields of inquiry. In order to answer this question a brief exposition of the approach is necessary, particularly with respect to the nature of urbanism.

In his elegant critique of theory in urban sociology Castells (1968, 1969, this volume) concludes that earlier traditions lack a distinctive *urban* focus, that is, an "object" that is at once theoretical (or conceptual) rather than concrete and urban rather than societal. Consequently, urban sociology is "ideology" rather than theory or science in the special sense that it provides "displaced knowledge"; knowledge that is useful, perhaps important, but that is incorrectly or spuriously interpreted for want of incorporation in an adequate theory. For example, there *is* a "culture of urbanism" but, rather than arising from size and density of the city itself, "the fundamental features of this urban culture are the direct consequences of industrialization, and, in certain cases, of capitalist industrialization." Studies of urban culture, descriptively accurate as they may be, constitute ideologies to the extent that they fail to locate this "object" in its proper causal nexus. Presumably, then, industrialization provides the underpinnings of things urban.

Nevertheless, urban research has focused on two important kinds of problems, spatial relationships and the process of collective consumption (i.e., of collective goods such as transportation, education, health, etc.) The question then becomes how the results of this useful research, this "raw material" (which is another way in which "ideology" is characterized) can be incorporated into theory. At this juncture it is helpful to

switch to the work of a like-minded French scholar where one answer to
the question posed comes through more clearly.

Lojkine (1972) attempts to sketch a theory of capitalist urbanization
by extending Marx's analysis of the mechanisms for increasing productivity within the workship to the operation of parallel mechanisms in
society as a whole. Among these *general conditions* of production Marx
stressed the importance of the means of communication and transportation, but Lojkine feels that

> this restriction of the scope of the concept [general conditions of production]
> is put into question today by the appearance of factors which are of equal
> importance and which are likewise *necessary conditions* for the overall repro-
> duction of developed capitalist formations. We are referring on the one hand
> to *collective means of consumption* which must be added to means of *social*
> and *material* circulation [in Marx], and on the other hand to the *spatial
> concentration* of the means of production and reproduction of capitalist social
> formations.

These two foci, also identified by Castells, characterize what is unique
historically about the capitalist city. That is, the growing concentration of
the collective means of consumption and of the spatial distribution of the
means of production and reproduction explain, respectively, the novelty
of urban life and why the city, as a social form for reducing the time and
costs of capital circulation (thus increasing productivity), is necessary in
capitalist society. Stated differently, the city

> is thus in no sense an autonomous phenomenon governed by laws of develop-
> ment totally seperate from the laws of capitalist accumulation: it cannot be
> dissociated from the tendency for capital to increase the productivity of labor
> by socializing the *general conditions* of production of which urbanization, as
> we have seen, is an essential component.

Here it should be stressed that Lojkine (and Castells) are not equating
capitalism and urbanization as cause and effect. It is recognized that cities
or urban forms existed long before capitalism became the dominant form
of economic organization in certain societies, just as they exist in contemporary noncapitalist societies. The social division of labor based fundamentally on a division between town and country "is part of the economic
formations of the most diverse societies." Nevertheless, the characteristic
features of capitalist cities are to be explained by the increasing concentration of the several factors mentioned.

The capitalist city thus appeared as the direct effect of the need to reduce indirect costs of production, and costs of circulation and consumption in order to speed up the rate of rotation of capital and thus increase the period during which capital was used productively.

For Lojkine and Castells the central feature of the contemporary (capitalist) city is the growing concentration of the means of collective consumption and of the spatial organization of production and consumption. These result from the "laws" of capital accumulation. Consequently, to account for the special character of contemporary urbanism and to place in proper perspective earlier "ideologies" of urbanism, urban phenomena assume a somewhat secondary, though crucial place in a more general theory of accumulation.

It might be observed at this point that we begin to verge on circularity, namely that capitalism produces capitalist cities. Such a judgement, however, would be unfair since the intent of these analyses is less to explain the origins of various urban forms than to characterize the processes shaping contemporary Western cities. Theoretical thinking scarcely ends here; rather, on this foundation it begins to analyze the *contradictions* inherent in this form of urbanism and to research the *variable* and *conditional* circumstances under which those contradictions are dealt with.

Understanding that the work reviewed so far is concerned mainly with characterizing the nature of urbanism in capitalist societies and developing a broader systemic explanation of the urbanization process, we turn finally to a more general formulation. Consistent with the previous writers and the political economy approach as a whole, Harvey (1973) treats urbanism as a social form "broadly consistent with the dominant mode of production." Nevertheless, "like any social form, urbanism can exhibit a considerable variety of forms within a dominant mode of production, while similar forms can be found in different modes of production." This is due to both the wide variety of historical, physical, or cultural conditions affecting particular cities, and the vagueness of the term "mode of production." In view of the latter Harvey follows Polanyi and Fried by distinguishing three forms of "economic integration"; reciprocity, redistributive integration, and market exchange. Reciprocity may be balanced or imbalanced but involves the transfer of goods and services according to custom. Such societies are egalitarian. Redistributive integration is based on prestige and the flow of goods to support an elite. These may be rank or stratified societies. Finally, market exchange involves the exchange of goods and services based upon price-fixing markets and the social organization of scarcity (i.e. power). These are stratified societies. The relationship between these types of economic integration, society, and urbanism are as follows:

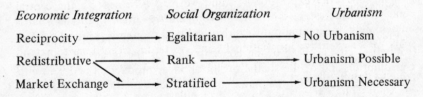

Economic Integration	Social Organization	Urbanism
Reciprocity ⟶	Egalitarian ⟶	No Urbanism
Redistributive ⟵	Rank ⟶	Urbanism Possible
Market Exchange ⟶	Stratified ⟶	Urbanism Necessary

Importantly, any concrete society will present some combination of these forms of economic integration such that it is necessary to

> interpret the historically occuring forms of urbanism by evaluating the balance of influence among various modes of economic integration at a particular time and by examining the form assumed by each of the modes at that time.

And this analytic suggestion points to the more fundamental conception of cities as the nodes of concentration of economic surplus or surplus value. Illustratively,

> cities are built forms created out of the mobilization, extraction and geographic concentration of significant quantities of the socially designated surplus product.

> Urbanism can assume a variety of forms depending upon the particular function of the urban center with respect to the total pattern of circulation of the socially designated surplus product.

> If there is no geographic concentration of the socially designated surplus product there is no urbanism.

In short, Harvey develops a broader perspective which in its general outline would allow analysis of a variety of urban forms as these are conditioned by different types of economic integration (including but not restricted to industrial capitalism) and different "balances of influence" of these types within a given historical society. Yet, Harvey's method is perfectly consistent with the political economy of urbanism approach; most notably in his emphasis on locating the explanation of urban forms in more general principles of economic and social organization. Moreover, like other exponents of the approach, Harvey's main concern is with urbanization in capitalist societies since it is in these societies that the city is most essential and indispensable as a mechanism for the concentration and circulation of surplus. Given that this is increasingly the function of cities in a market exchange system, he goes on to analyze its consequences in the production of particular "forms of urbanism" in the presence of growing class stratification and spatial segregation of economic activities and residential areas.

With this brief exposition in mind we may turn next to the central concern of this essay, directions in *comparative* urban research. What is immediately apparent about the urban political economy approach to date is its rather exclusive intranational focus. Little has been done to extend this type of analysis to cross national urban hierarchies or world urban systems despite the fact that the fundamental process of concern is clearly, in Amin's (1974) words, one of "accumulation on a world scale." Obviously, there is a vast literature on imperialism and a burgeoning recent one on dependency and underdevelopment. What is missing or largely underemphasized in these treatments of accumulation internationally, however, is the place of urban hierarchies in the process. More pointedly, theories of imperialism and neocolonialism, in Dos Santos' (1969) opinion, tend to view the international extension of capital exclusively from the point of view of the imperialist countries. The effects of this expansion are assumed to be relatively homogeneous across dependent societies leading to the systematic destruction of precapitalist forms of production and relegating the cities of dependent countries to the common mechanical task of passing the surplus upward through a nested set of metropolitan-satellite relationships. Much recent research and criticism has challenged this rather undifferentiated view stressing that peripheral economies may be more autonomous and adaptive than assumed, that cities exhibit variegated roles in the international economy, and that political factors mediate the accumulation process (e.g., c.f. Balán, 1975; Booth, 1975; Chilcote, 1974; Clammer, 1975; Dos Santos, 1969; Leeds, this volume; O'Brien, 1975; Roberts, 1975; Walton, 1976). Neverehtless, systematic comparative research aimed at explaining these alternatives has yet to appear.

All of this suggests a promising new direction for comparative urban research; one that is theoretically fertile in that it suggests the richness urban forms may be encompassed by more fundamental explanatory principles, and one that is methodologically innovative in that it moves from the city as the unit of analysis to cross national exchange processes in which cities assume particular roles. Stated as a set of premises and a conclusion; if it is granted that cities cannot be studied as autonomous units, if it makes sense theoretically and/or empirically to view urbanism/ urbanization as a social form significantly conditioned by economic forces, and if these forces operate cross nationally, then cities need to be studied from the standpoint of how they operate within and are shaped by international hierarchies linked by economic process. Harvey (1973) puts this succinctly with the observation. "The reputation and significance of individual cities rest to large degree upon their location with respect to the geographical circulation of surplus." Moreover, when patterns of the circulation of surplus change due to new resources, technologies and so forth, cities rise and fall as Wallerstein (1974) has shown in his study of the origins of the European world economy in the sixteenth century. Quoting Harvey (1973) once more, it seems that the new direction for comparative urban research is fully contained in the observation that

> urbanism, as a general phenomenon should not be viewed as the history of particular cities, but as the history of a system of cities within, between and around which the surplus circulates.

Assuming that this is a provocative lead, the question remains how particular research strategies might proceed from the theory.

In schematic terms we begin with the exchange or accumulation process as the unit of analysis. While comparative urban research on noncapitalist societies is probably the most serious lacuna in our present knowledge, for most purposes let us assume we begin with the capitalist process of accumulation as it interacts with "precapitalist social formations" (Amin, 1974). From here research could proceed in at least two directions.

First, an analysis of urban forms in cities selected according to their role in the accumulation process, and second an analysis of selected socioeconomic process that affect urbanism at various levels of society.

In the first case three practical strategies are suggested. Historical research could be undertaken focused on the rise and fall of cities as a result of changes in the nature of the circulation of surplus. In this regard Wallerstein's (1974) work is exemplary but much remains to be done on nature of urban structure in these cities during their rise and fall (c.f. Child, 1942; Adams, 1966).

Second, beyond the historical role of cities in the exchange process, the nature of urbanism might be compared in cities that serve distinctive functions in this process. For example, what differences might be noted in spatial organization or class structure of ports, manufacturing centers, commercial centers of agricultural regions, political-administrative centers (e.g. Brasilia), or multinational corporate enclaves (e.g., Dunkirk, France or Aratu near Salvador, Brazil). According to the theory developed here such cities should assume quite distinctive forms that can be explained by, among other things, their function in the total pattern of the circulation. And, of course, an equally compelling question is what "other things" (e.g. physical features, historical legacies, political decisions, legal traditions, etc.) may assume explanatory importance, whether these are mediating factors, semi autonomous forces or whatever.

A third alternative based on the logic of comparing cities according to their role in the exchange process would entail the selection of localities with different historical experiences such as with colonialism. Area studies, the practical difficulties of doing comparative work, and the vested interests of researchers have, sadly, mitigated against comparisons of Latin American and African cities, for example. While the following examples are not crucial, it would be most instructive to compare Buenos Aires, Argentina and Lagos, Nigeria; how their urban forms differ as a result of different colonial experiences; how they are variously affected by metropolitan economies; how they, in turn, influence urbanism in the second cities of Córdoba and Ibadan. In a similar vein, what comparisons might obtain between Havana, Cuba, Dar es Salaam, Tanzania or Addis Ababa, Ethiopia as they attempt urban reform following on national efforts to replace the capitalist accumulation model. Clearly these are amibitious suggestions, but they do point to the fundamental issues in comparative urban research.

A second general direction for comparative work is the analysis of Migration is, perhaps, the choicest example of such a process since it spans many levels with origins in the changing conditions of rural economic organization and consequences per rapid urbanization and international migration. Yet, there are a variety of comparable processes that affect urbanism and can be traced to changing patterns of accumulation for example, trade relations, the expansion of multinational corporations, and so forth.

An observation that seems to apply to studies of urbanism generally is that they have focused on the city in isolation from its surrounding environment and the role it plays in the larger carrying society. Increasingly comparative urban research is discovering the obvious, but methodologically troublesome, fact that much of what is often crucial in explaining local phenomena is extra-local in origin. International economic interests and policies, national political decisions on developmental strategies or infrastructure services, and technological change in the countryside, all set up a series of reverberating forces that combine in the city. While urban studies that employ the city as a geo-political unit of analysis are capable of noting the consequences of this confluence of forces acting upon local conditions, they are hardpressed to explain them since their causes or origins lie outside methodologically proscribed limits of inquiry.

What is called for, then, is a unit of analysis based on distinctive *vertically integrated processes* passing through a network from the international level to the urban hinterland. At least four nodes of this network that would be included *within* the vertically integrated unit of analysis are the international, national, urban/regional, and urban hinterland. In substantive applications of this unit of analysis specific actors and influence processes would be identified and traced through the levels.

A prime illustration of the approach is the case of the local impact of a foreign industry. Instructive earlier studies have dealt with the consequences of exogenous industrialization for local communities (e.g., Nash, 1958). The new research approach suggested here would extend the analytic unit upwards and downwards. At the international level it would determine the aims of the corporation in establishing foreign subsidiaries, reasons for choosing the particular site and the role of the subsidiary within the larger corporate strategy. At the national level it would investigate the negotiations between corporate and political leaders, under what terms the business was permitted entry, what concessions were obtained on both sides, how the decision articulated with national developmental strategies, what interests participated and benefited from the decision. At the actual locational level, what impact did the subsidiary have on the economy, did it create jobs and tax revenue, complement local initiatives, or monopolize some productive activity, what linkage effects did it create, how much control over local economic policy was relinquished, how did it affect (or imbalance) the labor force distribution and wages, what were the net costs and benefits to the indigenous economy? Finally, with respect to the urban hinterland, what effects might be traced to the enterprise in terms of migration, market expansion *into* the hinterland as well as new markets for hinterland commodities, etc? All of these developments highlighted by the vertically integrated unit of analysis affect the accumulation process in ways that also transform urban structures.

Here we have only sketched some of the research implications that follow from a theory of urbanism based on forms of economic integration and, particularly, capitalist accumulation. These research strategies do not depend upon any orthodox acceptance of the theory. In fact, they seem like interesting paths to follow quite apart from one's theoretical side bets. Among other things they would encourage authentically comparative research as opposed to "area studies." But, they also engage the theory and provide suggestions for how it might be elaborated, refined or corrected.

The political economy of urbanism developed in the early portions of this essay appears promising as one relatively powerful device for organizing our chaotic urban social science. But much of this work is new and the theory needs to be further developed and evaluated empirically. If the theory is to live up to its promise at least two of its facets will require more systematic attention. First, a much more elaborate conceptualization of the patterns of circulation of surplus is necessary. This is true not only in the more familiar case of Western societies but, as Castells (1969) observes "whereas the scientific theory of the capitalist mode of production has been partly developed (in *capital*), an equivalent theory of the socialist mode of production is lacking." Harvey's three-fold typology of forms of economic integration is obviously a useful beginning, but further differentiation of dominant forms is needed as well as empirical demonstration of "the balance of influence among various modes of economic integration at a particular time" and "the form assumed by each of the modes at that time."

Second, more attention is due those "mediating factors" that intervene between forms of economic integration and urban structure. As we have suggested, any number of considerations (physical, cultural, legal, etc) might be introduced here, but crucial importance would seem to attach to public policy or the role of the state as it is fashioned in the interplay between elites and popular social movements, that is, in class struggles the outcomes of which may be quite variable.

In short, a great deal needs to be done. Nevertheless, we have the beginnings of a theory which may make sense of our disparate and piecemeal knowledge of cities around the world. That theory needs to be engaged. Whatever the outcome of such engagement we are likely to understand more fully the nature of cities and their role in the larger social order.

REFERENCES

ADAMS, R. M. (1966) The Evolution of Urban Society. Chicago: Aldine.

AMIN, S. (1974) Accumulation on a World Scale. New York: Monthly Review.

ARMER, M. and A. D. GRIMSHAW (1973) Comparative Social Research: Methodological Problems and Strategies. New York: John Wiley.

BALAN, J., H. L. BROWNING, and E. JELIN (1973) Men in a Developing Society: Geographic and Social Mobility in Monterey, Mexico. Austin: University of Texas Press.

––– (1975) "Regional urbanization under primary sector expansion in neo-colonial societies," in A. Portes and H. L. Browning (eds.) Current Perspectives in Latin American Urban Research. Austin: University of Texas Press.

BOOTH, D. (1975) "Andre Gunder Frank, "An introduction and appreciation," in I. Dxaal et al. (eds.) Beyond the Sociology of Development: Economy and Society in Latin America and Africa. London: Routledge & Kegan Paul.

CASTELLS, M. (1968) "Y a-t-il une Sociologie Urbaine?" Sociologie du Travail No. 1: 72-90. (Trans. by Christopher G. Pickvance [ed.] Urban Sociology: Critical Essays, Methune, 1976.)

——— (1969) "Theorie et Ideologie en Sociologie Urbaine." Sociologie et Societes Vol. 1: 171-190. (Trans. by Christopher G. Pickvance [ed.] Urban Sociology: Critical Essays, Methune, 1976.)

——— (1972) Imperialismo y Urbanización en America Latina. Barcelona: Editorial Gustavo Gili.

——— (1973) La Question Urbaine. Paris: Francois Maspero.

——— and E. CHERKI, F. GODARD, and D. MEHL (1976) Sociologie des Mouvements Sociaux Urbaines: Enquete Sur la Region Parisiene. Vol. 1, Crise du Logemant et Movements Sociaux. Paris: Mouton.

CHILD, V. G. (1942) What Happened in History. Harmondsworth, Middlesex: Penquin.

CHILCOTE, R. H. (1974) "A critical synthesis of the dependency literature." Latin American Perspectives 1: 4-29.

CLAMMER, J. (1975) "Economic anthropology and the sociology of development: "liberal" anthropology and its French critics," in I. Oxaal et al. (eds.) Beyond the Sociology of Development: Economy and Society in Latin America and Africa. London: Routledge & Kegan Paul.

DOS SANTOS, T. (1969) "La Crise de la Theorie du Developpement et les Relations de la Dependance en Amerique Latine," L'Homme et la Societe 12 (Avril-Mai-Juin).

GORDON, D. M. (1971) Problems in Political Economy: An Urban Perspective. Lexington, Mass: D. C. Heath.

HARLOE, M. (1976) Captive Cities. London: Methuen.

HARVEY, D. (1973) Social Justice and the City. Baltimore: Johns Hopkins University Press.

——— (1975) "The political economy of urbanization in advanced capitalist societies: the case of the United States," in G. Gappert and H. Rose (eds.) The Social Economy of Cities, Urban Affairs Annual Reviews, Vol. 9 Beverly Hills: Sage Publications.

HILL, R. C. (1976) "State capitalism and the urban fiscal crisis in the United States," in L. Sawyers and W. Tabb (eds.) Megalopolis and Marx (forthcoming).

LOJKINE, J. (1972) "Contribution a une Theorie Marxiste de L'Urbanisation Captialiste," Cahiers Internationaux de Sociologie, Vol. 52: 123-146. (Trans. by Christopher Pickvance (ed.) Urban Sociology: Critical Essays. London: Methuen.)

MARSH, R. M. (1967) Comparative Sociology: A Codification of Cross-Societal Analysis. New York: Harcourt, Brace & World.

MOLLENKOPF, J. (1976) "The post war politics of urban development," Politics and Society 5, 3.

NASH, M. (1958) Machine Age Maya: The Industrialization of a Guatemalan Community. Chicago: Univ. of Chicago Press.

O'BRIEN, P. J. (1975) "A critique of Latin American theories of dependency," in I. Oxaal et al. (eds.) Beyond the Sociology of Development: Economy and Society in Latin America and Africa. London: Routledge & Kegan Paul.

PICKVANCE, C. G. (1974) "On a materialist critique of urban sociology." Sociological Review 22 (May): 203-220.

——— (1976) Urban Sociology: Critical Essays. New York: St. Martins Press.

PREZWORSKI, A. and H. TEUNE (1970) The Logic of Comparative Inquiry New York: John Wiley.

ROBERTS, B. (1976) "The provincial urban system and the process of dependency," in A. Portes and H. L. Browning (eds.) Current Perspectives in Latin American

Research. Austin: University of Texas Press.

SAWYERS, L. and W. TABB (1976) Megalopolis and Marx (forthcoming).

WALLERSTEIN, I. (1974) The Modern World-System: Capitalist Agriculture and the Origins of the European World Economy in the Sixteenth Century. New York: John Wiley.

WALTON, J. (1973) "Standardized case comparison: observations on method in comparative sociology," in M. Armer and A. O. Grimshaw (eds.) Comparative Social Research: Methodological Problems and Strategies. New York: John Wiley.

––– (1975) "Problems of method and theory in comparative urban studies." Urban Affairs Quarterly 11, (September): 3-12.

––– (1976) Elites and Economic Development: Comparative Studies on the Political Economy of Latin American Cities. Austin: University of Texas Press.

ABOUT THE CONTRIBUTORS

JANET ABU-LUGHOD is Professor of Sociology and Urban Affairs at Northwestern University, where she also directs the Comparative Urban Studies Program of the Center for Urban Affairs.

MICHAEL AIKEN is Professor of Sociology at the University of Wisconsin, Madison. His research interests include urban politics, organizations and comparative urban.

CORALIE BRYANT is Associate Professor in the School of Government and Public Administration at the American University in Washington, D.C. She is currently studying the role of international assistance in urban development.

MANUEL CASTELLS is Professor of Sociology at the École des Hautes Études en Sciences Sociales in Paris. He has published in English, French and Spanish on the sociology of social movements, urban sociology and comparative political processes.

WAYNE A. CORNELIUS is Assistant Professor of Political Science at the Massachusetts Institute of Technology. His recent publications include *Politics and the Migrant Poor in Mexico City* (Stanford University Press, 1975) and *Urbanization and Inequality: The Political Economy of Urban and Rural Development in Latin America* (Sage Publications, 1975).

RONALD S. EDARI is Assistant Professor of Sociology at the University of Wisconsin, Milwaukee. He is currently examining theoretical and methodological issues surrounding the study of urbanization in Third World countries. A recent book is entitled *Social Change* (Wm. Brown, 1975).

HANS-DIETER EVERS is Professor of Development Studies in the Department of Sociology at the University of Bielefeld in Wels Germany. He is the editor of *Modernization in Southeast Asia* (Oxford University Press, 1975) and several other works in German on comparative urban ecology.

WILLIAM G. FLANAGAN is a doctoral candidate in the Department of Sociology at the University of Connecticut. He is a coauthor of *Urbanization and Social Change in West Africa* (Cambridge University Press, 1976).

PHILIP E. JACOB is Professor of Political Science at the University of Hawaii, Manoa. He is a co-investigator for a multi-nation study of automation and industrial workers sponsored by the International Social Science Council.

PETER KOEHN is Assistant Professor of Political Science at the University of Montana. His research interests are in comparative local government, Ethiopian politics and urban development and adminstration.

ANTHONY LEEDS is Professor of Anthropology at Boston University. His research focuses on the evolution of society from loosely linked, ecologically localized primordial human settlements to the present ecologically-universalized, tightly interlinked, multisystemic world groupings of societies.

ELIZABETH R. LEEDS is a graduate student in the Department of Political Science at Massachusetts Institute of Technology. Her research interests are urban proletarian political organization, relationships between national housing policies and migration patterns and international migration in Southern Europe.

BRUCE LONDON is a doctoral candidate and teaching assistant in the Department of Sociology at the University of Connecticut. His dissertation, which is near completion, is entitled "Metropolis and Nation—An Ecological Analysis of Primate in City-Hinterland Relationships in Thailand."

LOUIS H. MASOTTI is Professor of Political Science and Urban Affairs and Director of the Center for Urban Affairs at Northwestern University. He serves as editor of *Urban Affairs Quarterly*. His recent books include *Urban Problems and Public Policy* (D. C. Heath, 1975) and *Toward a New Urban Politics* (Ballinger, 1976).

CHRISTOPHER G. PICKVANCE is Lecturer in Interdisciplinary Studies and Chairman of the Urban Studies Committee at the University of Kent in England. His recent publications include *Urban Sociology: Critical Essays* (St. Martins Press, 1976).

JOHN WALTON is Professor of Sociology and Urban Affairs at Northwestern University. His major research interests are political and urban sociology, comparative studies and the politics of development. His recent publications include *Elites and Economic Development* and (with Alejandro Portes) *Urban Latin America* (both Texas, 1976).

LOUISE G. WHITE is Adjunct Professor and Director of Undergraduate Programs in the School of Government and Public Administration at the American University in Washington, D.C. Her research interests are the influence of government jurisdiction and policy output on popular participation, economic models of participation, and the interaction of planning and participation.